The Origins of the Federal Theology in Sixteenth-Century Reformation Thought

The Origins of the Federal Theology in Sixteenth-Century Reformation Thought

David A. Weir

The Frank S. and Elizabeth D. Brewer Prize Essay of the American Society of Church History

CLARENDON PRESS · OXFORD

1990

Oxford University Press, Walton Street, Oxford OX2 6DP
Oxford New York Toronto
Delhi Bombay Calcutta Madras Karachi
Petaling Jaya Singapore Hong Kong Tokyo
Nairobi Dar es Salaam Cape Town
Melbourne Auckland
and associated companies in
Berlin Ibadan

Oxford is a trade mark of Oxford University Press

Published in the United States
by Oxford University Press, New York

British Library Cataloguing in Publication Data
Weir, David A.
The origins of the federal theology in sixteenth-
century Reformation thought.
1. Protestant theology, history
I. Title
230'.044'09
ISBN 0–19–826690–1

Library of Congress Cataloging in Publication Data
Weir, David A.
The origins of the federal theology in sixteenth-century
Reformation thought / David A. Weir.
Originally presented as the author's thesis (Ph.D–St. Andrews, 1984).
Bibliography. Includes index.
1. Covenants (Theology)—History of doctrines—16th century.
2. Reformed Church—Doctrines—History—16th century.   3. Theology,
Doctrinal—Germany (West)—Palatinate—History—16th century.
4. Palatinate (Germany)—church history—16th century.
5. Reformation—Germany (West)—Palatinate.   I. Title.
BT155.W43 1990   231.7'6'09031—dc20   89–35814
ISBN 0–19–826690–1

Typeset by Pentacor Limited, High Wycombe
Printed in Great Britain by
Biddles Ltd., Guildford & King's Lynn

Dedicated to the memory of my maternal grandparents:

John Crawford
1882–1977

Alice Robertson Crawford
1890–1980

'But the steadfast love of the LORD is from everlasting to everlasting upon those who fear him, and his righteousness to children's children, to those who keep his covenant and remember to do his commandments.'

Psalm 103: 17–18

Preface

THIS book had its origins as a dissertation submitted to the University of St Andrews in 1984. It is the first of what it is hoped will be a series on the importance of the theme of covenant in early modern European and colonial American history. As such it represents a specific study of a broader theme of human and divine commitment in the Judaeo-Christian tradition. The thesis of this book is that the prelapsarian 'covenant of works' or 'covenant of nature' is the key identifying feature of the federal theology, a type of theology which formed, and still forms, one of the basic theological frameworks for much of Protestant theology from the seventeenth century to the present.

The first part of the book outlines the implications of the federal theology for sixteenth- and seventeenth-century Reformed thought. According to the federal theology, the prelapsarian covenant was made with Adam and is still binding upon all men, even after the Fall of Adam into sin. The postlapsarian covenant of grace is made with Jesus Christ, the second Adam, who keeps the original prelapsarian covenant of works, takes upon himself the penalty for breaking it, and then applies this work of redemption to his elect people only. While John Calvin and the earlier Reformers discussed the importance of the postlapsarian covenant of grace, they never taught the federal theology with its prelapsarian covenant motif. Yet over eighty years after Calvin's death (1564) the Westminster Confession of Faith stated that the federal theological system was part of Reformed orthodoxy. The purpose of this book is to find the origins of the prelapsarian covenant concept, and therefore of the federal theology, and to show its importance for future generations of Protestant Reformed theologians and laity, especially as they developed their ecclesiology, sacramental doctrine, Church and State relations, confessions and catechisms, evangelistic methods, and moral and ethical standards within the matrix of the federal theology.

The prelapsarian 'covenant of works' motif originated between 1560 and 1590 in the Palatinate, one of several intellectual centres of Calvinism besides Geneva. There were two stages to its development. The first stage is its proposal in 1562 by Zacharias Ursinus after a decade of controversy over the sovereignty of God and Adam's Fall. While we cannot document an absolutely certain relationship between this controversy and the proposal of the prelapsarian covenant idea, we can ascribe a high degree of probability to this relationship. The controversy surrounding the Fall is the only doctrinal controversy dealing with Adam that I can find in Reformed thinking during the years preceding 1562.

One of the reasons that we cannot document some of the things we would like to know about Ursinus's thinking is that he left few written manuscripts. All we have are some letters, which are largely uninformative. Other manuscripts were lost during his frequent moves, destroyed at the time of his death (at his request), or destroyed in the Thirty Years War (1618–48).[1]

The second stage of the origins of the federal theology is the use of the prelapsarian covenant as a commonplace of theology between 1584 and 1590. Since the prelapsarian covenant idea is novel for the sixteenth century, one can clearly trace this second stage in four theologians who, in various ways, had connections with Ursinus and the Reformed Church of the Palatinate: Caspar Olevianus, Thomas Cartwright, Dudley Fenner, and Franciscus Junius.

After 1590 the federal theology blossomed all over Europe; it is impossible to draw historical connections between the various concepts of covenant after 1590 because after that date the prelapsarian covenant, and the federal theology, quickly became commonplaces of Reformed theology. The ramifications of the federal theology would be worked out in the seventeenth century, especially by the Puritans in England and New England and by the Presbyterians in Scotland.

Various organizations and individuals have given generously of their time and financial aid as I worked towards the completion of this project. The Saint Andrew's Society of the State of New York awarded me a graduate fellowship for study in Scotland for the year 1980-1. Without their assistance I could never have gone to Scotland. Professor James Kerr Cameron of the Department of Ecclesiastical History of Saint Mary's College of the University of St Andrews gave generously of his time and advice; while I struggled with the various concepts of covenant over a 150-year period he continually pointed me back to Heidelberg and the late sixteenth century as the seminal period for the federal theology. My parents, Richard B. and Jean C. Weir, have supported me faithfully while I was in Scotland and then during the last eight years as I worked off and on on the project. My father, Associate Professor of English at The King's College in Briarcliff Manor, New York, read the manuscript for style and grammatical accuracy, and my mother proof read the final drafts.

Mrs J. H. H. Burns of St Andrews was a gracious hostess during my time there. Paul and Marilyn Copeland, formerly of Wishaw, Scotland, allowed me to spend a summer with their family, for which I am grateful. Professor John F. Wilson and Dr William J. Edgar read parts of my manuscript in its earlier stages. My thanks also go to Professor Richard Luman of Haverford College, Haverford, Pennsylvania and Professor S. Bruce Willson, President Emeritus of the Reformed Presbyterian Theological Seminary, Pittsburgh, Pennsylvania, both of whom shared with me their love for ecclesiastical and theological history. Debbie Helgesen was a faithful and efficient typist amidst mountains of Latin quotations. Norman Birkett laboured assiduously to provide solutions to some thorny computer problems having to do with transfer of text.

Professor Michael McGiffert of the College of William and Mary, Williamsburg, Virginia, Professor John von Rohr, formerly of the Pacific School of Religion, Berkeley, California, and Professor Lyle Bierma of the Reformed Bible College, Grand Rapids, Michigan, carefully read the manuscript and gave invaluable critical suggestions. I am grateful to Professors McGiffert and von Rohr for sharing with me some of their work in progress on the covenant theme prior to publication. Professor Edward Dowey of Princeton Theological Seminary, Princeton, New Jersey, gave critical comments orally. So did Professor Fred Klooster of Calvin Theological Seminary, Grand Rapids, Michigan, when the thesis of this book was presented at the 1984 meeting of the Sixteenth-Century Studies Conference held at Concordia Theological Seminary, St Louis, Missouri. I extend my thanks to Professor Derk Visser of Ursinus College, Collegeville, Pennsylvania for inviting me to present that paper there. Many errors were caught by these readers, for which I am thankful. The responsibility for any remaining errors is of course my own.

The texts of quotations in languages other than English have been quoted in the notes. When published translations existed I relied on them, and these translations are cited in the notes, but in the case where no English translation exists the translations are my own; I was assisted in the task of translating by Mr Richard Jeffery of the Oxford University Press; his helpfulness saved me from many errors of detail and substance.

Several libraries gave me invaluable assistance over the last eight years. The University of St Andrews Library helped me in many ways. I am especially grateful to the Inter-Library Loan Division, which tracked down numerous books for me. Mr Geoffrey Hargreaves and the Rare Book Division gave generously of their help and time. In Scotland I was also allowed to use the University of Glasgow Library, the New College Library, and the National Library of Scotland. I was able to visit the Cambridge University Library in England for a period of three days. In the United States I have roamed freely in the vast resources of the Firestone Library of Princeton University. Again, I would like to the thank the Inter-Library Loan Division for securing books which the Firestone Library did not have. The Speer Library of Princeton Theological Seminary has been a major resource in this study. I have also availed myself of the collections of the Union Theological Seminary Library in New York, the Library of the Reformed Presbyterian Theological Seminary in Pittsburgh, Pennsylvania, and the New Brunswick Theological Seminary Library in New Brunswick, New Jersey.

On 5 November 1983 I had the privilege of attending a conference commemorating the 400th anniversary of the death of Zacharias Ursinus. The conference was held at Ursinus College in Collegeville, Pennsylvania and was sponsored by Ursinus College and the United Church of Christ. The discussions at that conference were very helpful to me as I tried to fit Ursinus into the broader framework of sixteenth-century European history.

The revisions to the manuscript for its publication as a book were done at the Center of Theological Inquiry in Princeton, New Jersey, where I was a Member from 1985 to 1987. I am grateful for the post-doctoral appointment which I enjoyed there. Professor R. Paul Ramsey and Dr James I. McCord were most helpful during my tenure at the Center. I regret that Professor Ramsey did not live to see the finished product of this book. The Centenary College Alumni Association generously gave a contribution from its Faculty Development Fund towards photocopying expenses and postage as the manuscript went back and forth across the Atlantic Ocean several times. The manuscript was awarded the Brewer Prize of the

American Society of Church History for the year 1983. This included a publishing subvention, for which I am grateful. It was also awarded the Samuel Rutherford Distinguished Thesis Prize of the University of St Andrews for 1984.

Finally, Anne Ashby, Molly Scott, Richard Jeffery and Jane Stuart-Smith have been faithful and patient editors as they have guided, from a distance, the publication of my first book.

D. A. W.

Centenary College
Hackettstown, New Jersey
June 1989

[1] D. Visser, *Zacharias Ursinus: the Reluctant Reformer* (New York, 1983), pp. xiv–xvii.

Contents

Abbreviations

ADB	*Allgemeine deutsche Biographie*
AGH	*Archive für die Geschichte der Stadt Heidelberg*
AGL	*Allgemeine Gelehrten Lexicon* (Jöcher)
AHR	*American Historical Review*
AJT	*American Journal of Theology*
APG(F)	Abhandlungen zur Philosophie und ihrer Geschichte (Leipzig)
APSR	*American Political Science Review*
AQ	*American Quarterly*
ARG	*Archive für Reformationsgeschichte*
Athenae Cantab.	*Athenae Cantabrigienses*
AThR	*Anglican Theological Review*
AusSemBul	*Austin Seminary Bulletin*
AV	Authorized Version (1611)
BFChTh	Beiträge zur Förderung christlicher Theologie (ser. 1)
BFChTh.M	Beiträge zur Förderung christlicher Theologie (ser. 2)
BFER	*The British and Foreign Evangelical Review*
BGLRK	Beiträge zur Geschichte und Lehre der reformierten Kirche
BHRef	Bibliotheca humanistica (et) reformatorica
BHTh	Beiträge zur historischen Theologie
BPfKG	*Blätter für pfälzische Kirchengeschichte*
BPW	Beiträge zur politischen Wissenschaft
BQ	*Baptist Quarterly*
BRR	*Baptist Reformational Review*
BS	*Bibliotheca Sacra*
BSHST	Basler Studien zur historischen und systematischen Theologie (Basler und Berner Studien zur historischen und systematischen Theologie)
BSRK	*Die Bekenntnisschriften der reformierten Kirche*
BWPGN	*Biographisch woordenboek van protestantsche godgeleerden in Nederland*
CBTEL	*Cyclopaedia of Biblical, Theological and Ecclesiastical Literature*
ChH	*Church History*
CJT	*Canadian Journal of Theology*
CO	Calvini Opera
Com.	*Commentary*
CR	*Corpus Reformatorum*

Creeds	Schaff, *The Creeds of Christendom*
CTJ	*Calvin Theological Journal*
DBF	*Dictionnaire de biographie française*
DLV	*Dignorum laude virorum*
DNB	*Dictionary of National Biography*
DTT	*Dansk teologisk tidsskrift*
EC	*The Encyclopedia of Christianity*
EDR	*Encyclopedic Dictionary of Religion*
EETh	Einführung in die evangelische Theologie
EHR	*English Historical Review*
EKL	*Evangelisches Kirchenlexicon*
ELH	*English Literary History*
EQ	*Evangelical Quarterly*
ERE	Hastings, *Encyclopaedia of Religion and Ethics*
Found.	*Foundations*
FThSt	Freiburger theologische Studien
GThT	*Gereformeerd theologisch tijdschrift*
HdJb	*Heidelberger Jahrbücher*
HistJ	*Historical Journal*
HMPEC	*Historical Magazine of the Protestant Episcopal Church*
HThR	*Harvard Theological Review*
HZ	*Historische Zeitschrift*
JAAR	*Journal of the American Academy of Religion*
JBS	*Journal of British Studies*
JCR	*Journal of Christian Reconstruction*
JDTh	*Jahrbücher für deutsche Theologie*
JEH	*Journal of Ecclesiastical History*
JETS	*Journal of the Evangelical Theological Society*
JHI	*Journal of the History of Ideas*
JHKGV	*Jahrbuch der hessischen kirchengeschichtlichen Vereinigung*
JPH	*Journal of Presbyterian History*
JR	*Journal of Religion*
KHS	Kieler historische Studien
LASRK	Leben und ausgewählte Schriften der Väter und Begründer der reformierten Kirche
LCC	The Library of Christian Classics
LPT	A Library of Protestant Thought
LQHR	*London Quarterly and Holborn Review*
MCJN	*Milton Center of Japan News*
MennEnc	*Mennonite Encyclopedia*
MennQR	*Mennonite Quarterly Review*
MercQR	*Mercersburg Quarterly Review*
MHVPf	*Mitteilungen des historischen Vereins der Pfalz*

NA	*Nassauische Annalen*
NAGH	*Neues Archiv für die Geschichte der Stadt Heidelberg und der rheinischen Pfalz*
NatLF	*Natural Law Forum*
NDB	*Neue deutsche Biographie*
NE	*The New Englander*
NEHGR	*New England Historical and Genealogical Register*
NEQ	*New England Quarterly*
NHdJb	*Neue Heidelberger Jahrbücher*
NIDCC	*The New International Dictionary of the Christian Church*
NIDNTT	*The New International Dictionary of New Testament Theology*
NNBW	*Nieuw nederlandsch biografisch woordenboek*
NSGTK	Neue Studien zur Geschichte der Theologie und Kirche
NSHE	*The New Schaff-Herzog Encyclopedia of Religious Knowledge*
PastPres	*Past and Present*
Pensiero Polit.	*Il Pensiero Politico*
PresRev	*The Presbyterian Review*
PubColSocMass	*Publications of the Colonial Society of Massachusetts*
QGP	Quellenschriften zur Geschichte des Protestantismus
RE	*Realencyklopädie für protestantische Theologie und Kirche*
RefR(H)	*Reformed Review* (Holland, Michigan)
RGG	*Die Religion in Geschichte und Gegenwart*
RGST	Reformationsgeschichtliche Studien und Texte
RKZ	*Reformierte Kirchenzeitung*
RSV	Revised Standard Version
RThPh	*Revue de Théologie et de Philosophie*
SchHE	*A Religious Encyclopaedia or Dictionary of Biblical, Historical, Doctrinal and Practical Theology* (2nd and 3rd edns.)
SCH(L)	Studies in Church History (London)
SCH(L) subs.	Studies in Church History (London), Subsidia
ScHR	*Scottish Historical Review*
SCJ	*The Sixteenth Century Journal*
SDGSTh	Studien zur Dogmengeschichte und systematischen Theologie (Zürich)
SHCT	Studies in the History of Christian Thought
SJTh	*Scottish Journal of Theology*
SMRT	Studies in Medieval and Reformation Thought
Spec.	*Speculum*
SS	*Shakespeare Survey*

SST	Studies in Sacred Theology (The Catholic University of America)
SVRG	Schriften des Vereins für Reformationsgeschichte
TARWPV	*Theologische Arbeiten aus dem rheinischen Wissenschaftlichen Prediger-Verein*
TBLNT	*Theologisches Begriffslexicon zum Neuen Testament*
TBSL	*Transactions of the Bibliographical Society of London*
TCERK	*Twentieth Century Encyclopedia of Religious Knowledge*
TDNT	*Theological Dictionary of the New Testament*
TDOT	*Theological Dictionary of the Old Testament*
TEH	*Theologische Existenz heute*
ThJb(T)	*Theologische Jahrbücher* (Tübingen)
ThQ	*Theologische Quartalschrift* (Tübingen)
THR	Travaux d'humanisme et renaissance
ThSt(B)	Theologische Studien (Zürich)
ThStKr	*Theologische Studien und Kritiken*
ThWAT	*Theologisches Wörterbuch zum Alten Testament*
ThWNT	*Theologisches Wörterbuch zum Neuen Testament*
ThZ	*Theologische Zeitschrift*
TRE	*Theologische Realenzyklopädie*
TvG	*Tijdschrift voor geschiedenis*
VVKGB	Veröffentlichungen des Vereins für Kirchengeschichte in der evangelischen Landeskirche Badens
WCF	*Westminster Confession of Faith*
WDCH	*The Westminster Dictionary of Church History*
WdF	*Wege der Forschung*
WKL	*Weltkirchenlexicon*
WMQ	*William and Mary Quarterly*
WThJ	*Westminster Theological Journal*
YSRE	Yale Studies in Religious Education
ZBRG	Zürcher Beiträge zur Reformationsgeschichte
ZHTh	*Zeitschrift für historische Theologie*
ZKG	*Zeitschrift für Kirchengeschichte*
Zwing.	*Zwingliana*

Introduction: The Problem Stated

Forasmuche as that, which may be knowen of God, is manifest
in them: for God hathe shewed it vnto them. For the inuisible
things of him, that is, his eternal power and Godhead, are seene
by the creation of the world, being considered in his workes, to
the intent that they shoulde be without excuse. . . .

Romans 1: 19–20 (Geneva Bible, 1560)

In the past century there has been much discussion of the sixteenth-
and seventeenth-century concept of covenant and what relation it
has to Protestant dogmatics. One of the basic theological shifts in
those centuries was the manner in which Reformed Protestant
theologians of northern Europe divided biblical time. Whereas John
Calvin (1509–64), in his *Institutes of the Christian Religion*, spoke
of an Old Covenant which extended from after the Fall to Christ
and then of a New Covenant which extended from Christ to the
Day of Judgement,[1] the Westminster Confession of Faith, written
eighty years later, spoke of a covenant of works and a covenant of
grace.[2] There were basic differences between these two concepts,
differences which affected the way Calvinists thought and acted.

Most of the research done on this transformation of looking at
biblical time has been written in relation to other subjects. The vast
amount of writing on Puritanism, for instance, has brought out the
fact that from about 1585 onward many of the younger English
Puritans believed in a covenant of works and a covenant of grace. As
various aspects of the Puritan movement have been studied—
sacramental theology, the process of conversion and preparation for
conversion, science, the civil realm and its role—the fundamental
concepts of the covenant of works and the covenant of grace
consistently come to the forefront.[3]

Historians have often categorized Calvinist thinkers by national
origin, but it has become increasingly apparent that this is a
problematic grouping. While different Reformed Churches faced
different problems in different countries, their theologians were
united by Latin, a language which had been taught to them since
childhood. Although the Reformers were renowned for stressing

the language of the common people, their technical treatises were written in Latin. Using Latin they were able to communicate their ideas to each other and to form a spiritual brotherhood which extended from Geneva to Aberdeen. The Reformation might have proceeded more slowly had there not been this fluidity of communication. This phenomenon of a web of communication and its resulting unity can be observed by looking at the biographies of English and Scottish theologians in the *Dictionary of National Biography*: many of them spent time on the Continent and had gone to school there. In the biographies of countless Reformed theologians in Britain and on the Continent the same names, places, and schools keep recurring. The same is true for dedications and obituaries found in their theological works.[4]

The distinction between the covenant of works and the covenant of grace, therefore, is not simply an Anglo-American Puritan distinction, as Perry Miller implies.[5] The federal schema of theology was also a key element in Continental European Reformed dogmatics of the seventeenth century.[6] However, it was the Puritans in England and America and the Presbyterians in Scotland who popularized the idea for the common people by removing it from the domain of Latin treatises and placing it in the forefront of popular piety. For example, the Westminster Confession and Catechisms often had published with them other documents which served as appendices. One of these was 'The Sum of Saving Knowledge', which is designed for the layman as a short summary of the gospel. A summary of its contents can be found at the beginning of this short tractate:

'The Sum of Saving Knowledge' may be taken up in these four heads:—1. The woeful condition wherein all men are by nature, through breaking of the covenant of works. 2. The remedy provided for the elect in Jesus Christ by the covenant of grace. 3. The means appointed to make them partakers of this covenant. 4. The blessings which are effectually conveyed unto the elect by these means.—Which four heads are set down each of them in some few propositions.[7]

Thus far no one has explored thoroughly the origins of the shift from the Old Covenant/New Covenant distinction to the covenant of works/covenant of grace distinction, and where the covenant of works or prelapsarian covenant idea had its origin.[8] It is the purpose of this book to explore as thoroughly as possible the origin of and the reasons for this transformation in theological thinking, and to show some of the implications it would have for Protestant Reformed thought. This was an important change in a basic presupposition of Calvinist thought, and has implications for every part of life: doctrine, preaching, the understanding of the civil and ecclesiastical realms, the perception of God, and the purpose of man's existence.

In the various discussions encountered in the secondary sources,[9] there is much confusion as to what is meant by 'the federal theology', 'covenant theology', and the 'covenant idea'. This confusion has consequently led many people to trace the origins of the shift from a postlapsarian covenant schema to a prelapsarian/postlapsarian covenant schema to earlier periods in history than can be warranted.[10] W. Adams Brown, writing in 1911, distinguishes very clearly between (*a*) the covenant idea and (*b*) the covenant theology.[11]

The covenant idea is a common inheritance of the Judaeo-Christian tradition found in the Bible. In recent decades the meaning of covenant has been expanded to include a much richer Near Eastern conception of commitment.[12] Covenant theology grows out of the covenant idea. Covenant theology is a theological system in which the covenant forms the basic framework and acts as the controlling idea in that theological system. Almost all Christian theologians ultimately practice some form of covenant theology, in that they must somehow distinguish themselves as Christians and not as believers under the Old Testament dispensation. Martin Luther, for instance, saw this distinction in terms of Law and Gospel. John Calvin described it in terms of Old Testament and New Testament. The federal theology is a specific type of covenant theology, in that the covenant holds together every detail of the theological system, and is characterized by a prelapsarian and postlapsarian covenant schema centred around the first Adam and the second Adam, who is Jesus Christ.

It will be helpful if a description is given of the classic seventeenth-century confessional version of the federal theology, for that is the federal theology in its fullest bloom, and many of the implications of the federal theological system founded in the sixteenth century were being worked out during the seventeenth.[13]

'The federal theology', in this book, refers to the doctrine that God, immediately after creating Adam, made a covenant with Adam before his Fall into sin. This covenant is similar to, if not the same as, the Mosaic covenant made at Mount Sinai, and emphasizes the idea of conditionality: God says to the creatures made in his image that if they obey him, then God will bless them and they will live. But if they disobey him, then God will curse them and they shall die. The test of obedience is found in Genesis 2: 16–17: 'And the LORD God commanded the man, saying, "You may freely eat of every tree of the garden; but of the tree of the knowledge of good and evil you shall not eat, for in the day that you eat of it you shall die" ' (RSV). Furthermore, part of the covenant before the Fall involves the giving of the moral law, the Decalogue, to Adam, and laying it on his heart; in his perfect estate Adam knew the moral law perfectly and obeyed it perfectly.

Finally, this covenant was binding upon all men at all times in all places, both before and after the Fall, by virtue of their descent from Adam. If Adam had not fallen, his children would have been obligated to keep this Edenic covenant. Adam fell, but still his children are obligated to keep the prelapsarian covenant.

The Westminster Confession of Faith (1647) states the doctrine in this manner:

Chap. VII.
Of God's Covenant with Man.

1. The Distance between God and the Creature is so great, that although reasonable Creatures do owe Obedience unto him as their Creator, yet they could never have any Fruition of him as their Blessedness and Reward, but by some voluntary Condescension on God's Part, which he hath been pleased to express by way of Covenant.

2. The first covenant made with Man, was a Covenant of Works, wherein Life was promised to Adam, and in him to his Posterity; upon Condition of perfect and personal Obedience. . . .

Chap. XIX.
Of the Law of God.

1. God gave to Adam a Law as a Covenant of Works, by which he bound him and all his Posterity to personal, entire, exact and perpetual Obedience; promised Life upon the fulfilling, and threatened Death upon the Breach of it; and indued him with Power and Ability to keep it.

2. This Law after his Fall, continued to be a perfect Rule of righteousness, and [as such] was delivered by God upon Mount Sinai. . . .

5. The Moral Law doth for ever bind all, as well justified Persons as others, to the Obedience thereof; and that not only in regard of the Matter contained in it, but also in respect of the Authority of God the Creator who

gave it. Neither doth Christ in the Gospel any way dissolve, but much strengthen this Obligation.[14]

Man, however, broke this covenant of works and fell into sin. Therefore man needs God's grace to be restored to his original estate of perfection and happiness. Thus God makes with man a second covenant:

Chapter VII.
Of God's Covenant with Man.

. . .

3. Man by his Fall made himself incapable of Life by that Covenant, the Lord was pleased to make a second, commonly called the Covenant of Grace: Wherein he freely offereth unto Sinners Life and Salvation by Jesus Christ: . . .

5. This Covenant was differently administered in the time of the Law, and in the time of the Gospel: . . . There are not therefore two Covenants of Grace differing in Substance, but one and the same under various Dispensations.[15]

Thus we see that the classical distinctions between the Old Testament and the New Testament (and the Mosaic Old Covenant and the Christian New Covenant) are subsumed under one covenant, the postlapsarian covenant of grace, and that the new element in Calvinist thinking is that of the prelapsarian covenant of works. In the federal schema the covenant of grace now consists of Jesus Christ, the covenant-keeper, keeping and fulfilling the prelapsarian covenant of works as the second Adam. Christ takes Adam's place as the obedient God-man and fulfils the prelapsarian covenant where Adam failed. This was known as the active obedience of Christ. Furthermore, Christ takes upon himself the punishment, anger, and wrath of God which Adam deserves for his disobedience, even though Christ was sinless. This was known as the passive obedience of Christ. This gracious work of redemption was then applied to the elect of God's sovereign choice.[16] The postlapsarian covenant of grace is really therefore the prelapsarian covenant of works in disguise, but a new Adam (Christ) was needed to keep the covenant which God had established with man at the beginning of the world. Once the prelapsarian covenant of works is established it can never be broken.

It is important to note several aspects and implications of the idea of the prelapsarian covenant or covenant of works. The first aspect of the federal theological system that we should notice is that the prelapsarian covenant of works binds all men, before and after the Fall.[17] Christian and Pagan, Turk and Jew, king, queen, and commoner—all must obey it. Each man and woman will stand before the judgement seat of Christ on the basis of whether or not he or she has obeyed the covenant of works. While because of Adam's Fall no one can be totally obedient to its stipulations, nevertheless each man is bound to them. The ramifications of this idea are extremely important. Through the idea of all men being required to obey the covenant of works through Adam versus some men enjoying the covenant of grace through Christ, one now had a potential basis for the State: the State, being the government of all men, could be founded on the covenant of works and the law of God, whereas the Church could be founded on the covenant of grace. The State could be entrusted with enforcing the law of God.[18]

An example of this concept can be found in the conflict in early seventeenth-century England over the sabbath day. Most people would agree with such commandments of the Decalogue as 'Do not lie' and 'Do not steal', but when it came to keeping a day of the week holy, with no recreation or work, the issue became much more sensitive and problematical. Most federal theologians came to the conclusion that all people, both members and non-members of the Church, must keep the sabbath, and that this commandment should be enforced by the State. Historians of Puritanism and Presbyterianism have traced the growth of 'hyper-Sabbatarianism' in the late sixteenth and early seventeenth centuries among these groups. The sabbath issue rises to the forefront concurrently with the rise of the federal theology between 1590 and 1640, and it seems that extreme Sabbatarianism had its roots in the federal theology.[19]

Another aspect of the covenant of works motif which must be noted is that man now becomes basically a legal creature from the very beginning—at creation. The Reformed camp is confirming its belief that the law of God was written on the heart of man in the estate of perfection, not simply given for the first time at Mount Sinai. This strongly reinforced the Calvinist antipathy towards antinomianism and its extreme logical conclusion: libertinism.[20]

The final aspect which we should note about the covenant of works is that it becomes, in some sense, the primary covenant which God has made with man. The Adamic relationship of perfection in Eden takes on greater weight than the Abrahamic relationship of grace. Grace is, as it were, a remedy to correct creation's fall into sin. The eschatological importance of the covenant of works thus becomes significant: man is being restored, after the Day of Judgement, to the relationship which he enjoyed with God prior to the Fall—with some differences. The federal theologian thus interpreted Jeremiah 31: 31–4 as, in some sense, a return to the covenantal state of Eden, when the law of God will be written on the hearts of the redeemed elect.[21]

This new schema of biblical history has extensive implications, some of which have not yet been explored, and most of which came to fruition in the seventeenth century. As a consequence of this transformation of thought, there is a shift in the importance of certain *loci* of scripture. The doctrine of creation, and the relationship between Adam and Christ, took on greater importance.[22] While exegetes continued to discuss the importance of the covenants with Noah, Abraham, Moses, and David (as aspects of the postlapsarian covenant of grace), there was now a place for a doctrine of nature and a theology of creation: creation and redemption each had its proper place. Christianity spoke both to the areas of the created world and to the areas of grace and redemption. The federal theologian now has the potential for a basic world view which includes 'nature' and 'grace'. According to this schema most men live only under nature, but the redeemed live under both the spheres of nature and of grace. Areas such as science, politics, law, and logic had roots in the covenant of works in creation. At times, the covenant of works was called the 'natural covenant' or the 'covenant of creation'. Theology and religious activity could be related to the covenant of grace. Ideally the categories were not to conflict (e.g., the Church-State problem is a major consideration at this juncture), but both should complement and assist each other, and both were under God and his law. There would come a time, in the new heavens and the new earth—the *eschaton*—when there would be no conflict between the two spheres, because the sphere of grace will have restored fallen nature to its original perfection.[23]

The federal theology potentially provided an adequate base for the reconstruction of northern European Protestant society and culture. With the loss of the traditional institutions of the Church and its sacraments, and the demise of canon law, northern European society was searching for an adequate base for its social ethic. How

could men be forced to live a Christian life-style when you were not
sure that they were under the covenant of grace and that their hearts
were 'turned unto the Lord'? The medieval way was to count men
as included under grace through the means of external signs—the
sacraments and outward behaviour. If a man was regularly
observing the sacraments and not living in heinous sin, he was to be
considered a Christian. The Reformed Protestant, however, was
much more concerned with the heart. Not all men had 'hearts
turned unto the Lord', yet the Protestant wanted all men to live
godly lives. One possible solution for the Reformed camp was to
adopt the idea of the covenant of works, which bound all men to
keep the law of God through Adam and yet did not place them,
perhaps falsely, in the realm of grace.[24]

The conflict between the Separatists and Non-Separating Puritans
in England is a good example of this dilemma. The Separatists
insisted upon withdrawing from the world and the Church to a pure
society of saints, whereas the Non-Separating Puritans insisted
upon participating actively in redeeming the world and reforming
the Church. While they were often distressed at the behaviour of
various churchmen, the Non-Separating Puritans still did not
withdraw to a separate existence. The only exceptions were the
saints who went to New England, and even they insisted that they
were not separating. The Anglicans were generally at the opposite
pole from the Separatists, in that they followed the medieval pattern
of maintaining that the Church was essentially coextensive with
society.[25]

In Anglo-American Puritan theology, the method of evangelistic
preaching to the unconverted underwent some definite shifts. The
means through which a man was thought to be converted became
more complicated and thus evangelistic technique became more
sophisticated: unconverted man first must be shown that through
Adam he has broken and cannot keep the covenant of works, and
that he thus stands condemned. He must therefore flee to the
covenant of grace. Before he can do so, however, some preachers,
especially Puritans, felt his heart must be 'prepared': there was
much discussion as to what this involved, but in brief the covenant
of works became a means to prod the unconverted to grace, in that
it prepared him for conversion by showing him his lost condition.
Concomitant with that is the notion of a man 'co-operating' with
nature and natural means as much as possible to bring him to the

point of conversion. Currently a fascinating history of the Puritan doctrine of preparationism and conversion is being explored and investigated.[26]

Before the rise of the federal theology in the late sixteenth century there were various theological conceptions of the covenant, and even some precursors to the idea of a covenant in Eden. It is to these concepts that we now turn. We will briefly examine the views of the covenant idea which were circulating amongst theologians prior to the crucial year 1562, when the prelapsarian covenant was first introduced into Reformed theology. Since we have distinguished between a prelapsarian and a postlapsarian covenant, we will follow that distinction in our investigation.

Both John Calvin and Heinrich Bullinger (1504–75) believed in a postlapsarian covenant of grace. Calvin explicated his doctrine of the covenant in Book II of the *Institutes*: 'The Knowledge of God the Redeemer in Christ, First Disclosed to the Fathers Under the Law, and Then to Us in the Gospel.'[27] Chapters 10 and 11 of Book II deal with the similarity and differences between the Old and New Testaments: 'The Similarity of the Old and New Testaments . . . The Difference Between the Two Testaments.'[28] But in both of these testaments all of God's people are in intimate covenant with him: 'Now we can clearly see from what has already been said that all men adopted by God into the company of his people since the beginning of the world were covenanted to him by the same law and by the bond of the same doctrine as obtains among us.'[29]

The two testaments form a unity: they are exactly the same in (1) substance (*substantia*) and (2) reality (*re ipsa*). However, they do differ in dispensation (*administratio*). Under the section dealing with differences Calvin lists five:

1. The Old Testament is dispensed in a physical way; the New Testament is dispensed in a spiritual way.[30]

2. The Old Testament is the shadow of the truth; the New Testament is the substance of the truth.[31]

3. The Old Testament is the letter of the law; the New Testament is the spirit of the law.[32]

4. The Old Testament leads to fear; the New Testament leads to freedom.[33]

5. The Old Testament deals only with one nation; the New Testament deals with many nations.[34]

Calvin makes no mention in any of his works of a prelapsarian covenant with Adam.[35] However, there is evidence that, at least to a certain degree, Calvin considered the Edenic relationship between God and Adam to be covenantal in nature. This can be found in the *Institutes*, in the section devoted to the sacraments. For Calvin, a sacrament is a sign of a covenant between God and man. Sometimes sacraments are miraculous (the light in the smoking firepot given to Abraham—Genesis 15: 17); at other times sacraments are natural (baptism and the Lord's Supper):

The term 'sacrament', as we have previously discussed its nature so far, embraces generally all those signs which God has ever enjoined upon men to render them more certain and confident of the truth of his promises. He sometimes willed to present these in natural things, at other times set them forth in miracles.[36]

As an example of a natural sacrament Calvin points to the tree of life: 'Here are some examples of the first kind. One is when he gave Adam and Eve the tree of life as a guarantee of immortality, that they might assure themselves of it as long as they should eat of its fruit (Gen. 2: 9; 3: 22).'[37] This is the only evidence that I know of in Calvin's writing which points to any conception of a prelapsarian covenant in paradise.

Heinrich Bullinger also gave the idea of covenant a central position in theology.[38] He took Zwingli's use of the covenant to defend infant baptism and expanded it into a much broader concept. He used it for a unified vision of history: history, for Bullinger, is not marked by radical discontinuity between the Old and New Testaments, but by unity and continuity. The crucial starting-point for Bullinger is the covenant with Abraham. Bullinger points out interesting parallels between the Old and New Testaments:

1. God concludes the covenant with Abraham appearing as El Shaddai, God Almighty; when Jesus Christ is incarnated he appears as God Almighty.

2. The covenant with Abraham is directed toward all nations, not just the Jews. When Christ comes, he comes to offer the gospel to all nations, not just to the Jews.

3. A condition is laid upon Abraham: 'Walk before me and be blameless.' Jesus Christ fulfils that condition.

4. Circumcision is made the sacrament of the Old Testament, which has its parallel with baptism in the New Testament.[39]

If Abraham and Christ are the two basic *loci* of history for
Bullinger, why was the law given to Moses? Bullinger takes the
Mosaic law as a concession to human weakness. The children of
Israel had been led astray by the sinfulness of Egypt, and so the
Abrahamic covenant to be strengthened with guide-lines of
conduct.

Bullinger makes no reference to a prelapsarian covenant with
Adam. Mark Walter Karlberg, in his recent dissertation,[40] tries to
show that Bullinger made some sort of reference to a prelapsarian
covenant with Adam in his treatise *De testamento Dei unico et
aeterno* (1534):

> As far as we can discover, there is only one instance in which he alludes to
> the covenant prior to the fall, the 'most ancient of all covenants with
> Adam,' which covenant was reestablished by the finger of God upon tables
> of stone. The context of this reference emphasizes the temporal, peda-
> gogical function of the Mosaic law specifically in regard to the ceremonial
> law.[41]

Karlberg is referring to the following passage in Bullinger's *De
testamento*:

> Primum ergo ipsa prisci foederis capita restituit, sed copiosius exposuit,
> inque tabulos lapideas proprio digita inscripsit. In his autem nulla adhuc
> ceremoniarum mentio. Sat enim praescriptum erat fidelibus. Verum dum
> isti infideles et perfidi esse pergerent, iniectum est humeris miserorum onus
> ceremoniarum, quo caruere prisci. Atqui in hunc finem atque hoc consilio
> iniectum ex caussa impellente constat, ne alienis deis instituerent sacra:
> propria erga instituit, eaque sibi ad tempus correctionis placere pronuncia-
> vit quae sine vero spiritu et sine vera fide perfecta adeoque sine Christo
> negligebat, ut vel ista ratione testamentum confirmaret, praeterea et Christi
> mysterium hisce velut typis inuolueret, essentique sacramenta et verba
> quaedam visibilia.[42]

However, we fail to see the validity of this assertion. There is no
mention in the text of the most ancient of all covenants 'with
Adam', but simply of the most ancient covenant, which would refer
to the covenant of grace. If we read this carefully we see that
Bullinger is speaking of the ignorance of the Israelites in Egypt, and
how God had to teach them anew of the covenant with Abraham.
Lillback translates the passage in this manner:

> First, therefore, He re-established the very heads of the ancient covenant,
> but He explained it more fully, and He wrote in tables of stone with His
> own finger. Moreover, in these things there is no mention thus far of

ceremonies. Indeed, it is enough that the written rule was for the faithful. Truly, while they continued to be unbelieving and unfaithful, the burden of the ceremonies was imposed by the arms of pity, which the ancients never had. Both to this end and by this counsel, He established the imposition out of an urgent cause, that they not institute the worship of a foreign god. Therefore, He established a special thing, and by this He declared Himself to be pleased for the time of correction, which He was passing over without the true Spirit and without the true completed faith and thus without Christ, so that He might establish the testament even with that plan (Ps. 98: 8–11.) Further, by this He might cover the mystery of Christ even as by figures, and there might be certain sacraments and visible words.[43]

J. Wayne Baker, in his extensive study of Bullinger's doctrine of the covenant, has not found any reference to a prelapsarian covenant.[44]

Wolfgang Musculus (1497–1563) comes close to the conception of a covenant binding all men when he points out in his *Loci Communes* of 1563 that the covenant with Noah is made with all men while the covenant of Abraham is made only with the elect:

Of the Couenant and Testament of God.

Thirdly, I finde that the couenant of God is of two sortes. One is generall, another is speciall and euerlasting. The general couenant is that, which he made with this whole frame of the earth and all that dwelleth therein, as well beastes as men, with the day also and the night, winter and sommer, cold and heate, seed time and haruest . . . This couenant is general, bicause it concerneth the whole worlde: and it maye be called earthly and temporall, bicause it doth touch the stedfastness of earthly matters, as it appeareth by the very wordes: and it dureth no longer than the standyng of this worlde, which shal once perish . . . The speciall and euerlasting couenant, is the same which he hath vouchesauyd to make with his elect and beleuing.[45]

Thus we see that the Reformers connected the idea of covenant with a postlapsarian dispensation of grace, as an antidote to sin.[46]

At least two theologians, however, explicitly proposed the idea of a prelapsarian covenant with Adam before Zacharias Ursinus (1534–83) did so in 1562. The first was St Augustine (354–430). The second was the Tridentine prelate Ambrosius Catharinus (1487–1553).

It is remarkable that, with one exception, no one has noted the fact that Augustine, alone amongst the fathers of the Church, spoke of a prelapsarian covenant with Adam.[47] Actually, for Augustine it was a prelapsarian *testamentum*. In his *Civitas Dei*, Book XVI, Chapter 27, Augustine makes one very short reference to a 'first covenant': 'But the first covenant, made with the first man, is certainly this: "On the day you eat, you will surely die." '[48] This is placed in the context of a discussion of the Abrahamic covenant and its relationship to circumcision, in which the question of infant salvation is brought forward. The entire passage is as follows:

'The perishing of the male child, if not circumcised on the eighth day.' Another question may cause perplexity. How are we to interpret the statement in this passage that 'the male child who is not circumcised in the flesh of the foreskin on the eighth day, his soul will perish from his people, because he has broken my covenant'? Now this is in no way the fault of the infant whose soul is said to be doomed to perish; and it is not the infant himself who has broken the covenant of God; it is his elders, who have not taken care to circumcise him. That is, unless it is because even infants have broken the covenant, not in consequence of any particular act in their own life but in consequence of the origin which is common to all mankind, since all have broken God's covenant in that one man in whom all sinned. Now it is true that many covenants are called God's covenants, apart from the two principal ones, the Old and New, which anyone may get to know by reading them. But the first covenant, made with the first man, is certainly this: 'On the day you eat, you will surely die.' Hence the statement in the book called Ecclesiasticus. 'All flesh grows old like a garment.' For the covenant from the beginning is, 'You will surely die.' Now, seeing that a more explicit law was given later, and the Apostle says, 'Where there is no law, there is no law-breaking', how can the psalm be true, where we read, 'I have counted all sinners on earth as law-breakers'? It can only be true on the assumption that those who are held bound by any sin are guilty of a breach of some law.[49]

Augustine goes on to argue that an infant has original sin because in Adam the infant has broken the covenant which God made with Adam. Augustine never develops the idea further, however. N. Diemer is the only modern scholar who has noted the existence of this passage.[50] In my research thus far the sixteenth- and seventeenth-century federal theologians seem to be oblivious to it.

The question came up again within the same context at the Council of Trent in 1546, again during the discussions of transmission of original sin. We know this fact from the 1619 history of the Council of Trent by Paolo Sarpi (1552–1623), originally written in Italian.[51] Sarpi was not present at the Council; however, he maintains that he read all public records available, the writings of various prelates who were members of the Council, the letters written between the Pope and the Council, and an unpublished register of notes and letters of members of the Council.[52] His account, translated into English by Nathanael Brent,[53] gives us an account of daily Council proceedings.

Sarpi says that Ambrosius Catharinus, a Nominalist theologian, was troubled by the Realist view of the transmission of sin, and that therefore he suggested that in the same way that God had made a covenant with Abraham, God has also made a covenant (*patto*) with Adam:

And hee explained his opinion in this forme: that as God made a covenant with Abraham and all his posteritie, when he made him father of the faithfull, so when he gave originall righteousnesse to Adam and all mankinde, he made him seale an obligation in the name of all, to keep it for himselfe and them, observing the commandements; which because he transgressed, he lost it as well for others as himselfe, and incurred the punishments also for them; the which as they are derived into every one, so the very transgression of Adam belonged to every one; to him as the cause, to others by vertue of the covenant; so that the action of Adam is actuall sinne in him, and imputed to others, is originall; because when he sinned, all mankind did sinne with him.[54]

According to George Park Fisher, Sarpi observes that

the opinion of Catharinus was best understood, 'because it was expressed by a political conceit of a bargain made by one for his posterity, which being transgressed, they are all undoubtedly bound; and many of the Fathers did favor that; but perceiving the contradiction of the other divines, they durst not receive it.'[55]

Catharinus was opposed by the orthodox theologian Petrus de Soto (1500–63), who upheld the Augustinian idea of all men being *in* Adam, not just simply being represented *by* Adam, as Catharinus was saying. Catharinus himself, however, tried to use Augustine as an authority, according to Sarpi:

Hee proved the covenant of God with Adam, by a place of the Prophet Osea, by another of Ecclesiasticus, and by many places of St. Austin. That the sinne of every one is the act onely of the transgression of Adam, he proved by St. Paul, when he saith, That by the disobedience of one man, many are made sinners . . .[56]

It is interesting to note that Catharinus also referred to Hosea as an authority. This would be a reference to Hosea 6: 7, which in the Vulgate reads: 'Ipsi autem sicut Adam transgressi sunt pactum; ibi praevaricati sunt in me.' The Westminster Assembly of Divines did not use this verse as a defence of the prelapsarian covenant. Indeed, the Protestant tradition did not regard this verse as a reference to a prelapsarian covenant with Adam at all. The Authorized Version of 1611 reads as follows: 'But they like men have transgressed the

covenant; there have they dealt treacherously against me.' Only
when the concept had been questioned did certain churches and
theologians add Hosea 6: 7 as a proof text.[57]

Whether the Reformed theologians of the late sixteenth century
were aware of this discussion is not known. However, the idea of a
prelapsarian covenant is rarely introduced into Reformed theology
in the context of the discussion of Pelagianism. Charles J. Butler has
commented:

> Although Catharinus originally deduced a covenant with Adam to handle
> the problem of human guilt from the parallel to the covenant with
> Abraham, the appearance of the covenant of works in Reformed circles
> came later. It depended on the law principle and the principle of
> representation. Traditional Augustinian Realism with its understanding of
> Adam as the natural head of the race seemed to retard the concept of him as
> federally representative of the race. This grew from thought on Christ as
> mediator of the covenant of grace. Until that came, Reformed thinkers,
> moved like Catharinus to seek a legal base for mankind's responsibility and
> guilt—especially as they limited the covenant of grace more and more to
> the elect—struggled first to a covenant of nature resting on man through
> creation either along with the entire world or pressed directly on him as
> part of God's image.[58]

Butler shows the connection of the covenant of works concept with
an explanation of the transmission of Adam's guilt and mankind's
guilt. But another way of interpreting the rise of the prelapsarian
covenant concept is to connect the covenant of works concept with
an explanation of Adam's original guilt, for after 1555 Reformed
theologians were faced with Beza's supralapsarian interpretation of
the eternal decrees of God. However, further exploration of the
relationship between the Pelagian question and the federal theology
should be pursued. Certainly the idea of the covenant of works
being binding upon all men is parallel to the problem of sin being
imputed to all men by virtue of their descent from Adam. If the sin
of Adam and its punishment are to be meted out to all men, could it
not be said that the obligation of Adam is also meted out to all men?

It is the contention of this book that the development of the
prelapsarian covenant of works idea in the second half of the
sixteenth century came as a result of a desire by orthodox Reformed
theologians to postulate for Adam in his Edenic state of perfection
what they had postulated for all mankind in its fallen and sinful
estate. Calvin and others had affirmed two realities for the fallen
world: the utter sovereignty of God over human action, without

God being the author of sin, on the one hand, and the utter responsibility of man for his conduct, on the other. For the Calvinist, both statements were true, making it, not a paradox (in which two statements appear true yet contradictory), but an antinomy (where two statements are true and contradictory). When Theodore Beza moved the discussion of predestination from Calvin's credal form to a situation where the doctrine of predestination is formulated around the decrees of God, there was much greater danger for falling into the error of ascribing to God responsibility for sin, especially Adam's original sin. The prelapsarian covenant with Adam was a means by which orthodox Calvinists of the late sixteenth century, some of whom adopted the Bezan form of explaining predestination, could maintain the tension between prelapsarian Adamic human responsibility and divine sovereignty. Late sixteenth-century Reformed theology taught that God, in his mercy and providence, condescended to Adam in a way that was comprehensible to him, that is, in terms of covenant. This covenant gave moral responsibility to Adam, and yet it was also the means by which the sovereign decrees of God concerning Adam were carried out. For the Calvinist of whatever variety, the prelapsarian covenant with Adam did not 'soften' the decree of God concerning the Fall; rather, it affirmed it, expanded it, explained it, and worked it out.

In order to elaborate upon this theme, it is necessary first to define certain terms and concepts which will be used throughout this essay, terms and concepts which from c.1550 were the basic presuppositions of most orthodox Calvinistic theologians.[59]

The orthodox Reformed Protestant believed in providence. That is, he maintained that nothing happens without God's being, somehow, sovereignly in control. God was infinitely just, infinitely wise, and infinitely good. There was no evil in him, nor was he responsible for evil. Yet evil exists, and Adam fell, and in some secret way this all fell into the sovereign plan of God. The French Confession of Faith stated a belief in providence in this manner in 1559:

Article VIII

We believe that he not only created all things, but that he governs and directs them, disposing and ordaining by his sovereign will all that happens in the world; not that he is the author of evil, or that the guilt of it can be imputed to him, as his will is the sovereign and infallible rule of all right and justice; but he hath wonderful means of so making use of devils and sinners that he can turn to good the evil which they do, and of which they are guilty. And thus, confessing that the providence of God orders all things, we humbly bow before the secrets which are hidden to us, without questioning what is above our understanding; but rather making use of what is revealed to us in Holy Scripture for our peace and safety, inasmuch as God, who has all things in subjection to him, watches over us with a Father's care, so that not a hair of our heads shall fall without his will. And yet he restrains the devils and all our enemies, so that they can not harm us without his leave.[60]

The doctrine of predestination fell within the realm of providence. Whereas providence dealt with the whole creation of God, predestination concerned individual human beings. Reformed theologians believed that God, from all eternity, predestined certain people to salvation of his own free mercy and good pleasure, without foreseeing that they would turn to the gospel of their own free will, since their will was bound to evil because of the Fall. God also, from all eternity, passed over some and predestined them to everlasting wrath in hell. However, those who ended up in hell could not complain: all men are sinners because of Adam's Fall, and as a consequence all men by nature hate God. God cannot be considered a tyrant; because of every man's sin he has every right to cast the entire world into hell. On the contrary, God should be worshipped for his mercy to the elect saints. But for the grace of God the elect would end up in hell too. God did not have to save them if he did not so desire.[61]

While other theologians had a difficult time explaining the hardening of Pharaoh's heart in Exodus and the hardening of Israel's heart in Isaiah 6, Reformed theology had a definite answer for this problem. God had every right to harden Pharaoh's heart and thus allow Pharaoh to sin more. Why? Because Pharaoh, because of Adam's Fall, was a wicked sinner already. God was simply giving him up to the lusts of his heart, as in Romans 1: 24. God was not the author of Pharaoh's sin; he was simply permitting Pharaoh to follow his own wicked nature. Yet God had planned the hardening of Pharaoh's heart from all eternity. To deny this doctrine would be to deny God's sovereignty, omnipotence and omniscience. God knew that Adam would fall, and as a result of the Fall man's will, and Pharaoh's will, would be bound to sin. In the eyes of God Pharaoh could do nothing but sin, and God in his justice had a right to punish him by hardening his heart.

There were, however, various permutations of this doctrine. Some theologians made a distinction between single predestination and double predestination. Single predestination referred to election to salvation only. It did not mention predestination to damnation, maintaining that the Scriptures were relatively quiet about this matter and that therefore theologians should not step where angels fear to tread. The Thirty-Nine Articles of the Church of England provide a good example of this more moderate doctrine:

XVII.

Of predestination and election.

Predestination to lyfe, is the euerlastyng purpose of God, whereby (before the foundations of the world were layd) he hath constantly decreed by his councell secrete to vs, to deliuer from curse and damnation, those whom he hath chosen in Christe out of mankynd, and to bryng them by Christe to euerlastyng saluation, as vessels made to honour. Wherefore they which be indued with so excellent a benefite of God, he called accordyng to Gods purpose by his spirite workyng in due season: they through grace obey the callyng: they be iustified freely: they be made sonnes of God by adoption: they be made lyke the image of his onelye begotten sonne Jesus Christe: they walke religiously in good workes, and at length by Gods mercy, they attaine to euerlastyng felicitie.[62]

Double predestination includes both the decrees of election and of reprobation, as stated above. Election, sometimes used interchangeably with the word predestination, refers usually to the choice of God for salvation only; the word, however, would be used by both single and double predestinarians. High Calvinism held to double predestination. In England a group of dissatisfied English Calvinists tried to change the Thirty-Nine Articles from a document teaching single predestination to a document teaching double predestination. They proposed the Lambeth Articles in 1595. The first of the Lambeth Articles stated: '1. God from eternity hath predestinated certain men unto life; certain men he hath reprobated.'[63]

The doctrine of predestination was also explained in various ways. In the earlier part of the sixteenth century, theologians tended to explain predestination around the outlines of the creed: Father, Son, and Holy Spirit and the Holy Catholic Church. By the end of the sixteenth century, the decrees themselves and the order of the decrees provided the framework of explanation for many Calvinists, so that those who adopted this framework were ultimately grouped into a school of thought called 'High Calvinism.'

High Calvinists, along with those who believed in double predestination, split into two groups at the end of the sixteenth century: infralapsarians and supralapsarians. The differences between these two groups, both of whom were considered orthodox, arose over the way God viewed man when he elected or reprobated him in the counsels of eternity.[64] The supralapsarian maintained that God's ultimate purpose was the revelation of his glory through the salvation of some men and the reprobation of others, and that everything in his providence happens with that object in mind. The infralapsarian preferred not to speculate concerning God's ultimate providential plan: God's main purpose may be to manifest his glory by saving some and reprobating others, but on the other hand it may be something else, totally hidden to the mind of man and not mentioned in the Scriptures.[65]

The order of God's decrees can therefore be summarized in this manner:

Infralapsarianism
1. The decree to create man.
2. The decree to permit the Fall of man.
3. The decree to elect some of these fallen men and to pass by the rest.
4. The decree to provide a redeemer for fallen men.
5. The decree to send the Holy Spirit to apply this redemption to the elect.

Supralapsarianism
1. The decree to elect and save men, who are spoken of as 'creatable'.
2. The decree to create man.
3. The decree to permit man to fall.
4. The decree to send Christ to redeem the elect.
5. The decree to send the Holy Spirit to apply to the chosen of God the redemption to be procured by Christ.[66]

The basic question at stake was this: does God look at man as an uncreated being whom he will then purpose to create and then redeem or send to hell, or does he look at man, in the eternal counsel of his will, as a sinner having fallen because of Adam's sin, heading towards hell and therefore in need of redemption?[67]

Arminianism was considered by High Calvinism to be a heresy, and was condemned as such at the Synod of Dort (Dordrecht in the Netherlands) in 1618–19. Arminianism was a rebellion against the Calvinistic doctrine of grace and predestination, and was centred upon the following five theological points:

1. Man is not totally depraved; he has some ability to choose God and his grace.
2. God elected man on the basis of foreknowledge; he saw ahead of time that certain men would, of their own free will, choose to repent and come to Christ for salvation.
3. The atonement of Christ was for all men, not just the elect. Christ's blood was shed for all men, and it was the responsibility of each man to use his or her free will to repent.
4. God's grace is not irresistible: man, of his own free will, could choose to reject the gospel.
5. Some Arminians taught that a saint's salvation was mutable; one could be redeemed and then, somehow, fall from grace by an exceedingly wicked sin. This therefore gave Christians an impetus to obey the law of God and to live morally upright lives, lest they fall into reprobation and the flames of hell.[68]

The precise links between Arminianism and the supralapsarianism versus infralapsarianism controversy have not yet been explicitly delineated in a historical manner. Neither is there a careful study of the early stages of Arminianism in the 1590s.[69]

Antinomianism was at the other end of the spectrum from Arminianism, at least in its view of ethical conduct. There were basically three types. The first type held that the law was completely abrogated with the coming of Christ, and that it was not needed in the preaching of the gospel. This variety set itself against both Lutheranism and Calvinism. The second type held that the law was needed in the preaching of the gospel and was relevant until the time of conversion, but that the believer, after his redemption, was in no way obligated to keep the law, especially the Decalogue. His life in Jesus Christ took care of his own personal moral responsibility; he no longer had to worry about ethics and ethical questions at all, at least consciously. The third type grew out of determinism, or a Calvinism construed as deterministic. Those who took this position argued that since everything was predestined, there was no reason to bother to live moral lives, to repent, or, as in the case of hyper-Calvinism, to preach the gospel. The extreme logical conclusions of antinomianism could be libertinism, but not all antinomians became libertines. Most antinomians lived very moral and law-abiding lives.[70]

The key event in all of these questions is the Fall of Adam. It is Adam's Fall which changes everything. For the Reformed Protestant, any good thing which happens after Adam's Fall is purely from the mercy and providence of God; anything bad which happens man deserves, because he is a sinner. The bad thing may have been planned from all eternity by God (without God being construed in any way as being responsible for evil), but it was always with the knowledge that he knew Adam would fall, and that therefore man would be a sinner when the bad thing happened. The Fall was of the utmost importance to the Reformed world view, for it radically altered man's relationship to God, a relationship which would not be corrected until after the Day of Judgement, in the new heavens and the new earth. Every problem in the world comes as a result of Adam's Fall: sickness, political strife, wars, heretical theology, marital problems. Indeed, the reason man gets lost trying to untangle the maze of God's providential ways is that he is a sinner and has a myopic view of God's mercy and justice.

It was an important doctrine of Reformed belief that God's providence ruled over the world after the Fall. But did God's providence cover Adam's sin and Adam's will? Providence *had* to rule over the will of fallen man, because for the Calvinist the result of Adam's sin was that man's will was bound and prone to all sorts of wickedness. There could be no salvation for fallen men but for the providence of God.

But what about Adam's will and God's providence? Before the Fall was it not free? What about original sin? Was it fair for Adam—and for the rest of mankind—to have God's sovereign providence extend over the Fall? Should it not be that Adam had absolute and total free will in that one crucial decision? But then how does one reconcile the sovereignty of God and the original Fall of man? Is it not fair to say that the Fall was the one thing which God foreknew, and that with this knowledge he then, in the secret counsel of his will, predestined in his providence all things which come to pass, including the salvation of the elect and the reprobation of the lost?

This was a crucial question being discussed among intellectuals and theologians of northern Europe during the period 1550–1600. The Reformation had now been established, and the lines between Roman Catholicism, Lutheranism, Calvinism, and the various sects had been established. The several camps were now entrenching themselves to do battle. It is the contention of this book that the idea of the covenant of works, or prelapsarian covenant, was introduced by Reformed theologians to help resolve this question of God's providence and Adam's original sin.

The earliest reference to a covenant with Adam before the Fall, in Reformed theology of the sixteenth century, is found in the *Catechismus Maior* or Major Catechism of Zacharias Ursinus, written in 1561–2. The catechism appeared at a crucial period in the history of Reformed dogmatics and its doctrine of providence, predestination, and election. By 1600 the idea of the prelapsarian covenant was accepted as basic orthodoxy by a host of Calvinist theologians.

We have established the fact that the identifying feature of the federal theology is the prelapsarian covenant of works. The various secondary sources tend to emphasize the postlapsarian covenant of grace as the important feature of the federal theology. Since this is a study in the origins of the federal theology, and therefore a study in the origins of the prelapsarian covenant with Adam, it is important that we identify those secondary sources which deal with the history of the prelapsarian covenant and which are of critical importance and then examine their treatment of the concept. The number of these sources is somewhat limited, for most of the scholarly work done thus far has dealt with the far more commonplace postlapsarian covenant of grace.[71]

Heinrich Heppe, one of the founding scholars of the history of Reformed dogmatics, deals with the federal theology in his 1857 work *Dogmatik des deutschen Protestantismus im sechzehnten Jahrhundert*.[72] Heppe's work is groundbreaking in several respects. He is the first to identify with precision some of the basic writings which can be considered federalistic in nature, and points us to Zacharias Ursinus and Caspar Olevianus as the originators of the federal theology. Heppe is very much oriented towards studying the development of a German dogmatic tradition with its own specific peculiarities; the chapter which deals with the early federal theology is entitled 'The Beginning and Development of German Reformed Dogmatics',[73] and Heppe's goal is for the reader to see

German theology as a separate entity: 'Rather the same is only to be understood from the entire development and from the history of German Protestantism, and thus the German Reformed theology will have received its title.'[74] Nevertheless, we shall see that it is more accurate to speak of a theology which arose in certain key cities and universities of the Holy Roman Empire and was developed by certain key thinkers of various national origins, than it is to speak of an intrinsically German theology.[75]

Heppe feels that this German Reformed theology arose in response to certain key questions which were being discussed throughout the European Reformed world. These key questions were four in number. (1) The 'determinism and predestination' discussions of Luther, Melanchthon, and Bucer. Related to these were the questions of election, perseverance of the saints, the Fall of Adam and God's providence, and double predestination. (2) The sacramental disputes of the sixteenth century, in which the nature of 'testament' or 'covenant' was being explored. (3) The need for a sense of personal union with Christ other than in a sacramental way. (4) The rise of scholasticism in theology and theological method.[76] Heppe also identifies four movements which were interacting over the federal theology at the time: (1) Melanch-thonianism; (2) 'rejuvenated' Melanchthonianism; (3) the federal theology; and (4) scholasticism.[77] From his perspective, the federal theology is an orthodox 'softening' of Bezan hyper-scholasticism and High Calvinism.[78] Heppe realizes the importance of the idea of a prelapsarian creation covenant, and points it out as a distinguish-ing feature of the federal theology, and therefore of German Reformed theology. He sees the 'German Reformed theologians' as postulating the creation order as the basis for the covenant, the Church, and the kingdom of God during the postlapsarian covenant of grace.[79]

Gottlob Schrenk, in his 1923 work *Gottesreich und Bund im älteren Protestantismus, vornehmlich Johannes Cocceius*,[80] gives one of the most commonly cited secondary accounts of the history of the federal theology. Schrenk's focus is on the federal theology of Johannes Cocceius, who lived a century after the federal theology first arose, but he provides a short history of the federal theology as an introduction to his main subject.[81] Schrenk first traces the history of the idea of the covenant from Zwingli up to Ursinus and Olevianus, but he realizes that the true federal theology consists of a prelapsarian covenant with Adam and then a postlapsarian covenant of grace—the so-called *Doppelbund* schema. Schrenk correctly identifies Ursinus as the first person to utilize this idea in any systematic manner. When Schrenk considers Ursinus and Olevianus, he sees the rise of the federal theology as an attempt to connect justification to the personal salvation experience of the believer.[82] After the *Doppelbund* schema was proposed it was consolidated by later dogmaticians, some of whom were teaching at Herborn in Nassau and Neustadt an der Hardt. Schrenk, however, does not really give a satisfactory reason as to why the *Doppelbund* schema arose. To relate a prelapsarian covenant to the salvation experience of the believer as a form of opposition to scholasticism is not sufficient explanation for the origins of the federal theology. We shall see, however, that the personal realization of some sort of covenant experience is related to the origins of the federal theology, but not in a direct way.

N. Diemer is the only modern scholar who has taken the prelapsarian covenant idea seriously enough to isolate it from all other theological discussions. His 1935 monograph, *Het scheppings-verbond met Adam (het verbond der werken)*,[83] is largely unavailable to the English-speaking world because it is written in Dutch, and few copies are readily available. Diemer's work is an analysis of sixteenth-century covenant thinking against the backdrop of medieval scholastic thought about the paradisal state. Diemer points out that medieval scholastic teaching, as exemplified, for instance, in the *Sentences* of Peter Lombard,[84] teaches that there were two aspects to the Edenic state: 'Nature' and 'Grace', and that Adam and Eve needed a *donum superadditum* of grace to keep from sinning. The early Reformers broke from that tradition, and Diemer sees four successive stages in which the doctrine of Edenic perfection slides into 'declension'. The stages move as follows: (1) The 'pure Reformed' doctrine of the covenants (Zwingli, Calvin, and Bullinger). (2) 'Humanistic federalism', exemplified by Melanchthon and his legalistic conception of the law of nature. (3) The 'weakened' Reformed standpoint, emanating from the Herborn school. (4) The 'Reformed standpoint abandoned', found in the seventeenth-century dogmatics of men such as Wollebius, Martinius, and Cocceius. Diemer classifies the various conceptions of the covenant of creation using the categories 'organic' versus 'legal and mechanistic', with the result that his analysis should be approached cautiously.[85]

While Diemer's categorization of covenantal thinking requires reconsideration, he does draw attention to a significant problem for the sixteeenth-century theologian, whether he was Roman Catholic, Lutheran or Reformed. What was the relation of God to man in paradise? For the sixteenth-century Christian theologian, there are essentially three possibilities. (1) Man is in a state of pure grace, in which he must be upheld in righteousness by the grace of God. However, to make God so intimately involved with man and man so dependent upon God will lead to problems when the delicate question of Adam's Fall comes up. (2) Another possibility is the Roman Catholic conception of man's existing in a dualistic state of nature and grace, in which there is a 'natural' aspect to man and a 'grace' aspect to man. The Protestants rejected this conception, but the Roman Catholic Church continued to struggle with it. (3) The third possibility is that man is in a state of nature, in that being in the image of God he is created into a state of godly independent perfection. Diemer then categorizes various Protestant theologians of the sixteenth century in this framework, exploring their doctrine of paradise.[86]

Perry Miller has written one of the most influential accounts of the covenant theology,[87] and while his synthesis has been questioned in many details,[88] his 1937 and 1939 expositions of the covenant theology are still of tremendous critical importance for today. Miller's focus, however, is mainly on the seventeenth century, and, even more, on the postlapsarian covenant of grace. He does not discuss in any great detail the origins of the federal theology, nor does he interact at all with the broader vision of the prelapsarian/postlapsarian covenant schema, except for acknowledging its existence.[89] He does include a bibliographical appendix in *The New England Mind* called 'The Federal School of Theology', but, like his chapters, it mainly deals with the postlapsarian covenant of grace.[90]

Peter Y. De Jong deals with the history of the covenant idea in his book entitled *The Covenant Idea in New England Theology 1620–1847*.[91] The origins of the federal theology are a side issue for De Jong, but he briefly considers the problem, following the pattern of Heppe and Schrenk. De Jong deals with the history of the federal theology using a person-by-person method. He points out that the doctrine of the covenant is essentially a Reformed or Calvinistic doctrine, and not a Lutheran one. De Jong feels that the doctrine was applied to several areas of theological importance: '(1) the nature and extent of sin; (2) the relationship between God the Creator and man the creature; (3) the bond between Christ and the race; (4) the doctrine of the church and the means of grace; (5) the doctrine of the Christian life; (6) the place of children in the church; (7) the Christian philosophy of history.'[92]

Leonard J. Trinterud wrote a provocative article in 1951 entitled 'The Origins of Puritanism'.[93] Trinterud postulates that there were two developments of the covenant idea taking place at the same time: one emanating from Calvin, Beza, and Genevan orthodoxy and the other emanating from Zwingli, Bullinger, Zurich, and the cities of the Rhineland, where such theologians as Leo Jud (1482–1542), John Oecolampadius (1482–1531), Wolfgang Capito (1478–1541), Martin Bucer (1491–1551), and Peter Martyr Vermigli (1500–62) were working. Trinterud sees the two schools as offering counterposing arguments:

Calvin and the Genevan theologians
1. The covenant is unilateral.
2. The covenant is God's unconditional promise to man.
3. The burden of fulfilling the covenant rests on God.
4. The covenant is fulfilled in Christ's Incarnation, Crucifixion, and Resurrection.

Zwingli, Bullinger, and the Rhineland theologians
1. The covenant is bilateral.
2. The covenant is God's conditional promise to man and man's response (a mutual pact or treaty).
3. The burden of fulfilling the covenant rests on man.
4. The covenant is fulfilled in the obedience of the individual.[94]

Trinterud does give the impression that the covenant theology and the federal theology are essentially the same, but he also understands the importance of the rise of the prelapsarian covenant. He also notes the importance of the implications of this idea, and relates it to the rise of the covenant as a socio-political idea.[95] Trinterud realizes the important implications of the prelapsarian covenant of works motif, and he rightly points to the years 1570–90 as the time that this idea arose, but he gives no adequate explanation for its rise to prominence. His vision remained fixed on the Rhineland theologians of the period 1520–40 as the originators of the federal theology.

Holmes Rolston III published a book in 1972 entitled *John Calvin versus the Westminster Confession.*[96] Rolston approaches the subject of the federal theology dogmatically, not historically, but he is very sensitive to the implications of the federal theology. He takes as his two poles of reference the works of John Calvin and the Westminster Confession of Faith. In comparing the two theological traditions and their teaching about Adam, he concludes that the idea of the prelapsarian covenant of works is invalid and has radically changed Calvin's original conception of man in the perfect estate of paradise. From a dogmatic standpoint, Rolston is very perceptive in seeing that the federal theology is concerned at its very root level with a 'concept of a responsible man', and that the prelapsarian covenant lies at the very foundation of such a concern.

Rolston maintains that Calvin perceived the Edenic state as a state of pure grace; that is, in Eden man was essentially dependent upon God. On the other hand the federal theologians, according to Rolston, saw man as being in a state of 'natural independence' in Eden, and it is only after the Fall that man needs God's grace. According to Rolston, while the federal theologian might pay lip-service to the idea that Adam was dependent on God, he was really maintaining that God had created man with everything he needed and that part of being the true *imago Dei* was to be an independent perfect being. This problem is of particular importance to our identification of the origins of the federal theology, for the question of the dependence or independence of Adam upon God's grace is related to the origins of the prelapsarian covenant. According to Rolston,

with the twin covenants, there has now crept into Reformed theology a concept of the primal relationship between God and man, and a corresponding statement of the ability and merit of man, that is not only absent from Calvin, it is alien to his thought. The double covenant fabric not only modified, it reverses much of Calvin's thought about man's primal relationship to his God.[97]

Rolston spends a lot of time attempting to prove that Calvin looked upon the Fall as a collection of sins in Adam (faithlessness, which leads to disobedience, which leads to concupiscence, which leads to ingratitude). On the other hand, the federal theologian looked upon Adam's sin as one sin: disobedience, and the breaking of a legal contract.[96] Rolston maintains that the result for the Reformed faith is a 'stuffy legalism':

The argument of this chapter is that the order of the Confession—law, law broken, then grace—was substituted for Calvin's grace, grace lost in ingratitude, and grace restored.

  The end result was the making of the first and most fundamental relationship between God and man legal, not gracious . . . What for Calvin is man's chief sin is, by the time we reach the Westminster Confession, his chief duty.[99]

Rolston does not treat the work of Calvin using historical methodology, nor does he handle the Reformed theological writings of the seventeenth century in a historical manner. His goal, rather, is that of a dogmatic study. But his work is important in that he brings to our attention an important feature of federal theological thinking: what is the *purpose* of applying covenantal status to Adam in creation? Why did Reformed theologians postulate, between the death of Calvin and the formulation of the Westminster Confession of Faith, a prelapsarian covenant? If one approaches the Edenic state from the viewpoint of John Calvin and Theodore Beza and asserts that it is a state of grace, then how did the Fall happen? How involved is God in the Fall: Did God withdraw his grace? To what point does his grace extend? Did God foreknow the Fall? Or does he permit the Fall? Or does he decree it through his providence without being responsible for it? While Rolston does not identify the origins of the federal theology or place them within the context of the development of Reformed historical theology in any extensive manner, he has raised some fundamental questions.

  William K. B. Stoever deals with the history and significance of the federal theology in his 1970 dissertation 'The Covenant of Works in Puritan Theology: The Antinomian Crisis in New England'.[100] Stoever focuses on a period of three years in the history of the Massachusetts Bay Colony, when Anne Hutchinson was agitating the colonial community with her 'antinomian' leanings. By this time, the federal theology had had time to develop, and the idea of the prelapsarian covenant is of great importance for the main burden of his study, which is the 'relation of created nature to divine power in the regeneration of sinful men'.[101] Stoever recognizes the prelapsarian covenant of works as the governing concept of the federal theology, and he perceives this covenant as the manifestation of the dialectic between 'nature' and 'grace'— between the normal world and the miraculous working of God in the hearts of men.[102] Stoever points to the covenant of works as the primary means by which this tension was resolved:

> The covenant of works with Adam was regarded as the primary *modus* by which God is related to and deals with humanity. God was held, in covenanting with man for salvation, to have taken man's distinctive capacities deliberately into account, and to have secured man's perpetual moral obligation to the moral law. After the Fall, redemption unfolds in accordance with the conditions established in the first covenant. Thus elaborated, the covenant motif provided a means of maintaining proper tension in the dialectic of nature and grace.[103]

The rest of Stoever's thesis consists of a consideration of how this idea of the prelapsarian covenant of works was worked out and utilized in the antinomian controversy in New England. Stoever maintains that there are great implications once one thinks in terms of a prelapsarian covenant 'of nature', because the natural world includes so many things of both a 'religious' and a 'secular' nature.

R. Sherman Isbell added to the scholarship on this problem with a 1976 Master of Theology thesis that had the title 'The Origin of the Concept of the Covenant of Works'.[104] However, Isbell's exploration is brief and cursory; he simply gives a summary of what various sixteenth-century theologians had written about the prelapsarian covenant. He examines neither the possible motivations for the proposal of the prelapsarian covenant of works in Reformed theology nor the implications of such an idea.

Mark W. Karlberg's recent 1980 dissertation, 'The Mosaic Covenant and the Concept of Works in Reformed Hermeneutics: A Historical-Critical Analysis with Particular Attention to Early Covenant Eschatology',[105] approaches the federal theology in terms of a dogmatic study with a historical background. Influenced by the work of N. Diemer, Karlberg considers in great detail the interaction between the Mosaic covenant and the prelapsarian covenant of works motif as manifested in the apparent law-grace conflicts of the various covenantal dispensations.

Karlberg considers several historical-theological problems and issues which arise out of the federal theology. His most important consideration is the question of whether or not the Garden of Eden was the final state for Adam if Adam had not sinned, or whether it was a means to a higher eschatological existence.[106] While we must remember that his is a dogmatic study, the question of whether the early federal theologians adopted a Thomistic Nature and Grace stance in respect to the covenant of works is important. Karlberg concludes that the idea of a covenant of nature implies a dualistic state of Nature and Grace in paradise, that the covenant of nature as a means to a higher end makes the 'covenant of nature' situation 'unstable', and that therefore Adam needed grace.

The second question which Karlberg raises is the nature of the Mosaic covenant: is it legal or evangelical? Is it exclusively pedagogical and tutelary, or does it have power to justification? Thirdly, Karlberg considers the question of the utilization of 'merit' for Adam's complete obedience to the divine law. When Adam is in the state of perfection does he stand before God on his own merits or does he stand before God by God's grace? The fourth question which Karlberg considers is the connection between the covenant conception and predestination. We shall see that this is of primary importance, but he does not treat the subject at any great length. He does state, however, that 'the distinctive character of German Reformed theology is evident in the discussions of the relation between the idea of the covenant of creation and the doctrine of predestination'.[107]

Karlberg also considers five other issues in passing: (1) the Anabaptist conception of the covenant versus that of the magisterial reformers; (2) the connection between natural law and the doctrine of civil righteousness as a manifestation of 'common grace'; (3) the related question of the principles of theocratic law being implemented in the course of the establishment of the Reformed faith; (4) the struggles with the antinomians, which were complicated by the differing interpretations of the Mosaic covenant; and finally (5) the doctrine of 'preparation for salvation' and the movement from a 'state of law' to a 'state of grace'.[108] Karlberg does not attempt to pinpoint the origins of the federal theology, and he assumes that the idea of a prelapsarian covenant of works was first proposed by a posthumous publication of a work by Ursinus in 1584, a date which we shall challenge.[109]

Another work which should be considered was also completed in 1980 and was written by Lyle D. Bierma. His dissertation, entitled 'The Covenant Theology of Caspar Olevian', is the only careful study on the early federal theology which has appeared to date.[110] Bierma's work is extremely useful in that it carefully lists and considers the entire corpus of Olevianus's writings. He also takes into consideration the work of Ursinus, who was Olevianus's colleague at the Collegium Sapientiae in Heidelberg. Bierma came to three major conclusions in his study. (1) Olevianus was neither a founder nor a final architect of the federal theology, but was a key intermediary figure between the Swiss theologians of the covenant and the second generation of the Herborn and Puritan federal theologians. (2) Olevianus's 'theological corpus appeared after the first attempt to employ the covenant as a central theme of a theological system (Ursinus) but actually before the first attempt to use it as an *organizing* principle for an entire system (the Herborn federalists)'. (3) 'Most important of all, Olevianus helped to change the complexion of Reformed covenant theology by shifting the focus away from the origins and development of covenant history to the meaning of the covenant for the present-day believer.'[111] Bierma considers *only* the federal theology of Olevianus and Ursinus in any detail, and his methodology does not allow for a chronological examination of the development of the federal theology. However, his work is extremely important and useful, and we will return to it later.

J. Wayne Baker has also recently published an important work on the covenant idea: *Heinrich Bullinger and the Covenant: The Other Reformed Tradition*.[112] Baker adopts the Trinterud thesis that there is a basic difference between Genevan orthodoxy and Rhineland teaching as regards the covenant. First, according to Baker, Calvin, Beza and their followers believed in a unilateral covenant; Bullinger was one of the few sixteenth-century theologians who believed in a bilateral covenant. Second, Bullinger and his followers differed from Genevan orthodoxy over the issues of justification and predestination.[113] The third area in which Bullinger differed from Calvin is the nature of the covenant as being the basis for a Christian republic and community. This question had important ramifications for the relationship between Church and State in Zurich and Geneva.

Throughout the volume Baker deals with these questions, with his focus on Bullinger. His discussion of the various meanings of the words is very helpful, and we get a look at the predestination controversies of the 1560s from a different perspective. Baker confirms for us the relationship between covenant and predestination, and notes the rise of double predestination as the standard of orthodoxy after 1560.

However, the most important part of Baker's work for us is the 'Epilogue'[114] and the final appendix.[115] In these sections Baker explains the rise of the federal system of theology as a school of thought in opposition to the predominance of absolute double predestination. He notes: 'The theological idea of the covenant, as expressed by Bullinger, paled as the sixteenth century wore on, even taking on the hues of heterodoxy late in the century.'[116] However, he then goes on to show how the proponents of the federal theology combined their double covenant schema with the doctrine of double predestination. For Baker, double predestination led to a 'paralysis' of the covenant idea. However, we will show that the double covenant schema was an attempt to bridge both worlds: that of unilateral covenant and that of bilateral covenant.

The work of Peter Alan Lillback on the origins of the covenant of works is especially pertinent to our discussion.[117] In a 1981 article and his 1985 dissertation, Lillback argues that the influence of Philip Melanchthon was important but not unique, and that actually Calvin's underdeveloped notion of the prelapsarian covenant of works influenced Ursinus much more. Calvin's teaching proves that he was a covenant theologian who could even be classified as one of the federal theologians, according to Lillback. The evidence for a prelapsarian covenant conception in Calvin's writings is, for the most part, the evidence that we have already considered. Lillback's most significant problem in his valuable and exhaustive study is that he makes larger claims in his introduction and conclusion than he can back up. In his dissertation he identifies Calvin as the 'great architect of the covenant theology',[118] yet in his close critical analysis he admits that Calvin's doctrine of the prelapsarian covenant is, at best, 'inchoate'.[119] Lillback seems to be determined to include Calvin amongst the federal theologians and to harmonize Calvin's theological system with the system of the Westminster Confession of Faith. The problem is that the evidence Lillback presents does not back up the conclusions that he reaches. Calvin did not set up the covenant theology that he held to as the basic structure for his work, nor did he add anything of particular importance to his contemporaries' understanding of the post-lapsarian covenant of grace. Nor did Calvin use any form of the prelapsarian covenant/postlapsarian covenant as a structural component of his thought. Indeed, as we shall see, he chose instead to follow the pattern of the Apostle's Creed for his *Institutes*. Lillback's account of Ursinus's trip in *c.*1558, however, does remind us that Ursinus was influenced by Calvin and by others, and one of those others was Sebastian Castellio (1515–63). While Lillback looks to Ursinus's visit to Calvin as the key influence on Ursinus's thinking about the covenant, we will look to Castellio as the figure of chief influence for Ursinus and Ursinus's teaching on the covenant. We agree that that trip was critical, but we want to present a different candidate for the critical person whom Ursinus encountered.[120]

Paul Helm comes to essentially the same conclusion as Lillback does in his article published in 1983.[121] Helm feels that while Calvin did not use the terms 'covenant of nature' or 'covenant of works', he taught nothing that contradicted the features of the federal theological system, and that most of the features of the federal theology are present in his writings. However, Helm does not address the question of the purpose of the covenant which Calvin does speak about, which is a postlapsarian covenant. The crucial question is this: Is the covenant used as the *basis* for establishing one's relationship with God and for the founding of society? Or is it used as an instrument of redemption to save man from sin and restore him to that original state? It seems that for Calvin the latter conception of covenant was the meaning of covenant in the Scripture: the biblical covenant's function was redemptive and salvific, not original and fundamental.

R. W. A. Letham contributes to this discussion in his article on some factors accounting for the development of the prelapsarian covenant.[122] Letham identifies the various schools of thought in the discussion and then tentatively points out four conclusions: the covenant idea was used to defend infant baptism by the early Reformers; the covenant idea was used by the Reformers to defend the unity of the law; the Decalogue began to be constructed in covenantal terms; and finally, through the influence of Ramistic methodology, the entire creation was viewed in a legal and covenantal mode of thought. Letham is correct in asserting that the Heidelberg theologians were the disseminators of the prelapsarian covenant idea in northern Europe, and that this dissemination was encouraged by Ramistic methodology, but he does not make clear how these Reformed theologians moved from viewing the events of Mount Sinai as being a covenant to viewing the Edenic state as being a covenant. Letham is on the right track, but more explication needs to be done about this shift in covenantal thinking.

Derk Visser has made a contribution to this discussion with a careful examination of the covenant idea, and specifically the prelapsarian covenant idea, in the works of Zacharias Ursinus.[123] Like Letham, Visser maintains that Ursinus's prelapsarian covenant motif emerged from a concern with legalism and not with predestination. Visser points out that the prelapsarian covenant of creation motif does not occur in the theological treatises which Ursinus himself published. Visser further maintains that the doctrine appeared too quickly after Ursinus's death to have its origins in the 1584 appearance of the *Catechismus Maior*, and that the origin of the idea emanates from Ursinus's pastoral concerns with the celebration of the Christian sabbath. Visser's conclusions are tentative, and show the need for a larger investigation on the doctrine of the covenant in the thought of Ursinus.

Finally, Michael McGiffert maintains in a recent article that the origins of the prelapsarian covenant, and some of its implications, emerged out of English Puritanism between 1585 and 1600.[124] McGiffert holds that the prelapsarian covenant did not come from a discussion of Adamic responsibility and divine sovereignty, but from the moralistic theories of English Puritans anxious to include all men under a general moral order. According to McGiffert, the Edenic covenant came from an attempt by certain Elizabethan Puritans to push back the Sinaitic covenant to the prelapsarian Edenic state.

Several characteristics of the secondary literature considered above should be noted. (1) Except for a few recent works, the history of the early federal theology and the prelapsarian covenant is always found within the context of another study dealing with a related subject. (2) Most historians have accurately pinpointed 1560–5 as the time when the prelapsarian covenant idea became important in Reformed theology, and have rightly looked to Zacharias Ursinus as the one who brought it to prominence. (3) No real reason has been given as to *why* the idea arose or *how* it came to prominence. (4) The methodology employed in the consideration of the early federal theology is theologian-by-theologian. The result is to view the federal theology as isolated in various individual theologians and their works rather than as a theological movement. In examining the development of an individual theologian over time, one loses the sense of the flow of the movement and fails to recognize that that individual interacted with other individuals and their writings year by year.[125]

The main part of this treatise will be a study of a slice of history and historical theology thirty years in length, from 1560 to 1590, with references to the decades before and after this period. It is during this time that the transition from the Old Testament/New Testament (or old covenant/new covenant) schema to the covenant of works/covenant of grace schema occurred. The old and new covenants as found in the Old and New Testaments were considered to be one covenant of grace, and the new idea is that of the prelapsarian covenant with Adam.

Chapter 1 will be devoted to a study of the lexicographical and biblical treatment in the sixteenth century of the various words used in connection with the idea of covenant: *berith, diatheke, foedus,* and *testamentum.* Such a study might seem an unnecessary redundancy dealing with obvious evidence, but when one explores this neglected evidence carefully one comes up with some interesting observations. The words mentioned above were undergoing careful examination and scrutiny during the period before and after 1561, and even as early as the time of Luther's conversion. The evidence points us in the direction of what was up to now an unlikely figure in the origins of the federal theology: Sebastian Castellio. While Castellio is mainly remembered for his stance for religious toleration and humanistic liberalism, some of the central issues over which he argued have often been forgotten; it could be said that he seems to have acted as a catalyst for the beginnings of the federal theology.

Chapter 2 will deal with the predestination controversies of the decade between 1550 and 1560, controversies in which Castellio played a large part. Other figures in this scenario will be John Calvin, Albertus Pighius (*c.* 1490–1542), Jerome Bolsec (d. 1584), and Theodore Beza (1519–1605). The problem of Adam's Fall was one of the chief controversies of this period. The stage is set for the introduction of the idea of a covenant with Adam before the Fall, by Ursinus, in 1562. Chapter 3 will deal with the introduction of the idea of a prelapsarian covenant in the works of Zacharias Ursinus, the originator of the Reformed federal theology. Chapters 4 and 5 will continue this study, as we see the federal school of theology rise out of three key Reformed schools in the German Rhineland: Heidelberg, Neustadt an der Hardt, and Herborn in Nassau. We will see that there were two stages to the growth of the federal theology: the first in 1561–3, as Ursinus first proposes the idea; the second in 1584–90, when the idea becomes accepted and becomes integrated into the theological thinking of Reformed systematic theologians. Four men especially played a role in the spread of the prelapsarian covenant idea: Caspar Olevianus (1536–87), Thomas Cartwright (1535–1603), Dudley Fenner (1558?–1587), and Franciscus Junius (1545–1602).

In contrast to previous studies, we will attempt a chronological methodology, and focus on the interactions of various individuals as each decade passed. Our cut-off date will be 1590; after that year the idea of a prelapsarian covenant flowered everywhere in Reformed theology, and it is impossible to draw historical connections after that time. By then the earliest federal theologians were dead, and the Palatinate teachers and students had disseminated themselves to other geographical areas.

Finally, an assessment will be made of the early federal theology and its influence, and we will attempt to see why the federal theology became accepted in Reformed Protestantism. By applying covenantal status to Adam in creation, and then binding that status upon all his descendants, the federal theology came up with a balanced system which kept almost everybody satisfied. Orthodox theologians were pleased because it upheld God's absolute sovereignty and man's utter responsibility, both before, during, and after the Fall. The problem of Adam's Fall was more fully explained. Antinomians could no longer say that the law of God was not binding upon them, whether they were believers or unbelievers. And finally, God dealt with man in two ways: through a prelapsarian covenant of works and a postlapsarian covenant of grace.

Notes

1. References to Calvin will be from the standard *Joannis Calvini opera quae supersunt omnia*, ed. G. Baum, E. Cunitz, and E. Reuss, 59 vols., *CR* xxix–lxxxvii (Brunswick, 1863–1900). The section where Calvin deals with the Old and New Testaments is as follows: *Institutes*, ii. 10–11, *CO* ii. 313–40. English

translation: John Calvin, *The Institutes of the Christian Religion*, 2 vols., ed. J. T. McNeill, trans. F. L. Battles (Philadelphia, 1960).

2. *WCF*, chs. 7 and 9. The text of the Confession can be found in *BSRK*, which contains: (*a*) the Latin and English texts of the Confession, pp. 542–612; (*b*) the Latin text of the Larger Catechism, pp. 612–43; and (*c*) the English text of the Shorter Catechism, pp. 643–52. The Latin and English texts of the Confession, along with the Latin and English texts of the Shorter Catechism, can be found in Schaff, *Creeds*, iii. 598–704. Schaff does not include the Larger Catechism. Also relevant is Schaff, *Creeds*, i. The *WCF* also often appears with other important documents, viz. *The [Westminster] Confession of Faith; The Larger and Shorter Catechisms ... With The Sum of Saving Knowledge ... Covenants, National and Solemn League; Acknowledgement of Sins, and Engagement to Duties; Directories for Publick and Family Worship; Form of Church Government, etc.; Of Publick Authority in the Church of Scotland; With Acts of Assembly and Parliament, Relative To, and Approbative of, the Same* (Belfast, 1933).

3. C. Burrage, *The Church Covenant Idea* (Philadelphia, 1904); P. Miller, 'The Marrow of Puritan Divinity', *PubColSocMass*, 32 (1935), 247–300. See the shortened version of this article in Miller, *The New England Mind*, i (Cambridge, Mass., 1939), 365–431, 501–5; P. Y. De Jong, *The Covenant Idea in New England Theology* (Grand Rapids, 1945); W. W. McKee, 'The Idea of Covenant in Early English Puritanism 1580–1643' (Diss. Yale, 1948); L. J. Trinterud, 'The Origins of Puritanism', *ChH* 20 (1951), 37–57; J. C. Brauer, 'Reflections on the Nature of English Puritanism', *ChH* 23 (1954), 99–108; A. Simpson, 'The Covenanted Community', in *Puritanism in Old and New England* (Chicago, 1955), 19–38; G. F. Nuttall, *Visible Saints: The Congregational Way* (Oxford, 1957), 73–82; W. G. Wilcox, 'New England Covenant Theology' (Diss. Duke, 1959); H. S. Burstyn and R. S. Hand, 'Puritanism and Science Reinterpreted', *Actes du XI*ᵉ *Congrès International d'Histoire des Sciences* (1965), no. 2, 139–43; J. G. Møller, 'The Beginnings of Puritan Covenant Theology', *JEH* 14 (1963), 46–67; E. S. Morgan, 'The Half-Way Covenant', in *Visible Saints: the History of a Puritan Idea* (New York, 1963), 113–38; C. J. Sommerville, 'Conversion, Sacrament and Assurance in the Puritan Covenant of Grace, to 1650' (MA thesis, University of Kansas, 1963); J. F. H. New, *Anglican and Puritan* (Stanford, 1964), 91–4, 127–8; G. Yule, 'Developments in English Puritanism in the Context of the Reformation', *Studies in the Puritan Tradition* (Chelmsford, 1964), 8–27, esp. 21–4; C. C. Cherry, 'The Puritan Notion of the Covenant in Jonathan Edwards' Doctrine of Faith', *ChH* 34 (1965), 328–41; J. von Rohr, 'Covenant and Assurance in Early English Puritanism', ibid. 195–203; D. L. Beebe, 'The Seals of the Covenant' (Diss. Pacific School of Religion, 1966); N. Pettit, *The Heart Prepared* (New Haven, 1966); C. J. Sommerville, 'Conversion versus the Early Puritan Covenant of Grace', *JPH* 44 (1966), 178–97; R. L. Greaves, 'John Bunyan and Covenant Thought in the Seventeenth Century', *ChH* 36 (1967), 151–69; V. L. Priebe, 'The Covenant Theology of William Perkins' (Diss. Drew, 1967); R. L. Greaves, 'The Origin and Early Development of English Covenant Thought', *The Historian*, 31 (1968), 21–35; R. G. Pope, *The Half-Way Covenant* (Princeton, 1969); I. Breward (ed.), *The Work of William Perkins* (Appleford, England, 1970); J. S. Coolidge, *The Pauline Renaissance in England: Puritanism and the Bible* (Oxford, 1970), 99–140; W. K. B. Stoever, 'The Covenant of Works in Puritan Theology' (Diss. Yale, 1970), and *'A Faire and Easie Way to Heaven'* (Middletown, Conn., 1978); L. J. Trinterud (ed.), *Elizabethan Puritanism* (New York, 1971), 302–14; T. H.

Breen, 'English Origins and New World Development', *PastPres* 57 (1972), 74–96; H. Rolston III, *John Calvin versus the Westminster Confession* (Richmond, 1972); E. B. Holifield, *The Covenant Sealed* (New Haven, 1974); J. F. Veninga, 'Covenant Theology and Ethics in the Thought of John Calvin and John Preston' (Diss. Rice, 1974); C. J. Butler, 'Religious Liberty and Covenant Theology' (Diss. Temple, 1979); R. T. Kendall, *Calvin and English Calvinism to 1649* (Oxford, 1979); J. Morgan, 'Puritanism and Science', *HistJ* 22 (1979), 535–60; M. McGiffert, 'Covenant, Crown and Commons in Elizabethan Puritanism', *JBS* 20 (1980), 32–52; R. A. Muller, 'Covenant and Conscience in English Reformed Theology', *WThJ* 42 (1980), 308–34, and 'The Spirit and the Covenant', *Found.* 24 (1981), 4–14.

4. Cf. D. Baker (ed.), *Reform and Reformation* (Oxford, 1979); I. Breward, 'Introduction and Biography', *The Work of William Perkins*, 16–19, 23; J. K. Cameron (ed.), *Letters of John Johnston . . . and Robert Howie* (Edinburgh, 1963); C. D. Cremeans, *The Reception of Calvinistic Thought in England* (Urbana, 1949); C. Cross, 'Continental Students and the Protestant Reformation in England in the Sixteenth Century', in Baker, *Reform and Reformation*, 35–58; C. R. Dodwell (ed.), *The English Church and the Continent* (London, 1959); A. L. Drummond, *The Kirk and the Continent* (Edinburgh, 1956); W. Goeters, *Die Vorbereitung des Pietismus in der reformierten Kirche der Niederlande* (Leipzig, 1911); H. Heppe, *The Reformers of England and Germany in the Sixteenth Century*, trans. H. Schmettau and B. H. Cowper (London, 1859); J. M. Krumm, 'Continental Protestantism and Elizabethan Anglicanism', in F. H. Littell (ed.), *Reformation Studies* (Richmond, 1962), 129–44; F. H. Littell, 'What Calvin Learned at Strassburg', in J. H. Bratt (ed.), *The Heritage of John Calvin* (Grand Rapids, 1973), 74–86; C. Miller, 'The Spread of Calvinism in Switzerland, Germany and France', in J. H. Bratt (ed.), *The Rise and Development of Calvinism* (Grand Rapids, 1959), 27–62; J. G. Møller, 'The Beginnings of Puritan Covenant Theology', 58–9; M. Prestwich (ed.), *International Calvinism* (Oxford, 1985); F. Smithen, *Continental Protestantism and the English Reformation* (London, 1927); T. C. Smout (ed.), *Scotland and Europe, 1200–1800* (Edinburgh, 1986); K. L. Sprunger, *Dutch Puritanism* (Leiden, 1982); W. C. Taylor, 'Scottish Students in Heidelberg, 1386–1662', *ScHR* 5 (1907–8), 67–75, 250–1; D. Visser (ed.), *Controversy and Conciliation* (Allison Park, Pa., 1986).

5. P. Miller, *The New England Mind*, i. 374.

6. This can be seen by examining the section on the covenant of works in H. Heppe, *Die Dogmatik der evangelisch-reformirten Kirche* (Elberfeld, 1861; rev. 2nd edn., Neukirchen, 1935), 224–54; English translation (rev.) of 2nd edn.: *Reformed Dogmatics*, ed. E. Bizer, trans. G. T. Thompson (London, 1950), 281–319. A large number of the quotes are from Continental, not British, divines.

7. 'The Sum of Saving Knowledge', in *The [Westminster] Confession of Faith*, 252.

8. Cf. P. Toon's statement: 'There does not yet exist a satisfactory study of the origins and early development of Federal Theology', *God's Statesman* (Exeter, 1971), 169 n. 1. G. Schrenk has discussed it briefly, dealing mainly with the Continental theologians, but the main part of his work centres upon the federal theology of the seventeenth century, particularly the school of Johannes Cocceius (1603–69): *Gottesreich und Bund im älteren Protestantismus, vornehmlich bei Johannes Cocceius* (Gütersloh, 1923). A. J. van t'Hooft explores the dichotomy of a covenant of works and a covenant of grace, but he does so in a book devoted to Bullinger: *De theologie van*

Heinrich Bullinger in betrekking tot de Nederlandsche Reformatie (Amsterdam, 1888), 1–95, 130–240.

9. See the Appendix for a basic bibliography on the federal theology and the covenant idea in the sixteenth, seventeenth, and eighteenth centuries.

10. This tendency can be seen in E. von Korff, *Die Anfänge der Föderaltheologie und ihre erste Ausgestaltung in Zürich und Holland* (Bonn, 1908). Another misconception is that the federal theology originates with the work of Johannes Cocceius. K. R. Hagenbach makes this error: 'Ein eigenthümliches System gründete J. Coccejus, die sogenannte Föderalmethode . . . ', *Lehrbuch der Dogmengeschichte* (Leipzig, 1840–1), ii. 2, sec. 221, 31. There were various revised German and English editions of this work. The discussions of the federal theology did not substantially change in any of them. Johannes Cocceius actually departed from the federal theology as articulated in the *WCF* by saying that the covenant of works becomes less binding as biblical history develops. He develops a theology of *Heilsgeschichte*, or 'salvation history', which sees the various covenants in the Old Testament and New Testament as an unfolding of God's revelation. Cf. C. S. McCoy, 'The Covenant Theology of Johannes Cocceius' (Diss. Yale, 1957); also his two other essays about Cocceius: 'Johannes Cocceius: Federal Theologian', *SJTh* 16 (1963), 352–70; *History, Humanity and Federalism in the Theology and Ethics of Johannes Cocceius* (Philadelphia, 1980).

11. W. A. Brown, 'Covenant Theology', *ERE* iv. 216–24. See also C. S. McCoy, 'The Covenant Theology of Johannes Cocceius', 59.

12. D. R. Hillers, *Covenant: The History of a Biblical Idea* (Baltimore, 1969); M. Weinfield, 'Berith', *TDOT* ii. 253–79; T. E. McComiskey, *The Covenants of Promise* (Grand Rapids, 1985); M. Kline, *Treaty of the Great King: The Covenant Structure of Deuteronomy* (Grand Rapids, 1963); E. W. Nicholson, *God and His People: Covenant and Theology in the Old Testament* (New York, 1986); D. J. McCarthy, *Treaty and Covenant* (Rome, 1978).

13. See G. Vos's work on the covenant idea for a good understanding of the nature and especially the implications of the federal theology: *De verbondsleer in de gereformeerde theologie* (1891; repr. Rotterdam, 1939); English translation: 'The Doctrine of the Covenant in Reformed Theology', in *Redemptive History and Biblical Interpretation: The Shorter Writings of Geerhardus Vos*, ed. R. B. Gaffin (Philipsburg, NJ, 1980), 234–67.

14. *WCF* 7 and 19; *BSRK* 558–60, 581–4; Schaff, *Creeds*, iii. 616–18, 640–3. The Larger Catechism covers the prelapsarian covenant in Questions 20 and 97 (*BSRK* 614 and 625). It is interesting to note that the Shorter Catechism calls the prelapsarian covenant a *foedus vitae*, a 'covenant of life' (*BSRK* 644; Schaff, *Creeds*, iii. 678).

15. *WCF* 7; *BSRK* 558–60; Schaff, *Creeds*, iii. 616–18.

16. *WCF* 8; *BSRK* 560–3; Schaff, *Creeds*, iii. 619–22; cf. R. A. Muller, *Dictionary of Latin and Greek Theological Terms, Drawn Principally from Protestant Scholastic Theology* (Grand Rapids, 1985), 205–6.

17. J. F. Veninga, in 'Covenant Theology and Ethics in the Thought of John Calvin and John Preston', is less than accurate when he tries to explain the ethical consequences of the federal theology: 'with man's sin, the covenant of works becomes obsolete, although the obligatory ethic associated with it continues its validity as the standard of conduct for the regenerate' (p. 203). He goes on to maintain that the theology of Calvin and the federal theology are virtually the same, and attempts to prove it by an examination of two ethical systems, that of John Calvin and that of John Preston. It might have been more helpful if Veninga had taken several Puritan ethical systems instead of that of

Preston alone. What Veninga fails to realize is (*a*) the significance of the fact that Calvin never taught the idea of a prelapsarian covenant or covenant of works; and (*b*) that the federal theologians believed that the covenant of works was binding upon all men—regenerate and unregenerate—after the Fall, and that they are obligated to keep it, whether they are members of the Church or not. Such a mandate affects an ethical system drastically. Cf. also P. Miller, *The New England Mind*, i. 384.

It was Andreas Hyperius (1511–64) who made Adam's Fall a major structural component of systematic theology. In his *Methodi theologiae* (1566; Basle, 1568) he makes the Fall a central point in his theological system. His work is divided up into six *Loci*, which are then subdivided into *ante lapsum* and *post lapsum* sections: '1) Deus; 2) Creatura; 3) Ecclesia; 4) Doctrina Legis et Evangelica; 5) Signa, seu Sacramenta; 6) Consummatio . . .' All six sections are considered before the Fall and after the Fall, e.g.: 'Creatura: Homo ante lapsum; Homo post lapsum; Doctrina: Doctrina ante lapsum; Doctrina post lapsum; Lex ante lapsum; Lex post lapsum; Evangelium ante lapsum; Evangelium post lapsum; . . . Signa, seu Sacramenta: Signa ante lapsum; Signa post lapsum.' While the idea of a prelapsarian covenant was already proposed four years before Hyperius's work was published (by Z. Ursinus in 1562), it serves to show that theologians of the time were looking at the Fall as an event of crucial importance, and this is reflected in their theological systems; cf. H. Heppe, *Dogmatik des deutschen Protestantismus im sechzehnten Jahrhundert* (Gotha, 1857), i. 144–8.

18. Cf. J. W. Baker, *Heinrich Bullinger and the Covenant* (Athens, Ohio, 1980); H. Baron, 'Religion and Politics in the German Imperial Cities during the Reformation', *EHR* 52 (1937), 405–27, 614–33, and 'Calvinist Republicanism and its Historical Roots', *ChH* 8 (1939), 30–42; F. S. Carney, 'The Associational Theory of Johannes Althusius' (Diss. University of Chicago, 1960); D. J. Elazar, *From Biblical Covenant to Modern Federalism* (Philadelphia, 1980), and 'The Political Theory of Covenant', *Publius*, 10 (1980), 3–30; H. Eulau, 'Theories of Federalism under the Holy Roman Empire', *APSR* 35 (1941), 643–64; O. von Gierke, *The Development of Political Theory*, trans. B. Freyd (New York, 1939); H. Höpfl and M. P. Thompson, 'The History of Contract as a Motif in Political Thought', *AHR* 84 (1979), 919–45; T. Hüglin, 'Johannes Althusius: Medieval Constitutionalist or Modern Federalist?', *Publius*, 9 (1979), 9–42; 'Althusius, Federalism and the Notion of the State', *Pensiero Polit.* 13 (1980), 225–32, and *Covenant and Federalism in the Politics of Althusius* (Philadelphia, 1980); D. Little, *Religion, Order and Law* (New York, 1969); R. W. Lovin, 'Covenantal Relationships and Political Legitimacy', *JR* 60 (1980), 1–6; M. McGiffert, 'Covenant, Crown and Commons'; S. Mogi, *The Problem of Federalism*, 2 vols. (New York, 1931); G. L. Mosse, *The Holy Pretence* (Oxford, 1957); R. H. Murray, *The Political Consequences of the Reformation: Studies in Sixteenth Century Political Thought* (London, 1926); D. Neri, 'Antiassolutismo e federalismo nel pensiero di Althusius', *Pensiero Polit.* 12 (1979), 393–409; G. Oestrich, 'Die Idee des religiösen Bundes und die Lehre vom Staatsvertrag', in W. Berges and C. Hinrichs (edd.), *Zur Geschichte und Problematik der Demokratie* (Berlin, 1958), 11–32; V. Ostrom, 'Hobbes, Covenant and Constitution', *Publius*, 10 (1980), 83–100; A. F. S. Pearson, *Church and State* (Cambridge, 1928); P. Riley, 'Three 17th Century German Theorists of Federalism', *Publius*, 6 (1976), 7–41.

The first political thinker to articulate a federal theory of the state was the first professor of law at Herborn, Johannes Althusius (*c*.1557–1638). We can see Althusius struggling with this problem in his *Politica Methodice digesta*. Althusius does not speak of a prelapsarian covenant of works, but he does maintain that the civil magistrate must enforce the Decalogue. For Althusius the state is based on a covenant. There is no doubt in my mind that the Heidelberg and Herborn federal theologians whom we shall consider later influenced Althusius with their discussion of covenant in theology. A thorough Calvinist in his ecclesiastical commitment, he makes several references to the Reformed theologians and teachers residing in the Palatinate. C. J. Butler has commented: 'After the idea of a federal representative had become familiar in Christology, it was simple to pit the law–grace concepts versus each other in the covenant of works–covenant of grace theology with the representative functioning in parallel fashion in each. When that occurred (*c.* 1580s) the natural law principle which had functioned by itself and in the civil covenant theories of the fifties and seventies could be linked to the covenant of works and used to press religious responsibilities upon man either personally or corporately' ('Religious Liberty and Covenant Theology', 19–20).

    Concerning covenantal bases for government, cf. L. G. Williams, '*Digitus Dei*: God and Nation in the Thought of John Owen' (Diss. Drew, 1981); J. B. Torrance, 'Calvinism and Puritanism in England and Scotland', in *Calvinus Reformator: His Contribution to Theology, Church and Society* (Potchefstroom, 1982), 264–86.

19. Cf. R. D. Brackenridge, 'The Development of Sabbatarianism in Scotland, 1560–1650', *JPH* 42 (1964), 149–65; P. Collinson, 'The Beginnings of English Sabbatarianism', in C. W. Dugmore and C. Duggan (edd.), SCH(L) 1 (London, 1964), 207–21; J. T. Dennison, Jun., 'The Puritan Doctrine of the Sabbath in England, 1532–1700' (Master of Theology thesis, Pittsburgh Theological Seminary, 1973) and 'The Perpetuity and Change of the Sabbath', in R. C. Sproul (ed.), *Soli Deo Gloria: Essays in Reformed Theology* (Nutley, NJ, 1976), 146–55; R. L. Greaves, 'The Origins of English Sabbatarian Thought', *SCJ* 12 (1981), 19–34; C. Hill, 'The Uses of Sabbatarianism', in *Society and Puritanism in Pre-Revolutionary England* (New York, 1964), 145–218, and 'Seventeenth-Century English Society and Sabbatarianism', in J. S. Bromley and E. H. Kossmann (edd.), *Britain and the Netherlands*, ii. 84–108 (Groningen, 1964); D. S. Katz, *Sabbath and Sectarianism in Seventeenth-Century England* (Leiden, 1988); W. A. Leaper, 'The Growth of Sabbatarianism in England from 1558 to 1658' (MA thesis, National University of Ireland, 1919); M. Levy, *Der Sabbath in England* (Leipzig, 1933); J. H. Primus, 'Calvin and the Puritan Sabbath', in D. E. Holwerda (ed.), *Exploring the Heritage of John Calvin* (Grand Rapids, 1976), 40–75; K. L. Sprunger, 'English and Dutch Sabbatarianism and the Development of Puritan Social Theology', *ChH* 51 (1982), 24–38; W. B. Whitaker, *Sunday in Tudor and Stuart Times* (London, 1933).

    W. U. Solberg, in *Redeem the Time* (Cambridge, Mass., 1977), points out the parallel rise of Sabbatarianism and the federal theology: 'After a brief discussion of certain distinctive ways of thinking about and observing holy days during the long pre-Reformation period, the three main expressions of the Continental Reformation are analyzed with a view to showing that the Sabbath flowered best in an environment of Reformed theology and even better still in alliance with covenant theology . . .' (p. x). '. . . Scholars differ as to how Puritan divines drew on Reformed covenant thought, and despite considerable attention given it over several decades, we lack a satisfactory general account of this development. It seems clear that covenant theology was highly conducive to a type of piety which encouraged a rigorous sabbatarianism . . .' (p. 39). Solberg points to the years 1585–8 as the period of the genesis of the Puritan doctrine of the sabbath, precisely the time when the federal theology was first being articulated into a system of theology (p. 56). However, K. L. Parker's Cambridge dissertation challenges this observation and maintains that in England a sabbath doctrine extended back into the Middle Ages ('The English Sabbath: 1558–1640', Diss. Cambridge, 1984).

20. Cf. E. F. Kevan, *The Grace of Law* (1964; repr. Grand Rapids, 1976). See also the following for discussions of the Protestant conception of natural law: J. D. Eusden, 'Natural Law and Covenant Theology', *NatLF* 5 (1960), 1–30; L. W. Gibbs, 'The Puritan Natural Law Theory of William Ames', *HThR* 64 (1971), 37–57; O. von Gierke, *Natural Law and the Theory of Society*, trans. E. Barker (1934; repr. 2 vols. in 1, Cambridge, 1950); A. Lang, 'The Reformation and Natural Law', trans. J. G. Machen, in W. P. Armstrong (ed.), *Calvin and the Reformation* (New York, 1909), 56–98; J. T. McNeill, 'Natural Law in the Thought of Luther', *ChH* 10 (1941), 211–27, and 'Natural Law in the Teaching of the Reformers', *JR* 26 (1946), 168–82; A. Passerin-D'Entreves, *Natural Law* (London, 1951); M. Schmidt, 'Biblizismus und natürliche Theologie in der Gewissenslehre des englischen Puritanismus', *ARG* 42 (1951), 198–219; 43 (1952), 70–187; P. Sigmund, *Natural Law in Political Thought* (Cambridge, Mass., 1971); J. B. Torrance, 'Calvinism and Puritanism in England and Scotland' (op. cit.), 'Strengths and Weaknesses of the Westminster Theology', in A. I. C. Heron (ed.), *The Westminster Confession in the Church Today* (Edinburgh, 1982), 40–54, and 'The Incarnation and "Limited Atonement" ', *EQ*, 55 (1983), 83–94.

21. Thus W. K. B. Stoever states: 'The "covenant of works" with Adam was regarded as the primary *modus* by which God is related to and deals with humanity . . . After the fall, redemption unfolds in accordance with the conditions established in the first covenant. Thus elaborated, the covenant motif provided a means of maintaining proper tension in the dialectic of nature and grace' (Stoever, 'The Covenant of Works in Puritan Theology', 10–11); cf. M. W. Karlberg, 'The Mosaic Covenant and the Concept of Works in Reformed Hermeneutics' (Diss. Westminster Theological Seminary, 1980).

22. The typology and imagery of the first and second Adam are discussed in J. Rosenmeier, 'New England's Perfection', *WMQ*, 3rd ser., 27 (1970), 435–59; see also J. A. Galdon, *Typology and Seventeenth-Century Literature* (The Hague, 1975), 77–94; R. Prins, 'The Image of God in Adam and the Restoration of Man in Jesus Christ: A Study in Calvin', *SJTh* 25 (1972), 32–44. The first and second Adam theme plays an especially important role in the New England Antinomian Controversy: cf. Stoever, *'A Faire and Easie Way to Heaven'*.

23. Cf. especially Stoever, *'A Faire and Easie Way to Heaven'* and 'The Covenant of Works in Puritan Theology', 7–9; J. Platt, *Reformed Thought and Scholasticism* (Leiden, 1982); W. van 't Spijker, 'Natuur en Genade in de Reformatorische Theologie', *Theologia Reformata*, 22 (1979), 176–90; J. B. Torrance, 'Calvinism and Puritanism in England and Scotland', 'Strengths and Weaknesses of the Westminster Theology', and 'The Incarnation and "Limited Atonement" '.

24. J. W. Baker, *Heinrich Bullinger and the Covenant*, xxiii and 107–40; G. D. Henderson, 'The Idea of the Covenant in Scotland', *EQ* 27 (1955), 2–14; B. Moeller, *Reichsstadt und Reformation* (Gütersloh, 1962) and *Imperial Cities and the Reformation*, trans. H. C. E. Midelfort and M. U. Edwards, Jun. (Philadelphia, 1972); L. J. Trinterud, 'The Origins of Puritanism'; G. Oestrich, 'Die Idee des religiösen Bundes'.

25. P. Miller, *Orthodoxy in Massachusetts, 1630–1650* (Cambridge, Mass., 1933) and *The New England Mind*, i.

26. See N. Pettit, *The Heart Prepared* (New Haven, 1966); P. Miller, ' "Prepar-

ation for Salvation" in Seventeenth Century New England', *JHI* 4 (1943), 253–86; J. R. Fulcher, 'Puritan Piety in New England' (Diss. Princeton University, 1963); J. S. Bray, 'The Value of Works in the Theology of Calvin and Beza', *SCJ* 4 (1973), 77–86; R. T. Kendall, *Calvin and English Calvinism*; J. H. Gerstner and J. N. Gerstner, 'Edwardsean Preparation for Salvation', *WThJ* 42 (1979–80), 5–71; L. B. Tipson, Jun., 'The Development of a Puritan Understanding of Conversion' (Diss. Yale, 1972); R. W. A. Letham, 'Saving Faith and Assurance in Reformed Theology', 2 vols. (Diss. Aberdeen, 1979); C. L. Cohen, *God's Caress* (New York, 1986); P. Caldwell, *The Puritan Conversion Narrative* (Cambridge, 1983); H. S. Stout, *The New England Soul* (New York, 1986).

27. 'De cognitione Dei redemptoris in Christo, quae patribus sub lege primum, deinde et nobis in evangelio patefacta est' (Calvin, *Institutes*, ii; *CO* ii. 175–6; English translation: Battles). For further discussion of Calvin's doctrine of the covenant see: W. van den Bergh, *Calvijn over het genade verbond* (The Hague, 1879); M. Simon, 'Die Beziehung zwischen Altem und Neuem Testament in der Schriftauslegung Calvins', *RKZ* 82 (1932), 3. 17–21, 4. 25–8, 5. 33–5; I. Török, 'Die Bewertung des Alten Testamentes in der Institutio Calvins', in V. Zsigmond (ed.), *Kálvin és a Kálvinizmus* (Debrecen, 1936), 121–39; F. W. Dillistone, 'The Covenant Conception in Calvin', in *The Structure of Divine Society* (Philadelphia, 1951), 117–29; E. H. Emerson, 'Calvin and Covenant Theology'; W. Niesel, *The Theology of Calvin*, trans. H. Knight (1938; Philadelphia, 1956), 39–53, 92–109; P. Prins, 'Verbond en verkiezing bij Bullinger en Calvijn', *GThT* 56 (1956), 97–111; H. H. Wolf, *Die Einheit des Bundes* (Neukirchen, 1958); A. A. Hoekema, 'Calvin's Doctrine of the Covenant of Grace', *RefR(H)* 15 (1962), 1–12; F. Wendel, *Calvin: the Origins and Development of his Religious Thought*, trans. P. Mairet (New York, 1963); A. A. Hoekema, 'The Covenant of Grace in Calvin's Teaching', *CTJ* 2 (1967), 133–61; J. W. Baker, 'Appendix B: Covenant and Testament in Calvin's Thought', in *Heinrich Bullinger and the Covenant*, 193–8; M. E. Osterhaven, 'Calvin on the Covenant', *RefR(H)* 33 (1980), 136–49; P. A. Lillback, 'Ursinus' Development of the Covenant of Creation', *WThJ* 43 (1981), 247–88; P. Helm, 'Calvin and the Covenant', *EQ* 55 (1983), 65–81; P. A. Lillback, 'The Binding of God' (Diss. Westminster Theological Seminary, 1985).

28. 'De similitudine veteris et novi testamenti . . . De differentia unius testamenti ab altero' (Calvin, *Institutes*, ii. 10 and 11; *CO*, ii. 313–29, 329–40; English translation: Battles).

29. 'Ex superioribus liquere iam potest, quoscunque ab initio mundi homines Deus in populi sui sortem cooptavit, eadem lege atque doctrinae eiusdem quae inter nos viget vinculo fuisse ei foederatos' (Calvin, *Institutes*, ii. 10. i; *CO* ii. 313; English translation: Battles).

30. *Institutes*, ii. 11. i-iii; *CO* ii. 329–31.

31. *Institutes*, ii. 11. iv-vi; *CO* ii. 331–4.

32. *Institutes*, ii. 11. vii-viii; *CO* ii. 334–5.

33. *Institutes*, ii. 11. ix-x; *CO* ii. 335–7.

34. *Institutes*, ii. 11. xi-xii; *CO* ii. 337–8.

35. It is at this point that I disagree with P. Lillback's recent dissertation and article ('The Binding of God' and 'Ursinus' Development of the Covenant of Creation'). Lillback is determined to classify Calvin amongst the federal theologians, and makes a rather circuitous argument to justify this classification. An evaluation of his work is included in the section on secondary sources at the end of this Introduction.

36. 'Sacramenti nomen, ut de eius ratione hactenus disseruimus, omnia generaliter

signa complectitur quae unquam hominibus mandavit Deus, ut certiores securosque de promissionum suarum veritate redderet. Ea vero in rebus naturalibus nonnunquam exstare voluit, nonnunquam in miraculis exhibuit' (*Institutes*, iv. 14. xviii; *CO* ii. 955; English translation: Battles).

37. 'Prioris generis exempla sunt, ut quum Adae et Hevae arborem vitae in arrhabonem immortalitatis dedit, ut eam secure sibi promitterent, quamdiu ederent ex illius fructu (Gen. 2, 17 et 3, 3)' (*Institutes*, iv. 14, xviii; *CO* ii. 955; English translation: Battles).

38. For discussion of Bullinger's handling of the covenant theme, see: van t'Hooft, *De theologie van Heinrich Bullinger*; Prins, 'Verbond en verkiezing'; E. Koch, *Die Theologie der Confessio Helvetica Posterior* (Neukirchen, 1968), 383–437; J. W. Baker, *Heinrich Bullinger and the Covenant*; D. C. Steinmetz, 'Heinrich Bullinger', in *Reformers in the Wings* (Philadelphia, 1971), 133–42; J. W. Cottrell, 'Is Bullinger the Source for Zwingli's Doctrine of the Covenant?' in U. Gäbler and E. Herkenrath (edd.), *Heinrich Bullinger*, i (Zurich, 1975), 75–83.

39. Steinmetz, *Reformers in the Wings*, 133–42.

40. Karlberg, 'The Mosaic Covenant'.

41. Ibid. 63–4.

42. Heinrich Bullinger, *In epistolas apostolorvm Bvllingeri* (1558), 163. An English translation of this work can be found in Lillback, 'The Binding of God', 498–527.

43. Lillback, 'The Binding of God', 515.

44. J. W. Baker, 'Covenant and Society', in *Heinrich Bullinger and the Covenant*.

45. 'De Foedere ac Testamento Dei. Tertio, foedus Dei duplex invenio. Generale unum, speciale ac sempiternum alterum. Generale est, quod pepegit cum universa hac terre machina, omnibusque; illam inhabitantibus, tam bestiis quam hominibus: cum die etiam et nocte, hyeme et aestate, frigore et aestu, semente ac mense, etc. . . . foedus hoc generale est, quia totum orbem complectitur, terrenumque vocare potest ac temporarium, propterea quod terrenarum rerum stabilitatem concernit, quemadmodum ex verbis ipsis patet, nec durat ultra mundi huius statum aliquando interiturum . . . Foedus speciale est ac sempiternum, quod cum electis ac credentibus sancire dignatus est . . .' (W. Musculus, *Loci communes sacrae theologiae* (Basle, 1560), 142–3; English translation: *Commonplaces of Christian Religion gathered by Wolfgang Musculus*, trans. J. Man (London, 1563), fos. 120–1.

46. Details of other Protestant theologians' conceptions of the covenant can be gleaned from the following: J. W. Cottrell, 'Covenant and Baptism in the Theology of Huldreich Zwingli' (Diss. Princeton Theological Seminary, 1971); R. L. Greaves, 'John Knox and the Covenant Tradition', *JEH* 24 (1973), 23–32; K. Hagen, 'From Testament to Covenant in the Early Sixteenth Century', *SCJ* 3 (1972), 1–24, and *A Theology of Testament in the Young Luther* (Leiden, 1974); P. A. Laughlin, 'The Brightness of Moses's Face' (Diss. Emory, 1975); M. McGiffert, 'William Tyndale's Conception of Covenant', *JEH* 32 (1981), 167–84.

47. Calvin, in his commentary on Hosea, made reference to 'others' who maintained that Hosea 6: 7 referred to a prelapsarian covenant. Nevertheless, he never identifies who these commentators are: 'Others explain the words thus, "They have transgressed as Adam the covenant." But the word, Adam, we know, is taken indefinitely for men. This exposition is frigid and diluted, "They have transgressed as Adam the covenant"; that is, they have followed or imitated the example of their father Adam, who had immediately at the beginning transgressed God's commandment. I do not stop to refute this

comment; for we see that it is in itself vapid.' 'Alii exponunt, Transgressi sunt pactum sicut Adam. Sed scimus nomen Adam indefinite sumi pro hominibus: et illa est frigida ac diluta expositio, Transgressi sunt sicut Adam pactum: hoc est, sequuti sunt, vel imitati exemplum patris sui Adam, qui etiam statim ab initio transgressus est mandatum Dei. Ergo non insisto in refutatione illius commenti: per se enim videmus esse frigidum' (Calvin, *In Hoseam*, CO xlii. 332–3; English translation: *Commentaries on the Twelve Minor Prophets* (Edinburgh, 1846) i. 235–6; English translation: Owen).

48. 'Testamentum autem primum, quod factum est ad hominem primum, profecto illud est: "Qua die ederitis, morte moriemini" ', *De civitate Dei*, Vol. vii of *Sancti Aurelii Augustini Hipponensis episcopi opera omnia* (Paris, 1838), 700; English translation: Augustine, *Concerning the City of God against the Pagans*, trans. H. Bettenson (Baltimore, 1967), 688. For a good summary of patristic teaching on the covenant, see Z. Thundyil, *Covenant in Anglo-Saxon Thought* (Madras, 1972), 97–120.

49. ' "De masculo, qui si octavo die non fuerit circumcisus, perit anima ejus, quia testamentum Dei dissipavit." ' 'Item potest movere, quomodo intelligi oportet quod hic dictum est, "Masculus qui non circumcidetur carnem praeputii sui octavo die, interibit anima illa de genere ejus, quia testamentum meum dissipavit": cum haec nulla culpa sit parvuli, cujus dixit animam perituram; nec ipse dissipaverit testamentum Dei, sed majores qui eum circumcidere non curarunt: nisi quia etiam parvuli, non secundum suae vitae proprietatem, sed secundum communem generis humani originem, omnes in illo uno testamentum Dei dissipaverunt, in quo omnes peccaverunt. Multa quippe appellantur testamenta Dei, exceptis illis duobus magnis, vetere et novo, quod licet cuique legendo cognoscere. Testamentum autem primum, quod factum est ad hominem primum, profecto illud est: "Qua die ederitis, morte moriemini." Unde scriptum est in libro, qui Ecclesiasticus appellatur, "Omnis caro sicut vestis veterascit." Testamentum enim a saeculo, "Morte morieris." Cum enim lex evidentior postea data sit, et dicat Apostolus, "Ubi autem non est lex, nec praevaricatio": quo pacto quod legitur in Psalmo verum est "Praevaricatores aestimavi omnes peccatores terrae"; nisi quia omnes legis alicujus praevaricatae sunt rei, qui aliquo peccato tenentur obstricti?" ' (Augustine, *De civitate Dei*, 700; English translation: *Concerning the City of God*, 689).

50. N. Diemer, *Het scheppingsverbond met Adam (het verbond der werken), bij de theologen der 16e, 17e, en 18e eeuw in Zwitserland, Duitschland, Nederland en Engeland* (Kampen, 1935), 7.

51. The history was published in 1619; we are using the 1974 critical edition: Paolo Sarpi, *Istoria del Concilio Tridentino*, ed. C. Vivanti, i (Turin, 1974).

52. Ibid. i. 5–6.

53. Sarpi, *The Historie of the Councel of Trent* (3rd edn.), trans. N. Brent (London, 1640).

54. 'Et esplicò la sua sentenza in questa forma; che sì come Dio statuí e fermò patto con Abrahamo e con tutta la sua posterità, quando lo constituí padre dè credenti, così, quando diede la giustizia originale ad Adam e a tutta l'umanità, pattuí con lui in nome di tutti un'obbligazione di conservarla per sé e per loro, osservando il precetto, il quale avendo transgredito, la perdette tanto per gli altri quanto per se stesso et incorse le pene anco per loro; le quali, sí come sono derivate in ciascuno, cosí essa transgressione d'Adamo è anco di Ciascumo; di lui come di causa, degli altri per virtu del patto; sí che l'azione d'Adamo, peccato attuale in lui, imputata agli altri, è il peccato originale, perché peccando

lui, peccò tutto 'l genere umano' (Sarpi, _Istoria_, i. 299–300; English translation: Brent, 175–6).

55. G. P. Fisher, _History of Christian Doctrine_ (New York, 1896), 351.

56. 'Il patto di Dio con Adamo lo provava per un luogo del profeta Osea, per un altro dell'Ecclesiastico e per diversi luoghi di sant'Agostino; il peccato di ciascuno esser il solo atto della transgressone d'Adamo, lo provava san Paulo, quando dice che "per l'inobedienza d'un uomo moli sono fatti peccatori", . . .' (Sarpi, _Istoria_, i. 300; English translation: Brent, 176).

57. Schaff, _Creeds_, iii. 617.

58. Butler, 'Religious Liberty and Covenant Theology', 19–20.

59. The most helpful recent study which explains these terms fully is by J. S. Bray, _Theodore Beza's Doctrine of Predestination_ (Nieuwkoop, 1975). See also B. G. Armstrong, _Calvinism and the Amyraut Heresy_ (Madison, 1969); J. P. Donnelly, SJ, _Calvinism and Scholasticism in Vermigli's Doctrine of Man and Grace_ (Leiden, 1976); Heppe, _Reformed Dogmatics_; Muller, _Dictionary of Latin and Greek Theological Terms_.

60. 'Article VIII: Nous croyons que non-seulement il a créé toutes choses, mais qu'il les gouverne et conduit, disposant, ordonnant selon sa volonté, de tout ce qui advient au monde; non pas qu'il soit auteur du mal, ou que la coulpe lui en puisse être imputée, vu que sa volonté est la règle souveraine et infaillible de toute droiture et équité; mais il a des moyens admirables de se servir tellement des diables et des méchants, qu'il sait convertir en bien le mal qu'ils font, et duquel ils sont coupables. Et ainsi en confessant que rien ne se fait sans la providence de Dieu, nous adorons en humilité les secrets qui nous sont cachés, sans nous enquérir par-dessus notre mesure; mais plutôt appliquons à notre usage ce qui nous est montré en l'Ecriture sainte pour être en repos et sûreté, d'autant que Dieu, qui a toutes choses sujettes à soi, veille sur nous d'un soin paternel, tellement qu'il ne tombera point un cheveu de notre tête sans sa volonté. Et cependant il tient les diables et tous nos ennemis bridés, en sorte qu'ils ne nous peuvent faire aucune nuisance sans son congé.' (_BSRK_ 233); Schaff, _Creeds_, iii. 364; English translation: Schaff); cf. also R. J. VanderMolen, 'Providence as Mystery, Providence as Revelation', _ChH_ 47 (1978), 27–47.

61. Bray, _Theodore Beza's Doctrine of Predestination_, 89.

62. _BSRK_ 511–2; Schaff, _Creeds_, iii. 497–9.

63. _BSRK_ 525; Schaff, _Creeds_, iii. 523.

64. The most extensive discussion of infralapsarianism and supralapsarianism is K. Dijk, _De strijd over Infra- en Supralapsarisme in de Gereformeerde Kerken van Nederland_ (Kampen, 1912); cf. also K. Barth, _Church Dogmatics_, ed. and trans. G. W. Bromiley and T. F. Torrance (Edinburgh, 1957), vol. ii, part ii, 33, sec. 1, 127–45. Cf. also H. E. Weber, _Reformation, Orthodoxie und Rationalismus_, iii (1951; repr. Darmstadt, 1966). The section on infralapsarianism versus supralapsarianism is found on pp. 119–28. Barth's discussion is mainly from a dogmatic point of view; however, he includes much historical theology and history. Both the infralapsarians and the supralapsarians believed that God was sovereign over the Fall and yet was not responsible for it; sometimes it is thought that infralapsarianism teaches that God was not sovereign over the Fall; cf. B. B. Warfield, _Calvin and Calvinism_ (New York, 1931), 364.

65. Barth, _Church Dogmatics_, vol. ii, part ii, 129.

66. Armstrong, _Calvinism and the Amyraut Heresy_, 41–2.

67. Hyper-Calvinism developed in the late seventeenth century out of the various forms of Calvinism. In England it particularly took hold amongst Dissenters and Particular Baptists. In certain instances it led to antinomianism, libertin-

ism, and the rejection of human ethical responsibility; in other instances it led to the renunciation of evangelism and the free offer of the gospel. The justification for both was a deterministic predestinarianism. Cf. P. Toon, *The Emergence of Hyper-Calvinism in English Nonconformity* (London, 1967).

68. 'Articuli Arminiani sive Remonstrantia', Schaff, *Creeds*, iii. 545–9. For a discussion of the Reformed doctrine of the perserverance of the saints, see J. Moltmann, *Prädestination und Perseveranz: Geschichte und Bedeutung der reformierten Lehre 'der perseverantia sanctorum'* (Neukirchen, 1961); Letham, 'Saving Faith and Assurance in Reformed Theology'.

69. The best study which I can find is that by C. Bangs, *Arminius: A Study in the Dutch Reformation* (Nashville, 1971). Cf. also id., 'Arminius and the Reformation', *ChH* 30 (1961), 155–70; A. W. Harrison, *The Beginnings of Arminianism to the Synod of Dort* (London, 1926) and *Arminianism* (London, 1937); F. E. Pamp, Jun., 'Studies in the Origins of English Arminianism' (Diss. Harvard, 1951); W. R. Godfrey, 'Tensions within International Calvinism' (Diss. Stanford, 1974)—Godfrey's superb bibliography gives all the relevant primary and secondary sources; R. A. Muller, 'The Federal Motif in Seventeenth Century Arminian Theology', *Nederlands Archief voor Kerkgeschiedenis*, 62 (1982), 102–22; J. Hicks, 'The Theology of Grace in the Thought of Jacobus Arminius and Philip van Limborch' (Diss. Westminster Theological Seminary, 1985); G. J. Hoenderdaal, 'Arminius . . . Arminianismus', *TRE* iv (1979), 63–9; N. Tyacke, *Anti-Calvinists: The Rise of English Arminianism c.1590–1640* (Oxford, 1987).

70. For an explanation of antinomianism, see A. H. Newman, 'Antinomianism and Antinomian Controversies', *NSHE* i (1908), 196–201; Stoever, *'A Faire and Easie Way to Heaven'*, 161–3, 181–3.

71. See Appendix.

72. Heppe, *Dogmatik des deutschen Protestantismus*, i. 139–204.

73. 'Die Entstehung und Ausbildung der deutschreformirten Dogmatik' (ibid. 139).

74. 'Vielmehr is dieselbe allein aus der inneren Gesammtentwicklung und aus der Geschichte des deutschen Protestantismus zu begreifen, und wird daher die deutschreformirte Theologie gennant' (ibid. 139–40).

75. This matter will be discussed in some detail later, but see C.-P. Clasen, *The Palatinate in European History, 1559–1660* (Oxford, 1963), 33–45.

76. Heppe, *Dogmatik*, i. 140.

77. Ibid. 143–4.

78. 'The federal theological method is the opposite of the scholastic. The latter views the complex of dogmatic truths as a traditional object for systematic arrangements. Dogmatic theology stands as an object over against the dogmatist, who deals with it according to the rules of science as with every other intellectual object. In comparison, on the other hand, the federal theology behaves differently. It handles religious truth not as an object set forth to speculate, systematize, and teach, but as an available good in the living possession of believers and of their regenerated awareness. It presents Dogmatics as that which is demonstrated in the personal religious knowledge and in the living practical experience of the regenerate Christian.' 'Die föderaltheologische Methode ist das Gegenteil der scholastischen. Die letztere betrachtet den Complex der dogmatischen Wahrheiten als ein gegebenes Objekt systematisirender Bearbeitung. Die Glaubenslehre steht als Objekt dem Dogmatiker gegenüber, der mit demselben nach den Regeln der Wissenschaft verfährt wie mit einem jeden andern geistigen Objekt. Anders dagegen verfährt die Föderaltheologie. Sie behandelt die Glaubenswahrheit

nicht als ein zum Speculiren, Systematisiren und Dociren hingestelltes Objekt, sondern als ein im lebendigen Besitze des Gläubigen und seines wieder-geborenen Bewusstseins vorhandenes Gut. Sie stellt die Dogmatik als das dar, als was sie sich im persönlichen Glaubensbewusstsein und in der lebendigen Erfahrung des wiedergeborenen Christen erweist' (ibid. 152).

79. 'In general the original German Reformed Dogmatics are characterized in this way: (1) they lay out an idea, that expresses the true purpose of creation and redemption as the basic idea in which all of the individual parts have their inner unity, and so all of the propositions refer back to this. This is the idea of the covenant of God, the Church, or else the kingdom of Christ.' 'Im Allgemeinen charakterisirt sich die ursprüngliche deutschreformirte Dogmatik dadurch: 1) dass sie einen Begriff, der den eigentlichen Schöpfungs- und Erlösungszweck ausspricht, als Grundbegriff ausstellt, in welchem alle ihre einzelnen Teile ihre innere Einheit haben, auf den daher auch alle ihre Sätze zurückweisen. Es ist diese der Begriff des foedus Dei, der ecclesia, oder des regnum Christi' (ibid. 143–4).

80. Schrenk, *Gottesreich und Bund*.

81. Ibid. 36–82.

82. 'The Connection of the Covenant to the Personal Salvation Experience of Believers: Ursinus, Olevianus, Sohnius.' 'Die Beziehung des Bundes auf die persönliche Heilserfahrung der Gläubigen: Ursinus, Olevianus, Sohnius' (ibid. 57).

83. Diemer, *Het scheppingsverbond met Adam*.

84. Ibid. 7–8.

85. M. W. Karlberg interacts extensively with Deimer's thinking in his dissertation ('The Mosaic Covenant').

86. Cf. A. Williams, *The Common Expositor* (Chapel Hill, 1948), 246–50; Miller, *The New England Mind*, i. 183–4; H. Heppe, *Dogmatik* i, 338–59.

87. Miller, *The New England Mind*, i. 365–462, and 'The Marrow of Puritan Divinity'.

88. G. M. Marsden, 'Perry Miller's Rehabilitation of the Puritans: A Critique', *ChH* 39 (1970), 91–105; J. von Rohr, *The Covenant of Grace in Puritan Thought* (Atlanta, 1986), 17–21.

89. Miller, *The New England Mind*, i. 376–7, 384–5.

90. Ibid. 502–5.

91. De Jong, *The Covenant Idea*.

92. Ibid. 50–61.

93. Trinterud, 'The Origins of Puritanism'.

94. As summarized by L. D. Bierma, 'The Covenant Theology of Caspar Olevian' (Diss. Duke, 1980), 25.

95. 'As these men, and their theologian colleagues, sought to weave together one complete theological-political-social theory the older theological doctrine of the covenant could not be used, for it was a covenant of redemption restricted entirely to the elect. Increasing mention is found during these years of a "covenant of creation", "covenant of nature", and similar ideas. But, it was not until 1580 that a wholly systematic re-organization of the covenant theology emerged. . . . By the 1580s the idea of a "covenant of works" so-called, made between God and Adam, had begun to have considerable vogue on the Continent. This covenant of works provided a theological basis for a moral, civil, and religious obligation binding upon all men, elect or non-elect, regenerate or unregenerate, professedly Christian or pagan. Into this covenant of works the whole state contract theory was incorporated by the theologians. The natural law of the state contract was also the natural law of the covenant of works. On the Continent the practical applications of this new covenant

scheme were never very fully exploited. Puritanism, however, was anything but blind to the possibilities which were inherent in this new scheme' (Trinterud, 'The Origins of Puritanism', 48).

96. Rolston, *John Calvin versus the Westminster Confession*; see also his article 'Responsible Man in Reformed Theology', *SJTh* 23 (1970), 129–56.

97. Rolston, 'Responsible Man', 142–3; cf. Diemer, *Het scheppingsverbond*, and Karlberg's assessment of Diemer, 'The Mosaic Covenant', 22–8. Rolston does not seem to be aware of the work of Diemer, although they both deal extensively with the same topic.

98. Rolston, *John Calvin versus the Westminster Confession*, 34, 36, 38. Rolston has commented: 'First, there is little thought of God's goodness as putting man under obligation; duty is now defined in terms of law, because duty is derived from law . . . Secondly, duty shifts to focus on man's initiative. The man who was in Calvin's thought to seek and receive all good from the hand of God, and thankfully to acknowledge it, has now to do it for himself. The burden of achieving life is laid squarely on his own shoulders. . . . Calvin and the Calvinists, despite superficial similarities, have fundamentally different ways of describing the fundamental sin' ('Responsible Man', 136–7).

99. Rolston, 'Responsible Man', 133.

100. Stoever, 'The Covenant of Works'. See also his published work, *'A Faire and Easie Way to Heaven'*. Some of Stoever's conclusions can also be found in his 1975 article: 'Nature, Grace and John Cotton', *ChH* 44 (1975), 22–34.

101. Stoever, 'The Covenant of Works', iii.

102. 'Puritanism as it developed encountered a two-fold dilemma. On the one hand was the political-ethical problem of living responsibly in the world, of participating fully in social, political and economic activity, without becoming "worldly". The world was understood as God's deliberate creation, and therefore as essentially good, and secession from the created order as though it were perishing or polluted would be blasphemous. The world was indeed perishing, but God alone knew the moment of dissolution; and the Christian dare not opt out of normal historical existence before the last trump. In the meantime, however, all his activity must be conscientiously referred to God who is both beginning and end of creation.

'On the other hand was the theological dilemma of maintaining justification by faith alone, the gratuity of grace, and the sovereign freedom of God's will in all phases of redemption, without violating the created order either onto-logically or deontologically. God's redemptive activity must be so conceived that (*a*) the integrity of creatures, in respect of their own proper natures conferred at creation, does not suffer before the divine omnipotence, and that (*b*) the moral order given at creation, which defines man's relationship to God, is not dissolved. On the first count, man by nature possesses both reason and will, in which his distinctiveness consists, and in which he is, of all creation, uniquely fitted to enjoy communion with God. Adam's fall destroyed man's ability to achieve blessedness by his own endeavour, but did not alter his nature as man, and his redemption may not proceed contrary to the normal structure of that nature. On the second count, God, in the garden, promised Adam (and mankind in him) blessedness on condition of perfect obedience to the moral law written in his heart at creation. Adam failed, bringing upon himself and his posterity the threatened punishment for disobedience; but that did not alter the status of the law as God's immutable will for human conduct, nor did it alter the terms of blessedness, which remain contingent upon obedience to that law. Such was the problem of human salvation as it appeared to the puritan theological mind, a mind which was characteristically, if not uniquely, dominated by the conception of God as absolute, all-sovereign will, and which habitually represented God's intentions for man in terms of law' (ibid. 7–9).

103. Ibid. 10.
104. Master of Theology thesis, Westminster Theological Seminary (1976).
105. Karlberg, 'The Mosaic Covenant'.
106. 'The first matter pertains to the notion of two distinct states or stages of creation, the state of nature and the state of grace. Recent covenant theologians describe the first state as the initial order of moral government and the second as the subsequent order of covenant arrangement, corresponding to the Thomistic nature-grace dualism. The idea of a pure state of nature is opposed to the biblical doctrine of creation, which is characteristically eschatological. In the biblical view there is movement from creation to consummation and glorification. This eschatological aspect is diametrically opposed to the scholastic nature-grace dichotomy which was applied to the covenant of works idea during the course of the first period of federal theology' (ibid. 4–5). Cf. also Vos, 'The Doctrine of the Covenant', 234–43.
107. Karlberg, 'The Mosaic Covenant', 6.
108. Ibid. 7–8.
109. Ibid. 95.
110. Bierma, 'The Covenant Theology of Caspar Olevian'.
111. Ibid., pp. iv-v.
112. Baker, *Heinrich Bullinger and the Covenant*.
113. 'The key Reformation principles of justification by faith alone through grace alone seemed endangered by the idea of a bilateral covenant. The Protestant logic appeared to be on the side of a theology of testament. Calvin's theology of testament within the confines of double predestination clearly avoided any weakening of the distinctive Protestant doctrine of justification. For Calvin, predestination implemented *sola fide* and protected *sola gratia*. Bullinger, while not avoiding the issue, did not attempt to solve the tensions, which he thought were also found in the Scripture, between conditional covenant and *sola gratia*. For Bullinger, the covenant was the exclusive vehicle through which God worked in history with His people. Bullinger held to a conditional covenant on the one hand and to *sola gratia* encased within a carefully stated doctrine of single predestination on the other hand' (ibid., pp. xxii-xxiii).
114. Ibid. 165–7.
115. Ibid., App. C, 'Calvinist Orthodoxy and the Paralysis of the Covenant Idea', 199–215.
116. Ibid. 165.
117. Lillback, 'Ursinus' Development of the Covenant of Creation' and 'The Binding of God'.
118. Lillback, 'The Binding of God', 496.
119. Ibid. 467.
120. Lillback, 'Ursinus' Development of the Covenant of Creation', 259.
121. Helm, 'Calvin and the Covenant'. This article appears in an issue especially devoted to Calvin and his 'Calvinistic' successors.
122. R. W. A. Letham, 'The *Foedus Operum*: Some Factors Accounting for its Development', *SCJ* 14 (1983), 457–67.
123. D. Visser, 'The Covenant in Zacharias Ursinus', *SCJ* 18 (1987), 531–44.
124. M. McGiffert, 'From Moses to Adam: The Making of the Covenant of Works', *SCJ* 19 (1988), 131–55.
125. Exceptions are De Jong, *The Covenant Idea*; Stoever, 'The Covenant of Works'; Karlberg, 'The Mosaic Covenant'; Letham, 'The *Foedus Operum*'; and McGiffert, 'From Moses to Adam'.

I

The Lexical and Biblical Evidence

Beholde, the daies come, saith ye Lord, that I wil mak a newe
couenant with the house of Israel, and with the house of Iudah,
Not according to the couenant that I made with their fathers, . . .

Jeremiah 31: 31–2 (Geneva Bible, 1560)

THE original Old Testament word for covenant is *berith*. However,
the primary import of the meaning of the word *berith* was lost as it
was translated into various languages, particularly Greek and Latin.
In the Septuagint *berith* was translated by the word *diatheke*, which
has slightly different connotations from the Hebrew word. With the
translation of the scriptures into Latin these two words had three
possible Latin translations: *foedus*, *pactum*, and *testamentum*. The
purpose of this chapter is to explore the way the sixteenth-century
student of the Bible perceived and understood these words.[1]

Much modern attention has been focused on the biblical meaning
of these words, and there has been a growing realization among
historians of the Reformation that they took on greater and greater
significance as the sixteenth century advanced. Research on the
Reformation understanding of covenant has centred mainly upon
tracts and treatises of various theologians.[2] We will confine ourselves,
however, simply to the evidence found in the lexicons and biblical
translations of the period, for these were the basic working tools of
Reformed, Lutheran, and Roman Catholic theologians alike. While a
theologian might not have had access to a treatise like Bullinger's *De
testamento seu foedere Dei unico et aeterno* (1534), he would be more
likely to have Hebrew, Greek, and Latin lexicons available to him,
along with several versions of the Bible.

The Lexical Evidence

1. Consideration will first be given to the word *berith*. *Berith*
indicates an agreement between two parties, usually God and man

or man and man. In the case of the God–man relationship the bond is imposed upon the inferior party, which is man. Man has no option. God makes the covenant for man. God commands and establishes the covenant totally of his gracious and free will.[3]

The first printed Hebrew lexicon appeared in 1506 and was produced by Johannes Reuchlin (1455–1522). His entry for *berith* is very brief:

> . . . *Foedus. pactum.* as in Jeremiah 31. Behold the days are coming, says the Lord, that I will make a new covenant (*foedus*) with the house of Israel and the house of Judah, not according to the covenant (*pactum*). Here the same word is translated in two ways.[4]

Reuchlin sets a pattern for other sixteenth- and seventeeth-century lexicons in that he does not go into extensive explanation of the word but simply quotes key scriptural passages which use the word *berith*. In this case it is the passage from Jeremiah 31: 31–4, a key passage which we will quote here for future reference:

> Behold, the days come, saith the Lord, that I will make a new covenant with the house of Israel, and with the house of Judah: Not according to the covenant that I made with their fathers in the day that I took them by the hand to bring them out of the land of Egypt; which my covenant they brake, although I was an husband unto them, saith the Lord: But this shall be the covenant that I will make with the house of Israel; After those days, saith the Lord, I will put my law in their inward parts, and write it in their hearts; and I will be their God, and they shall be my people. And they shall teach no more every man his neighbour, and every man his brother, saying, Know the Lord: for they shall all know me, from the least of them unto the greatest of them, saith the Lord: for I will forgive their iniquity, and I will remember their sin no more. (Jeremiah 31: 31–4, AV.)

The number of times *berith* is used in the Old Testament is extensive, and therefore the passages used to illustrate the word are of particular importance. These passages were impressed upon the consciousness of the theologian repeatedly. It is significant, therefore, that in the case of *berith* the earliest lexicon does not use the examples of the covenant with Abraham or Moses or David, but the example of the coming ideal state, in which the law of God will be written upon the heart of the believer, and each man shall 'know the Lord'.

The next lexicon of significance is one compiled by Alphonso Zamorensis (c.1474–c.1531). It appears in 1515 at the end of the *Complutensian Polyglot*. The entry for *berith* is more extensive, and refers to the plurality of the uses of the word: a covenant can be made with God, with death, with another person, etc. Much of the entry is a discussion of the concept of a sign of the covenant and not the covenant itself. The author draws a relationship between cutting (*percutere*) and covenant (*foedus, pactum*) and notes the famous example of God confirming the covenant to Abraham by walking between the two halves of slain animals (Genesis 15). Again, the concluding reference is to Jeremiah 31.[5]

Sebastian Münster (1488–1552) published his *Dictionarium Hebraicum* in 1523. His discussion of the word *berith* is not extensive, but he continues the confusion surrounding the understanding of the word by maintaining, as the Vulgate does, that *testamentum* is an acceptable translation for *berith*. His only scriptural reference is to Jeremiah 31.[6]

Sanctus Pagninus (1470–1536) produced his *Thesaurus Linguae Sanctae* in 1529. His lexicon has a Latin index to correspond with the Hebrew listing of words. *Foedus* and *pactum*, as could be expected, are the two Latin words which are related to *berith*.[7] However, it is significant that the word *testamentum* is not listed as a possible translation of *berith*. Furthermore, the earlier lexicons of 1506 and 1515 do not translate *berith* as *testamentum*. The Münster lexicon of 1523 does. This indicates to us that the linguists of the period did realize the difference between the two words: that *berith* is an agreement between two consenting parties while *testamentum* has the meaning of a disposition to one party after the death of the other party who made the testament.

Pagninus's second biblical reference, to 'Psalm 79: 9' (78: 10, RSV; 77: 10, Vulgate), indicates an interest in another important theme that will start to dominate the theological thinking of orthodox Calvinist theologians of a slightly later period: the interrelationship, or equivalence, between covenant and law. This important relationship, combined with the idea that the law of God was written on Adam's heart before the Fall, will contribute to the postulation of a prelapsarian covenant with Adam in later decades. For now, the idea is simply dormant. The idea is emphasized again by Pagninus's reference to Deuteronomy 4: 13 later. Pagninus's focus is on the two parties, God and man, faithfully keeping the covenant that has been made.[8]

The final sixteenth-century lexicon which we will consider is that of Robert Stephanus (Estienne) (1503–59). It is actually not a

lexicon but a collection of Hebrew phrases: *Phrases Hebraicae*.[9]
This collection was published in 1558, just before the crystallization
of the federal scheme, which occurred between 1560 and 1590.
Stephanus recognizes both *pactum* and *foedus* as legitimate translations of *berith*. He covers the same passages as the previous
lexicographers did, but this time in a more thorough way. Most
significant about how Stephanus approaches the word is that he
emphasizes that the covenant has precepts and conditions, and that
these precepts equal the law of God. Under *foedus* we find these
words:

Covenant, for tables of the covenant. That ark in which is the covenant, I
Kings 8:21, that is, the tables on which were the precepts and conditions of
the covenant. Covenant, for the Jews. His heart against the holy covenant,
Daniel 2:28 and 30 [*sic*; Daniel 11:28 and 30], that is, so that he may harm
the Jews who worship the true and living God, according to his Law.[10]

And under *pactum* we find a similar section:

Pactum see *Foedus*. A perpetual covenant of salt, Numbers 18:19. See salt.
Keeping his covenant and his testimony, Psalm 25:10, that is the laws of
God: for God cuts a covenant with us, for this reason, that we should
observe his laws or covenant, or else covenant signifies 'the conditions of
the covenant'.[11]

Stephanus gives only a short paragraph to the idea that *testamentum*
can be a valid translation of *berith*, probably because the Vulgate
sometimes translates it as such. His references under *testamentum*
amount to only two passages, both in the Psalms.[12]

By 1558 the idea of conditionality, of 'If . . . then . . . ', plays a
much more important role in the lexicographical understanding of
berith. This development should not be surprising, as we shall see.
The same idea of conditionality and law is continued by Johannes
Buxtorf the Elder (1564–1627) in his *Lexicon Hebraicum et
Chaldaicum* of 1607.[13] Buxtorf is the first lexicographer to use the
term *foedus gratiae*, although only in his introduction.[14] By 1669
Johannes Cocceius, who proposed modifications to the classical
federal theology, could maintain that covenant included three
elements: (*a*) *stipulatio*; (*b*) *promissio*; and (*c*) *adstipulatio*.[15]

Several things can be said in summary about the sixteenth-
century lexical understanding of the word *berith*:

(i) All of them translate the Old Testament word by the words
foedus or *pactum*. Very little attention is given to the word

testamentum as a viable translation. However, *testamentum* is sometimes used freely and interchangeably with *foedus* in the Vulgate Old Testament (especially in the Psalms) as an accepted translation of *berith*. This indicates that the linguists of the period were aware of the subtle differences between the various words, and that the meanings of these several words were undergoing examination, scrutiny, and discussion.

(ii) The lexicographers did not give detailed explanations of the word that they were defining. Rather, after a brief explanation they gave various examples of how that word was used in Scripture. In the case of *berith* there was a general pattern to the scriptural examples which they selected: (*a*) some of the lexical entries deal with the relationship between God and his people. In this case a tension appears between passages illustrating God's free and gracious choice of his people (Abraham and Genesis 15–17) and the responsibility of his people to be obedient to him (Moses and Deuteronomy 29). The former seems to illustrate predestinating, unconditional love. The latter seems to illustrate conditional love. The antinomian controversies of the sixteenth and seventeenth centuries focused on this problem, and one of the goals of the federal theology was to resolve this tension. (*b*) Some of the entries mention the signs and seals of the covenant. (*c*) Most deal with the idea that a covenant with God involves law and precepts, which act as conditions of the covenant. (*d*) Some give examples of covenants other than those between God and man: man–man; God–nature; husband–wife; and so forth.

(iii) As the century progressed the idea of a conditional covenant became more important. Words such as 'precepts', 'law', and 'conditions' creep into the lexicons. This should be expected, for there is a definite shift in the understanding of covenant during this period.

(iv) It is of particular interest and importance that Jeremiah 31: 31–4 is mentioned in virtually all of the lexicons. This illustrates the pivotal influence of that passage for the lexicographers. The old covenant and even the new covenant are imperfect. What the Christian really wants is the everlasting covenant, the eschatological covenant, the covenant of God with perfected humanity after the Day of Judgement in the new heavens and the new earth. This covenant involves the restoration to the perfection of the Edenic state and more. It is achieved through Christ, the second Adam, who kept the law for his people and writes it on their hearts. It is this covenantal relationship which will form the model and pattern for the prelapsarian covenant of the early federal theologians.

2. The lexical evidence for *diatheke* is briefer. Its meaning is slightly different from that of *berith*. Whereas *berith* implies the notion of 'imposition', 'liability', or 'obligation', *diatheke* technically refers to a last will and testament, while it

is properly dispositio, or 'arrangement' made by one party with plenary power, which the other party may accept or reject, but cannot alter. A 'will' is simply the most conspicuous example of such an instrument, which ultimately monopolized the word just because it suited its differentia so completely.[16]

Berith does not include any sense of last will and testament. Unlike *berith* there is more room for rejection in *diatheke*: the terms on which a party may inherit its inheritance never change, but a party might decide to reject the inheritance. Rejection of the terms of *berith* leads to certain destruction. At the same time *diatheke* was the term that the translators of the Septuagint chose for *berith*. Johannes Behm has remarked:

The remarkable fact that *diatheke* is not an unequivocal concept in the LXX, but hovers between the senses of 'covenant' and 'disposition', is not based solely on the fact that the Greek term embraces both possibilities; it is to be explained finally in terms of the complex content of the word *berith* which the translators were trying to grasp.[17]

It is particularly important that the Septuagint rarely uses *suntheke* for a translation of *berith* between God and man. *Suntheke* refers to a contract or treaty in which the parties are equal and bargain with one another, eventually binding themselves together on mutual conditions to effect some future result. There is no sense of obligation or imposition. Each party is free. Each is independent of the other. The obligations to each other are conditional, and thus there is no room left for gracious giving. It is a legal agreement: 'If you . . . then I . . .' and 'If you do not . . . then I will not . . .'

Berith and *diatheke*, at least in the God–man relationship, are unconditional. They are unilateral agreements. God makes his covenant for his people out of his sovereign pleasure and grace. However, how does one explain the passages of the Bible in which God's covenant seems to be based upon conditions rather than grace, on *suntheke* rather than *diatheke* or *berith*? This tendency is most clearly illustrated by the Book of Deuteronomy. For the orthodox Calvinist of the day this problem of meaning was particularly acute. Two basic presuppositions undergirded his faith: the total inability of man to save himself and to obey the covenant; and God's sovereign and predestinating grace choosing out the elect. How could God place conditions in his covenant with man when he also plainly taught that no matter how hard one tried man could not keep the covenant? The confusion comes when the contractual *suntheke* appears to be equivalent to the covenant of grace. The classic struggle between works and grace, between *opera* and *gratia*, is apparent.

James B. Torrance has attempted to show that during this period the later Reformers confused *diatheke* with *suntheke*, and that consequently there was a greater emphasis on the conditionality of the covenant than on the graciousness of the covenant: the imperatives of grace preceded the indicatives of grace, and not vice versa.[18] However, it is more than a small confusion of words, as Torrance to a certain degree realizes. Torrance is correct in his observation, but he does not expose the roots of this tendency. The federal theology arose precisely because of the conflict (not the confusion) between *diatheke* and *suntheke*. It was an attempt to explain why God seemed to show two faces: one of predestinating grace through his sovereign decrees and another of conditional love. The Calvinist wanted an orthodox answer as to why God could show both appearances at the same time.

A sampling of Greek lexicons will be sufficient to explain the understanding of *diatheke*. Because of the association with last will and testament *diatheke* is immediately connected to *testamentum*. *Foedus* recedes into the background. However, the differences between these words is understood. Here is one lexical example from 1572:

Diatheke and *diathekai*, variously, testament, tables, inheritance which descends by way of the testament . . .
. . . Symmachus translates as covenant: it does not mean only a last will of the deceased, but a covenant of the living, for the Hebrew word means more 'pact' or 'covenant' rather than 'testament'.[19]

Suntheke is also listed, and the translation given for it is *foedus* or *pactum*.

The most extensive explanation of *diatheke* can be found in the *Thesaurus Graecae linguae* (1572) of Henry Stephanus (Estienne) (1528–98). Stephanus realizes that the more technical meaning of *diatheke* in secular Greek literature is *testamentum*, and he realizes that the Bible utilizes it for the more precise *berith*:

> *Diatheke, he*, the testament . . . With the Greeks, however, the interpreta-
> tion in the Bible of *diatheke* is the same as what *suntheke* means, that is,
> covenant, pact . . . that in many places in the Scriptures testament does not
> mean the will of the dead, but the covenant of the living. Likewise certainly
> *he kaine diatheke* means more 'new covenant' rather than 'new
> testament'.[20]

The link between *diatheke* and *testamentum* served to set the word *foedus* by itself. As the knowledge of Hebrew and the Hebrew Bible increased among the theologians of the later part of the sixteenth century these theologians did not have to depend on the Vulgate for the words of Scripture. They were finding that in the Vulgate the word *berith* is translated often by *foedus*, sometimes by *testamentum*. By 1590 the early federal theologians were not speaking of a *testamentum operum* or a *testamentum gratiae*; they were speaking of a *foedus gratiae*. In the terminology of the federal theology and in the covenant idea *testamentum* went out of use, as a result of the shifting understanding of and emphasis upon the various terms for covenant.

The Biblical Evidence

How were these words used in the Latin biblical translations of the sixteenth century? Between 1515 and 1580 several Latin translations of the Bible other than the Vulgate were published.[21] When one examines their use of the words *testamentum* and *foedus* one finds that they followed the Vulgate consistently. There is one exception, and that is the translation of Sebastian Castellio.

Bonifatius Fischer, in a recent critical concordance to the Vulgate, has shown that *foedus* appears many times in the Vulgate Old Testament, but that in the Vulgate New Testament it appears only once.[22] The Vulgate New Testament exclusively translates *diatheke* by the word *testamentum*. Castellio flies directly in the face of this precedent. His translation of the Bible is known for its classical eloquence and tendency to paraphrase, traits which orthodox Reformed men such as Calvin and Beza violently condemned.[23] But what Castellio did in this particular case, hitherto neglected by modern research, is something which some orthodox Calvinists might approve of. He abandoned the word *testamentum*, except in a few key places, and used *foedus* as a translation of *berith* and *diatheke*. Consequently, a crucial passage such as Matthew 26: 27–8 reads like this in the Vulgate: 'Et accipiens calicem gratias egit et dedit illis dicens bibite ex hoc omnes hic est enim sanguis meus novi testamenti qui pro multis effunditur in remissionem peccatorum',[24] whereas in Castellio's transation it reads like this: 'Deinde, capto poculo, actisque laudibus, dedit eis, dicens: bibite ex eo omnes: hic est enim sanguis meus novi foederis, pro multis effundendus ad veniam peccatorum.'[25] The most hotly disputed words of the sixteenth century had been altered.[26] Such a radical break with centuries of tradition could not fail to go unnoticed. The change was reiterated when, in the midst of controversy over his translation, he changed the title of the corpus of New Testament writings to *novus foedus*: *Sebastiani Castellionis defensio suarum translationum Bibliorum, et maxime Noui Foederis*.[27]

It is Sebastian Castellio, known much more for his championing of religious liberty and freedom of conscience than for his linguistic ability, who affirms that *foedus* is a better translation than *testamentum* for *berith* and *diatheke*. Indeed, the only time Castellio uses *testamentum* is in Hebrews 9. He changes all the instances of *testamentum* in the Vulgate Old Testament to *foedus*. What he did contradicted the translators of the Septuagint, for he affirms that *foedus* expresses *berith* better than *testamentum* or *diatheke* does, and that *berith* is an Old Testament concept which has been obscured by *diatheke* and which is illuminated by *foedus*.

Like the lexical evidence, this word-substitution indicates that there was much more discussion than appears in print over these words, and that there was an awareness of the different definitions and connotations. Theologians were questioning what exactly was a *testamentum* or *foedus*, and whether they were adequate translations of the original concept of *berith*.

It is most interesting that Zacharias Ursinus, who was the first Protestant theologian to propose a prelapsarian covenant, visited Castellio in Basle just as he (Ursinus) was making the decision to leave the Lutheran fold and join the High Calvinists.[28] Furthermore, Ursinus's visit coincided with the height of the burning controversy over God's sovereignty and Adam's Fall, which pitted men like Castellio against Calvin and Beza.

Notes

1. For a summary of the major features of sixteenth-century biblical scholarship, see R. Bainton and D. P. Lockwood, 'Classical and Biblical Scholarship in the Age of the Renaissance and Reformation', *ChH* 10 (1941), 125–43; *The Cambridge History of the Bible*, iii (Cambridge, 1963).
2. In particular see two works by K. Hagen, 'From Testament to Covenant' and *A Theology of Testament*. Cf. also Baker, 'Appendix A: Covenant and Testament in the Early Reformation', in *Heinrich Bullinger and the Covenant*, 181–91; M. Greschat, 'Die Bundesgedanke in der Theologie des späten Mittelalters', *ZKG* 81 (1970), 44–63; H. A. Oberman, 'Wir sein pettler. Hoc est verum', *ZKG* 78 (1967), 232–52.
3. For a modern understanding of the word, see M. Weinfield, 'Berith', in *ThWAT* i. 781–808; English translation in *TDOT* ii. 253–79; also D. J. McCarthy, SJ, 'Covenant in the Old Testament', *Catholic Biblical Quarterly*, 27 (1965), 217–40; this was extensively revised and translated as: *Der Gottesbund im Alten Testament* (Stuttgart, 1967); English translation: *Old Testament Covenant* (Richmond, 1972); Hillers, *Covenant: The History of a Biblical Idea*; G. W. Buchanan, *The Consequences of the Covenant* (Leiden, 1970); McCarthy, *Treaty and Covenant* (new edn., Rome, 1978); W. J. Dumbrell, *Covenant and Creation* (Nashville, 1984); McComiskey, *The Covenants of Promise*.
4. J. Reuchlin, *De rudimentis linguae Hebraicae una cum lexico* (n.p., 1506), i. 93: '. . . Foedus. pactum. ut Ieremie XXXi. Ecce dies venient dicit dominus, Et feriam domui Israel et domui Iuda foedus novum, non secundum pactum ecce. idem vocabulam dupliciter traduxit.'
5. A. Zamorensis, *Uocabularium Hebraicum et Chaldaicum totius Ueteris Testamentum*, vol. vi of *Uetus Testamentum multiplici lingua nunc primo impressum* (Alcalá, 1515), fo. xix.
6. S. Münster, *Dictionarium Hebraicum* (Basle, 1539), fos. 64–5.
7. S. Pagninus, *Thesaurus linguae sanctae* (Lyons, [1529]), col. 284.
8. 'And he declared to you his covenant, which he commanded you to perform, that is, the ten commandments; and he wrote them upon two tables of stone' (Deut. 4: 13, RSV).
9. O. R. Stephanus (Estienne), *Phrases Hebraicae . . . Thesauri linguae Hebraicae altera pars* (Geneva, 1558).
10. 'Foedus, pro tabulis foederis. Ipsi arcae in qua est foedus, I Regem 8: 21 id est, tabulae in quibus erant praecepta et conditiones foederis. Foedus, pro Iudaeis. Cor eius contra foedus sanctum, Daniel 228 et 30 [*sic*; Daniel 11: 28 and 30] id est, ut noceat Iudaeis qui colunt Deum verum et vivam, iuxta Legem ipsius', ibid. 366.
11. 'Pactum, vide foedus. Pactum salis perpetuum, Numeri 18: 19 vide sal. Custodientibus pactum eius et testimonia eius. Psalmi 25: 10 id est, leges Dei: quod ea ratione percutiat foedus nobiscum Deus, ut leges eius observemus aut pactum, sive foedus significat conditiones foederis', ibid. 649–50.
12. Ibid. 892. The references are to Psalm 22: 16 and Psalm 25: 10; the numbering is according to the Hebrew and English versions, not the Latin Vulgate. The reference to Psalm 22: 16 ('Aruit tanquam testa fortitudo mea') is inaccurate as a reference to *testamentum*.
13. J. Buxtorf, *Lexicon Hebraicum et Chaldaicum . . . editio quinta* (Basle, 1645).
14. Ibid. 88.
15. J. Cocceius, *Lexicon et commentarius sermonis Hebraici et Chaldaici Veteris Testamenti* (Leiden, 1669), 114–16.

16. G. Quell and J. Behm, 'diatheke', *ThWNT* ii. 105–37; English translation: *TDNT* ii. 106–34; this particular quote is from *TDNT* ii. 125; cf. also L. Coenen, J. Guhrt, and O. Becker, 'Bund', *TBLNT* i. 157–65; English translation: 'Covenant, Guarantee, Mediator', *NIDNTT* i. 365–76.
17. *TDNT* ii. 126–7.
18. 'Covenant or Contract?', *SJTh* 23 (1970), 51–76.
19. 'Διαθήκη et Διαθήκαι, Pluraliter testamentum, tabellae haereditas quae testamento obvenit . . . Symmachus pactum interpretatur: nec voluntatem tantum defunctorum sonat, sed pactum uiuentium, nam uox Hebraea magis sonat pactum aut foedus quam testamentum', G. Budaeus *et al.*, *Dictionarium Graecolatinum* (Basle, 1572). There are no page numbers.
20. H. Stephanus (Estienne), *Thesaurus Graecae linguae* (Geneva, 1572), iii. 1492–3. 'Διαθήκη, ἡ, Testamentum . . . Apud Graecos autem Bibliorum interpretes διαθήκη idem significat quod συνθήκη id est Foedus, Pactum . . . in plerisque Scripturarum locis Testamentum non voluntatem defunctorum sonare, sed pactum viventium. Itidem certe ἡ καινή διαθήκη sonat potius novum foedus quam novum testamentum.'
21. The following Latin translations were consulted: *Biblia cum concordantiis veteris et novi testamenti* (Leiden, 1523); *Biblia sacrosancta Testamenti Veteris et Noui*, trans. L. Jud *et al.* (Zurich, 1544); *Biblia . . .*, trans. R. Estienne (Paris, 1545); *Biblia . . .*, ed. and trans. S. Castellio (Basle, 1554); *Testamenti veteris Biblia sacra*, trans. I. Tremellius and F. Junius (London, 1580).
22. B. Fischer, *Novae Concordantiae Bibliorum Sacrorum iuxta Vulgatam versionem critice editam* (Stuttgart, 1977), ii. 2130 and v. 5166–7.
23. See, for instance, T. Beza, *Responsio ad defensiones et reprehensiones Sebastiani Castellionis* (Geneva, 1563).
24. The edition of the Vulgate which I am using is the standard *Biblia Sacra iuxta Vulgatam versionem*, 2 vols. (Stuttgart, 1969).
25. *Biblia . . .*, ed. and trans. S. Castellio.
26. Castellio is consistent in his change: cf. Mark 14: 24, Luke 22: 20, and 1 Corinthians 11: 25 in his translation, among other passages.
27. S. Castellio, *Defensio suarum translationum Bibliorum* (Basle, 1562).
28. Cf. 'Das Stammbuch des Zacharias Ursinus (1553–1562 und 1581)', ed. W. H. Neuser, *BPfKG* 31 (1964), 101–55; E. Sturm, *Der junge Zacharias Ursin* (Neukirchen, 1972), 109; Visser, *Zacharias Ursinus*.

2

The Background to the First Proposal
of the Prelapsarian Covenant in
Reformed Theology

Also we knowe that all things worke together for the best vnto
them that loue God, euen to them that are called of his
purpose.

Romans 8: 28 (Geneva Bible, 1560)

THE *foedus* made with Adam before the Fall is a covenant which
deals with creation and nature. Through it, man stands before God
on his own merits; coming from sixteenth-century Reformed
theology that sounds heretical, but it must be borne in mind that we
are not speaking here of a doctrine of grace. There is no place here
for justification by grace through faith, because there is no need for
justification. Man is perfect; he stands holy before a holy God. In
fact, a whole array of Christian doctrine is not necessary at this
stage for a 'Church' with two members. There is no sin to call a man
out of, no repentance necessary, no sanctification needed, and no
ecclesiology required. Depending on how you approach the
paradisal state there might be room for 'eschatology', in that the
Edenic state might be a means to an even higher state, but that is
totally within the area of speculation.[1] Man is in perfect covenantal
harmony with God.

Previous Reformed theologians had spoken of the doctrine of the
covenant as one doctrine among many. With the rise of the federal
theology historians have noted how the idea of covenant began to
have a controlling influence in the systematic ordering of doctrine.[2]
This should not be surprising, for once the doctrine of a covenant
before the Fall of creation is postulated, then covenant becomes the
primary way in which God relates to man. After the Fall it is logical
that God should relate to man in terms of covenant; God simply
continues what he had been doing before the Fall. Covenant thus
becomes the primary instrument or means by which God deals with
man, both before and after the Fall. The importance of the Fall is

again emphasized in this schema, for it is the crucial point which separates a world ruled by one covenant (works) from a world ruled by two covenants (works and grace).

It is therefore of particular importance that in this study we should be aware of important questions being discussed by Reformed theologians in the area of the doctrine of creation. The Bible was looked upon mainly as a book of grace, a vast exposition and unfolding of the covenant of grace. The Bible did, however, give information about three worlds: (1) the created world before the Fall; (2) the fallen world of the present; and (3) the perfect world of the future. Its emphasis naturally is on the middle world. The perfect world of the future is most fully delineated in the Book of Revelation. Apart from what the Bible revealed, the Reformed theologian could say very little about the first state. He had only the first three chapters of Genesis.

However, there was one controversy agitating the Reformed world which serves as the backdrop against which the idea of a prelapsarian covenant developed: the problem of reconciling God's providential sovereignty and the Fall of Adam. It is the contention of this book that the doctrine of a *foedus* with Adam developed in response to this problem as a 'milder' orthodox elaboration and explanation of the seemingly harsh decretal doctrines of Theodore Beza. The covenant with Adam comes out of the thought patterns and manner of argumentation of the second half of the sixteenth century. Once the prelapsarian covenant had developed into a theological 'commonplace' (*locus communis*) it was utilized further in the 'scholastic' debates, disputations, and discussions of theology of the period between 1560 and 1600. Once this novel idea entered into the theological systems of the time, it quickly assumed a powerful and prominent place in the structure of Reformed dogmatics, for it was one of the bases of the theology of nature, which in turn was the framework and foundation for the theology of grace. Grace meant nothing unless there was something to be gracious to, in this case fallen nature and fallen man.

The doctrine that the Fall of Adam was somehow ordained by God in his plan and purpose without God being responsible for evil is not a new one in the history of Christian doctrine. It emerges in such areas as the discussion of the idea of the *felix culpa*, or 'happy fall'. Commenting upon the roots of the *felix culpa* idea in relation to Milton's *Paradise Lost*, Arthur O. Lovejoy has pointed out that for centuries the doctrine of the wisdom of God in the permission of sin was recited as part of the *Exultet* in the Easter Eve service of the medieval Roman Catholic Church.[3]

In the second edition of the *Institutes* (1539) John Calvin made it very clear that he held to the position that Adam's Fall fell within God's sovereign plan without God being responsible for evil.[4] Calvin did not believe in a *felix culpa*—for him the Fall was an unmitigated disaster—but he is able to assert that in the sovereignty of God the Fall happened so that God could be enabled to show forth his rich mercy and abounding love by giving his Son for the redemption of his people. While this was a doctrine dealing with creation and the created order, the doctrine of Adam's Fall for Calvin was always soteriologically and Christologically oriented, not theologically oriented. To place this assertion of antinomy or contradictory truths under God and creation rather than under Jesus Christ and redemption would have been to give the doctrine over to speculative, philosophical theology, which is often tempted to see God as a cold, terrifying Lord executing his sovereign terrible decrees by his sheer majestic will. Linking the idea to Christ modified and mollified the formidable problems, pastoral and theological, associated with such an assertion. By 1580, however, many orthodox theologians were placing the doctrine in the former position, under the doctrine of God.

In 1542 Albertus Pighius, a Roman Catholic theologian, wrote a treatise entitled *De libero hominis arbitrio et diuina gratia, libri decem*.[5] In ten books he attacked Calvin's entire corpus of views on (1) the bondage of the will (2) predestination, and (3) providence, found in the editions of the *Institutes* so far printed. Pighius's first six books dealt with the freedom or bondage of the will after the Fall, and therefore with the doctrine of election. The argument went along the same lines as that between Luther and Erasmus.[6] Pighius died soon after, but Calvin replied in 1543 with an answer to the first six books: *Defensio sanae et orthodoxae doctrinae de servitute et liberatione humani arbitrii adversus calumnias Alberti Pighii Campensis*.[7] The work, dedicated to Philip Melanchthon, dissects Pighius's work book by book. Pighius's main concern in the first six books was that the doctrine of the bondage of the will negated human moral responsibility and left in despair those who wanted to forsake sin.

Theodicy questions came up again in 1551, however, and would remain as centres of controversy for the rest of the decade in Geneva and other urban centres of the Reformation.[8] This time the disturbance was caused by Jérome Bolsec, a member of the Geneva community itself. Bolsec's views are contained in the various papers recorded as the 'Procès de Bolsec' in the *Calvini Opera*.[9] Bolsec maintained that God looked upon a person as elect or reprobate by foreseeing his belief or unbelief, and that it was a new and heretical idea that God from all eternity would determine the eternal destiny of a man simply on the basis of his sovereign will. Bolsec further maintained that Calvin's doctrine made God a tyrant, in that his sovereignty over the sin of fallen man made him the author of sin, and also gave no moral inducement to an individual. Man could use predestination as an excuse for sin, which was a form of antinomianism.

Bolsec was also concerned about the idea of a hidden will of God: he maintained that very little of it is mentioned in Scripture and wondered how Calvin knew so much about it.[10] But most importantly Bolsec brought up the problem of the Fall again. He realized rightly that the Fall was a key event:

If there is an explicit text in the aforesaid Holy Scripture which teaches what he has written in his *Institutes*, that is, that God not only foresaw the Fall of Adam and in it the ruin of all his descendants, but also willed it so and had ordained and determined it so in his counsel: let him state the text explicitly and clearly.

What cause was there in Adam why he must not only be abandoned by God but also compelled to sin, considering that in him there was no original sin, which is the cause that God can justly abandon and damn the children of the said Adam?[11]

Calvin responded to this challenge by writing *De aeterna Dei praedestinatione, qua in salutem alios ex hominibus elegit, alios suo exitio reliquit* (1552).[12] This work is actually a reply to the final four books of Pighius's *De libero hominis arbitrio*, which deal with providence, predestination, and foreknowledge. In refuting Pighius, Calvin was also refuting Bolsec. Bolsec seems to have been promoting many of Pighius's ideas in Geneva.

Pighius had maintained that man did have a free will after the Fall, and that the stance of Calvin regarding the sin of man was absurd, in that man was being punished for sins which he could not help and which had been decreed by God before the foundation of the world.[13] Furthermore, Pighius maintained that Calvin misunderstood the true meaning of the term 'predestination'. For Pighius predestination was only single predestination. Furthermore, there was no such thing as particular election, but only 'general election': foreseeing the Fall, God elected the whole human race in Christ so that none would perish unless a man failed to respond in faith. The image of the potter and the vessels in Romans 9 is based on foreknowledge and not on divine sovereignty. Reprobation, for Pighius, is outside of the will of God; he therefore rejects the doctrine that God does not wish all men to be saved.

However, in the section on the Fall, Pighius contended that God did not foreknow the Fall and what man would do with his freedom. He held that God had the power to prevent the Fall, and that if he had foreknown it he would in effect have caused it by allowing it to happen, therefore making himself the author of evil. Thus, there is a conflict in Pighius's treatise over whether or not God foreknew the Fall.

Calvin again argues against Pighius, and indirectly Bolsec, point by point in the *De aeterna praedestinatione*. With respect to the Fall and Adam's responsibility, Calvin reaffirmed God's ordination of the Fall and yet Adam's responsibility by postulating a 'proximate cause' directly in Adam and a 'hidden' or 'remote' cause in God's providence:

I reply that it is no wonder that Pighius should indiscriminately (to use his own word) confuse everything in the judgements of God, when he does not distinguish between causes proximate and remote. By looking round here and there, men do not find how they can transfer the blame for their destruction, because the proximate cause resides in themselves. For if they should complain that the wound is inflicted on them from another quarter, the internal sense of their mind will hold them bound to the conclusion that evil arose from the voluntary defection of the first man. I know the insolence of the carnal mind cannot be prevented from immediately protesting: If God foreknew the Fall of Adam and was willing to apply no remedy, we innocently perish from His eternal decree rather than render the just penalty of sin. And, supposing no such thing to be foreseen by God, none the less the same complaint against original sin remains. For impiety will object to God: Why did not Adam sin in solitude so as alone to bear the penalty? why did he involve us unmerited in participation in the same disaster? indeed by what right does God transfer to us the penalty of another's fault? But when all has been said, the internal feeling of the heart does not cease to urge on everyone the conviction that no one, even being his own judge, may be absolved. Nor truly can anyone contend against this. For as on account of the sin of one man a lethal wound was inflicted on all, so all men acknowledge God's judgement to be just. We cannot avoid concluding that the first origin of ruin is in Adam and that we individually find the proximate cause in ourselves. What can then prevent our faith adoring from afar with due humility the hidden counsel of God by which the Fall of man was foreordained, and yet acknowledging what appears to be our own part, that the whole human race in the person of Adam is bound to the penalty of eternal death and therefore subject to death? Therefore Pighius has not shattered, as he thought, the splendid and fitting symmetry in which the causes proximate and remote agree with one another. . . .

. . . But I affirm both these propositions which Pighius disputes to be the truth. For what he holds out as disagreement between the two propositions is none at all. We say that man was created in such a condition that he is unable to complain to his creator. God foresaw the fall of Adam; He did not suffer him to fall but by His will.[14]

Calvin affirms that God is the cause of all happenings, and yet not the author of evil. It is important to take especial note of his elaboration of 'proximate' and 'remote' causes, for this is something to which we shall want to return:

Further what I said before is to be remembered, that since God manifests His power through means and inferior causes, it is not to be separated from them. It would be foolish to think that, because God has decreed what is future, all care and endeavour on our part is rendered superfluous. If there was anything that we must do, He prescribed it, and willed us to be the instruments of His power; and it is right for us not to separate what He has joined together.[15]

Bolsec was banished from Geneva in 1552, but the controversy was opened again the same year by Jean Trolliet (no dates known). Trolliet focused specifically on the doctrine of the Fall being ordained by God. Like Pighius and Bolsec, he affirmed that such a doctrine would lead men to irresponsible moral behaviour and would make God the author of evil. The substance of the dispute from Trolliet's viewpoint is given in Letter 1658 of the *Calvini Opera*:

This is true to which before my very revered lords and masters I sign the following propositions: speaking of the doctrine of Mr Calvin I maintain that in his *Institutes* he penned the following propositions: that Adam stumbled by will of God. He wrote this in the chapter on predestination, in his *Institutes*, in his own translation from Latin into French found on folio 461, recto, saying: that when the sinful perish in their corruption, this is nothing else but that they bear the calamity in which Adam by the will of God has stumbled and has ruined all of his successors. I confess, he says, that it was by the will of God that all the children of Adam have been included in this misery in which they are maintained continually. . . .

. . . Why, they say, should God impute to men as sin, the things which he has imposed on them by necessity through his predestination? For what could they do? Might they be able to resist his decrees?[16]

Calvin had written to the Senate on 6 October 1552 describing the idea of God being the author of sin as 'un blaspheme par trop execrable'.[17] The challenge by Trolliet led the Genevan authorities to take more definite measures. On 9 November 1552 the Little Council declared that Calvin's *Institutes* taught the truth about predestination and that from now on no one should speak contrary to this truth.

Sebastian Castellio took up the cause of dissent from Calvin's doctrine in 1554, but this time safely from within the walls of Basle.[18] Castellio had departed from Geneva in June 1544 after a series of controversies and confrontations with Calvin and the Genevan authorities over his translation of the New Testament, the rejection of his application to become a hospital chaplain to those stricken with plague, and most importantly, his doctrine of Christ's descent into hell and his interpretation of the Song of Solomon. There was no mutual admiration and respect between Castellio and Geneva.[19] In 1554 Castellio published his Latin edition of the Bible, to which he attached a long note on Romans 9 which dealt mainly with predestination after the Fall.[20] These issues need not detain us here.

Castellio did maintain that God has a permissive will, and that to deny this permissive will in favour of an ordaining will—therefore making the Fall part of the plan of God—was to make God the author of evil. We will return to this discussion of Romans 9 at a later stage, because Martin Borrhaus (1499–1564) attacked this interpretation and Castellio replied to Borrhaus with a letter defending his views, a letter which was not published until 1578, fifteen years after Castellio's death.[21]

The same year two anonymous tracts appeared before the Genevan authorities: it was assumed that both of them were written by Castellio. As far as is known Castellio never denied authorship of these two brief attacks. The first one was written in Latin, and thus far is lost.[22] The second one was written in French and was entitled: *Traité du veil et du nouvel homme. Conseil a la France désolee, requeil latin de certains articles et arguments extraits des livres de M. J. Calvin.*[23] As in the *Annotationes* on Romans 9, both of them fiercely attacked the doctrine of the sovereignty of God as expounded by Calvin.

We can get a sense of how much this question of theodicy was bothering the Reformed Church by seeing other theologians

entering the fray. In his *Loci Communes* of 1555 Philip Melanchthon (1497–1560) included a whole chapter on the subject. He
makes these statements:

> Of the Origin of Sin, that Man was not and Furthermore is not Forced to
> Sin, and of 'Contingentia'. A sixth thing, of which we must also speak, and
> about which great strife has often arisen in the world, is this: Whenever
> someone says that God upholds all created things, someone else immediately
> asks about the origins of sin . . . It is very necessary to recognize that sin is
> not caused by God. God has no pleasure in it, does not will it, and does
> nothing to effect it; he neither compels nor drives anyone to sin. On the
> contrary, he is an earnest enemy and punisher of sin. Man's will and the
> devil's will are the sources of sin! First the devils and then men themselves,
> of their *own free wills, unforced by God*, departed from God and fell into
> sin.[24]

Melanchthon passes over the problem, for the moment, of the 'very
complicated arguments' about '*necessitate et contingentia*', but is
careful to exhort the pious that God hates sin.[25]

That same year, Theodore Beza was writing and outlining a work
which was to have a great effect on the Reformed doctrine of
predestination during the coming years: his *Svmma totius Christianismi*.[26] In this particular case, the sum total of Christianity for
Beza was completely summarized in terms of the doctrine of
predestination. Included in this work was a table outlining in
precise form the eternal decrees of God.[27] At the top was God, and
emanating from him were two streams. On one side was the stream
dealing with the elect: this included such things as 'calling', 'faith',
and so forth—things which lead to eternal life. On the other side
was the stream dealing with the reprobate: it included such things as
induratio—the hardening of the heart, and ultimately eternal death
and destruction in hell. Each item on each side had its logical
counterpart on the other side, and the ultimate goal was the glory of
God and the manifestation of his mercy and justice.[28] (See Fig. 1.)

It is during this time—between 1550 and 1580—that some
scholars maintain that there was a shift in orthodox Reformed and
orthodox Protestant thinking, a shift from 'humanistic' patterns of
thought to 'scholastic' patterns of thought. Brian G. Armstrong,
and John S. Bray after him, have postulated six basic tendencies
which reflect Protestant scholasticism.[29]

(1) The first characteristic is 'an approach to religious truth which
stresses the need to discover basic assumptions or principles on

which one may build a logical system of belief that would be capable of rational defense. This approach usually assumed some form of syllogistic reasoning.'[30]

(2) Secondly, there is strong reliance on the methodology and philosophy of Aristotle. Many feel that the impetus for this Aristotelian revival came through Melanchthon, but recently there has been a challenge to this assumption. The Aristotelianism used was not the Aristotle of the medieval schoolmen but the Aristotle of the Italian Renaissance as presented by such men as Francesco Zabarella (1360–1417) and Pietro Pomponazzi (1464–1525).[31]

(3) A third characteristic is a great stress on the use of reason and logic in religion. This could lead to the elevation of reason to the same status as revelation, and thus result in less of an emphasis upon Scripture as the absolute authority. While orthodox Reformed theologians habitually said that their reason and intellectual abilities were limited, whether they believed it or not is another matter. The works of orthodox Calvinists were marked by an increasing desire for logical consistency, a development which can be traced decade by decade in the sixteenth century.

(4) The fourth characteristic is a concern for speculative metaphysical questions, which often centred upon the will of God. This was not so prevalent in the sixteenth century, but in the seventeenth century every Reformed academy of higher education had a chair of metaphysics.[32] For instance, at the French national Synod of Alès (1620) the synod decreed 'that every Reformed academy would have a professor of theology whose task it would be to expound the "commonplaces" as succinctly as possible, in a scholastic manner, in order that the students may be profited as much as possible and that they may be enabled to apply themselves most forcefully to disputes and metaphysical distinctions'.[33]

(5) We can quote Bray for the fifth characteristic: 'an interpretation of Scripture which tended to define Scripture in an unhistorical fashion as a body of propositions once and for all delivered by God, the purpose of which was to provide an inerrant, infallible base upon which a solid philosophy could be constructed'.[34]

(6) Finally, scholasticism tended to be drawn toward a new doctrine of faith, a doctrine in which faith was one doctrine amongst many and not a primary, cardinal doctrine, as was the case for Calvin and Luther.[35]

Bray has explored the writings of Beza carefully and concluded that Beza embraced Protestant scholasticism to a qualified extent.[36]

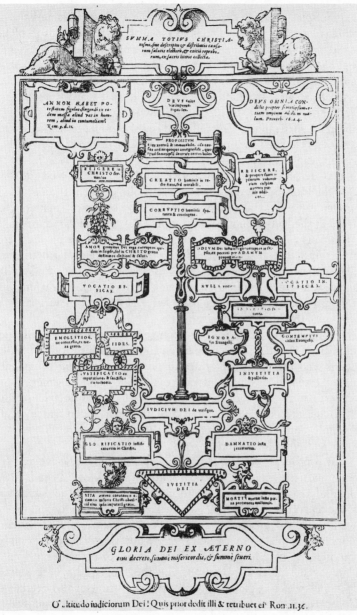

Fig. 1. The chart from Theodore Beza, *Svmma totius Christianismi* (1555) as reproduced by Beza in his *Volumen ... tractationum theologicarum* (Geneva, 1582), Vol. i, Page 170. (Speer Library, Princeton Theological Seminary, Princeton, New Jersey).

The *Svmma* of 1555 certainly has some of the characteristics of scholasticism: precise organization, the rational exploration of the mysteries of God, the articulation of basic presuppositions and their logical conclusions, and so forth. Beza felt that he was perpetuating and defending the system put forth by Calvin, and indeed in many respects he was. Beza affirmed everything that Calvin taught. For Beza, however, the *methodology* of defending Calvin's doctrine was different. First, in the *Tabula* found in the *Summa totius Christianismi* of 1555, Beza organized his material in a different manner than Calvin did in his *Institutes*. Calvin organized his *Institutes* essentially on the lines of the creed: God the Father, God the Son, God the Holy Spirit, and the Holy Catholic Church. Beza's table is a much more rational and logical exposition of subject-matter. One looks at the layout and connecting lines of the *Tabula* and thinks: '*If* there is a God, and that God is sovereign, *then* he must control everything that happens in the world. The central doctrine of Christianity is salvation, and then reprobation. *Therefore*, God has decreed to save some and to damn others.' This yearning for organization and consistency is evidence of the first characteristic of scholastic thinking outlined above.

Second, Beza was forced to rearrange his placement of predestination from that of Calvin's arrangement. Up to this point (1555–6) Calvin had placed his doctrines of predestination *and* providence under the rubric of the doctrine of God as Redeemer. Both predestination and providence were soteriological doctrines, with Christ at the centre. Sin came into the world that grace might abound, and grace was manifest through the Crucifixion and Resurrection of Jesus Christ.

But for Beza both predestination and providence have as their object not the glory of God through the work of Christ but the glory of God through the salvation of the elect and the damnation of the reprobate. One focuses on the Cross, the other focuses on the destiny of two groups of people. Predestination and providence must now be placed by Beza under the doctrine of God, not under the doctrine of Christ. Predestination and providence no longer serve as the chief explanations for the Cross; they are simply doctrines which explain rationally the execution of the decrees of God made before the foundations of the world in the counsels of eternity.

Finally, Beza made a distinction between the divine decrees and the *execution* of the divine decrees, and it is on this distinction that he then elaborated his table in 1555.[37] The decree to elect some to salvation and some to damnation is a decision, according to Johannes Dantine, which is 'précédant toutes les autres causes'.[38] Thus Beza was the first Reformed theologian to espouse supralapsarianism. All events stem and flow from this decision. However, set between the decrees and the execution of the decrees are 'secondary causes'. The terms used by Beza are various: *causae mediae*; *causae intermediae*; *causae secundae*; *instrumenta*; *instrumenta media*. Never, interestingly enough, does he use the term which Calvin used: *causae inferiores*.[39] By using this distinction Beza could affirm that evil fitted into God's plan through secondary causes which were free and contingent, but at the same time God was not responsible for evil. Dantine has stated: 'Thus God is able to act through the means of evil without being the author of evil. God disposes, therefore, absolutely all things without removing their responsibility and their contingence.'[40] For Beza, therefore, the Fall had to happen, but the reason it had to happen was so that God's glory might be manifest in the salvation of the elect through Christ's work and in the just reprobation of the damned. The Fall happened through secondary means: the means of Adam's free will.

Bray has maintained that various commentators have given us a distorted picture of Beza's doctrine of predestination.[41] In his exploration of all of Beza's writings he found that as a pastor Beza rarely preached about reprobation, predestination, and similar matters. The same was true for his commentaries. Furthermore, there is little evidence of scholastic thinking in these works. Scholasticism does, however, come out in his systematic works and polemical works, including the *Summa* of 1555. Bray admits that Beza believed Aristotelianism to be true. Beza insisted that Aristotle's works should be the basis for the logic and moral philosophy taught at Geneva.[42] Bray also admits that Aristotle had a tremendous influence on Beza.[43] While it may be true that modern commentators have had a distorted picture of Beza's doctrine of predestination, it could also be true that Beza's contemporaries themselves had this distorted perception of Beza's position. It was a lot easier to digest his brief table outlining predestination than it was to read his biblical commentaries.[44] It must be remembered, however, that Beza was careful not to apply Aristotelian reasoning to God and his decrees; Aristotelian reasoning was only applied to the *execution* of the decrees. The task of the theologian was to study, using Aristotelian logic, the secondary means by which God executed his decrees.[45]

Otto Grundler has shown that this was one of the basic differences between Girolamo Zanchius (1516–90) and Beza. Zanchius applied Aristotelian logic to God himself; he maintained that man could know God in his essence, and not just in his appearance—i.e. the way he revealed himself to man.[46] Consequently there was not much room for a hidden decree, and the doctrines of predestination, providence, and Adam's Fall are given another subtle addition. With Zanchius there is no opportunity to let God work out the problem of evil and of Adam's Fall in God's hidden and secret will. Consequently, if God is not to be in any way responsible for evil and for Adam's Fall the need for a doctrine of secondary causes becomes more urgent.

The controversy did not end with Beza's *Tabula*. It was continued in 1557 when Calvin wrote his *Response a certaines calomnies et blasphemes, dont quelques malins s'efforcent de rendre la doctrine de la predestination de Dieu odieuse*.[47] This particular treatise does not deal with the problem of the Fall, but only with three points which are specifically attributed to Castellio: (1) God has created all the world for salvation; (2) man does not totally lose the image of God after the Fall (and therefore does not lose the power of his will); and (3) 'un horrible blaspheme' of Castellio: that if God has created men for damnation, God's will and Satan's will are the same.

That same year Calvin wrote another reply to Castellio, this time in Latin, entitled *Brevis responsio ad diluendas nebulonis cuiusdam calumnias quibus doctrinam de aeterna Dei praedestinatione foedare conatus est*.[48] Calvin's main line of defence is that Castellio has misread him, and in misreading him he is misreading the fathers of the Church, the Bible, and God himself. Calvin maintains that Castellio is accusing him of making God the author of sin. Calvin says that he is doing no such thing; God is omnipotent over sin, but

Calvin everywhere sharply repudiates and affirms to be detestable the idea of the absolute power of God which is propounded in sophistic schools, because the power of God cannot be rightly separated from his wisdom and justice . . . For righteousness pleases God, just as iniquity is an abomination to him. But how by his secret judgement he overrules all the things that men do wrongly is not for us to define, except that we must affirm that, whatever he does, he never deviates from his own justice.[49]

If God had only absolute power and sovereignty and not perfect justice and wisdom,˙ then Castellio would have a solid case, according to Calvin. But neither Calvin nor the Church has ever separated God's power from his mercy and justice.

The treatise goes on to deal with the Fall of Adam:

> After he has babbled out his calumnies for long enough, he draws nearer, and affirms that some men in these perilous times, though they do not dare to teach openly that God is the cause of evil, suggest the same thing by other forms of speech. They say that Adam sinned by the will of God, and that the impious not merely by God's permission but by his impulse perpetrate all their wickedness. Here this fine rhetorician exclaims with dismay: O wretched man! how can it be that God willed this, when he had created Adam in his own image. As if it were for me to render a precise reason for the hidden judgements of God, so that mortal men might understand to a nicety that heavenly wisdom, whose height they are commanded to adore. No: let Moses rather intervene upon this foolish garrulity, with an exact reply, when he says: 'The secret things belong unto the Lord our God: but those things which are revealed belong unto us' (Deut. 29: 29).[50]

For Calvin, the reason for Adam's Fall remains hidden in the secret will of God; he does not propose any 'secondary causes' as Beza did two years earlier.

The question of Adam's sin being perpetrated not only by the will of God, but by his impulse, appears in the same paragraph. That brings God even closer to being the author of sin.[51] But Calvin still maintains that man should not explore such a great mystery. He even argues against the distinction Castellio made between God's permissive will and his effectual will.[52] Calvin finally tries to settle the question of Adam's Fall with this authoritative paragraph:

> Nor will Calvin concede that God wills what is evil in itself, that is in so far as it is evil; but the judgements of God shine forth in the crimes of men, as when he punished David's adultery by the incestuous licentiousness of Absalom. God therefore, commanding Adam not to eat of the tree of good and evil, exacts and tests obedience. Meanwhile he not only knew what was about to happen, but decreed it. If this seem harsh to our fastidious censor, let him attribute it to his own peevishness and distaste, rather than to the savour of the doctrine. For when he wants to bludgeon the hearts of all with the weighty iron hammer of his words, declaring that the will of God is one only, and this he will make plain by the prophets and Christ himself, Augustine bravely repels the attack with his authority. These, he says, are the mighty works of the Lord, perfected of his desires, and so wisely perfected that, when the angelic and human creation had sinned, that is had done not what God willed but what it itself willed, even through the same creaturely will by which was done what the Creator did not wish, he

fulfilled what he willed, as the supreme good using even evil deeds well, for the damnation of those whom he justly predestined to punishment, and for the salvation of those whom he graciously predestined to grace. As regards themselves, they did what God did not will; as regards God's omnipotence, they were by no means able to prevail against it. In this itself they did what was against the will of God; yet through them God's will was done. Therefore the mighty works of the Lord are carried out according to all his desires, so that in a marvellous and ineffable way even what is done against his will is not done beyond his will; because it would not be done did he not allow it. Nor does he allow it unwillingly but willingly. Nor as good would he allow evil to be done, unless as omnipotent he were able to make good out of the evil.[53]

In the year 1558 four more treatises appeared, in an intense exchange of cross-fire over the general question of predestination. First of all, in January, Calvin came out with a work entitled *Calumniae nebulonis cuiusdam adversus doctrinam Iohannis Calvini de occulta Dei providentia*.[54] This is a much more extensive treatise than the earlier ones and shows that Calvin is taking his opposition much more seriously. The tract is directed against Castellio, but Calvin continually speaks in the plural of 'others' who maintain the same teaching as Castellio. The work opens up with a list of the major points of contention: 'Articles Extracted from the Latin, as well as the French, Books of John Calvin on Predestination'.[55] Note the verb *decerpti*, which means 'plucked out of'. The implication is that the arguments are taken out of their context, and that if they are left in their context they would make sense and be true. In this work we can see how much the question of the Fall of Adam has risen to the fore by 1558.

These are the first two propositions attacked by Calvin's accusers:

I. God of his pure and mere will created the greatest part of the world to perdition.
II. God not only predestinated even Adam to damnation, but to the causes of that damnation also, whose fall he not only foresaw, but he also willed by his secret and eternal decree and ordained that he should fall, which fall, that it might, in its time, take place, God placed before him the apple, which should cause that fall.[56]

The two propositions are related, of course, for in order to uphold the first proposition you must have Adam's Fall ordained for reprobation to be accomplished. One wonders whether the accusers have Theodore Beza in mind, with the emphasis on the purposes of

God being the salvation of a few and the reprobation of most of the world. Calvin also lists individually the objections to each article, and the 'generally accepted' alternatives put forward by his opponents:

I. Against the First. Your opponents maintain that this article is contrary to nature, and contrary to the Scripture.
II. Against the Second. Your opponents say that this second article is the doctrine of the devil, and they demand of me, Calvin, that I would tell them where, in the divine Scriptures, the substance contained in this article is written?[57]

Calvin then gives an extensive rebuttal of each point, with reasons. In reference to the second article, Calvin does not add much more to what he has said before. He reiterates the total sovereignty of God: 'Whereas, God himself, ever vindicating to himself the right and the act of holding the helm of all things which are done in the whole world, never permits a separation of his prescience from his power!'[58] At the same time he reminds his adversaries of Proverbs 16: 4: 'The Lord has made everything for his own purpose, even the wicked for the day of evil.' He refers to the judgements of God as a 'profound abyss', and reminds them that while he is not able to cite a passage in Scripture which shows that God, although he does not wish the Fall, yet did not stand in its way, nevertheless God 'will have mercy on those whom he will have mercy':

You demand of me to cite the place in the Holy Scriptures by which I prove that God did not prevent the fall of Adam, because His will was not to prevent it. Just as if that memorable reply of God to all such inquiries and inquirers did not contain in itself an all-sufficient proof: 'I will have mercy on whom I will have mercy.' From which the apostle Paul at once concludes, and justly so, that God hath not mercy upon all, because He wills not to have mercy upon all.[59]

Finally Calvin concludes that God alone is a law to himself.

The importance of this work is not so much what Calvin says, but the manner in which he says it. The objections of the last seven years are taken one by one and countered by Calvin in a systematic, substantial fashion. There is much less invective and name-calling in this treatise than there is in Calvin's earlier treatises. Evidently the opposition was getting serious. Honest answers were required for honest questions.

Castellio replied to this defence of orthodoxy by writing another treatise: *Harpago, sive defensio ad autorem libri cui titulus est*

'*Calumniae nebulonis*'.[60] According to Buisson, this treatise was never published, but was passed around among Castellio's friends and opponents.[61] Again, Castellio takes Calvin's points one by one and rejects them. At this point Beza entered the fray again, with his *Ad sycophantarum quorundam calumnias, quibus unicum salutis nostrae fundamentum, id est aeternam Dei praedestinationem euertere nituntur, responsio Theodori Beze Vezelii*.[62] While Castellio's name was not mentioned in the 1558 edition, it was obvious that he was Beza's target. Later, his name was replaced for 'sycophantarum' in the collected works of Beza.[63] That same year, 1558, Castellio rewrote his *Harpago* and this time attached to it an appendix which is his reply to Beza.[64] The arguments were simply repetitions of previous ones, but more refined and sophisticated.

The final edition of Calvin's *Institutes* was published in 1559, and in that edition Calvin makes a radical change that stems directly from this whole controversy. In the earlier editions of the *Institutes* Calvin had placed his discussions of the doctrines of providence and predestination together, under soteriology. This served to place the focus on Christ: providence, and predestination as its direct manifestation, made all things which happen in the world, including the Fall, lead to the Crucifixion and Resurrection of Christ.[65] In the 1559 edition of the *Institutes* this order is changed. The doctrine of providence is placed under the doctrine of God the Creator, while the doctrine of predestination remained under the doctrine of God the Redeemer. The result was to move in the direction that Beza was moving several years earlier in his *Tabula*: the decrees of God are seen not so much as being connected with the Crucifixion and the Resurrection of Christ but as being part of the mysterious *primum mobile*.[66]

Interestingly enough, the doctrine of the Fall of Adam is still kept with the doctrine of predestination under the doctrine of Christ, and it is not put forward as a cardinal point. Rather, it is dealt with under 'objections':

They say it is not stated in so many words that God decreed that Adam should perish for his rebellion. As if, indeed, that very God, who, Scripture proclaims, 'does whatever he pleases' [Ps. 115: 3], would have created the noblest of his creatures to an uncertain end. They say that he had free choice that he might shape his own fortune, and that God ordained nothing except to treat man according to his own deserts. If such a barren invention is accepted, where will that omnipotence of God be whereby he regulates all things according to his secret plan, which depends solely upon itself? Yet predestination, whether they will or not, manifests itself in Adam's posterity. For it did not take place by reason of nature that, by the guilt of one parent, all were cut off from salvation. What prevents them from admitting the whole human race? For why should they fritter away their effort in such evasions? Scripture proclaims that all mortals were bound over to eternal death in the person of one man [cf. Rom. 5: 12 ff.]. Since this cannot be ascribed to nature, it is perfectly clear that it has come forth from the wonderful plan of God. It is utterly absurd that these good defenders of God's righteousness hang perplexed upon a straw yet leap over high roofs! Again I ask: whence does it happen that Adam's fall irremediably involved so many peoples, together with their infant offspring, in eternal death because it so pleased God? Here their tongues, otherwise so loquacious, must become mute. The decree is dreadful indeed, I confess. Yet no one can deny that God foreknew what end man was to have before he created him, and consequently foreknew because he so ordained by his decree. If anyone inveighs against God's foreknowledge at this point, he stumbles rashly and heedlessly. What reason is there to accuse the Heavenly Judge because he was not ignorant of what was to happen? If there is any just or manifest complaint, it applies to predestination. And it ought not to seem absurd for me to say that God not only foresaw the fall of the first man, and in him the ruin of his descendants, but also meted it out in accordance with his own decision. For as it pertains to his wisdom to foreknow everything that is to happen, so it pertains to his might to rule and control everything by his hand. And Augustine also skillfully disposes of this question, as of others: 'We most wholesomely confess what we most correctly believe, that the God and Lord of all things, who created all things exceedingly good [cf. Gen. 1: 31], and foreknew that evil things would rise out of good, and also knew that it pertained to his most omnipotent goodness to bring good out of evil things rather than not to permit evil things to be . . ., so ordained the life of angels and men that in it he might first of all show what free will could do, and then what the blessing of his grace and the verdict of his justice could do.'[67]

1559 was also the year that the first of a series of confessions appeared from the Continental Reformed churches. The French Confession of Faith was adopted in the spring of 1559. There are two elements which make it different from previous Reformed confessions. First, it adds natural revelation as a valid means of God's communication to man:

As such this God reveals himself to men; firstly, in his works, in their creation, as well as in their preservation and control. Secondly, and more clearly, in his Word, which was in the beginning revealed through oracles, and which was afterward committed to writing in the books which we call the Holy Scriptures.[68]

It is significant that Calvin apparently drafted a version of this Confession, and that the synod expanded the first two chapters into six chapters.[69] The original draft did not have any reference to natural revelation. Why did the synod feel that it had to add this feature, something that no other Reformed confession had done? Certainly one of the contributing factors must have been the persistent problem of predestination. Adding natural revelation would give man, both before and after the Fall, less excuse for his rebellion against God (cf. Romans 1). Indeed, it would make Adam doubly responsible: he had perfect communion with God, and he also could see God's revelation through the creation. Reformed theologians seemed to be looking for some way to explain the decrees of God.

The second element in this confession was a much larger and fuller chapter on the doctrine of providence. At the same time that the Synod was affirming the doctrine of natural revelation, it still wanted to remain totally orthodox in its perception of God's sovereignty:

We believe that he not only created all things, but that he governs and directs them, disposing and ordaining by his sovereign will all that happens in the world; not that he is the author of evil, or that the guilt of it can be imputed to him, as his will is the sovereign and infallible rule of all right and justice; but he hath wonderful means of so making use of devils and sinners that he can turn to good the evil which they do, and of which they are guilty. And thus, confessing that the providence of God orders all things, we humbly bow before the secrets which are hidden to us, without questioning what is above our understanding; but rather making use of what is revealed to us in Holy Scripture for our peace and safety, inasmuch as God, who has all things in subjection to him, watches over us with a Father's care, so that not a hair of our head shall fall without his will. And yet he restrains the devils and all our enemies, so that they can not harm us without his leave.[70]

Such an article had never before appeared in a Reformed confession.[71]

Joachim Staedtke and others have shown that Geneva and Basle were not the only places where this problem of predestination and providence was being discussed. During the period 1550–60 these matters were also causing problems in Zurich, England, and Scotland. The Zurich controversy culminated in 1560 with Heinrich Bullinger's rejection of the double decree of predestination (i.e. double predestination).[72] This decision had apparently come out of the influence of Theodor Bibliander (1504 [1509?]–1564), who had a conflict with Peter Martyr Vermigli over the subject. Vermigli maintained the strict orthodox teaching. It is therefore interesting to look at the Second Helvetic Confession of 1566, one of the last documents which Bullinger wrote, to see what Bullinger says about this matter.

Bullinger affirms that all things are governed by the providence of God, but he purposely leaves out any discussion of the problem of evil in relation to the doctrine of providence. He is very careful, however, to emphasize the 'means' by which God works:

Nevertheless, we do not spurn as useless the means by which divine providence works, but we teach that we are to adapt ourselves to them in so far as they are recommended to us in the Word of God. Wherefore we disapprove of the rash statements of those who say that if all things are managed by the providence of God, then our efforts and endeavors are in vain. It will be sufficient if we leave everything to the governance of divine providence, and we will not have to worry about anything or do anything.[73]

'Leaving everything to the governance of divine providence' was not good enough for the new, rising generation of Calvinist theologians. They desired much more precision.

Two chapters later Bullinger states that God is not the author of sin, and discusses the problem of the hardening of the heart, a question which is important only after the Fall. He considers the problem of the foreordination of the Fall as a 'curious question':

Other questions, such as whether God willed Adam to fall, or incited him to fall, or why he did not prevent the fall, and similar questions, we reckon among curious questions (unless perchance the wickedness of heretics or of other churlish men compels us also to explain them out of the Word of God, as the godly teachers of the Church have frequently done), knowing that the Lord forbade man to eat of the forbidden fruit and punished his transgression. We also know that what things are done are not evil with respect to the providence, will, and power of God, but in respect of Satan and our will opposing the will of God.[74]

For such an influential and important man as Bullinger to be 'weak' in this area of doctrine was a serious matter. The younger generation felt that it had a duty to uphold the teaching of Calvin in the face of attacks from heretics and 'softness' on the part of certain key leaders.

The next year, 1561, another important confession was adopted: the Belgic Confession of Faith. In many ways this document was patterned after the French Confession. Its chapter on revelation places an even greater emphasis on natural revelation:

We know him by two means: First, by the creation, preservation, and government of the universe; which is before our eyes as a most elegant book, wherein all creatures, great and small, are as so many characters leading us to contemplate the invisible things of God, namely, his eternal power and Godhead, as the Apostle Paul saith (Rom. 1. 20). All which things are sufficient to convince men, and leave them without excuse.[75]

The chapter on divine providence contains many of the same elements as does the French Confession's chapter, but this time in more detailed form. The chapter on man and his creation and Fall is also more extensive, and has certain interesting phrases which will be of interest to us further on in our study:

Article XIV.

We believe that God created man out of the dust of the earth, and made and formed him after his own image and likeness, good, righteous, and holy, capable in all things to will agreeably to the will of God. But being in honor, he understood it not, neither knew his excellency, but willfully subjected himself to sin, and consequently to death and the curse, giving ear to the words of the devil. For the commandment of life, which he had received, he transgressed; and by sin separated himself from God, who was his true life, having corrupted his whole nature, whereby he made himself liable to corporal and spiritual death. And being thus become wicked, perverse, and corrupt in all his ways, he hath lost all his excellent gifts which he had received from God, and only retained a few remains thereof, which, however, are sufficient to leave man without excuse; for all the light which is in us is changed into darkness, as the Scriptures teach us, saying: The light shineth in darkness, and the darkness comprehendeth it not: where St. John calleth men darkness.[76]

In future years theologians would be considering what this 'commandment of life' was, and what it meant to be created after 'God's own image and likeness, good, righteous, and holy'. The doctrine of man and how God relates to him is of prime importance, for it is this thinking which will lead to the idea of a 'covenant of works' or 'covenant of nature' made with man before the Fall.

The Heidelberg Catechism, written in part by the man who first proposed a prelapsarian covenant with Adam in Reformed theology, was published in 1563, two years after the Belgic Confession. Its doctrine of creation is brief and sparse, but revealing:

Question Six. Did God create man thus wicked and perverse? Answer. No; but God created man good, and after his own image—that is, in righteousness and true holiness; that he might rightly know God his Creator, heartily love him, and live with him in eternal blessedness, to praise and glorify him.[77]

That same year Sebastian Castellio died and the next year, 1564, Calvin himself died. But Reformed orthodoxy had decided what it believed about the Fall of Adam. It can be summarized in the following undated statements of Calvin, written some time during the ten-year controversy, but probably toward its end:

Before the creation of the first man God determined in the eternal counsel what he wished to be done to the entire human race.

This hidden plan of God was made so that Adam would defect from the original state of his nature and that by his defection he might drag all of his posterity into the state of eternal death.[78]

The next generation would elaborate on this teaching.

After the deaths of Castellio and Calvin the disagreements over predestination and the problem of Adam's Fall became less a focus of controversy. However, there is one further piece of evidence which we must consider. In 1578 the following work by Castellio was published posthumously: *Sebastiani Castellionis Dialogi IIII. De praedestinatione. De electione. De libero arbitrio. De fide. Eiusdem opuscula quaedam lectu dignissima.* The title-page contained a condensed form of the verse 2 Peter 3: 9: 'Dominus non vult ut quisquam pereat, sed ut omnes corrigantur'.[79] Several smaller works were added to this book. The one which will concern us will be the letter which Castellio wrote to Martin Borrhaus: *De paedestinatione scriptum. Sebastiani Castellionis ad D. Mart. Borrhavm.*[80] Later, in 1613, the *Dialogi IIII* were published again, and, in addition to the smaller works published in 1578, Castellio's 1554 comments on Romans 9 were also printed, but with separate pagination: *Annotationes Sebastiani Castellionis, in caput nonum ad Rom. quibus materia electionis et praedestinationis amplius illustratur.*[81]

Before we turn to these two works, let us give some attention to one of the four dialogues: *De praedestinatione.*[82] The dialogues are between two men, Federicus, who is actually Castellio, and Ludovicus, a Calvinist catechumen. For Castellio, the common sense of the common man is a far better guide to truth than the sophistries and subtleties of those who are educated in a formal way, and he states this at the beginning of the four dialogues.[83] The basic axiom by which Federicus makes Ludovicus look foolish is the law of non-contradiction. It is absolutely impossible for God to contradict himself, according to Castellio. This is what makes God the fair and just God that he is. Castellio takes aim at the seeming 'supralapsarianism' that Calvin is espousing. The basic issue keeps recurring: is man created for perfection or is he created for sin? An example can be cited here:

What if God were to say to Adam: 'I created you for sinning, and you can no more abstain from it than you can abstain from getting hungry. But take care that you do not sin. For if you sin, you will die'. Could a more absurd thing be thought?

  If man has been created in the image of God, then he has certainly been created for righteousness and not for sin. Is it [a sign that he was created for sin] when God gives him dominion over the earth and [other] creatures?[84]

The theme of absurdity is repeated in the *Annotationes* on Romans 9. This tract is about thirty pages long and deals with many other problems besides the Fall of Adam. But at the beginning of the work Castellio lays out the problem: that of the destiny of man. He is quick to point out that no matter what happens to other creatures of God who were created without conditions, man, the unique being made in God's image, was created with conditions: 'Those ones are predestined conditionally, the others infallibly and unconditionally; each of these kinds of predestination is distinguished in God.'[85] For man to be given conditions of obedience and then to have God working against man by predestinating man to break those conditions is logically contradictory and absurd. Adam had conditions in the garden and therefore it is logical to conclude that Adam sinned voluntarily:

Adam sinned voluntarily.

  However to have sinned voluntarily, God argues, God says that he had been more obedient to his wife, than to God himself. For indeed, obedience is voluntary. That it was against God's will that he sinned, is made known through the precept by which God had prohibited him to have eaten that fruit, so that indeed the will of God, as that of man, might be known from the precept. In the same way a rebuke appears, when God says that he had been disobedient to him: since he understands the will of God to have been, that he should not eat of that fruit. From these it appears that Adam had sinned, not by the predestination of God (who does not will sin) but by his own sin and will, and by no necessary compulsion. Someone will say: but if God had not wished it, he [God] would have been enabled to prevent it, that he [Adam] might not sin; I admit, if he had created him as a log, not as a man: or if he had killed him at once. But to create man, and to compel the same either towards sin or towards the doing of right, would be like creating a bird, and taking away from it free flight; this in truth is not to create a bird, but to create something else. But indeed God is able to do whatever he wills; this I acknowledge, but he wills nothing absurdly (even if men judge many of his works to be absurd) such as a thing not able to be done. Therefore that Adam should have had the power of sinning, or not sinning, was the will of God: but that he should not be capable of doing either, and nevertheless might have free will, this would be absurd, and just as if you would say 'He is able and not able'. Therefore that he was able to sin, he has this from God; but that he wished to sin, he had this from himself.[86]

Castellio maintains that God shows forth his precepts and his law—not to eat of the fruit—but in so doing he gives man *permission* to sin; however, man does not sin by the will of God. Man alone is responsible for his sin.

Martin Borrhaus (known also as Martin Cellarius) wrote a letter to Castellio, the date of which cannot be ascertained, and Castellio wrote a letter back to Borrhaus, which is one of the other items published in 1578. Borrhaus had criticized Castellio's interpretation of Romans 9, and affirmed the orthodox stance according to Calvin and Beza. Castellio replied not by answering Borrhaus point by point, but by asking Borrhaus two questions: (1) whether Borrhaus sees God to be the author of sin; and (2) whether God's commands contradict God's decrees.[87]

Castellio summarizes the first argument of Borrhaus in the following manner:

From this very position follows this argument: whatever happens by the counsel of God, the same is by God the author; nevertheless, Adam by the plan of God contracted a stain, that is, he sinned; therefore Adam sinned with God as the author.[88]

Although this letter cannot be dated with precision, one can note the syllogistic reasoning which Castellio extracts from Borrhaus. There is a great emphasis on the *consilio Dei* and the *decretum Dei*; this evidence seems to place it toward the end of Castellio's career, when questions were again beginning to be discussed in scholastic categories and with the use of scholastic methods. The second challenge is more serious: if God's commands and his decrees contradict each other, then God is a hypocrite, a *simulator*. Castellio puts it this way:

Whether God is a hypocrite is the second question.

Now we come to the other matter, which is a consequence of the prior, namely, that you make God a hypocrite: what indeed is deduced in this way: If God created some men for destruction, and he does not wish to save them, and yet he invites all without discrimination to justness, and further invites them to salvation, it follows, that he is a hypocrite: certainly he behaves, as if he wished all to be saved; when in fact he wishes only some.[89]

It is a general problem both before and after the Fall, and Castellio narrows down to the prelapsarian side of the problem very quickly:

God says: I do not wish the death of the wicked, but that he might live: but, lest by this condition you should escape he adds, that he should repent, and yet those wicked men of whom he speaks did not repent; from which you according to your doctrine state that God decreed it so that the wicked should continue in their way. Therefore he wills against his own statutes. He says to Adam: Do not eat of the tree of knowledge, and you say that he has decreed it so that Adam would eat of the tree of knowledge. Therefore, his precept is contrary to the decree. Which of them do you wish me to believe?[90]

Whom to believe, or which words of God to believe, was indeed a serious question.

Castellio keeps reiterating the fact that Adam lived in paradise on the basis of *conditionality*, and this assumes a central place in his treatise. To give man conditions gives him meaningful choice before God. Castellio challenged Borrhaus to show how God could give unchanging conditions to show his unchanging nature and yet at the same time have decreed the Fall of Adam from all eternity by his irrevocable decrees:

Moreover, you have taught that Adam sinned by the counsel of God and by his decree, just as we have shown above. But indeed in this very place itself, where you deal with conditionality, you say that God decreed what Paul refers to as being done. 'He includes all under unbelief, that he might have mercy on all.' In which, and in other similar places (for often you write the same thing), you pronounce that everything happens by the unchangeable and irrevocable decree of God; and indeed it thus happens so that nothing else can happen, than may happen, because by one word it is allowed to be said, that everything is done by necessity. But if everything happens by necessity nothing happens with a condition, and in fact not even God is able to do anything with a condition, or to do anything else, than as he does. For they are as much opposed as fire and water, to happen by necessity, and to happen by conditionality. For what is a condition? Define it for me, or hear me define it. A condition is an offering of the power of choosing to someone. But there is no place of choice where something happens by necessity; or perhaps you know that because, for example, of that small saying: 'Necessity does not have a law.' Because if by necessity, and by the ineluctable decree of God, Adam had sinned, and was ejected out of paradise because of that sin: he was not conditionally predestined to life, but was without any condition and by God's inescapable decree predestined to death. Otherwise, what sort of condition will it be, if God had addressed to Adam your doctrine: 'I place you, Adam, in paradise, so that you may live there, but on this condition, if you will obey my command. However, you will no more be able to obey me, than to conquer me. For you will sin by my immutable and unconquerable decree.' I beseech you, who would not deride this condition?[91]

Instead of God being forced to change his plans because of Adam's sin, as the Calvinists accused their opponents of asserting, Castellio was trying to show that really the Calvinists were saying that God himself changes, and indeed in an unfair way. Castellio was trying to force the Calvinists into asserting that God was a hypocrite, in that he decreed one way and yet unfairly gave Adam conditions by which to live. Therefore, Adam's Fall, and that of all men who fall with him, was a hypocritical act on the part of God; indeed, it was a cruel joke.

While this work was not published until 1578, it was written before Castellio's death in 1563, and we can be sure that even before these ideas were in print, they were circulating by means of his own lectures and public appearances and also through a network of like-minded friends. The orthodox Calvinist could not but be aware of Castellio's arguments and the threat they posed to orthodoxy. Some alternative theory, especially in the matter of Adam's Fall, had to be proposed to answer these questions and give orthodoxy a firmer footing.

It was against this background and scenario that Zacharias Ursinus, a new convert from Lutheranism to the Reformed faith, first proposed, in 1561 and 1562, the idea of a prelapsarian *foedus naturale* with Adam.

Notes

1. Diemer, *Het scheppingsverbond*; Karlberg, 'The Mosaic Covenant'; R. W. A. Letham, 'The *Foedus Operum*', cf. esp. 457.
2. Brown, 'Covenant Theology'.
3. A. O. Lovejoy, 'Milton and the Paradox of the Fortunate Fall', *ELH* 4 (1937), 161–79. The idea of *felix culpa* ('happy fall') is to be distinguished from the doctrine of God's sovereignty over the Fall. For Calvin, the Fall was not

'happy' in the later Miltonic sense, but God was still sovereign over it. For a discussion of the history of the predestination controversy throughout the centuries of Christian doctrine, see W. A. Copinger, *A Treatise on Predestination, Election and Grace* (London, 1889). While Copinger has several organizational peculiarities in his discussion, his chronological bibliography is especially helpful.

4. Calvin, *CO* i. 874. Discussions of Calvin's doctrine of predestination are legion. The most complete modern discussion in English is that by D. N. Wiley, 'Calvin's Doctrine of Predestination' (Diss. Duke, 1971), to which I am indebted. While his dissertation deals with many other matters, I have followed his meticulous historical outline of the sources on predestination throughout this chapter. See ibid, 136–7 for his brief discussion of predestination and the Fall in the 1539 *Institutes*. Another helpful work is R. Stauffer, *Dieu, la création, et la Providence dans la prédication de Calvin* (Berne, 1978). Stauffer has an excellent bibliography at the end. Cf. also Baker, *Heinrich Bullinger and the Covenant Idea*; J. Bohatec, 'Calvin's Vorsehungslehre', in *Calvinstudien*, ed. J. Bohatec (Leipzig, 1909), 339–441; J. Dantine, 'Die Prädestinationslehre bei Calvin und Beza' (Diss. Göttingen, 1965).

5. A. Pighius, *De libero hominis arbitrio et diuina gratia* (Cologne, 1542), fos. 138–9. See also G. Melles, *Albertus Pighius en zijn strijd met Calvijn over het liberum arbitrium* (Kampen, 1973); H. Jedin, *Studien über die Schriftsteller-tätigkeit Albert Pigges*, RGST 55 (1931); A. P. Linsenmann, 'Albertus Pighius und sein theologischer Standpunkt', *ThQ* 48 (1866), 571–644; P. A. Pidoux de Maduère, *Albertus Pighius, adversaire de Calvin* (Lausanne, 1932).

6. D. Erasmus, *De libero arbitrio* (Basle, Antwerp, and Cologne, 1524; Leipzig, 1910); M. Luther, *De servo arbitrio*, in *Werke*, xviii. 551–787. English translation of both: *Luther and Erasmus: Free Will and Salvation*, trans. and ed. E. G. Rupp, A. N. Marlow, P. S. Watson, and B. Drewery (Philadelphia, 1969).

7. The *Defensio* is found in *CO* vi. 225–404.

8. See U. Plath, *Calvin und Basel in den Jahren 1552–1556* (Zurich, 1974); cf. also vol. i of A. S. Schweizer, *Die protestantischen Centraldogmen in ihrer Entwicklung innerhalb der reformirten Kirche* (Zurich, 1854).

9. 'Actes du procès intenté par Calvin et les autres ministres de Genève à Jérome Bolsec de Paris, 1551', *CO* viii. 141–248. With regard to Bolsec, see: F. Blanke, 'Calvins Urteil über Zwingli', in *Aus der Welt der Reformation*, 5th edn. (Zurich, 1960), 32–5; E. Doumergue, *Jean Calvin*, vi (Neuilly-sur-Seine, 1926), 131–61; F. W. Kampschulte, *Johann Calvin*, ii (Leipzig, 1899), 125–50.

10. Wiley, 'Calvin's Doctrine', 137.

11. 'Sil y teste expres en ladicte escripture saincte quil enseigne ce quil a escript en son Institution assavoir que non seulement dieu a preveu la cheute d'Adam et en ycelle la ruyne de toute sa posterité mais encore quil lha ainsy voulu et quil lavoit ainsy ordonné et determiné en son conseil. Quil die le teste expretz et manifeste.

   'Quelle cause y avoit en Adam pour laquelle il dheut estre non seulement habandonné de dieu mais encores necessité à pecher veu que en luy ny avoit le peché originel qui est la cause pourquoy dieu iustement peult delaisser et damner les enfans dudict Adam', 'Actes du procès . . . Bolsec', *CO* viii. 179. I am indebted to Richard Jeffery of the Oxford University Press for his help in translating this paragraph of sixteenth-century French.

12. The *De aeterna Dei praedestinatione* is found in *CO* viii. 249–366. Two English translations exist: J. K. S. Reid (ed. and trans.), *Concerning the Eternal Predestination of God* (London, 1961), and H. Cole (trans.), *Calvin's Calvinism* (1856–7; repr. Grand Rapids, 1950), 13–186.

13. Pighius, *De libero hominis arbitrio*.

14. 'Respondeo, nihil mirum esse, si tam indiscriminate (ut eius verbis utar) omnia miscet Pighius in Dei iudiciis, quando inter causas propinquas et remotas non discernit. Postquam huc illuc circumspexerint homines, quo tamen interitus sui culpam transferant, non invenient: quia proxima in ipsis causa residet. Nam si aliunde inflictum sibi vulnus querantur, interior animi sensus constrictos tenebit, ex voluntaria primi hominis defectione exortum fuisse malum. Scio non posse carnis proterviam compesci, quin hic protinus obstrepat: Si Adae casum praescivit Deus, nec remedium adhibere voluit, nos ex aeterno eius decreto perire innoxios magis, quam iustas peccati poenas dare. Verum, ut demus nihil tale fuisse a Deo praevisum, eadem nihilominus de peccato originali querimonia manebit. Obiiciet enim Deo impietas: Cur non sibi privatim, ut solus damnum sentiret, peccavit Adam? Cur nos, qui nihil meriti eramus, in eiusdem cladis societatem involvit? Imo, quo iure alienae culpae poenam in nos Deus traiecit? Sed enim ubi omnia dicta fuerint, singulos interior cordis sensus urgere non desinet, qui neminem, vel se iudice, patitur absolvi. Nec vero controversiam de eo quisquam facit. Nam quum, ob unius hominis peccatum, inflictum omnibus fuerit lethale vulnus: rectum Dei iudicium omnes agnoscunt. Si nihil obstat, quominus et prima interitus origo ab Adam coeperit, et proximam in se causam singuli inveniant, quid etiam impediet, quin arcanum Dei consilium, quo praeordinatus fuerat hominis lapsus, qua decet sobrietate, procul adoret fides nostra, et tamen quod propius apparet, conspiciat: totum humanum genus in Adae persona aeternae mortis reatu constrictum esse, et propterea morti esse obnoxium? Non ergo discussit Pighius, sicuti putabat, optimam et aptissimam symmetriam, qua inter se causa propinqua remota congruunt. . . .

    '. . . Nam quod obtendit inter duas sententias dissidium, prorsus nullum est. Dicimus hominem hac conditione fuisse creatum, ut conqueri de suo opifice nequeat. Praevidit Deus Adae lapsum: nec certe nisi volens ruere passus est', Calvin, *De aeterna Dei praedestinatione*, CO viii. 296–7; Reid, *Concerning the Eternal Predestination*, 100–1; cf. Cole, *Calvin's Calvinism*, 90–1; English translation: Reid.

15. 'Ac memoria tenendum est, quod ante posui, ubi Deus per media et inferiores causas virtutem suam exserit, non esse ab illis separandam. Temulenta est ista cogitatio: decrevit Deus quid futurum sit, ergo curam ac studium nostrum interponere supervacuum est. Atqui, quum nobis quid agendum sit, prae-scribat, et virtutis suae organa nos esse velit: fas nobis esse ne putemus separare quae ille coniunxit', ibid., CO viii. 354; Reid, 170–1; Cole, 235; English translation: Reid.

16. 'Est vray que devant mes tres redoubtez seigneurs et superieurs je soubsigne parlant de la doctrine de Monsr. Calvin ay dict quil avoit escript en son Institution les propositions suyvantes: Assavoir: que Adam estoit trebuche par le vouloir de Dieu. Il la escript au chappitre de la predestination, en son Institution, par luy mesme translatee de latin en francoys feuillet 461 page primiere, disant: que quand les iniques perissent en leur corruption ce nest aultre chose sinon quilz portent la calamite en laquelle Adam par le vouloir de Dieu est trebusche et a precipite tous ses successeurs. Ie confesse, dict il, que ce a este par le vouloir de Dieu que tous les enfans d'Adam sont cheuz en ceste misere en laquelle ilz sont maintenant contenuz. . . .

    '. . . Pourquoy, disent ilz, Dieu imputeroit il vice aux hommes les choses desquelles il leur a impose necessite par sa predestination? car que pourroient ilz faire? resisteroient ilz a sez decretz?', 'Trolliet contra Calvin', CO xiv. 371–80. For information on Trolliet see Doumergue, *Jean Calvin*, vi. 162–9.

17. Doumergue, vi. 378.

18. The standard authority on Castellio is F. Buisson, *Sébastien Castellion* (Paris, 1892). Buisson's critique of Castellio's teaching on predestination is found in ii. 165–81. See also J. Maehly, *Sebastian Castellio* (1862; repr. Geneva, 1971); C. É. Delormeau, *Sébastien Castellion* (Neuchâtel, 1963); E. Giran, *Sébastien Castellion et la réforme calviniste* (Haarlem, 1913); A. Schweizer, 'Sebastian Castellio als Bestreiter der calvinischen Prädestinationslehre der bedeutendste Vorgänger des Arminius', *ThJb(T)* 10 (1850), i. 1–27; H. M. Stückelberger, 'Calvin und Castellio', *Zwing.* 7 (1939), 91–128. There are several authorities which give a partial and incomplete account of the Castellio controversy. See especially Baum, Cunitz, and Reuss, in *CO* ix, pp. xxvi ff.; J. K. S. Reid, in Calvin, *Theological Treatises* (Philadelphia, 1954), 331–2 (based on Baum, Cunitz, and Reuss); Wiley, 'Calvin's Doctrine', 140. Our purposes are not simply to see Calvin's doctrine of predestination versus a host of opponents, but to see the whole controversy as a dynamic force within the Reformed community, with Calvin at the centre. It is necessary to see Castellio and the others not simply as opponents of Calvin but as opponents of the Reformed camp. Various Reformed figures and synods will react to the controversy in slightly different ways, and thus colour the thinking on the various questions being considered at certain crucial points.

19. Cf. S. Ozment, 'Sebastian Castellio', in *Mysticism and Dissent* (New Haven, 1973), 168–202.

20. Part of this note is cited in Wiley, 'Calvin's Doctrine', 141–2. This treatise, thirty pages long, was reprinted in 1613 as 'Annotationes Sebastiani Castellionis, in caput nonum ad Rom. Quibus materia electionis et praedestinationis amplius illustratur', in *Sebastiani Castellionis Dialogi IIII* (Gouda, 1613), part 2, 1–30.

21. See nn. 80 and 87, below.

22. Cf. *CO* ix, pp. xxvi ff., and Calvin, *Theological Treatises* (ed. Reid), 332.

23. Cited by Wiley, 'Calvin's Doctrine', 140.

24. 'Von Ursach der Sünden, und das der Mensch nicht zur Sünde gezwungen ist, auch noch nicht gezwungen wird, und von der Contingentia.
    'Die sechste Erinnerung, davon zu reden seer nötig ist, und davon offt in der Welt grosse streit erreget sind, ist diese, Wenn man spricht, Gott erhelt alle erschaffene ding, so fraget man alsbald, von ursach der Sünden. . . .
    'Da von ist seer nötig zu wissen, und festiglich zu schliessen, Das die Sünde nicht von Gott geschaffen ist, Gott lesset sie im auch nicht gefallen, und wil sie nicht, thut auch nichts wircklich darzu, zwinget oder treibet niemand zu sündigen, sondern er ist ein ernster Feind und strasser der sünden, Aber des Teuffels und des Menschen wille sind ursache der sünden, Und sind erstlich die Teuffel und Menschen, selbs aus eigenem Freiem willen, ungezwungen von Gott abgewichen, und in die Sünde gefallen', P. Melanchthon, 'Loci Theologici Germanice: C. Tertia Eorum Aetas', in *Opera quae supersunt omnia* (ed. H. Bindseil), xxii. 136; English translation: *Loci Communes 1555*, ed. and trans. C. L. Manschrek (New York, 1965), 45; the German quotation is from the 1558 edition, which is the edition in the *Opera*.

25. Ibid.

26. T. Beza, *Svmma totius Christianismi, siue descriptio et distributio causarum salutis electorum et exitii reproborum ex sacris literis collecta et explicata* (Geneva, 1555); no extant copy of this tract survives. Cf. F. Gardy, *Bibliographie des œuvres théologiques, littéraires, historiques et juridiques de Théodore de Bèze* (Geneva, 1960), 47–53. English translation: *A briefe Declaraccion of the chiefe poyntes of Christian religion, set forth in a Table of Predestination* (Geneva, 1556).

The *Svmma* also appeared in *Volumen . . . tractationum theologicarum* (Geneva, 1582), i. 170–205. Cf. also Beza's later treatise: *De praedestinationis doctrina et vero usu tractatio absolutissima*, in ibid. iii. 402–47. The chart also appeared in Beza's 1570 edition of *Volumen tractationum theologicarum*; cf. Gardy, 144–7

27. A discussion of this table can be found in J. Dantine, 'Les Tabelles sur la doctrine de la prédestination par Théodore de Bèze', *RThPh*, 3rd ser., 16 (1966), 365–77.

28. Beza, *Volumen tractationum theologicarum*, i. 170. The chart is reproduced in H. Heppe, *Die Dogmatik der evangelisch-reformirten Kirche* (Elberfeld, 1861), 109; the chart is slightly modified in the 1935 edition edited by E. Bizer (Neukirchen, 1935), 119; cf. the English translation: *Reformed Dogmatics* (ed. E. Bizer, trans. G. T. Thompson; London, 1950), 147–8.

29. Armstrong, *Calvinism and the Amyraut Heresy*, 32 ff.; Bray, *Theodore Beza's Doctrine*, 12–15. Cf. also Platt, *Reformed Thought and Scholasticism*; T. H. L. Parker, 'The Approach to Calvin', *EQ* 16 (1944), 165–72.

30. Bray, *Theodore Beza's Doctrine*, 12.

31. Cf. O. Grundler, 'Thomism and Calvinism in the Theology of Girolamo Zanchi' (Diss. Princeton Theological Seminary, 1961), 1–15; cf. also Grundler, *Die Gotteslehre Girolamo Zanchis und ihre Bedeutung für seine Lehre von der Prädestination* (Neukirchen, 1965).

32. Bray, *Theodore Beza's Doctrine*, 14.

33. Ibid. 12.

34. Ibid. 14–15.

35. For a critique of this argument concerning scholastic methodology in Reformed theology, see L. C. Boughton, 'Supralapsarianism and the Role of Metaphysics in Sixteenth-Century Reformed Theology', *WThJ* 48 (1986), 63–96.

36. Bray, *Theodore Beza's Doctrine*, 120–31 and 137–43.

37. Dantine, 'Les Tabelles', 367.

38. Ibid. 368.

39. Ibid. 370 n. 1. Cf. also Calvin, *Institutes*, i. 17. ix; *CO* ii. 161.

40. 'Ainsi Dieu peut agir par des moyens mauvais sans être auteur du mal. Dieu dispose donc absolument de toutes les choses sans leur ôter leur responsabilité et leur contingence'; Dantine, 'Les Tabelles', 370.

41. Bray, *Theodore Beza's Doctrine*, 69–85.

42. Ibid. 122.

43. 'The most significant impact that Aristotle had upon Beza was in the areas of ontology and epistemology. For Aristotle, real knowledge was based upon discovering the ultimate cause of events, and that cause of events was, at the same time, its logical foundation. Until one had plumbed the depths of events and discovered the prime cause by which one could describe the logical necessity of events, one had not grasped reality. It was this drive toward the ultimate cause of events and the search for logical relations that pushed Beza beyond the position of Calvin on the question of predestination and resulted in the *Tabula* of 1555. That work may be viewed as a scientific system (in Aristotle's sense of the term) in which God has become the *causa summa* from whose qualities the logical necessity of all events may be drawn. The *causa summa* directs the entire predestination event by means of the middle secondary causes (*causae mediae*). It is for this reason that one finds in the *Tabula* an abundance of terms which connote logical necessity. Even God has been equated to providence and is depicted as an "unpredictable power" ', ibid.

44. A totally different interpretation of the shift in thinking on predestination is given by R. A. Muller, 'Predestination and Christology in Sixteenth Century Reformed Theology' (Diss. Duke, 1976). Muller's work on this topic is continued in *Christ and the Decree* (Durham, NC, 1986). For a summary of the discussion of the extent to which Beza differed from Calvin and to what degree the Calvinists differed from Calvin, see R. W. A. Letham, 'Theodore Beza: A Reassessment', *SJTh* 40 (1987), 25–40.
45. Bray, *Theodore Beza's Doctrine*, 125.
46. Grundler, 'Thomism and Calvinism'.
47. This is found in *CO* lviii. 199–206. In vol. ix of the *CO* Baum, Cunitz, and Reuss considered this treatise to be lost, as later did J. K. S. Reid.
48. The *Brevis responsio* is found in *CO* ix. 253–66. It has been translated by J. K. S. Reid as 'Brief Reply in Refutation of the Calumnies of a Certain Worthless Person in Which He Attempted to Pollute the Doctrine of the Eternal Predestination of God', in Calvin, *Theological Treatises*, 333–43. It has also been translated in Cole, *Calvin's Calvinism*, 187–206. Copinger dates this work to 1554: *Treatise on Predestination*, 'Bibliography', viii.
49. 'Passim Calvinus commentum de absoluta Dei potentia, quod in scholis suis ventilant sophistae, acriter repudiat, et detestabile esse asserit: quia ab aeterna Dei sapientia et iustitia separari non debeat potestas . . . Deo enim placet iustitia, sicuti abominationi est iniquitas. Quomodo autem occulto iudicio moderetur quaecunque perperam ab hominibus fiunt, nostrum non est definire, nisi quod statuere oportet, quidquid agat, eum nunquam deflectere a sua iustitia', Calvin, *Brevis responsio*, *CO* ix. 259; Reid, in Calvin, *Theological Treatises*, 335; Cole, *Calvin's Calvinism*, 192–3; English translation: Reid.
50. 'Postquam aliquamdiu suas calumnias blateravit, propius congreditur, quosdam his periculosis temporibus, quamvis non audeant aperte docere malorum causam esse Deum, idem innuere aliis loquendi formis, quod Adam Deo volente peccaverit, et impii non solum Dei permissu, sed etiam impulsu maleficia omnia perpetrent. Hic cum deploratione excipit bonus rhetor: O miser homo! qui fieri potuit Deum hoc voluisse, qui ad imaginem suam Adam creaverat? Quasi vero meum sit de absconditis Dei iudiciis exactam rationem reddere ut ad unguem teneant mortales coelestem illam sapientiam, cuius altitudinem suspicere iubentur. Quin potius stultam hanc garrulitatem praeciso responso abrumpat Moses, quum dicit: Abscondita sua sint Deo nostro: haec autem quae trado, vobis revelata sunt (Deut. 29, 29)', *CO* ix. 260; Reid, in Calvin, *Theological Treatises*, 336; Cole, *Calvin's Calvinism*, 194; English translation: Reid.
51. *CO* ix. 260; Reid, in Calvin, *Theological Treatises*, 336; Cole, *Calvin's Calvinism*, 194.
52. Ibid. (Cole, 194–5).
53. 'Neque enim malum per se, hoc est, quatenus malum est, Deum velle Calvinus concedet: sed in hominum sceleribus refulgere Dei iudicia, sicut per incestos concubitus Absalon Davidis adulterium punivit. Deus ergo Adae praecipiens ne gustaret de arbore scientiae boni et mali, obedientiam quam probabat exegit. Interea quid futurum esset non modo praescivit, sed etiam decrevit. Quod si asperum videtur delicatulo censori, non sapori doctrinae, sed morositati suae vel fastidio imputet. Quod enim verborum suorum pondere tanquam ferreo malleo infigere vult omnium cordibus, unicam esse Dei voluntatem quam nobis per prophetas et Christum patefacit, sua autoritate Augustinus fortiter repellit. Haec sunt, inquit, magna opera Domini, exquisita in omnes voluntates eius, et tam sapienter exquisita, ut quum angelica et humana creatura peccasset, id est, non quod voluit ille, sed quod voluit ipsa fecisset, etiam per eandem

creaturae voluntatem, qua factum est quod creator noluit, impleret ipse quod voluit: bene utens et malis tanquam summe bonus, ad eorum damnationem, quos iuste praedestinavit ad poenam, et ad eorum salutem, quos benigne praedestinavit ad gratiam. Quantum enim ad ipsos attinet, quod Deus noluit, fecerunt: quantum ad omnipotentiam Dei, nullo modo id efficere valuerunt. Hoc quippe ipso, quod contra voluntatem Dei fecerunt, de ipsis facta est voluntas eius. Propterea enim magna opera Domini, exquisita in omnes voluntates eius, ut miro et ineffabili modo non fiat praeter eius voluntatem quod etiam fit contra eius voluntatem: quia non fieret si non sineret. Nec utique nolens sinit, sed volens. Nec sineret bonus fieri male, nisi omnipotens de malo facere posset bene', CO ix. 262–3; Reid, in Calvin, *Theological Treatises*, 339; Cole, *Calvin's Calvinism*, 199–200; English translation: Reid.

54. The *Calumnia nebulonis* is found in CO ix. 269–318. A translation of it is found in Cole, *Calvin's Calvinism*, 207–350.

55. 'Articuli decerpti ex libris tum Latinis tum Gallicis Iohannis Calvini de praedestinatione', CO ix. 273; Cole, *Calvin's Calvinism*, 264. In the CO, the points are gathered together (CO ix. 273); in the translation by Cole, they are scattered out over pp. 257–350 of *Calvin's Calvinism* as headings to sections. I have used the Cole translation for the English quotations of this work.

56. 'I. Deus maximam mundi partem nudo puroque voluntatis suae arbitrio creavit ad perditionem. II. Deus non solum praedestinavit ad damnationem, sed et ad causas damnationis et Adamum, cuius non modo praevidit lapsum, sed voluit decreto aeterno et occulto, ordinavitque ut laberetur: quod ut suo tempore fieret, lapsus causa pomum proposuit', CO ix. 273; Cole, *Calvin's Calvinism*, 264 and 279.

57. 'I. Contra primum. Primum articulam dicunt esse contra naturam, et contra scripturam. II. Contra secundum. Secundum item dicunt esse doctrinam diaboli et petunt a nobis, Calvine, ut ostendamus ubinam id scriptum sit in libris divinis', CO ix. 275–6; Cole, *Calvin's Calvinism*, 264–5 and 279.

58. 'Deus ipse gubernacula totius mundi sibi vendicans, potentiam suam a praescientia separari non patitur', CO ix. 294; Cole, *Calvin's Calvinism*, 280–1.

59. 'Locum citari postulas quo probem Deum, quia noluerit, non prohibuisse Adae lapsum. Quasi vero ad id probandum non sufficiat memorabile illud responsum: Miserebor cuius miserebor: unde colligit Paulus non omnium misereri, quia non vult (Exod. 33, 19; Rom. 9, 15)', ibid. (Cole, 282).

60. Cf. Buisson, *Sébastien Castellion*, ii. 123–31. A copy of the manuscript of the *Harpago* and its addition (cf. n. 64 below), made in 1571, is found with the papers of David Joris in the Bibliothèque de Bâle (cf. Buisson, ii. 124).

61. Cf. Buisson, *Sébastien Castellion*, ii. 124.

62. The *Ad sycophantarum calumnias* was published in 1558 in Geneva; cf. Beza, *Volumen tractationum theologicarum*, 'Ad Sebastiani Castellionis calumnias', i. 337–424; cf. Gardy, *Bibliographie*, 55–8.

63. Cf. Beza, *Volumen tractationum theologicarum*, i. 337.

64. Cf. Buisson, *Sébastien Castellion*, ii. 128.

65. Calvin, *Institutes* (1534–54), CO li–lviii.

66. Calvin, *Institutes* (1559), i. 16–18; CO ii. 144–74.

67. 'Disertis verbis hoc exstare negant, decretum fuisse a Deo, ut sua defectione periret Adam. Quasi vero idem ille Deus, quem scriptura praedicat facere quaecunque vult, ambiguo fine condiderit nobilissimam ex suis creaturis. Liberi arbitrii fuisse dicunt, ut fortunam ipse sibi fingeret; Deum vero nihil destinasse, nisi ut pro merito eum tractaret. Tam frigidum commentum si recipitur, ubi erit illa Dei omnipotentia, qua secundum arcanum consilium,

quod aliunde non pendet, omnia moderatur? Atqui praedestinatio, velint, nolint, in posteris se profert. Neque enim factum est naturaliter ut a salute exciderent omnes, unius parentis culpa. Quid eos prohibet fateri de uno homine, quod inviti de toto humano genere concedunt? Quid enim tergiversando luderent operam? Cunctos mortales in unius hominis persona morti aeterna emancipatos fuisse scriptura clamat. Hoc quum naturae adscribi nequeat, ab admirabili Dei consilio profectum esse minime obscurum est. Bonos istos iustitiae Dei patronos perplexos haerere in festuca, altas vero trabes superare, nimis absurdum est. Iterum quaero, unde factum est ut tot gentes una cum liberis eorum infantibus aeternae morti involveret lapsus Adae absque remedio, nisi quia Deo ita visum est? Hic obmutescere oportet tam dicaces alioqui linguas. Decretum quidem horribile, fateor; infitiari tamen nemo poterit quin praesciverit Deus, quem exitum esset habiturus homo, antequam ipsum conderet, et ideo praesciverit, quia decreto suo sic ordinarat. In praescientiam Dei si quis hic invehatur, temere et inconsulte impingit. Quid enim, quaeso, est cur reus agatur coelestis index quia non ignoraverit quod futurum erat? In praedestinationem competit, si quid est vel iustae vel speciosae querimoniae. Nec absurdum videri debet quod dico, Deum non modo primi hominis casum, et in eo posterorum ruinam praevidisse, sed arbitrio quoque suo dispensasse. Ut enim ad eius sapientiam pertinet, omnium quae futura sunt esse praescium, sic ad potentiam, omnia manu sua regere ac moderari. Et hanc quoque quaestionem Augustinus, ut alias, scite expedit: saluberrime confitemur quod rectissime credimus, Deum Dominumque rerum omnium, qui creavit omnia bona valde, et mala ex bonis exoritura praescivit, et scivit magis ad' suam ϙmnipotentissimam bonitatem pertinere, etiam de malis benefacere quam mala esse non sinere: sic ordinasse angelorum et hominum vitam, ut in ea prius ostenderet quid posset liberum arbitrium, deinde quid posset gratiae suae beneficium iustitiaeque iudicium', Calvin, *Institutes*, iii. 23, vi–ix; *CO* ii. 703–6; the quotation is from *CO* ii. 704–5; English translation: Battles, 955–6.

68. 'Ce Dieu se manifeste tel aux hommes: Premièrement par ses œuvres tant par la création que par la conservation et conduit d'icelles. Secondement et clairement par sa parolle, laquelle au commencement revelee par oracles, a esté puis apres redigee par escrit es livres que nous appellons escripture saincte', *Confessio gallicana*, ch. 2; *BSRK* 221–2; Schaff, *Creeds*, iii. 360; *Reformed Confessions of the Sixteenth Century*, ed. A. C. Cochrane (Philadelphia, 1966), 144; English translation: Schaff. R. A. Muller ('Predestination and Christology', p. 154) points out that in 1560 Wolfgang Musculus published his *Loci Communes*, which display a liking for natural theology.

69. Cf. *Reformed Confessions*, ed. Cochrane, 138, and Armstrong, *Calvinism and the Amyraut Heresy*, 24–30. Cochrane considers 'natural revelation' to be a 'virus'!

70. 'Nous croyons que non-seulement il a ' cree toutes choses: mais qu'il les governe et conduit, disposant, et ordonnant selon sa volonte de tout ce qui advient au monde, non pas qu'il soit autheur du mal, ou que la coulpe luy en puisse estre imputee, veu que sa volonte est la reigle souveraine et infallible de toute droicture et equite. Mais il a des moyens admirables de se servir tellment des Diables et des meschans, qu'il scait convertir en bien le mal qu'ils font, et duquel ilz sont coulpables. Et ainsi en confessant, que rien ne se faict sans la providence de Dieu, nous adorons en humilité les secrets, qui nous sont cachez, sans nous enquerir par dessus nostre mesure; mais plustost appliquons à nostre usage, ce qui nous est monstre en l'Escripture saincte, pour estre en repos et scurete: D'autant que Dieu, qui a toutes choses subiectes a soy, veille

sur nous d'un soing paternel, tellement qu'il ne tombera point un cheveu de nostre teste sans son vouloir, Et cependant tient les diables, et tous noz ennemis bridez, ensorte qu'ilz ne nous peuvent faire aucune nuisance sans son conge', *Confessio gallicana*, ch. 8; *BSRK* 223; Schaff, *Creeds*, iii. 364; *Reformed Confessions*, 147; English translation: Schaff.

71. Cf. *The Harmony of Protestant Confessions*, ed. and trans. P. Hall (London, 1844). Appendix II of his Introduction is entitled 'Proper Catalogues of Each and Every Confession in This Harmony, After the Order Wherein They Were First Written', pp. xl–xlviii. Cf. also the articles on 'revelation' in the earlier confessions. For a discussion of the rise of natural theology during the second half of the sixteenth century, see W. Kickel, *Vernunft und Offenbarung bei Theodor Beza* (Neukirchen, 1967); P. Althaus, *Die Prinzipien der deutschen reformierten Dogmatik im Zeitalter der aristotelischen Scholastik* (Leipzig, 1914; repr. Darmstadt, 1967), 126–78.

72. J. Staedtke, 'Der zürcher Prädestinationsstreit von 1560', *Zwing.* 9 (1953), 536–45; cf. also Baker, 'Predestination and Covenant in Bullinger's Thought', in *Heinrich Bullinger and the Covenant*, 27–54, and 'Appendix C: Calvinist Orthodoxy and the Paralysis of the Covenant Idea', ibid. 199–215; M. A. Gooszen, *Heinrich Bullinger en de strijd over de praedestinatie* (Rotterdam, 1909); W. Hollweg, *Heinrich Bullingers Hausbuch* (Neukirchen, 1956); D. F. Keep, 'Henry Bullinger', *LQHR* (1966), 133–46; Koch, *Die Theologie der Confessio Helvetica Posterior*; P. Walser, *Die Prädestination bei Heinrich Bullinger im Zusammenhang mit seiner Gotteslehre* (Zurich, 1957).

For concurrent controversies and later developments see: G. Adam, *Der Streit um Prädestination im ausgehenden 16. Jahrhundert* (Neukirchen, 1970); Copinger, *A Treatise on Predestination*; (n.a.), 'The Confutation of the Errors of the Careless by Necessity', Baptist Historical Society, *Transactions* 4 (1914–15), 88–123; W. M. Dietel, 'Puritanism vs. Anglicanism' (Diss. Yale, 1956); O. T. Hargrove, 'The Doctrine of Predestination in the English Reformation' (Diss. Vanderbilt, 1966), 'The Predestinarian Offensive of the Marian Exiles at Geneva', *HMPEC* 42 (1973), 111–23, and 'The Predestinarian Controversy among the Marian Protestant Figures', *HMPEC* 47 (1978), 131–51; R. Kyle, 'The Concept of Predestination in the Thought of John Knox', *WThJ* 46 (1984), 53–77; J. C. McLelland, 'The Reformed Doctrine of Predestination According to Peter Martyr', *SJTh* 8 (1955), 255–74; R. A. Muller, 'Perkins' *A Golden Chaine*', *SCJ* 9 (1978), 68–81; H. C. Porter, *Reformation and Reaction in Tudor Cambridge* (Cambridge, 1958); D. D. Wallace, *Puritans and Predestination* (Chapel Hill, 1982).

73. 'Interim vero media per quae operatur divina providentia, non aspernamur, ut inutilia, sed his hactenus nos accomodandos esse docemus, quatenus in verbo Dei nobis commendantur. Unde illorum voces temerarias improbamus, qui dicunt, Si providentia Dei omnia geruntur, inutiles certe sunt conatus nostri et studia nostra. Satis fuerit, si omnia divinae permittamus providentiae gubernanda, nec erit quod porro simus solliciti de re ulla, aut quicquam faciamus', *Confessio helvetica posterior*, ch. 6; *BSRK* 176; Schaff, *Creeds*, iii. 245; Cochrane (ed.), *Reformed Confessions*, 233; English translation: Schaff.

74. 'Reliquas quaestiones, An Deus voluerit labi Adamum, aut impulerit ad lapsum? aut quare lapsum non impediverit? et similes quaestiones deputamus inter curiosas (nisi forte cum haereticorum aut alioqui importunorum hominum improbitas cogit ista etiam ex verbo Dei explicare, sicut fecerunt non raro pij Ecclesiae doctores), scientes Dominum prohibuisse, ne homo ederet de fructu prohibito, et transgressionem punivisse; sed et mala non esse quae fiunt, respectu providentiae Dei, voluntatis ac potestatis Dei, sed respectu satanae et

voluntatis nostrae, voluntati Dei repugnantis', *Confessio helvetica posterior*, ch. 8; *BSRK* 176; Schaff, *Creeds*, iii. 249; Cochrane (ed.), *Reformed Confessions*, 237; English translation: Schaff.

75. 'Art. II. Duobus autem modis eum cognoscimus: primo, per creationem, conservationem, atque totius mundi gubernationem: quandoquidem is coram oculis nostris est, instar libri pulcherrimi, in quo creaturae omnes, magnae minoresque, loco characterum sunt, qui nobis Dei invisibilia contemplanda exhibent; aeternam nempe eius potentiam et divinitatem, ut Paulus Apostolus loquitur, Rom. 1. Quae omnia ad convincendos, et inexcusabiles reddendos homines, sufficiunt', *Confessio belgica*, ch. 2; *BSRK* 233 (Latin); Schaff, *Creeds*, iii. 384; Cochrane (ed.), *Reformed Confessions*, 189–90; English translation: Schaff. The Belgic Confession shows evidence of scholastic influence, as does the French Confession. P. Hall records the first chapter of the Belgic Confession as being entitled 'Of the Essence or Nature of God', *The Harmony of Protestant Confessions*, xlv.

76. 'Art. XIV. Credimus, Deum ex terrae pulvere, hominem creasse, et ad suam imaginem et similitudinem fecisse atque efformasse; bonum nempe, iustum, et sanctum. Qui suo sese arbitrio ad divinam voluntatem per omnia componere posset. Verum, cum in honore esset, id ipsum non intellexit, nec excellentiam suam cognovit, sed seipsum, verbis diaboli aurem praebens, peccato, ac proinde morti et maledictioni, volens subiecit. Nam mandatum vitae quod acceperat, transgressus est: seseque a Deo, qui vera ipsius erat vita, peccato suo, penitus divulsit, totamque naturam suam corrupit. Quo se morti corporeae et spirituali obnoxium reddidit. Atque ita improbus perversusque effectus, et in viis studiisque suis corruptus, praeclara illa omnia dona, quae a Deo acceperat, amisit. Adeo ut ipsi tantum exigua quaedam illorum vestigia remanserint: quae tamen ad reddendum eum inexcusabilem sufficiant; quoniam, quicquid in nobis est lucis, in tenebras versum est ut Scriptura nos docet; dicens, Lux in tenebris lucet; et tenebrae eam non comprehenderunt. Ubi S. Iohannes homines tenebras appellat', *Confessio belgica*, ch. 14; *BSRK* 237–8 (Latin); Schaff, *Creeds*, iii. 398–9; Cochrane (ed.), *Reformed Confessions*, 198–9; English translation: Schaff.

77. '6. Frag. Hat denn Gott den menschen also böss unnd verkert erschaffen? Antwort. Nein: sonder Gott hat den menschen gut, unnd nach seinem ebenbild erschaffen, das ist, in warhafftiger gerechtigkeyt und heiligkeyt, auff dass er Gott seinen Schöpffer recht erkennte, und von hertzen liebte, und in ewiger seligkeyt mit jm lebte, jn zu loben und zu preisen', The Heidelberg Catechism, Question 6; *BSRK* 684; Schaff, *Creeds*, iii. 309; Cochrane (ed.), *Reformed Confessions*, 306; English translation: Schaff. The French Confession, the Heidelberg Catechism, and the Belgic Confession all have remarkably similar sections on providence. Especially notable is a sentence such as this from the first question of the Heidelberg Catechism: 'he protects me so well that without the will of my Father in heaven not a hair can fall from my head; indeed, that everything must fit his purpose for my salvation. Therefore, by his Holy Spirit, he also assures me of eternal life, and makes me wholeheartedly willing and ready from now on to live for him.' One wonders if martyrs such as those at Smithfield only a couple of years earlier (1555) might have provided the impulse for the assertion of providential protection.

78. 'Ante creatum primum hominem statuerat Deus aeterno consilio quid de toto genere humano fieri vellet.

'Hoc arcano Dei consilio factum est ut Adam ab integro naturae suae statu deficeret ac sua defectione traheret omnes suos posteros in reatum aeternae mortis', Calvin, 'Articuli de praedestinatione', *CO* ix. 713–14; cf. Calvin, *Theological Treatises*, ed. Reid, 178–80; English translation: Reid.

79. 'The Lord is . . . not wishing that any should perish, but that all should reach repentance' (2 Peter 3: 9, RSV).
80. Castellio, *Dialogi IIII* (Aresdorffii, 1578), 332–445, and (Gouda, 1613), 254–339.
81. Gouda, 1613. See n. 20 above.
82. Castellio, *Dialogi IIII*, 'De praedestinatione', 1–109.
83. Steven Ozment has stated it clearly: 'In the first of the *Four Dialogues*, "On Predestination," scholastic logic is taken over and given a commonsense twist to produce a kind of "mock scholasticism" by which Castellio's opponent is finally reduced to a self-confession of foolishness. Scholastic logical rigor and axioms are made to subserve the evident facts of daily experience (often with tongue-in-cheek) rather than the cogency of theoretical possibilities', *Mysticism and Dissent*, 175.
84. 'Quid enim absurdius vel cogitari posset, quam si Deus sic Adamum alloquatur? Ego te creavi ad peccandum, ita vt a peccato non magis abstinere possis quam ab esurie. Verumtamen caue ne pecces. Nam si peccaueris moriere.
    'Ergo si creatus fuit ad imaginem Dei, certe ad iustitiam creatus fuit, non ad peccatum. Iam imperium illud, quod ei dat Deus in terram et in animalia, estne peccatum?', Castellio, 'De praedestinatione', 41 and 20; English translation, Ozment, *Mysticism and Dissent*, 186.
85. 'Destinantur autem alia cum conditione, alia certo et sine conditione: quae utraque destinatio in Deo cernitur', Castellio, *Annotationes*, 10.
86. 'Adamus peccavit volens. Peccasse autem volentem, arguit Deus, qui dicit eum uxori magis obedivisse, quam ipsi Deo. Nam obedientia certa voluntaria est. Nolente Deo peccasse, ostendit praeceptum, quo Deus vetuerat ne fructum illum gustaret, ut enim hominis, sic et Dei voluntas cognoscitur ex praecepto. Idem ostendit reprehensio, cum dicit Deus eum non obedivisse sibi: ex quo intelligitur Dei voluntatem fuisse, ut non gustaret fructum illum. Ex his apparet Adamum peccasse, non destinatione Dei (qui peccatum non vult) sed voluntate culpaque sua, nulla necessitate cogente. Dicet aliquis: Sed si Deus noluisset, eum, quominus peccaret, impedire potuisset: Fateor, si eum stipitem, non hominem creasset: aut si eum statim interfecisset. Sed hominem creare, et eundem vel peccandum vel ad recte faciendum cogere, perinde fuisset, atque avem creare, et ei liberum volatum adimere, hoc vero esset non avem, sed aliud quidpiam creare. At enim Deus potest omnia quae vult: Fateor, sed nihil vult absurdum (etiam si homines multa eius opera absurda judicant) ut quod fieri non possit. Itaque ut Adam peccandi, aut non peccandi potestatem haberet, fuit voluntatis Dei: sed ut non utrumlibet posset, et tamen liberam voluntatem haberet, hoc esset absurdum, et perinde ac si dicas, potest et non potest. Igitur quod peccare potuit, hoc habuit a Deo: sed quod peccare voluit, hoc habuit a se ipso', ibid. 13–14.
87. Castellio, *De praedestinatione scriptum* (Gouda, 1613), 250–60.
88. 'Ex ista positione efficitur hoc argumentum: Quicquid Dei consilio sit, idem sit authore Deo; Atqui Adamus Dei consilio labem contraxit, hoc est peccauit: Ergo Adamus authore Deo peccauit', ibid. 257–8.
89. 'An Deus sit simulator, quaestio secunda. Iam ad alterum veniamus, quod ex priore consequitur, videlicet, quod Deum facias simulatorem: quod quidem sic colligitur; Si creavit Deus aliquos homines ad exitium eosque seruare non vult, et tamen omnes nullo discrimine ad iustitiam, et porro ad salutem inuitat, efficitur, vt sit simulator: quippe qui verbis ita se gerat, quasi velit omnes saluos fieri: cum revera non nisi certos velit'. ibid. 267.
90. 'Dicit Deus: Nolo mortem impii sed vt viuat: ac, ne hoc conditione quaeras effugium addit, ut se conuertat, et tamen non se conuerterunt illi impij de

quibus loquitur: ex quo tu secundum tuam doctrinam statues Deum decreuisse, ut impij esse perseuerarent. Vult ergo contra statutum suum. Dicit Adamo: Noli vesci arbore scientiae, et tu dicis, eum decreuisse ut vesceretur Adamus arbore scientiae. Est ergo eius praeceptum decreto contrarium. Utri vis vt credam?', ibid. 271.

91. 'Praeterea Adamum Dei consilio, atque docreto (*sic*) peccasse sicuti supra ostendimus, docuisti. Quin et hoc ipso in loco, vbi de conditione agis, dicis Deum decreuisse, quod Paulus refert, fieri. "Conclusit omne sub increduli- tatem, vt omnium misereatur." In quibus, et aliis similibus locis (nam saepe eadem scribis) pronuncias omnia immutabili, irreuocabilique Dei decreto fieri, et quidem ita fieri, vt nihil aliter fieri queat, quam sit, quod vno uerbo dicere licet, fieri omnia necessario. Atqui si fiunt omnia necessario, nihil fit cum conditione, ac ne Deus quidem quicquam cum conditione facere, aut aliter facere, quam facit, potest. Pugnant enim ista vt ignis et aqua, necessario fieri, et cum conditione fieri. Quid est enim conditio? Defini eam tu mihi, aut definientem audi. Conditio est oblata potestas aliquid eligendi. Atqui electionis nullus locus est vbi fit aliquid necessario: id quod vel ex trito illo dicto cognoscas: Necessitas non habet legem. Quod si necessario, et ineluctabili Dei decreto peccauit Adamus, et ob peccatum eiectus est ex paradiso: non fuit cum conditione destinatus vitae, sed fuit citra vllam conditionem ineluctabili Dei decreto destinatus morti. Alioquin qualis erit illa conditio, si Deus secundum doctrinam tuam sic alloquatur Adamum: Ego te Adame in paradiso colloco, vt ibi vivas, sed ea conditione, si mandato meo obediueris. Obedire autem non magis poteris, quam me vincere. Nam immutabili invictoque decreto meo peccabis. Quaeso te, quis conditionem hanc non derideat?', ibid. 284–5.

3

The Prelapsarian Covenant as Proposed by Zacharias Ursinus

> Then the Lord God toke the man, and put him into the garden
> of Eden, that he might dresse it and kepe it. And the Lord God
> commanded the man, saying, Thou shalt eat frely of euerie tre
> of the garden, But as touching the tre of knowledge of good
> and euil, thou shalt not eat of it: for whensouer thou eatest
> thereof, thou shalt dye the death.
>
> Genesis 2: 15–17 (Geneva Bible, 1560)

WE have seen that the distinguishing feature of the federal theology
is the application of covenantal status to the paradisal state, with
Adam as the responsible federal or covenant head who makes a
decision for all of creation. By federal or covenant head we mean
that in the economy of God's justice each person stands before God
through another person, either Adam or Christ. This question was
especially important with respect to the doctrine of the transmission
of original sin. Christian theologians have traditionally distinguished two ways of thinking about representation: all men are
either 'in' Adam when he makes the decision to sin, or all men are
'represented' by Adam as he decides to sin, in the same way that a
representative in a legislature represents a district. For classical
Christian theologians, coming to faith in Christ meant that a person
was united to Jesus Christ the God-Man, who is the second Adam,
and Christ acted as that person's covenant head or federal
representative before God, either realistically or representatively.

The constitutive elements of the prelapsarian covenant are
basically similar to those of other covenants in the Bible:

(1) The covenant had conditions; these conditions were expressed
in three ways: (a) the command not to eat of the tree of the
knowledge of good and evil; (b) the implicit command to keep the
seventh day holy as a sabbath of rest and as a creation ordinance;
and finally (c) the command to obey the Decalogue, which was
written upon Adam's heart—an idea derived mainly from New
Testament Pauline passages such as are found in Romans.

(2) There were two parties to this covenant, God and man.

(3) The prelapsarian covenant was essentially a covenant of conditionality. It could be characterized as dipleural or bilateral, as opposed to monopleural or unilateral. It thus possessed the characteristic of mutuality: man had conditions placed upon him, but so did God. God bound himself to keep his promise to man. Man promised to obey God. If man was obedient, God had to bless him. If man was disobedient, God had to curse him with death. God could not remain neutral. Both God and man were bound by covenant obligations. The postlapsarian covenant of grace, however, was thought of as an unconditional covenant. It was monopleural, or unilateral. Therefore it was non-mutual. God must graciously save man from his sin. Man could not keep the covenant, and he could not respond of his own free will to God. God must enable man to keep the covenant by keeping the prelapsarian covenant for him, through the work of Jesus Christ.

(4) The covenant was binding upon Adam and Eve and all their descendants, whether Adam sinned or whether he did not sin. Thus the covenant of works bound both the believer and the unbeliever. The covenant of grace bound only the believer. Two covenants were therefore binding upon man: one binding the entire human race; the other binding a smaller group within the human race. That small group, because they were saved by grace through the covenant of grace, had a special obligation and double responsibility to keep as best they could the conditions of the prelapsarian covenant. They were to show forth to the lost world the obligations binding upon all men, and work to make even the unregenerate obey the law of God. The tree of the knowledge of good and evil was no longer there to eat, but certainly the elect knew and could teach others the Decalogue, and certainly they could keep the sabbath day as a memorial of God's rest and of Jesus Christ's resurrection.

The combination of points (3) and (4) provided a way for the federal theologians to explain the tension found within Scripture between the phrases of conditionality ('If you keep the covenant, then . . .' and 'If you do not keep the covenant, then . . .') and graciousness ('I will establish my covenant with you . . .'). God could therefore say to men under grace 'Keep the covenant . . .', because they, as sons of Adam, were bound to keep the prelapsarian covenant; and at the same time he could say 'I will establish my covenant with you . . .', because they could not humanly keep the prelapsarian covenant and therefore needed God to make a new covenant of grace with them. The covenant of grace consisted of Jesus Christ keeping the prelapsarian Edenic covenant for the elect as the second Adam and then applying this work of redemption to his people.[1]

(5) The covenant had a sign attached to it: man was allowed to eat of the tree of life. In the covenant of grace this sign would be replaced by the Old Testament sacraments of circumcision and the Passover and the New Testament sacraments of baptism and the Lord's Supper.

The idea of a prelapsarian covenant is not an absolute novelty in the history of Christian doctrine, as shown by our brief exploration of Augustine, Calvin and Catharinus, but it was not utilized extensively in Reformed theology until the second half of the sixteenth century. There is no evidence of its use during the early Reformation.

Zacharias Ursinus is the theologian who first utilized the idea of a prelapsarian covenant to any great extent in the sixteenth century.[2] Very little study has been made of Ursinus's doctrine of the covenant and how and where it fits in with his other theological doctrines, particularly that of God's sovereignty.[3] The purpose of this chapter is to explore Ursinus's doctrine of the covenant, particularly the prelapsarian covenant, and examine it within the context of his doctrine of predestination.

Ursinus was born in Breslau, and grew up a Lutheran under the tutelage of Philip Melanchthon. However, between 1557 and 1561, when he was between the ages of 23 and 27, he adopted a Reformed theology in place of his earlier Lutheran commitments. Ursinus was Professor of Dogmatics from 1562 to 1568 at the University of Heidelberg. Between 1562 and 1576 he was also the Headmaster and Professor at the Collegium Sapientiae, a seminary for older teenagers preparing for the pastorate and for work at the University. In 1563 he also took on the duties of the preacher at the Peterskirche in Heidelberg. He is best known for the key role he played in the composition of the Heidelberg Catechism of 1563. In 1577 he became Professor of Dogmatics in the Casimirianum at Neustadt an der Hardt. This school was essentially a continuation of the Collegium Sapientiae and the Reformed Faculty of Theology of the University of Heidelberg after the Reformed teachers at Heidelberg were replaced by Lutheran teachers.

Ursinus's *Opera theologica* were published in 1612.[4] The editor, Quirinus Reuter, arranged the works in three volumes. The first contained Ursinus's discussion and teaching of basic doctrines of religion; the second his polemical works; and the third his commentary on Isaiah. This arrangement is significant and problematical, for there is no assurance that Reuter placed the works in chronological order of composition within each volume.

The following treatises are significant in Ursinus's discussion of the covenant; most of his other works are not relevant with respect to the federal theology and the covenant idea:

(1) 1561–2. *Catechesis, summa theologiae per quaestiones et responsiones exposita: sive, capita religionis Christianae continens.*[5] Often referred to as the Major Catechism, the first recorded publication we have of it is in Neustadt in 1584.[6] There is some confusion as to its date of composition, but this problem will be discussed below. This catechism is not the same as the Heidelberg Catechism, and it is easy to confuse it with the exposition of the Heidelberg Catechism. This is a *Summa theologiae*. The Heidelberg Catechism is a *Catechesis religionis Christianae*.

(2) 1562. *Catechesis minor perspicua brevitate Christianam fidem complectens. Scripto anno MDLXII. A. D. Zacharia Ursino. Iam primum ex autoris bibliotheca et autographo deprompta.* This small catechism, often referred to as the Minor Catechism, is much more of a parallel to the Heidelberg Catechism of 1563 than the Major Catechism is.[7]

(3) 1568. *D. Zachariae Ursini loci theologici traditi in academia Heidelbergensi.*[8]

(4) 1587. *[Explicatio] catechesis religionis Christianae.* The text of the Heidelberg Catechism, and Ursinus's discussion of it, are woven together to form the major part of the first volume of the *Opera theologica.* An earlier version of lecture notes on Ursinus's lectures appeared in 1584, right after his death, but the 1587 edition, edited by David Pareus, became the standard commentary on the Heidelberg Catechism. This is by far Ursinus's most popular and famous work, and it underwent many translations and editions.[9]

(5) 1589. *Zachariae Ursini, Uratislaviensis, scholasticarum in materiis theologicis exercitationum liber.*[10]

Ursinus wrote other works dealing with theological method, but we will not need to deal with them at this point. It is important to note, however, that Ursinus was a thoroughgoing Aristotelian and firmly condemned the new Ramistic philosophy and methodology which was being proposed at the University of Heidelberg during his professorship.[11]

The Major Catechism is the only treatise by Ursinus which teaches the prelapsarian covenant idea. In his other works the covenant of grace plays a key role, especially in relation to the doctrine of Jesus Christ as mediator, but the *foedus naturale* appears only in the Major Catechism. The dating of the Major Catechism is therefore of importance: given the scenario previously outlined, it is of crucial importance whether the catechism was written in 1562, as M. Lauterburg and A. Lang maintain,[12] or just before 1584, which is when Mark Walter Karlberg dates it, and when it was first published.[13] The discussion of the date of composition of the Major Catechism always comes as an appendage to the discussion of the more influential Heidelberg Catechism: the Major and Minor Catechisms are usually seen as source material for the Heidelberg Catechism. Virtually all the commentators simply assume that the Major Catechism came first, and that therefore it was written prior to 1563.[14] But how can we be sure that the Major Catechism came first and was not written toward the end of Ursinus's career, if it was first published posthumously in 1584?

In the 1612 edition of the *Opera theologica* the Minor Catechism is specifically dated 1562 by Ursinus himself: 'scripta MDLXII' is written at the top of the page.[15] There is no such heading for the Major Catechism. The most helpful authority on this question is the early article by M. Lauterburg published in 1901.[16] There he dates the Major Catechism to 1561, immediately after the arrival of Ursinus at Heidelberg. Lauterburg points out that Reuter wrote a preface to the Major Catechism in the *Opera* of 1612, which dates the catechism to Ursinus's early years and therefore before the Heidelberg Catechism of 1563.[17] According to Reuter:

Therefore Dr. Ursinus, not at all the least among the theologians of his time, at the command of the Chief Magistrate, put on paper and showed to those he should, a catechism, indeed the larger one, for adult students, and higher schools; the other smaller one accommodated to the artisan people, and to those of younger ages. And both are recommended, because they embrace the height of heavenly truth, and the level ground of sincere theological words. Out of this also many copies were made, to be a public catechism, by Friedrich III, in the year 1563.[18]

But how do we know that Reuter is correct, and that he is not just speculating or filling in what he thinks is the case? After all, he wrote the preface in 1612, exactly fifty years after the Minor Catechism appeared. Our assurance comes from the biography which we have of Reuter: Reuter was a student at the University of Heidelberg and studied with Ursinus, beginning in 1573.[19] He therefore learned theology using the Major Catechism. Whatever form the Major Catechism first took (perhaps printed booklets or printed sheets of paper?) no example survives for us today.

Erdman Sturm provides us with more evidence that the Major Catechism was written in 1561 or 1562. He points out that in his inaugural address at the Collegium Sapientiae Ursinus wished to finish two projects which he was working on: a catechism and a collection of *Loci Communes* which he wanted to develop into a *Summa* of Christian doctrine. Sturm connects this *Summa* with the Major Catechism.[20] We can therefore date the Major Catechism to as early as 1573, and we can be almost totally sure that the account which Reuter gives of the Major Catechism's being written in the early 1560s is accurate. Consequently, the idea of the prelapsarian covenant was proposed by Ursinus in 1561 or 1562, to his students of theology only, at the end of a decade of debate over the issue of God's sovereignty and Adam's Fall.

The Major Catechism has a fourfold structure which is outlined in its eighth and ninth questions:

8. How many are the headings, under which the whole doctrine of Christianity is contained? A. Four.
9. What are they? A. The summary of the divine law, or the Decalogue; the summary of the gospel, or Apostle's Creed; the invocation of God, or Lord's Prayer; and the institution of the ministry of the Church.[21]

Ursinus divides the basic tenets of Christianity into the law or Decalogue, the gospel, as summarized in the Apostle's Creed, the Lord's Prayer, and the Church. This is very different from the way Beza divides his *Svmma totius Christianismi*, which appeared six years earlier. For Beza the sum total of Christianity, at least in that tractate, is divided into the various decrees of God, which start with God and emanate from him to effect salvation for the elect and damnation for the reprobate.[22]

The idea of the prelapsarian covenant is found at the very beginning of the Major Catechism, in a question dealing with the purpose of the Decalogue:

What does the divine Law teach? A. What sort of covenant in creation God had entered into with man; by which pact man would have conducted himself in that service, and what God would require from him after beginning with him a new covenant of grace; that is, of what quality and for what purpose man might be established by God, and into which state he might be brought back; and by which pact one reconciled to God ought to arrange his life.[23]

At its very inception in Reformed dogmatics the prelapsarian covenant is associated with the Decalogue; furthermore, the conditions of the prelapsarian covenant are the same as the conditions of the postlapsarian covenant. It is significant that Ursinus does not state that the covenant was made with Adam (*cum Adamo*), but with man (*cum homine*). Thus the more general term indicates that the covenant is made with *man*—all men, of whom Adam is the progenitor. Lyle D. Bierma sees this concept—i.e. the covenant binding all men—as a progressive step in the history of the covenant idea.[24]

Ursinus also states clearly what he feels the prelapsarian existence of Adam and Eve consisted of: 'the true knowledge of God and of the divine will', and he feels that the Edenic state existed for the worship of God in 'eternal Beatitude':

11. In what state was man formed? A. After the image of God.
12. In what way is this an image? A. The true knowledge of God and of the divine will, and the whole inclination and striving of man to live according to this alone.
13. For what, however, was he formed? That he might worship God in eternal beatitude for the whole of his life.[25]

Ursinus says very little about whether he thought the Edenic state was temporary (leading up to the eternal state), or whether it was considered permanent (Eden itself being the eternal state). However, in Question 31 of the Major Catechism, which contains the second reference to the prelapsarian covenant, Ursinus hints that God promised a future 'eternal life', i.e. that Adam had not yet attained the state of eternal life in the garden:

36. What is the difference between the Law and the Gospel? A. The Law contains the covenant of nature, initiated in creation by God with men, that is, it is known to men by nature; and it requires from us perfect obedience to God, and it promises eternal life for those who keep it, and threatens eternal punishments for those who do not fulfil it. But the gospel contains the covenant of grace, that is, existing but not known naturally: it shows to

us the fulfilment in Christ of his justice, which the law requires, and its restoration in us through the Spirit of Christ; and it promises eternal life by grace because of Christ, to those who believe in him.[26]

Ursinus does not make any reference to Christ as the second Adam.[27] However, he very clearly points out that Christ is the only man who can completely obey the law of God, an idea articulated by the Lutherans as the active obedience of Christ:

18. Is any one of us able to fulfil this obedience? A. With Christ alone excepted, not one man in this life ever was able to fulfil it, nor will be able.[28]

Why does Ursinus use the novel idea of a covenant in creation or a natural covenant in one of his first theological treatises? We have shown that the word *foedus* was undergoing careful examination in the sixteenth century, and that Sebastian Castellio was the only Protestant Bible translator to change the word *testamentum* to *foedus* in certain key biblical passages. We know that Castellio was very much opposed to the teachings of Calvin and Beza on God's sovereignty. We also know something else: in 1557–8, at the height of the controversy about God's sovereignty and Adam's Fall, Zacharias Ursinus visited Sebastian Castellio in Basle after spending seven years with Melanchthon at Wittenberg. Derk Visser comments:

In 1557, after spending seven years in Wittenberg, Ursinus set out on a study trip that took him from Wittenberg to Worms and from there into the Rhine valley; into Switzerland (where he briefly visited Zurich and Geneva); into France (where he acquired the rudiments of Hebrew in Paris); and back again via Geneva, Zurich, and the Rhine valley. On this trip he made a point of visiting as many known figures as possible, among whom were not only Bullinger and Calvin but also Sebastian Castellio and the theologians of Tübingen. The conversations he had on this voyage—as well as those of his trip in 1561, when he met George Cassander—are an illustration of one of his favorite texts: 'Examine all things and retain what is good.'[29]

Melanchthon, with his doctrine of prevenient grace,[30] was certainly no High Calvinist, and even Bullinger had problems with the emerging system articulated by Beza. The list of people whom Ursinus visited is certainly varied,[31] and we also know that this was the period during which Ursinus was leaving Melanchthon's Lutheranism and going into the Reformed fold.[32] Certainly his concern over the question of Adam's Fall would match Castellio's, although he would approach the problem in a very different way from Castellio. While nothing definite can be said, could we perhaps see Castellio as a possible source—or catalyst—for Ursinus's proposal of a prelapsarian covenant in 1562? It was Castellio who gave evidence of having examined the word *foedus* very carefully, and it was Castellio, of course, who could not reconcile Adam's Fall and the absolute sovereignty of God. It seems that the prelapsarian covenant emerged in Ursinus's thought as a means of articulating the problem of theodicy.

Certainly theodicy is a theme in the Major Catechism. However, it does not come under the section of the law of God. Rather, it comes under the heading of the gospel, which in the Major Catechism consists of the Apostle's Creed. Like the Heidelberg Catechism, the Major Catechism has no sections which deal with the specific doctrine of predestination and election.[33] However, there is a section which deals with the providence of God.

In the Major Catechism Ursinus first defines what the providence of God is:

47. What do you call the providence of God? A. The eternal, immutable, most wise and best counsel of God, according to which all things happen and are directed for the glory of the Creator.[34]

However, the immediate questions after Question 47 attempt to dispel any thought that God is the author of evil:

48. Is this saying that the wicked also are ruled over by God? A. Indeed by his own power and counsel he thus effects through them what he wills, so that indeed they are not able to be moved without his very permission, but by his grace and his Spirit he neither sanctifies them nor leads them.
49. Is not therefore God the cause of the sins, of which they admit? A. Not at all. For God is able to institute and effect also through the most evil people nothing except what is best and most just. Because however while they themselves sin, yet God works good through them, nor is it the good will of God and his just judgement, but whatever depravity remains in them and is derived from them of their own accord.[35]

We see that Ursinus was concerned with the problem of evil, but the questions that he asks must be examined against the backdrop of the previous decade (1550–61) and its shifts in predestinarian dogma.

From the evidence presented in his early writings, including the Major Catechism, and from what he said in his later writings, we can conclude that Ursinus was an orthodox High Calvinist.[36] He believed that even the Fall of Adam was somehow included in God's providential plan. However, unlike Beza, he did not believe that the sum total of Christianity could be reduced to the decrees of God, or that the average lay person must have a precise grasp of Reformed theology and doctrine. The Major Catechism and the idea of a covenant in creation seem to be items reserved for the students of theology at Heidelberg: they were never translated into German by Ursinus or by any of his immediate contemporaries. On the other hand, the assurance and comfort of the covenant of grace is the main theme of the Heidelberg Catechism, which was intended both for trained students of theology and for the laity. Ursinus has been accused of being 'soft' on the system of High Calvinism; this is not the case. However, Ursinus does reserve the tough questions for his technical theological treatises and for those with the ability to read them.[37]

Jürgen Moltmann feels that the Heidelberg school with its federal theology was combined with Ramistic methodology to form an anti-Bezan, anti-Aristotelian opposition to Bezan High Calvinism.[38] However, we know that Ursinus was a High Calvinist and was opposed to Ramistic methodology. Olevianus was of a similar disposition. Beza and Olevianus were good friends. We can say, however, two things: (1) Ursinus and Olevianus, along with the other early federal theologians, were concerned to 'fill out' the stark teaching of Beza concerning God's sovereignty; (2) the federal theologians were more inclined to leave hard questions such as the problem of Adam's Fall to those trained in theology who had a knowledge of Latin. The result was that while they were not opposed to Bezan High Calvinism, their teaching appeared 'milder', less deterministic, and more pietistic in emphasis.[39]

Ursinus is more concerned with maintaining a proper balance with regard to God's sovereignty and man's freedom. Except for the one question on providence, the Heidelberg Catechism does not deal explicitly with such topics as predestination and election; however, in his technical theological treatises Ursinus is careful to assert God's absolute sovereignty, even over the Fall, along with a denial of God's responsibility for evil. At the same time he wants somehow to explain how the Fall happened. The prelapsarian covenant in creation does not mitigate the decree of God respecting the Fall; it merely explains it more fully.

In his *[Explicatio] catechesis religionis Christianae* Ursinus explains what a covenant is:

Question 18. What the covenant of God is. A. A covenant in general is a mutual pact between two parties, where one obligates the other to certain conditions for doing, giving, or receiving something, employing signs and external symbols for solemn testimony, as a confirmation that the promise may be inviolable. From here certainly the definition of the covenant of God is deduced. For it is a mutual pact between God and men . . .[40]

For Ursinus a covenant is an explicit formal agreement between God and man or between man and man, in which both parties know and accept certain conditions. Ursinus took this idea and applied it to the perfect relationship between man and God in Eden, and thereby Ursinus left Adam and Eve without excuse when they broke the covenant. He further realized that the prelapsarian covenant binding Adam and all his descendants left the entire human race without excuse. Ursinus taught this idea to a whole generation of students at the Collegium Sapientiae, the University of Heidelberg, and the Casimirianum at Neustadt an der Hardt, but the idea remained dormant until 1584, when the Major Catechism was first published after his death.[41]

Between 1584 and 1590 Ursinus's students and younger colleagues started to utilize the idea of a prelapsarian covenant in their systematic theological treatises. It is to this second stage in the origins of the federal theology that we now turn.

Notes

1. This explains more fully the contrast which L. J. Trinterud finds between 'contract' and 'covenant' in the full development of covenant theory; cf. 'The Origins of Puritanism'. Another way of describing this contrast is *diatheke* vs. *suntheke*; cf. Torrance, 'Covenant or Contract?'; cf. ch. 1 above.
2. The best biography in English of Ursinus is that by Visser, *Zacharias Ursinus*. Visser has also edited a collection of essays dealing with Ursinus and the Palatinate: *Controversy and Conciliation*. See also the following: M. Adam, 'Zacharias Ursinus', *DLV* 252–8; *AGL* iv. 1741–2; D. Agnew, 'Zacharias Ursinus', in *The Theology of Consolation* (Edinburgh, 1880), 367–8; G. A. Benrath, 'Die Eigenart der pfälzischen Reformation und die Vorgeschichte des Heidelberger Katechismus', *HdJb* 7 (1963), 13–32; C. J. Burchill, 'On the Consolation of a Christian Scholar', *JEH* 37 (1986), 565–83; J. F. A. Gillet, 'Ursinus (Zacharias)', *RE* (1st edn.), xvi. 754–61, and *Crato von Crafftheim und seine Freunde* (Frankfurt, 1860), i. 87–269 and ii. 97–167; J. F. A. Gillet and J. Ney, 'Ursinus, Zacharias', *RE* (2nd edn.), xvi. 238–43; M. Goebal, 'Dr. Zacharias Ursinus', trans. H. Harbough, *MercQR* 7 (1855), 629–36; J. F. G. Goeters, 'Entstehung und Frühgeschichte des Katechismus', in L. Coenen (ed.), *Handbuch zum Heidelberger Katechismus* (Neukirchen, 1963), 3–23; J.

I. Good, *The Heidelberg Catechism in its Newest Light* (Philadelphia, 1914), 242–82, and *The Origin of the Reformed Church in Germany* (Reading, Pa., 1887); E. Güder, 'Katechismus, Heidelberger oder Pfälzer', *RE* (2nd edn.), vii. 605–14, and 'Heidelberg Catechism', *SchHE* (2nd and 3rd edns.), ii. 959–60; F. Hauss, 'Zacharias Ursinus', *RGG* (3rd edn.), vi. 1204; W. Hollweg, *Neue Untersuchungen zur Geschichte und Lehre des Heidelberger Katechismus*, 2 vols. (Neukirchen, 1961 and 1968); A. Lang, *Der Heidelberger Katechismus und vier verwandte Katechismen* (1907; repr. Darmstadt, 1967) and *Der Heidelberger Katechismus zum 350jährigen Gedächtnis seiner Entstehung* (Leipzig, 1913); M. Lauterburg, 'Katechismus, Heidelberger oder Pfälzer', *RE* (3rd edn.), x. 164–73, and 'Heidelberg Catechism', *SchHE* v (1912), 204–6; D. Ludwig, 'Zacharias Ursinus', *RGG* (2nd edn.), v. 1419; E. J. Masselink, *The Heidelberg Story* (Grand Rapids, 1964); W. Metz, *Necessitas satisfactionis?* (Zurich, 1970); J. Moltmann, 'Zacharias Ursinus', *EKL* iii. 1596–7; Ursinus, 'Stammbuch', ed. Neuser; W. H. Neuser, 'Die Väter des Heidelberger Katechismus', *ThZ* 35 (1979), 177–94; J. W. Nevin, 'Zacharias Ursinus', *MercQR* 3 (1851), 490–512; T. J. Ney, 'Ursinus, Zacharias', *ADB* xxxix. 369–72, 'Ursinus, Zacharias', *RE* (3rd edn.), xx. 348–53, and 'Ursinus, Zacharias', *SchHE* xii. 111–12; G. W. Richards, *The Heidelberg Catechism* (Philadelphia, 1913); T. Schaller, 'Zacharias Ursinus', *RGG* (1st edn.), v. 1526; Sturm, *Der junge Zacharias Ursin*; K. Sudhoff, 'Heidelberger oder Pfälzer Katechismus', *RE* (1st edn.), v. 658–68, and *C. Olevianus und Z. Ursinus: Leben und ausgewählte Schriften* (Elberfeld, 1857); B. Thompson (ed.), *Essays on the Heidelberg Catechism* (Philadelphia, 1963); 'Ursinus (Beer), Zacharias' (n.a.), *CBTEL* x. 680–1; D. J. Toft, 'Zacharias Ursinus' (MA thesis, University of Wisconsin, 1962).

Various letters of Ursinus have been edited and published in scattered places: 'Zacharias Ursins Briefe an Crato von Crafftheim nach den in Breslau befindlichen Urschriften', ed. W. Becker, *TARWPV* 8 (1889), 79–121; 'Briefe des Heidelberger Theologen Zacharias Ursinus', ed. G. A. Benrath, *HdJb* 8 (1964), 93–141; 'Ein Brief an Henricus Stephanus', ed. C. Krafft, *TARWPV* 8 (1889), 121–3; 'Briefe des Heidelberger Theologen Zacharias Ursinus aus Heidelberg und Neustadt a. H.', ed. H. Rott, *NHdJb* 14 (1906), 39–172; 'Briefe des Heidelberger Theologen Zacharias Ursinus aus Wittenberg und Zürich (1560/1561)', *HdJb* 14 (1970), 85–119; 'Zacharias Ursins Briefe an Crato von Crafftheim nach den in Breslau befindlichen Urschriften', ed. W. Becker, *TARWPV* 12 (1892), 41–107 (continuation of Becker, 1889); Sturm, *Der junge Zacharias Ursin*, 11–13, 309–13.

3. The only exception is D. Visser, 'The Covenant in Zacharias Ursinus', *SCJ* 18 (1987), 531–44. Visser maintains that Ursinus was less of a federal theologian than has been thought (contrary to the argument of this book), and that Ursinus's doctrine of a prelapsarian creation covenant comes from his concern with God's law, not predestination.

4. D. *Zachariae Ursini opera theologica*, ed. Quirinus Reuterus (Heidelberg, 1612). Cf. F. W. Roth, 'Zur Geschichte der Heidelberger Buchdruckereien und Verlagsgeschäfte 1558–1618', *NAGH* 4 (1901), 226–55.

5. Ursinus, *Opera theologica*, i. 10–32. The text is also in Lang, *Der Heidelberger Katechismus und vier verwandte Katechismen*, 151–99.

6. Ursinus, *Volumen tractationum theologicarum* (Neustadt, 1584), 620–51. Cf. Lang, *Der Heidelberger Katechismus und vier verwandte Katechismen*, p. lxi; cf. also Sturm, *Der junge Zacharias Ursin*, 14–15 and 314.

7. Ursinus, *Opera theologica*, i. 34–9. The text is also in Lang, *Der Heidelberger Katechismus und vier verwandte Katechismen*, 200–18.

8. Ursinus, *Opera theologica*, i. 427–733.
9. The text of the Heidelberg Catechism was first published in Heidelberg in 1563. Various editions of Ursinus's commentaries and lectures on the Heidelberg Catechism appeared after his death. Several of his students took their lecture notes and published them; the most authoritative are the editions by David Pareus, but the various editions which he edited were altered and emended as the years passed. The following are significant; the data regarding each of the first editions are included: (*a*) *Doctrinae Christianae Compendium* (Geneva, 1584); this was the edition which was not done by Pareus, but by another of Ursinus's students; (*b*) *Explicationum Catecheticarum Z. Ursini* (n.p., 1586?; Cambridge, 1587); this is the Pareus edition, which found its way into the Ursinus *Opera* in 1612: Ursinus, *Opera theologica*, i. 46–413; cf. P. Schaff, *Creeds*, i. 529–30; this was reprinted under the title *Corpus doctrinae Christianae* beginning in 1612; (*c*) *The Svmme of Christian Religion*, trans. H. Parry, Bishop of Worcester (Oxford, 1587); (*d*) *Certaine learned and excellent discourses*, comp. D. Pareus (Oxford, 1600); (*e*) *Corpus doctrinae orthodoxae* (Heidelberg, 1612); (*f*) *Corpus doctrinae Christianae ecclesiarum* (Heidelberg, 1612); (*g*) *Het schat-boeck der Verclaringhen over de Catechismus* (Leyden, 1630); (*h*) *Corpus doctrinae ecclesiarum reformatarum* (Hanover, 1634); (*i*) *The Commentary of Dr. Zacharias Ursinus on the Heidelberg Catechism*, trans. G. W. Willard (2nd American edn.; Columbus, Ohio, 1852).
10. Neustadt, 1589.
11. Ursinus wrote two treatises on the subject of Ramism, one in 1570 and the other in 1586; they appeared as appendices to his 1586 edition of Aristotle's works on logic: *Organi Aristotelei, etc.* (Neustadt, 1586); cf. also J. I. Good, 'Peter Ramus and his Significance for the [Heidelberg] Catechism', *The Heidelberg Catechism in its Newest Light*, 102–20; W. J. Ong, *Ramus: Method, and the Decay of Dialogue* (Cambridge, Mass., 1958).
12. M. Lauterburg, 'Katechismus, Heidelberger oder Pfälzer', *RE* (3rd edn.), x. 164–73; Lang, *Der Heidelberger Katechismus und vier verwandte Katechismen*, pp. lxi–lxvii; M. Lauterburg, 'Heidelberg Catechism', *SchHE* v. 204–6; Lang, *Der Heidelberger Katechismus zum 350jährigen Gedächtnis seiner Entstehung*.
13. Karlberg, 'The Mosaic Covenant', 95.
14. Benrath, 'Die Eigenart der pfälzischen Reformation'; Goeters, 'Entstehung und Frühgeschichte'; J. I. Good, *The Heidelberg Catechism in its Newest Light*, 39–53, and *The Origin of the Reformed Church in Germany*; E. Güder, 'Katechismus, Heidelberger oder Pfälzer', *RE* (2nd edn.), vii. 605–14, and 'Heidelberg Catechism', *SchHE* (2nd and 3rd edns.), ii. 959–60; W. Henss, 'Der zeitgeschichtliche Hintergrund des Heidelberger Katechismus im Spiegel der Heidelberger Sammlungen', *Ruperto-Carola*, 15 (1963), 32–44; W. Hollweg, *Neue Untersuchungen*; Lang, *Der Heidelberger Katechismus und vier verwandte Katechismen* and *Der Heidelberger Katechismus zum 350-jährigen Gedächtnis seiner Entstehung*; M. Lauterburg, 'Katechismus, Heidelberger oder Pfälzer', *RE* (3rd edn.), x. 164–73, and 'Heidelberg Catechism', *SchHE* v (1912), 204–6; W. Neuser, 'Die Väter des Heidelberger Katechismus'; P. Schaff, 'Die ältesten Ausgaben des Heidelberger Katechismus', *ZHTh* 37 (1867), 113–24; Sturm, *Der junge Zacharias Ursin*; K. Sudhoff, 'Heidelberger oder Pfälzer Katechismus'; Thompson (ed.), *Essays on the Heidelberg Catechism*; A. J. C. Wolters, *Der Heidelberger Katechismus* (Bonn, 1864).
15. Ursinus, *Opera theologica*, i. 10–11.
16. Lauterburg, 'Katechismus, Heidelberger oder Pfälzer', *RE* (3rd edn.), x. 164–73.

17. Ibid. 166.
18. 'Itaque D. Ursinus, haud postremus inter ejus temporis Theologos, Magistratus summi jussu, Catechesin, unam quidem majorem, pro studiosis adultioribus, et scholis majoribus: alteram minorem, captui populi, et puerilis aetatis magis accommodatam, in chartam conjecit, et quibus oportuit exhibuit. Utraque probata, quod summam veritatis coelestis, sive sincerae Theologiae phrasi plana complecteretur. Ex hac etiam pleraque transcripta in publicam Catechesin, a Friderico III. Anno MDLXIII', Quirinus Reuter, in Ursinus, *Opera theologica*, i. 10–11.
19. J. Ney, 'Reuter: Quirinus', *ADB* xxviii. 328–9; cf. also G. Toepke, *Die Matrikel der Universität Heidelberg*, ii: *1554–1662* (Heidelberg, 1886), 65, no. 38 (1573).
20. Sturm, *Der junge Zacharias Ursin*, 239–41. The quotation is as follows: 'Mediam tamen viam cogitamus ingredi: capita religionis nostrae praecipua recensebimus, quae ad veram agnitionem Dei doctrina de creatione, lapsu et reparatione generis humani recte intelligendam requiruntur: neque omnes de his quaestiones persequemur, sed definitiones recitabimus, distinctiones necessarias, et si quae sunt aliae de singulis articulis sententiae ad fundamenta religionis pertinentes . . .'; 'However, we think to enter upon the middle way: we will review the principal headings of our religion, which are required for knowing correctly the true, magnificent doctrine of God from the Creation, Fall, and Redemption of the human race; nor will we pursue everything from these questions, but we will recite definitions, necessary distinctions, and whatever other sentences from single clauses which are pertinent for the foundation of religion'; *D. Zachariae Ursini Uratislaviensis theologi celeberrimi oratio habita in academia Heidelbergensi, cum auspicaretur locorum communium professionem. Calend. Septembr. Anno Domini MDLXII*, in *Opera theologica*, i. 414–23; this quotation is from p. 417.
21. '8. Quot sunt capita, quibus doctrinae Christianae summa continetur? A. Quatuor. 9. Qua sunt illa? A. Summa legis divinae seu Decalogus; Summa Evangelii seu Symbolum Apostolicum; Invocatio Dei seu precatio Dominica; et institutio ministerii Ecclesiae', Ursinus, *Catechesis, summa theologiae*, in *Volumen*, 620–1, *Opera theologica*, i. 10; Lang, *Der Heidelberger Katechismus und vier verwandte Katechismen*, 153.
22. T. Beza, *Svmma totius Christianismi, siue descriptio et distributio causarum salutis electorum et exitii reproborum ex sacris literis collecta et explicata* (Geneva, 1555); repr. in *Volumen tractationum theologicarum*, i. 170–205.
23. '10. Quid docet Lex divina? A. Quale in creatione foedus cum homine Deus iniverit; quo pacto se homo in eo servando gesserit et quid ab ipso Deus post initum cum eo novum foedus gratiae, requirat: hoc est, qualis et ad quid conditus sit homo a Deo, in quem statum sit redactus: et quo pacto vitam suam Deo reconciliatus debeat instituere', Ursinus, *Volumen*, 621, and *Opera theologica*, i. 10; Lang, *Der Heidelberger Katechismus und vier verwandte Katechismen*, 153.
24. Bierma, 'The Covenant Theology of Caspar Olevian', 87.
25. '11. Qualis est homo conditus? A. Ad imaginem Dei. 12. Qua hoc est imago? A. Vera Dei et divinae voluntatis agnitio, et secundum hanc solam vivendi, totius hominis inclinatio et studium. 13. Ad quid autem est conditus? A. Ut universa vita sua Deum in aeterna beatitudine colat', Ursinus, *Volumen*, 621, and *Opera theologica*, i. 10; Lang, *Der Heidelberger Katechismus und vier verwandte Katechismen*, 153.
26. '36. Quod est discrimen Legis et Evangelii? A. Lex continet foedus naturale, in creatione a Deo cum hominibus initum, hoc est, natura hominibus nota est; et

requirit a nobis perfectam obedientiam erga Deum, et praestantibus eam promittit vitam aeternam, non praestantibus minatur aeternas poenas. Evangelium vero continet foedus gratiae, hoc est, minime natura notum existens: ostendit nobis eius iustitiae, quam Lex requirit, impletionem in Christo, et restitutionem in nobis per Christi Spiritum; et promittit vitam aeternam gratis propter Christum, his qui in eum credunt', Ursinus, *Volumen*, 623, and *Opera theologica*, i. 14; Lang, *Der Heidelberger Katechismus und vier verwandte Katechismen*, 156.

27. At the end of his life Ursinus did develop the subject of the first Adam and second Adam more clearly, in a book of scholastic doctrinal exercises edited by his son and published in 1589: *Dispositiones declamationum in feriis natalis Domini, paschatis et pentecostes*, in *Zachariae Ursini, Uratislaviensis, scholasticarum in materiis theologicis exercitationum liber*, 81–227; the relevant section is no. 6: 'Collatio primi et secundi Adami, ex ad Rom. 5 et I Cor. 15', 120–31.

28. '18. Potestne quisquam nostrum hanc obedientiam praestare? A. Solo Christo excepto, nullus unquam hominum in hac vita eam praestare neque potuit, neque poterit', Ursinus, *Volumen*, 621, and *Opera theologica*, i. 11; Lang, *Der Heidelberger Katechismus und vier verwandte Katechismen*, 154.

29. D. Visser, 'Zacharias Ursinus, 1534–1583', in J. Raitt (ed.), *Shapers of Religious Traditions in Germany, Switzerland and Poland 1560–1600* (New Haven, 1981), 123–4. Cf. also Sturm, *Der junge Zacharias Ursin*, 109. Sturm also points out that Ursinus befriended Secundus Curio, who agreed with Castellio's unorthodox views at the time of Ursinus's visit. However, according to K. Benrath, Curio returned to orthodoxy: 'In his work *De amplitudine Dei* he deviated from rigid Calvinism in the doctrine of predestination, but in 1559 he asserted his orthodoxy in a public confession of faith'; Benrath, 'Celio, Secundus Curio (1503–1569)', in *NSHE* iii. 326. Visser comments in his recent biography of Ursinus: 'Back in Basel at the end of the month, he met Coelius Secundus Curio, Martin Cellarius, and Sebastian Chastellion. No theological significance can be attached to these brief encounters, which is fortunate, for it would challenge the imagination to determine the influence academicians with such divergent views may have had on Ursinus. Chastellion, according to Sturm, was befriended by Curio, but as Languet had brought Melanchthon in contact with Chastellion, who was a great advocate of tolerance, because a human being could scarcely know the truth in theological matters, it may have been Languet who made Ursinus go to see him. One would like to know what Ursinus talked about with Chastellion, who had become an open opponent of Geneva over Calvin's treatment of Michael Servetus, the anti-Trinitarian. Later, in 1571, Ursinus was to consign the opinion of the Heidelberg faculty against another anti-Trinitarian, who also was to be executed', Visser, *Zacharias Ursinus*, 68–9.

30. Cf. H. Engelland, 'Introduction', in Philip Melanchthon, *Loci Communes*, i–xli.

31. Ursinus, 'Stammbuch', (ed. Neuser).

32. Cf. Sturm, *Der junge Zacharias Ursin*.

33. Cf. W. H. Neuser, 'Die Erwählungslehre im Heidelberger Katechismus', *ZKG* 75 (1964), 309–26.

34. '47. Quid vocas Providentiam Dei? A. Aeternum, immutabile, sapientissimum et optimum Dei consilium iuxta quod omnia eveniunt, et ad gloriam Creatoris diriguntur', Ursinus, *Volumen*, 624, and *Opera theologica*, i. 15; Lang, *Der Heidelberger Katechismus und vier verwandte Katechismen*, 52. In the Lang edition the question numbers are not 47–9 but 52–4.

35. '48. An malos etiam a Deo regi dicendum est? A. Sua quidem potentia et consilio sic per eos quae ipse vult, efficit ut ne moveri quidem sine ipsius voluntate possint sed gratia et Spiritu suo ipsos neque sanctificat neque ducit. 49. An non igitur causa est Deus peccatorum, qua illi admittunt? A. Nequaquam. Deus enim etiam per pessimos quosque nihil nisi optimum et iustissimum instituere potest atque efficere. Quod autem peccant ipsi, dum Deus per illos agit bene causa non est bona Dei voluntas et iustum iudicium sed quae haeret in ipsis et ab ipsis ultro accersita est pravitas', ibid.

36. Cf. Pareus's account of Ursinus's discussion of providence in the *Explicatio*, Ursinus, *Opera theologica*, i. 136–7. Ursinus does discuss the problem of causation in one of his later theological treatises: *D. Zachariae Ursini loci theologici traditi in academia Heidelbergensi* (1568), in *Opera theologica*, i. 427–733; cf. 'De providentia Dei', i. 570–605.

37. R. A. Muller points out three levels in the study of theology during the sixteenth century. The first is catechetical, in which only the basic rudiments are provided. The second level is that in which difficult questions are resolved and questions of methodology, organization, and scope are discussed. Levels one and two, in turn, provide the framework and presuppositions for the advanced exegetical study of Scripture. Muller, 'Predestination and Christology', 252–3.

38. J. Moltmann, 'Zur Bedeutung des Petrus Ramus für Philosophie und Theologie im Calvinismus', *ZKG* 68 (1957), 295–318.

39. Bierma, 'The Covenant Theology of Caspar Olevian', 229–39.

40. 'Quaestio XVIII. Quod sit foedus Dei. Foedus in genere est mutua pactio duarum partium, qua altera alteri se certis conditionibus obligat ad aliquid faciendum, dandum vel accipiendum, adhibitis signis et symbolis externis ad solennem testificationem, confirmationis causa, ut promissio sit inviolabilis. Hinc facile colligitur definitio foederis Dei. Est enim mutua pactio inter Deum et homines . . .', Ursinus, *Explicatio*, in *Opera theologica*, i. 98; cf. Toft, 'Zacharias Ursinus', 61–85 for a discussion of Ursinus's conception of the covenant of grace. Visser, 'The Covenant in Zacharias Ursinus'.

41. For some comments on why Ursinus did not pursue the prelapsarian covenant of nature idea in his later work, cf. Bierma, 'The Covenant Theology of Caspar Olevian', 79–81.

4

The Early Federal Theologians

And these wordes which I commande thee this day, shalbe in thine heart. And thou shalt rehearse them continually vnto thy children, and shalt talke of them when thou tariest in thine house, and as thou walkest by the way, and when thou lyest downe, and when thou risest vp: . . .

Deuteronomy 6: 6–7 (Geneva Bible, 1560)

THE origins and development of the early federal theology, with its key identifying feature of a prelapsarian covenant, can be traced to a certain group of theologians of the late sixteenth century. Zacharias Ursinus was the first Reformed theologian to propose this idea, and it is logical to examine the view of some of his followers and colleagues to see whether they follow suit. All of these figures read each other's works and interacted intellectually with each other, often in formal theological disputations. After examining the theological works of Ursinus's colleagues, we will be able to affirm that the federal theology has its origins in the Palatinate of the Holy Roman Empire between 1560 and 1590.

The purpose of this chapter is threefold: first, to give a brief overview of the political and religious history of the Palatinate; second, to identify specifically the first generation of federal theologians emanating from Heidelberg; third, to give a brief survey of the history of the schools to which these theologians belonged: the Faculty of Theology of the University of Heidelberg, the Casimirianum in Neustadt an der Hardt, and the Herborn Academy.

The period 1560–90 is probably the only stage in the history of the federal theology in which one can trace its historical development with any precision: after 1590 the covenant idea blossoms all over Europe, and it is impossible to keep track of the manifold uses and conceptions of the covenant motif. However, in this situation we have an isolated, singular idea being proposed by a limited group of people in a very definite place, and therefore we can see almost year by year the development of the seminal idea of a prelapsarian covenant.

Political History of the Palatinate[1]

The Palatinate is a territory surrounding the city of Heidelberg in the Rhine Valley. In the sixteenth century it was ruled by one of the seven electors of the Holy Roman Empire, and at precisely the time that the federal theology was on the rise the Palatinate was at the height of its political and cultural prestige.

Claus-Peter Clasen has provided a good summary of the religious and political importance of the Palatinate in late sixteenth- and early seventeenth-century European history.[2] We will not be concerned with the place of the Palatinate in the broader context of European history,[3] nor will we concern ourselves greatly with the political and religious history of the Palatinate itself.[4] Rather, it is sufficient that we note certain chief characteristics of the Palatinate between 1560 and 1590.

Clasen notes that the history of the Palatinate must be set within two key trends of the period: (1) the fall of Spain and the rise of France as the leading power of Europe; and (2) the attempt of the Counter-Reformation to extirpate Protestantism.[5] While these two trends led to devastating wars in the Netherlands and in France, the Holy Roman Empire had a period of peace which lasted almost seventy years, from 1555 until the start of the Thirty Years War in 1618. It was an uneasy peace, but one which was desired by the Lutheran provinces of the Empire. There was one exception to this trend of pacifism amongst the leaders of the Empire: the Prince Elector of the Palatinate, who gathered around him a group of Reformed Protestants which became the central core of militant Protestantism in the Empire.[6]

Clasen traces this militaristic stance to the Calvinistic and Reformed theology of the rulers of the Palatinate, and analyses the 'causal relation' on three levels: the religious level, the political level, and the sociological level. On the religious level Clasen points to the inherent spirit of Calvinism, which saw any treaty with Rome as a compromise with Satan and the Antichrist. On the political level, Clasen feels that the Palatinate and its rulers felt more and more insecure in the face of the Counter-Reformation. They distrusted the Lutherans, and felt that the Treaty of Augsburg would not protect them in the coming years. On the sociological level Clasen examines the political rulers of the Palatinate between 1559 and 1576 and points out that there was a remarkable overlap of Church and State in the Palatinate.[7]

Friedrich III, the Pious (1515–76), ruled as Elector Palatine from 1559 to his death in 1576.[8] He was a very pious man who brought theological conceptions and viewpoints into all of his political decisions. In the political life of the Palatinate the nobility were displaced by theologians during this period. Only two politicians, Doctor Ehem and Licentiate Zuleger, played a leading role as advisers to Friedrich III. The theologians of the Collegium Sapientiae and the University of Heidelberg gave much more advice to Friedrich.[9]

Clasen points out three very interesting factors about this group of theologically trained advisers. (1) They were united by theological commitment and common experience. (2) None were born in the Palatinate, but they looked at the Palatinate as an instrument of the international expansion of Calvinism. (3) Several were very young when they held important positions in the Palatinate.[10] From 1559 until 1576 these theologians were the leading figures in the Palatinate; some of these same people were teaching at various intervals in the Collegium Sapientiae and in the Faculty of Theology of the University of Heidelberg.

In 1576, however, Friedrich III died, and his eldest son, Johann Ludwig VI (1539–83), took over as Prince Elector.[11] Ludwig was a Lutheran, and within weeks all Calvinistic theologians were exiled. For the next seven years, 1576–83, the Palatinate was officially a Lutheran state. Many of the leaders who advised Friedrich III moved to Neustadt an der Hardt, which was controlled by Ludwig's brother, Johann Casimir (1564–92).[12] Casimir formed his own Reformed theological school, the Casimirianum, which was faithful to the Calvinistic stance of his father.

In 1583, Johann Casimir's brother, Ludwig VI, died. Johann Casimir immediately rushed back to Heidelberg and seized control in the name of his young nephew, Friedrich IV (1574–1610), the future Prince Elector and the son of Ludwig VI.[13] Friedrich IV was brought up by Casimir as a Calvinist, and now the Lutheran theologians and politicians went into exile.

In 1592 Casimir died, and the policy of the Palatinate was conducted by Johann von Nassau (1536–1606)[14] and Ludwig von Wittgenstein (1532–1605), leaders of the Calvinistic group called the Counts of the Wetterau. Johann von Nassau is important to us because prior to this he had been instrumental in founding another Calvinistic academy at Herborn in Nassau in 1584, which employed a few of the theologians who previously had taught or been students at the Collegium Sapientiae, the University of Heidelberg, and the Casimirianum in Neustadt an der Hardt.

It was within this context that the early federal theologians developed their theological ideas. We will now give consideration to who these figures were by giving brief biographies of their lives and noting the works that deal with the federal theology and the idea of covenant.[15]

The Earliest Federal Theologians

I. Thomas Cartwright (1535–1603)[16] is much better known as one of the earliest English Puritans than as one of the first federal theologians. Born in Hertfordshire, England, he graduated from Cambridge University and was later elected Lady Margaret Professor of Divinity there. In 1569 he had a controversy with Dr Whitgift over clerical vestments, and after being deprived of his professorship went to Geneva, where he established a friendship with Theodore Beza. He returned to England in 1572, but left again in 1573. It was between 1573 and 1574 that Cartwright was associated with the University of Heidelberg, and thus would have had close contact with Zacharias Ursinus and Caspar Olevianus.[17] In 1574 he went to Antwerp, but in the same year was elected pastor of the English-speaking congregation in Middelburg. After remaining with that congregation from 1574 to 1576 he became pastor of the English-speaking congregation in Antwerp, beginning in 1576.

Those writings of his which teach the federal theology were published posthumously, beginning in 1604, but we know that in 1585 he published a letter as a preface to Dudley Fenner's *Sacra theologia*—a most important work in the history of the federal theology.[18] The composition date of these treatises cannot be fixed with any certainty. Of course, since they were published in 1604 and after, they did not have the impact that they might have had in 1580–90. But the fact that Cartwright was a colleague of Fenner and also of Ursinus, and also a federal theologian, gives us strong reason to give some consideration to his works, which we know were written before 1603, the date of his death. The pertinent works of Cartwright are as follows:

1. *A Methodicall Short Catechisme* (1604).

2. *Christian Religion: svbstantially, methodicallie, plainlie and profitablie Treatised* (1611).[19]

II. Dudley Fenner (1558?–1587).[20] Like Cartwright a graduate of Cambridge, Fenner was a follower of Cartwright and came to Antwerp to be with him in 1575, just after Cartwright had finished his visit to Heidelberg and his association with Ursinus and Olevianus. It is very possible that Cartwright and Fenner discussed the new ideas of Ursinus while in Antwerp. At any rate, his first work, on the first four commandments of the Decalogue (*A brief Treatise upon the first Table of the Lawe*),[21] was written 'when the author was under 20', which would place it around 1576–8. It does not espouse the federal schema. However, by 1585 Fenner had adopted Ramistic methodology and was the first to articulate the prelapsarian covenant motif utilizing the Ramistic system—a very important step in the history of the federal theology.[22] Perhaps both Fenner and Cartwright adopted the prelapsarian covenant idea between 1580 and 1585, with Fenner publishing in 1585 and Cartwright not being published until 1604, after his death. The relevant works of Fenner are as follows:

1. *The Artes of Logike and Retorike, plainly set foorth in the English toongue* (1584)

2. *Sacra theologia sive veritas quae est secundum pietatem ad unicae et verae methodi leges descripta* (1585 and 1589)

3. *The Sacred Doctrine of Divinitie* (1589)[23]

III. Franciscus Junius (François du Jon) (1545–1602)[24] was born in Bourges and first studied law before he studied theology at Geneva. Like Ursinus, Junius was a professor at the University of Heidelberg and one of the influential Calvinists who were not from the Palatinate but who played an important role in Palatinate political life. From 1573 to 1577 he was a translator of the Old Testament with Immanuel Tremellius (1510–80). From 1577 to about 1578 he was a professor at the Casimirianum in Neustadt an der Hardt. In 1584 he was appointed a professor at the University of Heidelberg and in 1592 he became a professor at the University of Leiden, where he died in 1602. Although he knew Ursinus at Heidelberg and at Neustadt an der Hardt, Junius does not speak of a prelapsarian covenant until after 1590. However, Junius is

important for two reasons: before 1590 he made several orations on
the topic of covenant, and an important feature of his theology was
High Calvinism; Junius confronted the problem of Adam's Fall and
the sovereignty of God head-on.[25]

IV. Caspar Olevianus (1536–87)[26] was a colleague of Ursinus in
Heidelberg and collaborated with him on the Heidelberg Catechism
which appeared in 1563. In 1560 he was appointed Director of the
Collegium Sapientiae and one year later was appointed Professor of
Dogmatics at the Faculty of Theology of the University of
Heidelberg. Some time later he became pastor of the principal
church in Heidelberg. Instead of going to the Casimirianum in 1577
Olevianus became a tutor at Berleburg, but from 1584 until his
death in 1587 he was a pastor at Herborn and a teacher in the
Herborn *Hochschule*, or Herborn Academy.

Lyle Dean Bierma[27] attempts to maintain that Olevianus taught a
prelapsarian covenant beginning in 1578, but there is no evidence of
such teaching until 1585, in one of his last works, which actually
centres around the covenant of grace:

1. *De substantia foederis gratuiti*[28]

Bierma does point out, however, that it was Olevianus who was the
first to emphasize the believer's *personal* acceptance of the covenant
of grace, which follows the general pattern of the very personal
nature of the Heidelberg Catechism.[29]

V. Zacharias Ursinus (1534–83).[30]

Table 1 illustrates the various links which tied these men together
by listing their institutional positions. As far as we can tell, only
these men, less Zanchius, Tossanus, and Junius, taught the idea of a
prelapsarian covenant between 1560 and 1590. Junius taught the
prelapsarian covenant after 1590. All other Reformed theologians
concerned themselves with the postlapsarian covenant of grace.

We have included Girolamo Zanchius in the table although he
represents a different stream of Reformed theology from that
usually found in Heidelberg; furthermore, Zanchius gives no
evidence of having adopted federal theological ideas.[31] According to
Otto Grundler,[32] between 1570 and 1580 Zanchius adopted an
extreme scholastic stance in his dogmatic theology, even going so
far as to use Aristotelian presuppositions and methodology to
analyse the very essence of God and his eternal decrees—something

TABLE 1. *The Sixteenth-Century Palatinate Theologians*

University of Heidelberg	Casimirianum at Neustadt an der Hardt	Herborn Academy
1561–77*		
Z. Ursinus		
C. Olevianus		
F. Junius		
D. Tossanus		
G. Zanchius		
T. Cartwright	1577–84*	
	Z. Ursinus	
1583–1602*	F. Junius	
F. Junius	1577–78? 1582–4	1583–7
1584–92		C. Olevianus
D. Tossanus	D. Tossanus	
1583–1602	G. Zanchius	

* Some theologians taught on a sporadic basis at each of these schools.

which even Beza did not do. Whereas Calvin would have maintained that 'the secret things belong to the Lord our God', Zanchius, in the new scholastic spirit of High Calvinism, was willing to begin to explore those mysteries. In so doing he was running against the stream of thinking which he found at Heidelberg. While Zanchius seemed to be following in the High Calvinist tradition of Geneva, the other theologians at Heidelberg wished to remain Reformed but at the same time give a plausible explanation for the decrees of God—decrees which included the Fall of Adam but which did not make God the author of sin—and also to make the doctrines of High Calvinism more personal and applicable, as evidenced by the first question of the Heidelberg Catechism of 1563.

We have included Daniel Tossanus (1541–1602) in the table because he also played a role in Palatinate Church life. Tossanus[33] was chaplain to Elector Friedrich III from 1573 to 1577. In 1577 he also went to Neustadt an der Hardt and became a professor at the Casimirianum and Inspector of the Churches for Casimir. From 1583 to 1602 he was a professor of theology at the University of

Heidelberg. However, the works of Tossanus are extremely rare, and F. W. Cuno does not include Tossanus in the general stream of the federal theology.[34] We can therefore safely conclude that his work has no bearing on our present study.

In this particular case we see that the educational institution is an effective disseminator of an idea and a means by which we can establish a historical context for its development. The University of Geneva (founded 1559) and the University of Heidelberg (founded 1386; became Reformed 1559–61; developed offshoots at Neustadt an der Hardt and Herborn in Nassau) were the only established schools of theology for Calvinists during much of the second half of the sixteenth century. Calvinists were in such minorities in other parts of Europe that they could not hope to dominate most established universities. The newer universities were founded at the latter end of the sixteenth century and needed time to become established. The University of Leiden was founded in 1574, while the University of Edinburgh was not founded until 1583. The University of Franeker was founded in 1585, while the Universities of Groningen, Utrecht, Amsterdam, and Harderwijk were not established until the seventeenth century. Heidelberg and Geneva were therefore the two great centres of Calvinist intellectual life for decades. Both were universities in which foreign students played an important role. While Geneva symbolized High Calvinist orthodoxy and was dominated by the figure of Beza for over forty years, Heidelberg, while still wishing to remain orthodox, tended to be less stringent and more 'pietistic' in its teaching of Reformed dogmatics and distinctive principles. The theologians of both schools were friendly with each other, as evidenced by Beza's introductions to several of Olevianus's works,[35] but in various ways the teaching at Heidelberg and in the Palatinate quietly diverged from the emphases found at Geneva. One divergence was Ursinus's proposal, without a lot of fanfare, of the idea of a prelapsarian covenant with Adam, which came after a decade of strife over whether Adam's crucial original sin was included in God's sovereign plan or not. It is important therefore to consider briefly the history of the three schools from which the federal theological system emanated: the Faculty of Theology of the University of Heidelberg, the Casimirianum at Neustadt an der Hardt, and the Herborn Academy.[36]

The University of Heidelberg[37]

The University of Heidelberg became a Reformed school of theology between 1559 and 1561. The school was under control of the State, and thus when Elector Otto Heinrich died in 1559 faculty appointments came under the control of the succeeding Elector, Friedrich III, the Pious. Friedrich wished to make the university a school which was distinctly Calvinistic in outlook, and so in the succeeding years he managed to draw men such as Ursinus, Olevianus, Zanchius, Tremellius, Tossanus, and Junius to the faculty.

If we run over its list of matriculants,[38] some interesting names emerge, names which will be influential in the Protestant world of the late sixteenth and early seventeenth centuries. Among them are Johannes Piscator (1546–1625), later to be a professor at the Herborn Academy; Samuel Huber (c.1547–1624) and Johannes Oldenbarnevelt (1547–1619), both of whom were to rebel against the system of High Calvinism; Thomas Erastus (1524–83), appointed Professor of Medicine in Heidelberg in 1558 and the theologian who felt that the State should dominate the Church; and David Pareus (1548–1622), who was to promulgate the Heidelberg Catechism widely and who took Ursinus as his mentor. Thus some of the international influence which the University of Heidelberg had via its graduates becomes apparent.

During the period that Ursinus was professor, the school did not concern itself at all with extensive discussion of covenant doctrine. Rather, its main discussions centred upon the sacramentarian controversy, the problem of anti-Trinitarianism and Arianism, the relation between Church and State, and the problem of Ramistic philosophy and methodology. The professors taught the Old Testament and New Testament, Greek, Hebrew, and the theological *loci*—themes or aphorisms of theological matter which were argued over and rearranged in various theological systems using Aristotelian methodology and presuppositions. These debates were known as 'disputations'.[39]

In 1576, Friedrich III died. His son, Johann Ludwig VI, was a convinced Lutheran, and sought immediately to make the university a Lutheran school. All the Reformed teachers and pastors were dismissed from their posts immediately; the situation reflected the policy of *cuius regio, eius religio*. Lutheran professors then took over the vacated positions.

The Casimirianum of Neustadt an der Hardt

However, Johann Ludwig's brother, Johann Casimir, kept to the Reformed faith of his father and invited the students and faculty of the Collegium Sapientiae at Heidelberg and the Reformed members and students of the Faculty of Theology of the University of Heidelberg to join him in founding a new school, the Casimirianum, to be located in Neustadt an der Hardt, one of the small cities of the Palatinate which Casimir controlled.[40]

However, the faculty was greatly reduced—only Ursinus, Junius, Zanchius, and Tossanus went to the Casimirianum to teach, and Junius left for a while. Furthermore, the school no longer had the status of a university and did not have the amenities that Heidelberg had: library, accommodation, and so forth. Both students and faculty viewed the situation as temporary. The building where the Casimirianum was located still stands today in Neustadt an der Hardt.

In 1583 Johann Ludwig VI died, and Johann Casimir took over Ludwig's position in the name of Ludwig's son, Friedrich IV, who was Casimir's nephew. Again, the tables were turned. All Lutheran professors and pastors had to leave, and Reformed teachers replaced them. However, the original Heidelberg group was never to return to prominence: Ursinus died at Neustadt an der Hardt, Olevianus went to Herborn, Zanchius remained at Neustadt an der Hardt; only Junius and Tossanus returned to Heidelberg, and then Junius departed for Leiden eight years later.

The Herborn Academy

However, in 1583, another school was founded by the House of Orange which would continue some of the teaching that had come out of Heidelberg. The Herborn Academy[41] was sponsored by the House of Nassau, specifically by Count Johann von Nassau, or Johann der Ältere. The school taught theology and jurisprudence, among other subjects. Its first theology professors were Olevianus and Johannes Piscator, who earlier had been a student at Heidelberg. Its first Professor of Jurisprudence was Johannes Althusius (c.1557–1638).[42]

While the school was strongly Reformed in doctrine, it adopted more modern methodological techniques, one of which was Ramistic philosophy, which was to have an important influence in the development of the federal theology. It was while teaching at this school that Olevianus published his work *De substantia foederis gratuiti inter Deum et electos* (1585), which is one of the first treatises to mention a prelapsarian covenant with Adam after the publication of Ursinus's *Major Catechism* in 1584. After the death of Johann Casimir in 1592, Johann der Ältere took over the direction of Palatinate policy in collaboration with Ludwig von Wittgenstein. Thus, during the decade before the seventeenth century began, the strongly Calvinistic Johann der Ältere was controlling three schools: the University of Heidelberg, the Casimirianum of Neustadt an der Hardt, and the Herborn Academy. The federal theology emerged out of these three schools, from whence it spread all over Europe. We are now able to consider the second stage in the development of the early federal theology.

Notes

1. For broader views of the history of late sixteenth-century Europe see: J. H. Elliot, *Europe Divided 1559–1598* (New York, 1968); S. Ozment, *The Reformation in the Cities* (New Haven, 1975); J. Bryce, *The Holy Roman Empire* (London, 1894); J. T. McNeill, 'Calvinism in Germany and Eastern Europe', in *History and Character of Calvinism* (New York, 1954), 268–89; J. Janssen, *Geschichte des deutschen Volkes seit dem Ausgang des Mittelalters*, iv and v (Freiburg im Bresgau, 1891–3); English translation: *History of the German People at the Close of the Middle Ages*, trans. A. M. Christie, vii–ix (London, 1905–6); Good, *Origin of the Reformed Church in Germany*.
2. Clasen, *The Palatinate in European History*.
3. See Clasen, *The Palatinate*; McNeill, 'Calvinism in Germany and Eastern Europe'; V. Press, *Calvinismus und Territorialstaat* (Stuttgart, 1970); H. Heppe, *Geschichte des deutschen Protestantismus in den Jahren 1555–1581* (Marburg, 1852–9).
4. For the religious and political history of the Palatinate see the following: H. Altingius, 'Historia Ecclesiae Palatinae' in *Monumenta pietatis*, ed. L. C. Mieg (Frankfurt, 1702), i. 129–250; *AGH* (Heidelberg, 1868–70); this was later continued as *NAGH* (Heidelberg, 1890–); Benrath, 'Die Eigenart der

pfälzischen Reformation'; R. Benz, *Heidelberg: Schicksal und Geist* (Constance, 1961); E. D. Bristley, 'Bibliographica Catechismus Heidelbergensis' (1983; manuscript on file, Library of Westminster Theological Seminary, Philadelphia, Pa.); Cameron (ed.), *Letters*; Clasen, *The Palatinate*; R. J. W. Evans, *The Wechel Presses* (Oxford, 1975); M. Goebal, *Geschichte des christlichen Lebens in der rheinischen-westphälischen Kirche*, i (Coblenz, 1849), 352–94; Good, *Origin*; J. B. Götz, *Die erste Einführung des Kalvinismus in der Oberpfalz*, RGST 60 (1933), and *Die religiösen Wirren in der Oberpfalz von 1576 bis 1620*, RGST 66 (1937); J. T. Gümbel, *Die Geschichte der protestantischen Kirche der Pfalz* (Kaiserslautern, 1885); L. Häusser, *Geschichte der rheinischen Pfalz* (1845; repr. Pirmasens, 1970); Heppe, *Geschichte des deutschen Protestantismus* (Marburg, 1852–9); J. Janssen, *Geschichte des deutschen Volkes*, iv. 184–202 and v. 488–94; English translation: vii. 313–27, viii. 394–5, and ix. 93–104; T. Karst, *Das kürpfalzische Oberamt Neustadt an der Haardt* (Speyer, 1960) and 'Pfalzgraf Johann Casimir und die Neustadter', *MHVPf* 76 (1978), 129–46; M. Kuhn, *Pfalzgraf Johann Casimir von Pfalz-Lautern* (Otterbach-Kaiserslautern, 1961); Masselink, *The Heidelberg Story; MHVPf* (Speyer, 1876–); Muller, 'Predestination and Christology', 243–315; Press, *Calvinismus und Territorialstaat*, 221–368; K. Schottenloher, *Pfalzgraf Ottheinrich und das Buch*, RGST 50/51 (1927); J. D. Seisen, *Geschichte der Reformation zu Heidelberg von ihren ersten Anfangen bis zur Abfassung des Heidelberger Katechismus* (Heidelberg, 1846); L. Stamer, *Das Zeitalter der Reform (1556–1685)*, iii. 1 of *Kirchengeschichte der Pfalz* (Speyer, 1955); B. G. Struve, *Ausführlicher bericht von der pfaltzischen kirchenhistorie* (Frankfurt, 1721), 68–526; Sudhoff, *Olevianus und Ursinus*; B. Thompson, 'The Palatinate Church Order', *ChH* 23 (1954), 340–57; Thompson (ed.), *Essays*, 8–82; D. J. Toft, 'Zacharias Ursinus', and 'Shadows of Kings: The Political Thought of David Pareus, 1548–1622' (Diss. University of Wisconsin, 1970), 30–5; Visser, *Zacharias Ursinus*; Visser (ed.), *Controversy and Conciliation*.

   For discussions of the religious and political history of Nassau, the province where Herborn is located, see: R. Glawischnig, *Niederlande, Kalvinismus und Reichsgrafenstand 1559–1584* (Marburg, 1973); *Nassauische Annalen: Jahrbuch des Vereins für Nassauische Altertumskunde und Geschichtsforschung* (Wiesbaden, 1827–).

5. Clasen, *The Palatinate*, 1.

6. 'Wherever we look, to German or Western European politics, the Palatinate distinguished itself by its militant and aggressive, anti-Catholic policy. In almost all cases the majority of the German Protestants strongly condemned the Palatine radicalism. This contrast between the Palatinate and the other German princes expresses itself even in the stereotyped formulas which constantly recur in the diplomatic correspondence. While the Palatines continually speak of the "advancement de la gloire de dieu et établissement de son église", the other German Protestants never cease to emphasize the "beständige erhaltung und vortpflanzung des geliebten friedens, ruhe und einigheit in enserem geliebten Vatterlande der teutschen nation" ', ibid. 5.

7. Ibid. 6–19.

8. See O. Chadwick, 'The Making of the Reforming Prince', in R. B. Knox (ed.), *Reformation, Conformity and Dissent* (London, 1977), 44–69; P. Fuchs, 'Friedrich III: der Fromme', *NDB* v. 530–2; Good, *Origin*; A. Kluckhohn, 'Friedrich III', *ADB* vii. 606–12, and *Friedrich der Fromme, Kurfürst von der Pfalz, der Schützer der reformirten Kirche 1559–1576* (Nördlingen, 1879); J. F. A. Gillet, 'Friedrich III, Kurfürst von der Pfalz, und der Reichstag zu Augsburg im J. 1566', *HZ* 19 (1868), 38–102; Agnew, 'Friedrick III, Elector

Palatine', in *The Theology of Consolation*, 266–71; W. J. Hinke, 'The Origin of the Heidelberg Catechism', *Reformed Church Review*, 4th ser., 17 (1913), 156–66.

    Cf. also Benrath, 'Die Eigenart der pfälzischen Reformation'; L. Coenen (ed.), *Handbuch zum Heidelberger Katechismus* (Neukirchen, 1963); Good, *The Heidelberg Catechism in its Newest Light*, 133–200; Hollweg, *Neue Untersuchungen*; Lang, *Der Heidelberger Katechismus zum 350jährigen Gedächtnis*; M. Lauterburg, 'Katechismus, Heidelberger oder Pfälzer', *RE* (3rd edn.), x. 164–73, and 'Heidelberg Catechism', *NSHE* v. 204–6; Masselink, *The Heidelberg Story*; Neuser, 'Die Väter des Heidelberger Katechismus'; Richards, *The Heidelberg Catechism*; Sudhoff, *Olevianus und Ursinus*; Thompson (ed.), *Essays on the Heidelberg Catechism*.

 9. 'Ehem and Zuleger were Frederick's closest counsellors. He decided practically all important questions of policy with these two men. But behind them was a shadowy group of Calvinist ministers who were not only used on diplomatic missions, but also exerted a considerable influence on the actual policy making. Among them we find the French pasteurs Daniel Toussaint, Pierre Boquin, Francois du Jon, the Dutchman Pierre de Berghen alias Dathenus, the Italians Hierinymo Zanchi and Immanuelo Tremellius and the German Olevian. All of them were in close contact with Calvin and Beze', Clasen, *The Palatinate* , 15.

10. '1. They were united not only by faith but by common experience. Almost all of them had been educated as Catholics and had been converted to Calvinism as adults. Furthermore they had been persecuted and had been forced to flee abroad. 2. Practically all of them were closely connected with France or the Netherlands. None of them was born in the Palatinate, few in Germany. Many had studied in Geneva or Bourges. Before coming to the Palatinate they had lived in Italy, Switzerland, the Netherlands, France and England. Their correspondence covered the whole of western Europe and centered in Geneva. These foreigners were bound neither by material interest nor by any patriotic sentiment to the Empire or even to the Palatinate. Their attention was fixed not on the tiny Palatinate church but on European Protestantism. To them the Palatinate was only an instrument to defend and expand Calvinism. Their greatest enemy was Spain, the strongest power of the Counter-reformation. Here the anti-Catholic and the anti-Hapsburg course of Palatine policy met. 3. Several of these theologian-politicians occupied the highest positions in the Palatinate at a surprisingly young age', ibid. 15–16.

11. F. von Bezold, 'Ludwig, Pfalzgraf bei Rhein', *ADB* xix. 577–80; Good, *Origin*, 232–52.

12. See G. Heyl, 'Johann Casimir', *NDB* x. 531–2; F. von Bezold, 'Johann Casimir, Pfalzgraf bei Rhein', *ADB* xiv. 307–14; Kuhn, *Pfalzgraf Johann Casimir*; Johann Casimir, *Briefe des Pfalzgrafen Johann Casimir*, ed. F. von Bezold (Munich, 1882–1903); Good, *Origin*; Karst, 'Pfalzgraf Johann Casimir'; Visser (ed.), *Controversy and Conciliation*.

13. M. Ritter, 'Friedrich IV', *ADB* vii. 612–21; P. Fuchs, 'Friedrich IV. der Aufrichtige', *NDB* v. 532–5; Good, *Origin*, 315–22.

14. R. Glawischnig, 'Johann VI, Graf von Nassau-Katzenelnbogen', *NDB* x. 500–1; Good, *Origin*, 256–9 and 262–6; P. L. Müller, 'Johann VI, Graf von Nassau-Dillenburg', *ADB* xiv. 254–8; F. W. Cuno, *Johann der Aeltere von Nassau-Dillenburg, ein fürstlicher Reformator* (Halle, 1869); Glawischnig, *Niederlande, Kalvinismus und Reichsgrafenstand*; K. Wolf, 'Aus dem Briefwechsel Christoph Pezels mit Graf Johann dem Älteren von Nassau-Dillenburg', *ARG* 34 (1937), 177–234.

15. Helpful biographies of various historical figures for this period can be found in the following: M. Adam, *DLV* (Frankfurt, 1706); *AGL*; D. Agnew, *The Theology of Consolation*; J. Raitt (ed.), *Shapers of Religious Traditions in Germany, Switzerland and Poland 1560–1600* (New Haven, 1981).

16. *AGL* i. 1709; K. Bauer, 'Cartwright, Thomas', *RGG* (2nd edn.), i. 1466; C. Borgeaud, 'Cartwright and Melville at the University of Geneva, 1569–1574', *AHR* 5 (1899), 284–90; B. Brook, *Memoir of the Life and Writings of Thomas Cartwright* (London, 1845); R. Buddensieg, 'Cartwright, Thomas', *RE* (3rd edn.), iii. 733–5; 'Cartwright, Thomas' (n.a.), *CBTEL* ii. 134–5; 'Cartwright, Thomas' (n.a.), *EKL* i. 669–70; *Cartwright and his Contemporaries* (n.a.) (London, 1848); P. Collinson, 'The Authorship of *A Brieff Discours off the Troubles begonne at Franckford*', *JEH* 9 (1958), 188–208; F. L. Colvile, *The Worthies of Warwickshire who Lived between 1500 and 1800* (London, 1870), 92–100, 878; C. H. Cooper, 'Thomas Cartwright', *Athenae Cantab.* ii. 360–6; B. Hanbury, *The Ecclesiastical Polity of R. Hooker Accompanied by a Life of T. Cartwright* (London, 1830), i, pp. cxxxiv-ccvi; O. Herz, 'Cartwright, Thomas', *RGG* (1st edn.), i. 1589; A. F. Johnson, 'Books Printed at Heidelberg for Thomas Cartwright', *The Library*, 5th ser., 2 (1947–8), 284–6; H. Jones, *Thomas Cartwright 1535–1603* (London, 1970); M. M. Knappen, *Tudor Puritanism* (Chicago, 1939); D. Little, *Religion, Order and Law* (New York, 1969), 84–104; J. B. Mullinger, 'Cartwright, Thomas (1535–1603)', *DNB* ix. 226–30; A. F. S. Pearson, *Thomas Cartwright and Elizabethan Puritanism* (Cambridge, 1925); *Cartwrightiana*, ed. A. Peel and L. H. Carlson (London, 1951); M. Schmidt, 'Cartwright, Thomas', *RGG* (3rd edn.), i. 1624; Sprunger, *Dutch Puritanism*; J. Strype, *Annals and Life of Whitgift* (Oxford, 1822); J. Venn and J. A. Venn, 'Cartwright, Thomas', *Alumni Cantabrigienses*, i. 303; H. F. Wijnman, 'Cartwright, (Thomas)', *NNBW* ix (1933), 130–1.

17. Toepke (ed.), *Matrikel der Universität Heidelberg*, ii. 69, no. 8 (1574), where the name 'Thomas Cartirrightus' is registered; cf. also Pearson, *Thomas Cartwright and Elizabethan Puritanism*, 129–66.

18. Thomas Cartwright, 'Epistle in Latin to Dudley Fenner', dated 3 Sept. 1583, and prefixed to Fenner's *Sacra theologia sive veritas* (London and Geneva, 1585); cf. Knappen, *Tudor Puritanism*, 373–4.

19. T. Cartwright, *A Methodicall Short Catechisme*, printed in numerous editions of John Dod and Robert Cleaver, *A Plaine and Familiar Exposition of the Ten Commandments* (London, 1604); I am quoting from the 18th edition (London, 1630). Cf. also *A Shorte Catechism* in *Cartwrightiana*, 159–73, which is not the same catechism; *Christian Religion: svbstantially, methodicallie, plainlie and profitablie Treatised*, ed. W. Bradshaw (London, 1611).

20. *AGL* ii. 568; R. Bayne, 'Fenner, Dudley (1558?–1587)', *DNB* xviii. 317–19; C. H. Cooper, 'Dudley Fenner', *Athenae Cantab.* ii. 72–4; Knappen, *Tudor Puritanism*; McGiffert, 'Covenant, Crown and Commons', esp. 40–2; W. Muss-Arnolt, 'Puritan Efforts and Struggles, 1550–1603: II', *AJT* 23 (1919), 471–99; Pearson, *Thomas Cartwright and Elizabethan Puritanism*, 272–6, 334–5; K. Sprunger, *Dutch Puritanism*; J. Venn and J. A. Venn, 'Fenner, Dudley', *Alumni Cantabrigienses*, ii. 130; H. F. Wijnman, 'Fenner, (Dudley)', *NNBW* ix (1933), 254.

21. D. Fenner, *A brief Treatise upon the first Table of the Lawe* (Middelburg, 1576); cf. J. D. Wilson, 'Richard Schilders and the English Puritans', *TBSL* 11 (1909–11), 65–134.

22. Fenner, *Sacra theologia*, 39–51.

23. D. Fenner, *The Artes of Logike and Retorike, plainly set foorth in the English toongue* (Middelburg, 1584); this was reprinted in *Four Tudor Books on*

Education, ed. R. D. Pepper (Gainesville, Florida, 1966), 143–80; *Sacra theologia*, see n. 18 above; *The Sacred Doctrine of Divinitie, Gathered ovt of the worde of God* (London, n.p., 1589; misprinted 1599); this is not a translation of *Sacra theologia*; *Dudley Fenner his Catechisme* (Edinburgh, 1592); Bayne (*DNB*, xviii. 317–19) ascribes this last item to Fenner, but I have not been able to locate it at all.

24. M. Adam, *DLV* ii. 96–101; *AGL* ii. 2024–6; F. W. Cuno, *Franciscus Junius der Ältere, Professor der Theologie und Pastor* (1891; repr. Geneva, 1971), and 'Junius, Franz', *RE* (3rd edn.), ix. 636–7; C. De Jonge, 'Franciscus Junius (1545–1602) and the English Separatists at Amsterdam', in D. Baker (ed.), *Reform and Reformation* (Oxford, 1979), 165–74, and 'De Irenische Ecclesiologie van Franciscus Junius' (Diss. Leiden, 1980; Nieuwkoop, 1980); Y. Destianges, 'Du Jon (François)', *DBF* xii. 48–9; W. Geesink, 'Franciscus Junius', in *Calvinisten in Holland* (1887; repr. Geneva, 1970), 1–51; J. F. G. Goeters, 'Junius (du Jon), Franciscus d. A. (1545–1602)', *RGG* (3rd edn.), iii. 1071; M. Haag, '[François] Du Jon', *La France protestante*, iv. 382–91; W. Hedorn, 'Junius, Franz (1545–1602)', *RGG* (1st edn.), iii. 866–7; 'Junius, Franciscus' (n.a.), *BWPGN* iv. 604–16; F. S. Knipscheer, 'Junius, (Franciscus)', *NNBW* ix. 481–3; A. Kuyper, 'Praefatio', *D. Francisci Junii opuscula theologica selecta* (New York, 1882), pp. v–xx; P. Merula, 'Vita Francisci Junii' (Leiden, 1595); published in F. Junius, *Opera theologica* (Geneva, 1608), i/B, 1–28 (vol. i of the 1608 edition has a triple pagination system: it starts out with columns 1–40, then goes to pages 1–28 for the biography, then starts out again with columns numbering from 1 to 1785 for the rest of the book. I am therefore calling the first section i/A, the second section i/B, and the third section i/C); W. Nijenhuis, 'Varianten binnen het Nederlandse Calvinisme in de zestiende eeuw', *TvG* 89 (1976), 358–73, esp. 365–6; English translation: 'Variants within Dutch Calvinism in the Sixteenth Century', *The Low Countries History Yearbook: Acta Historiae Neerlandica*, 12 (1979), 48–64, esp. 56–8; J. Reitsma, *Franciscus Junius, een levensbeeld uit de eersten eeuw der kerkhervorming* (Groningen, 1864); O. Ritschl, 'Junius, Franciscus (1545–1602)', *RGG* (2nd edn.), iii. 572; A. Schweizer, 'Junius, Franciscus (Du Jon)', *RE* (1st edn.), vii. 176, and 'Junius, Franziskus (Du Jon)', *RE* (2nd edn.), vii. 315; J. H. Worman, 'Junius, Franciscus', *CBTEL* iv. 1097.

25. The speeches are in the form of orations, and take up the pages forming i/A of the *Opera theologica* (1608). The first oration, 'De promissione et Federe Gratioso Dei cvm ecclesia' (*Opera theologica*, i/A, 13–22), is mainly about the postlapsarian state and the covenant of grace. Unfortunately we have no date for this oration. The second oration, also undated, shows that Junius was also interested in the various philological interpretations of the words for covenant: 'De federe et testamento Dei in ecclesia vetere, oratio secvnda', 'On the Covenant and Testament of God in the Old Church, a Second Oration' (*Opera theologica*, i/A, 22–30). It is a lexicographical discussion of *berith*, *diatheke*, *foedus*, and *testamentum*, but makes no mention of a prelapsarian covenant.

Junius's concern with the problem of Adam's first sin comes out in a discussion of the subject written in 1595: 'De peccato primo Adami, et genere cavsae qua ad peccandvm addvctvs est . . .', 'On the First Sin of Adam, and on the Kind of Cause by which he had been Led to Sin . . .' (*Opera theologica*, i/C, 1429–72; cf. Cuno, *Franciscus Junius der Ältere*, 250). Junius lists the four questions under consideration: 'Qvaestionis I: Quibus testimoniis vel rationibus ex Sacra Scriptura petitis probari possit Adamum necessario pecasse?

Qvaestionis II: Quae sit causa necessitas (*sic*: necessitatis) lapsus Adami: nudane Dei praescientia et voluutaria (*sic*) permissio, an decretum efficax? Qvaestionis III: Quomodo haec necessitas conueniat cum libero hominis arbitrio. Qvaestionis IV: Quomodo liber erit Deus a peccato Adami, si statuatur decretum eius causa lapsus.' 'Question I: By what testimony or reasons searched out of Holy Scripture is it able to be proven that Adam sinned by necessity? Question II: What might be the cause of the necessity for the Fall of Adam: the bare foreknowledge of God and his voluntary permission, or the efficacious decree? Question III: In what way this necessity agrees with the free will of men? Question IV: In what way God will be free from the sin of Adam, if it stands that his decree is the cause of the Fall?' (*Opera theologica*, i/C, 1435–6). While this treatise was written in 1595, which is past our cut-off date of 1590, and while there does not seem to be any mention of the prelapsarian state being covenantal, nevertheless it shows us that there is still a great concern over the question of Adam's sin and God's sovereignty.

I. Breward feels that Junius connects the prelapsarian/postlapsarian covenant doctrine with the larger doctrine of justification, not election (Breward, 'Introduction', *The Work of William Perkins*, 90 and 128). He bases this on the evidence found in the theological theses disputed in Leiden under the direction of Junius. This would date the theses after 1592, which is the year Junius became a professor at Leiden. The particular thesis is: 'De foederibus et testamentis divinis' (cf. *D. Francisci Junii opuscula theologica selecta*, ed. Kuyper, 183–90).

26. M. Adam, 'Caspar Olevianus', *DLV* i. 283–7; *AGL* iii. 1058; Agnew, 'Gaspar Olevianus, LL.D.' in *The Theology of Consolation*, 317–18; Benrath, 'Die Eigenart der pfälzischen Reformation'; Bierma, 'The Covenant Theology of Caspar Olevian'; F. Birkner, 'Olevianus, Kaspar', *RE* (1st edn.), x. 597–605; F. Birkner and C. O. Thelemann, 'Olevianus, Kaspar', *RE* (2nd edn.), xi. 21–3; Coenen (ed.), *Handbuch zum Heidelberger Katechismus*; F. W. Cuno, 'Olevian: Caspar D.', *ADB* xxiv. 286–9, and *Blätter der Erinnerung an Dr. Kaspar Olevianus* (Barmen, 1887); M. Goebal, 'Dr. Caspar Olevianus', trans. H. Harbough, *MercQR* 7 (1855), 294–306; J. F. G. Goeters, 'Olevian, Caspar', *RGG* (3rd edn.), iv. 1626; Good, 'Caspar Olevianus', in *The Heidelberg Catechism in its Newest Light*, 201–41, and *Origin*; E. Güder, 'Katechismus, Heidelberger oder Pfälzer', *RE* (2nd edn.), vii. 605–14, and 'Heidelberg Catechism', *SchHE* (2nd and 3rd edns.), ii. 959–60; H. Harbough, 'Olevianus', *CBTEL* vii. 343–5; Hollweg, *Neue Untersuchungen*; Lang, *Der Heidelberger Katechismus zum 350jährigen Gedächtnis* and *Der Heidelberger Katechismus und vier verwandte Katechismen*; M. Lauterburg, 'Katechismus, Heidelberger oder Pfälzer', *RE* (3rd edn.), x. 164–73, and 'Heidelberg Catechism', *NSHE* v. 204–6; D. Ludwig, 'Olevian, Caspar', *RGG* (2nd edn.), iv. 693; Masselink, *The Heidelberg Story*; J. Moltmann, 'Olevian, Caspar', *EKL* ii. 1688–9; Neuser, 'Die Väter des Heidelberger Katechismus'; T. J. Ney, 'Olevianus, Kaspar', *RE* (3rd edn.), xiv. 358–62; Richards, *The Heidelberg Catechism*; T. Schaller, 'Olevian, Caspar', *RGG* (1st edn.), iv. 948; H. Schlosser, 'Caspar Olevianus', *Nassauische Lebensbilder*, 1 (1940), 67–73; J. H. Steubing, 'Lebensnachrichten von der Herborner Theologen. I: Caspar Olevian und Johannes Piscator', *ZHTh*, 11, no. 4 (1841), 74–138; K. Sudhoff, 'Heidelberger oder Pfälzer Katechismus', *RE* (1st edn.), v. 658–68, *Olevianus und Ursinus*, and 'Sudhoff's Olevianus', trans. H. Rust, *MercQR* 8 (1856), 163–98; Visser (ed.), *Controversy and Conciliation*.

27. Bierma, 'The Covenant Theology of Caspar Olevian'. Bierma explores the following works of Olevianus for evidence of a prelapsarian covenant: *In*

epistolam D. Pauli Apost. ad Galatas notae, ex concionibus Gasparis Oleviani excerptae, et a Theodora Beza editae (Geneva, 1578); *Notae Gasparis Oleviani in evangelia* (Herborn, 1579); *In epistolam D. Pauli Apostoli ad Romanos notae* (1579; 2nd edn. Geneva, 1584); *In epistolas ad D. Pauli Apostoli ad Philippenses et Colossenses, notae* (Geneva, 1580).

28. Caspar Olevianus, *De substantia foederis gratuiti inter Deum et electos* (Geneva, 1585; 2nd edn. 1589, 'priore emendatior').

29. For example, the first question of the Heidelberg Catechism is stated in the first person: 'Was ist dein einiger Trost im Leben und im Sterben? Dass ich mit Leib und Seele, beides im Leben und im Sterben, nicht mein, sondern meines getreuen Heilandes Jesu Christi eigen bin, der mit seinem theuren Blute für alle meine Sünden vollkommen bezahlet . . .'; English translation: 'What is thy only comfort, in life and in death? Answer: That I, with body and soul, both in life and in death, am not my own, but belong to my faithful Saviour Jesus Christ, who with his precious blood has fully satisfied for all my sins . . .'; Schaff, *Creeds*, iii. 307.

30. Cf. the biographical section on Ursinus, ch. 3 above.

31. Cf. O. Grundler, 'Thomism and Calvinism' and *Die Gotteslehre*; cf. also C. Burchill, 'Girolamo Zanchi: Portrait of a Reformed Theologian and His Work', *SCJ*, 15 (1984), 185–207; J. Fischer, 'Zanchi, Girolamo', *NSHE* xii. 496–7; D. Schmidt, 'Girolamo Zanchi', *ThStKr*, 32 (1859), 625–708.

32. Grundler, 'Thomism and Calvinism' and *Die Gotteslehre*.

33. *AGL* iv. 1274–6; F. W. Cuno, 'Tossanus: Daniel', *ADB* xxxviii. 469–74, and *Daniel Tossanus der Ältere* (Amsterdam, 1898); F. Hauss, 'Toussain (Tossanus), 1. Daniel (1541–1602)', *RGG* (3rd edn.), vi. 964–5; D. Ludwig, 'Toussain (Tossanus), 1. Daniel (1541–1602)', *RGG* (2nd edn.), v. 1246; A. Müller, *Daniel Tossanus' Leben und Wirken* (Flensburg, 1882); T. Schaller, 'Toussain (Tossanus), 1. Daniel (1541 bis 1602)', *RGG* (1st edn.), v. 1308–9; C. Schmidt, 'Tossanus', *RE* (1st edn.), xvi. 204–6, and *RE* (2nd edn.), xv. 726–7; 'Toussain or Tussanus, Daniel' (n.a.), *CBTEL* x. 502–3; J. Vienot, 'Toussain (Tossanus), Daniel', *RE* (3rd edn.), xx. 3–5. According to Cuno (*Daniel Tossanus der Ältere*) Tossanus's works were published together in 1604: *D. Danielis Tossani S. Theologiae in academia Heidelbergensi doctoris et professoris primarii operum theologicarum* (Hanover, 1604).

34. Cf. Cuno, *Daniel Tossanus der Ältere*.

35. Beza wrote introductions to and participated in the publication of the following works by Olevianus: *In epistolam ad Galatas* (1578); *In epistolam ad Romanos* (1579); *In epistolas ad Philippenses et Colossenses* (1580). Moltmann feels that the Heidelberg school of thought was definitely antagonistic to the Genevan school of thought (cf. 'Zur Bedeutung des Petrus Ramus'), but recently there have been questions about the validity of his view.

36. For a general overview of the history of Protestant universities during the sixteenth century, see the following: G. A. Benrath, 'Die Universität der Reformationszeit', *ARG* 57 (1966), 32–51; Janssen, *Geschichte des deutschen Volkes*, vii; English translation: xiii and xiv; F. A. G. Tholuck, *Das akademische Leben des siebzehnten Jahrhunderts* (Halle, 1853–4); I. A. Dorner, *Geschichte der protestantischen Theologie, besonders in Deutschland* (Munich, 1867), 429–37; English translation: *History of Protestant Theology, Particularly in Germany*, trans. G. Robinson and S. Taylor (Edinburgh, 1871), ii. 9–22; P. Dibon, *La Philosophie néerlandaise au Siècle d'Or*, i: *L'Enseignement Philosophique dans les universités a l'époque précartésienne* (Paris, 1954); R. J. W. Evans, *Rudolf II and his World* (Oxford, 1973).

37. G. Hinz (ed.), *Aus der Geschichte der Universität Heidelberg und ihrer Fakultäten* (Heidelberg, 1961) and *Die Ruprecht-Karl-Universität Heidelberg*

(West Berlin, 1965); K. Bauer, *Aus der grossen Zeit der theologische Fakultät zu Heidelberg* (Lahr in Baden, 1938); E. Bizer, *Historische Einleitung zur Heinrich Heppes Dogmatik* (Neukirchen, 1958); Cameron (ed.), *Letters*; Clasen, *The Palatinate*; W. Doerr (ed.), *Semper Apertus: Sechshundert Jahre Ruprecht-Karls Universität Heidelberg, 1386–1986*, i: 1–70, 231–54; iv: 324–6 (New York, 1985); Evans, *The Wechel Presses*; Good, *Origin*; J. F. Hautz, *Geschichte der Universität Heidelberg*, ii: *1556–1803* (Mannheim, 1862), 43–152, 412–41; G. P. van Itterzon, *Franciscus Gomarus* (The Hague, 1930), 30–2; P. Moraw and T. Karst, *Die Universität Heidelberg und Neustadt an der Haardt* (Speyer, 1963); Sudhoff, *Olevianus und Ursinus*; Toepke (ed.), *Matrikel der Universität Heidelberg*, ii: *1554–1662*; E. Winkelmann (ed.), *Urkundenbuch der Universitaet Heidelberg*, ii (Heidelberg, 1886); H. Weisert, *Die Rektoren der Ruperto Carola zu Heidelberg und die Dekane ihrer Fakultäten, 1386–1968* (Heidelberg, 1968).

38. Toepke (ed.), *Matrikel der Universität Heidelberg*, ii.

39. See N. Fiering, *Moral Philosophy at Seventeenth-Century Harvard* (Chapel Hill, 1981) for a discussion of academic and theological disputation.

40. Cameron (ed.), *Letters*; Clasen, *The Palatinate*; F. J. Dochnahl and K. Tavernier, *Chronik von Neustadt an der Haardt nebst den umliegenden Orten und Burgen mit besonderer Berücksichtigung der Weinjahre* (Pirmasens, 1900); I. A. Dorner, *Geschichte der protestantischen Theologie*, 434–5 n. 1; English translation: ii. 14–16 n. 1; Good, *Origin*, 238–40; Gümbel, *Geschichte*, 409–33; Hautz, *Geschichte*, ii. 112–15; van Itterzon, *Franciscus Gomarus*, 23–7; Karst, *Das kürpfalzische Oberamt* and 'Pfalzgraf Johann Casimir'; M. Kuhn, *Pfalzgraf Johann Casimir*, 87–97 and 169–71; W. E. Moeller, *Reformation und GegenReformation*, vol. iii of *Lehrbuch der Kirchengeschichte* (Leipzig, 1894), 272–8; English translation: *History of the Christian Church*, trans. J. H. Freese (New York, 1900), iii. 302–5; Moraw and Karst, *Die Universität Heidelberg*; Press, *Calvinismus*; Tholuck, *Das akademische Leben*, ii. 312 ff.

41. Cameron (ed.), *Letters*; Cuno, *Johann der Ältere*; 'Festschrift zur 350Jährigen Wiederkehr Gründung der Hohen Schule zu Herborn', *NA* 55 (1935), 1–184; Good, *Origin*, 262–4; H. Grün, 'Geist und Gestalt der Hohen Schule Herborn', *NA* 65 (1954), 130–47, and 'Die theologische Fakultät der Hohen Schule Herborn 1584–1817', *JHKGV* 19 (1968), 57–145; C. Heiler, 'Der Herborner Student, 1584–1817', *NA* 55 (1935), 1–100; G. Menk, 'Der doppelte Johannes Althusius—eine ramistische Dichotomie?', *NA* 87 (1976), 135–42, 'Kalvinismus und Pädagogik', *NA* 91 (1980), 77–104, and *Die Hohe Schule Herborn in ihrer Frühzeit* (Wiesbaden, 1981); Moeller, *Reformation und GegenReformation*, 276–8; English translation, 305; *NA* (Wiesbaden, 1827–); A. von Reth, *Herborn, Dillenburg, Haiger* (Marburg/Lahn, 1970); H. Schlosser, 'Die Bedeutung der Hohen Schule Herborn für die Geschichte des deutschen Geistes', *NA* 55 (1935), 101–12; H. Steitz, *Geschichte der evangelischen Kirche in Hessen und Nassau* (Marburg, 1977); J. H. Steubing, *Kirchen- und Reformations-Geschichte der Oranien-Nassauischen Lande* (Hadamar, 1804) and 'Lebensnachrichten von den Herborner Theologen'; G. Zedler and H. Sommer (edd.), *Die Matrikel der Hohen Schule und des Paedagogiums zu Herborn* (Wiesbaden, 1908). 42. Cf. Introduction, n. 18.

42. Cf. Introduction, n. 18.

5
The Second Stage in the Development of the Federal Theology

> Moreouer I wil establish my couenant betwene me and thee, and thy sede after thee in their generacions, for an euerlasting couenant, to be God vnto thee and to thy sede after thee. And I wil giue thee and thy sede after thee the land, wherin thou art a stranger, euen all the land of Canaan, for an euerlasting possession, and I wil be their God.
>
> Genesis 17: 7–8 (Geneva Bible, 1560)

> Now therefore if ye wil heare my voyce in dede, and kepe my couenant, then ye shalbe my chief treasure aboue all people, thogh all the earth be mine. Ye shalbe vnto me also a kingdome of Priestes, and an holy nation. These are the wordes which thou shalt speake vnto the children of Israel.
>
> Exodus 19: 5–6 (Geneva Bible, 1560)

IN 1584 the idea of a prelapsarian covenant, as articulated by Zacharias Ursinus, appeared in the public domain of northern Europe when Ursinus's *Major Catechism* was published. By this time Ursinus was dead, but his colleagues continued to develop the covenant theme in Reformed theological thought. One of the most important was Caspar Olevianus, who by 1584 was teaching at the Herborn Academy. In 1585 he published his *De substantia*. A careful examination of the *De substantia* shows us that the idea of a prelapsarian covenant is mentioned six times, but that all the references are scattered; the theme is not developed in any specific way or place.[1] The result is that the prelapsarian covenant idea does not have a specific place in Olevianus's theological system; for Olevianus it is still a *locus communis*—a commonplace of theology to be developed and worked into a theological system.

If we are going to see how the prelapsarian covenant idea developed further it is important to understand Protestant theological methodology of the late sixteenth century.[2] Most of the earlier Reformers abandoned the scholastic methodology of medieval theology, but the second and third generation of Reformers readopted it, as Melanchthon had done in his *Book of Common-places*, first published in 1521.[3] A commonplace was an idea, usually dealing with one subject, which the student or theologian developed and used as an authority in his scholarly or theological work.[4] There were theological and non-theological commonplaces. For centuries commonplace-books which dealt with various areas were common. Usually appearing in the form of a blank book, they were used as places to file away information. The information would be culled from various sources—scripture, lectures, individual reading—and would be divided up by sections. The result would be a collection of fragmented ideas, which would then be used for development into a theological system. Thus, a theologian might write up a section for 'covenant', and anything about the theme of covenant which he read or heard would be written down in that section.

The issue arose, of course, whether this or that commonplace was true and authoritative, and so various Protestant theologians would publish their own books of commonplaces for theological students to work with and memorize. Thus, the idea that 'God made a covenant with Adam before his Fall into sin' could be considered a commonplace.

The theological schools of the day cultivated the Aristotelian method of dialectic, and the theological disputation was the chief method by which theology was taught. By applying the various techniques of argumentation, a conclusion was reached as to whether a commonplace was valid or not. If it held up to scrutiny, then it could be utilized in a system of theology. There again it would be scrutinized as to whether it held up in the entire system, and whether the system itself held up. Disputations could be formal, with elaborate rules enforced (e.g. two colleges at Cambridge or Oxford competing against one another), or they could be very informal. Because they were oral, there is not much evidence as to precisely what occurred at a disputation. What is known is that they formed the very warp and woof of theological education at the universities in the late sixteenth century.[5]

The idea of the prelapsarian covenant did not appear in a commonplace-book until after 1590, but it followed the same pattern as the other commonplaces. First it was written about in some authoritative book, in this case the works of Ursinus and Olevianus, and then the idea was utilized and developed in various theological systems.

The *De substantia* of Olevianus is divided up into two sections: the first part deals with Christ the mediator, and follows the outline of the Apostle's Creed. The second part deals with the various biblical references that deal with the idea of covenant between God and man.

The first references to the prelapsarian covenant are found at the beginning of the *De substantia*, in the section dealing with the Godhead and the phrase 'I believe in God the Father Almighty.' In affirming the theological point that the Godhead has three persons, Olevianus attacks those who deny this point. Even Satan admitted the Trinity as he deceived Adam and Eve and led them away from God and the covenant of creation:

When Satan had said, 'You will be as God', God repeats it and states: 'He has become like one of us.' I say this so that the impudence and blindness might become apparent of those who now are allowing themselves to be seduced from the true God and the covenant of redemption, by the negation of that truth by affirming which, approved fully by the mouth of God, nevertheless distorted in a perverse end, Satan first led man from God and from the covenant of creation.[6]

Olevianus does not in any way make special mention of the covenant of creation; it is mentioned almost as an aside. A few sentences later the same subject comes up, again in relation to how Satan has broken the covenantal relationship between God and man:

For we see that Satan, in order to overturn the first covenant or union which was between God and man established after the image of God, proposed to man the hope of equality with God and with his capacities, which men were not allowed to strive after: and thus he pushed the first parents and their own heirs into eternal destruction. The cause therefore of all dissension between God and men is sin, that is voluntary and plainly free defection from God, and the corruption of the whole man together with those actual sins that arise from this.[7]

Again, there is no special reference to the prelapsarian covenant; it is simply assumed that the Edenic relationship is a covenantal relationship.

The second reference to the prelapsarian idea comes soon after, when Olevianus is considering the reasons why the Incarnation is necessary. For Olevianus there are two reasons: first, expiation for the dissolved covenant of creation, and second, restoration to a state of immortal perfection:

And since not only was it proposed by God to restore us to integrity, but to the status of the sons of God, which is far higher and more firm than what we had received in the first creation of man: therefore he wished that the incarnate Son be the foundation of this most high and eternal covenant; the incarnate Son, I mean, was not only required to be the atonement for the broken covenant of creation, and its restoration; but also the duration of the atonement once for all accomplished was perpetual, and the restoration was into a larger and more excellent status according to Romans 5: 17.[8]

Again, there is no special chapter or heading for the covenant of creation theme; it is simply an aside, a mention of one idea among many ideas.

The third mention of the prelapsarian covenant comes at the beginning of the second half of the *De substantia*:

And firstly, indeed, although the Lord induced faith to his elect not in one way through the Word, but most of all as God the Father, Son and Holy Spirit administers the covenant of grace, so that according to his own eternal wisdom he prepares the hearts of the elect for possessing it; yet for others, however, he takes away every excuse by showing it was a covenant by nature, or an obligation of nature between God, since he is the creator, and men who are founded after his image: this is undoubtedly so that just as God reveals himself to them partly internally by his image within them, partly externally in the mirror of the maker of this world, so in turn he should be honoured and glorified by them. Of these natural obligations God wished testimony to appear partly in natural law written through fears, partly in law written on two tables, and by each of these laws of creation to oblige us (by the first all men in the universe, by the other peculiarly also those to whom it was brought) either for obedience or for punishment, that is, his curse or damnation on account of disobedience, or until there may be reconciliation; and indeed with the decision of the coming judgement already given beforehand, partly in conscience, in which God erected his own tribunal; partly through the laws sanctioned and enunciated by the mouth of God (Deuteronomy 27: 26) . . .

. . . Actual sin is whatever opposes the law of God, either in actions internal, such as thoughts piercing the heart, or external, through words and actions (Romans 3, 7, Deuteronomy 27: 26). All of these are lethal poisons and attacks against God, and they are fighting with the covenant of nature between God and us, or that conformity with God which once shone within his image.[9]

The final mention of the prelapsarian covenant comes further on in the second part: as in the earlier instances, there is reference by Olevianus to how Satan deceived Adam and Eve and led them out of covenantal perfection:

In the very beginning of the human race that old serpent by a false interpretation led men away from the Word of the law, and thus from the covenant of creation (for before the Fall there was no need of the gospel), the summary of which law, shining forth within the image of God, was that he should love the Lord his God with his whole soul (just as Moses repeated a summary, 'Now Israel what does God require from you but that you seek him with your whole heart') and in testimony of that love he might abstain from the use of that one tree, giving to God the glory of wisdom, etc.[10]

However, there is one difference in this case. The prelapsarian covenant is connected with the law of God, which is related to loving God. Nevertheless, we can conclude that the prelapsarian covenant was not a doctrine of fundamental importance for Olevianus.

Lyle D. Bierma concludes that Olevianus was a practical theologian, not a speculative, metaphysical theologian. He points out that several key aspects of the developed federal theological system are missing: (1) Olevianus never states that the prelapsarian covenant is a means to a higher state of grace. (2) He never identifies the prohibition from eating of the tree of the knowledge of good and evil (Genesis 2: 16–17) with the prelapsarian covenant; nor does he refer to Galatians 3: 10 as a viable proof text. (3) The prelapsarian *foedus creationis* is not a 'foil' for the postlapsarian covenant of grace. (4) Adam is not the federal head of the human race who imputes guilt to posterity.

For Bierma, Olevianus's contribution to the history of the covenant idea is that he made the covenant personal; that is, he applied the legal and gracious aspects of the covenant to the life of the believer.[11] Individual piety was Olevianus's focus; he never dealt with the problem of God's sovereignty and Adam's Fall, which tended to lead theologians into abstract speculation. However, he picked up the idea of the prelapsarian covenant from reading and dealing with Ursinus and his *Major Catechism*. Since Olevianus's main concern was practical piety, he did not realize the extraordinary power of the idea to which he was alluding.

Another figure did realize the power of the prelapsarian covenant idea, and he published his treatise in the same year (1585) as Olevianus's *De substantia*. Dudley Fenner's *Sacra theologia* represents the second watershed in the history of the early federal theology, for it was Fenner who (1) identified the prelapsarian covenant with key New Testament passages; (2) first called it the *foedus operum*, or covenant of works; and (3) first integrated the idea with Ramistic methodology.

The *Sacra theologia* was published in 1585 and republished in 1589 *(priore emendatior)*, 1604, and 1632.[12] According to Ronald Bayne, 'Fenner spent seven years on this work, and submitted it to the corrections of Cartwright and other friends.'[13] The *Sacra theologia* was therefore begun in 1578. Sometime between 1576 and 1585 Fenner became a federal theologian. His 1576 treatise, *A brief Treatise upon the first Table of the Lawe*, deals with the first four commandments, but does not relate the Decalogue to the prelapsarian covenant. In 1585 he does draw such a relationship in the *Sacra theologia*.

The *Sacra theologia* is divided into ten sections; these ten sections can in turn be divided into two parts: I–IV deal with theology proper, V–X deal with the government and polity of man and his institutions (State, Church, family) after the Fall.

The book utilizes the Ramistic system of dichotomies extensively, and it is in this way that the prelapsarian covenant is developed as a 'foil' to the postlapsarian covenant of grace. Ursinus and Olevianus, of course, were not Ramists, and so they never saw the potential of aligning the prelapsarian covenant and the postlapsarian covenant. Fenner did so, having one year before published a treatise which adopts and expounds the Ramistic system.[14]

Fenner's treatise is the first to place the covenant systematically within the context of the previous sixty years. Fenner is very definitely a High Calvinist, and he carefully combines High Calvinism and the federal theology, something which Ursinus never did. The covenant of works and covenant of grace flow out of the decrees and actions of God, and their relations to the Decalogue are drawn very explicitly.

Book I starts out with a definition of theology, and the binary method is immediately evident:

[Book I: On Divinity]

Diuinitie is the knowledge of the truth which is of God, to live well and blessedly. Tit. 1. 1; I Tim. 2. 16 et 6. 4; II Tim. 2. 18 Ioan 1. 2. 3

Thereof ther be two parts:

```
┌── The first concerninge God
│
└── The second concerninge the actions of God.
```

Psalm 78. 7 Prover. 2. 5. 10 Iud 1. 10. Colos. 2. 2 Deut 32. 2. 3. 4[15]

Theology is first the science of God, and then a study of his actions. When we get to Book II we find that God's actions are twofold: the decrees of God and the execution of the decrees:

[Book II: On the Actions of God]

The seconde parte of diuinitie, is that which giveth precepts of the actions of god.

The actions of god, is his worke or effect in all things to the revealing of his glorie. Roma. 11. 35

The action of God is two-fold

   ┌─ The decree Eph. 1. 11

   └─ The execution of the decree Act. 4. 28

The decree, is the action of God appoinetinge in him selfe from everlastinge accordinge to his will and pleasure all things, and all the circumstances of all things, by certayne and unchangeable counsaile. Act 2. 23 et 15. 18. Rom. 11. 32. 35

To this is praedestination subjected or put under. Rom. 8. 28. 29. 30. Praedestination, is the decree of God concerninge the everlastinge salvation and condemnation of the chiefe creaturs. I Thes. 5. 9. I Pet. 2. 8 Iud. 4. Rom. 9. 22. 23. Act. 4. 28 Mat. 45 (*sic*); 14. 41. Whereunto all other things are referred, as to their nearest end: whose nearest end also (as it is the last of all other) is the glorie of God. Rom. 9. 17.   1. 21. 23. 24. Prov. 16. 4.[16]

Fenner wastes no time in defining what predestination is; the division between the reprobate and the elect fits perfectly with the binary system of Ramism:

Therof ther be two parts

   ┌─ The decree of election

   └─ The decree of reprobation

The decree of election, is praedestination of the good-pleasure of the will of God, appoinetinge to choose certayne to aeternall salvation, which is to be perfected by [his] proper meanes, to the glorie of his grace Ephe. 1. 4. 5. 6. 7.

The decree of reprobation is praedestination of [his] purpose to hatred, appoinetinge to reject certaine to everlasting damnation for their meritt or desert, which is to be perfected by his proper meanes to the glorie of his justice. I. Ths. 5. 9. I. Pet. 2. 8. Iud. 4.[17]

Fenner immediately moves from the decrees themselves to the execution of the decrees. On the one hand is the execution of the decree to create the universe; on the other hand is the execution of the decree to govern the universe. In discussing the latter decree Fenner includes the idea of obedience as being a fundamental duty of all men toward God:

[Hitherto of the holiness of the nature of the chief creatures.]
It followeth of the holines of their actions.
That is obedience.

Obedience, is the perfect conformation or framing of all the motions and actions of the pure creature, to perfect the whole worke approved unto the glorie of god. I. Cor. 6. 20. et 10. 31 Col. 3. 17. I Sam. 15. 22. I. Cor. 7. 17. 18. 19. Mat. 6. 10. Num. 15. 39. Psal. 103. 20[18]

Further on Fenner deals with the law of God, the Decalogue, which is the rule of obedience:

[On the holiness of man]
The lawes therof be

    ⌐ Common Iud. 23. 24

    └ Special I. Thes. 9. 21. 23.

The common lawe of all holines is this. [a] Lett all the partes of the bodie, and all the actions of euerie one of them, and [b] to conclude all the whole nature of the whole man, be all most and apt helps and instruments to exprese outwardlie their owne holines. (a) Prov. 4. 22. 23. 24. etc. Rom. 6. 19. Psalm 119. 36. 37. Iob. 31. 1. (b) I. Cor. 6. 20. et 3. 16.[19]

Finally, Fenner concludes Book II by dealing with the Edenic state and such aspects as marriage, the sabbath, and the Fall, but not in covenantal terms. However, he does look upon the two trees as sacramental in nature:

The specials concerninge foode followe.
which is either

    ⌐ common to men, and other livinge creatures granted [to be] of herbs. Genes. II. 29. 30. 31

    └ Proper to man of all the fruicts of the trees in the garden, the fruict of the tree of the knowledge of good and evill, beinge excepted. [chapter 2. 17]

The specials concerninge the adjuncts of the worde, are

    ⌐ The signe of the tree of lyfe

    └ The confirmation of the word, of not eatinge of the fruict of the tree of the knowledge of good and evill.

The signe of the tree of life, is a signe sealinge unto man, remayninge in his

obedience, the free gifte of the aeternall lyfe of god, which cometh from the
father, through the sonne, by the holy ghost,
Gen. 2. 9 et 3. 22. 24. Apoc. 2. 7 I Ioh. 14. Prov. 8. 30. 31[20]

Book III deals with the Fall, and there is no doubt in Fenner's
mind that the Fall fits in with God's sovereignty:

[Book Three]: The fall and syne, although in the fulfillinge of praedestination, they are both decreed, [a] as also disposed of god, as means, [b] and in
them all particular actions are effectually by him performed: [c]
notwithstandinge they beinge voluntarie onely suffered of god, are directed
unto the last and furthest end. (a) Rom. 2: 32. I Petr. 2. 8. Matth. 25. 41.
cum Esa. 54. 16. (b) Rom. 11: 36 Eph. 2. 11. Exo. 10. 1. 20. et 2. 10 et 14. I
Sam. 2. 25. II Sam. 12. 11. Psal. 105. 25. Ioan. 12. 40. Gen. 3. (c) Iac. i. 13.
Act. 14. 16.[21]

However, immediately after discussing how sin and the Fall fit into
God's plan and decrees, Fenner in Book IV moves on to the theme
of the covenant:

The Fourth booke, of the couenant of god and of Christ. And hitherto of
synne so that out of these and the analogie of everie of the parts of the image
of god, the nature of all synnes may most easily be defyned, distinguished
and discerned: so that diligence in reed[in]ge, and meditation in the
scriptures, be added, or used.

Hitherto also of the fall, the common means of fulfillinge predestination in
the corrupte state of things: It followeth of the second, to witt, of the
covenant of god. Malach 2. 10. 11. Genes. 3. 7. cum Roman 2. 14. 15.
Genes. 4. 7. Romans 9. 4. 5. Ephes. 2. 12. Galat. 3. 19.

The couenant of god is the couenant made with man, and his seede, of lyfe
and death Genes. 2. 17. et 3. 15. et 17. 1. Galat. 3. 10. 11. Marc. 16. 26.[22]

At the very beginning Fenner makes clear that God strikes a
covenant with man and his seed: therefore, for Fenner, the covenant
is binding upon both Adam and his children. Fenner goes on to
outline the two sides to the covenant using the binary form of
Ramism. Fenner is careful to point out that God sets the
stipulations and man receives the stipulations:

The couenant of god is the couenant made with man, and his seede, of lyfe
and death.

The parts of the couenant are:

```
┌─── The action of god couenanting or solemnly promising
│                       Rom. 2. 12. 26.
│
└─── The action of man receyv[in]ge the couenante
                        Gen. 17. 1. Ex. 23. 8.
```

Deut. 26. 17. 18. Marc. 16. 16.

The action of god covena[ntin]ge, is the first parte of the covenante, wherby god solemnely promiseth and couenantith that he wilbe a god unto men, to the blessinge of lyfe, if they shall fulfill the condition annexed. [Ibid.] But if nott; contrariwise.

The action of man recyvinge the couenant, is the second parte of the couenante, wherby man undertaketh that he wilbe a people to god, to the blessinge of life, as he shall fulfill the condition annexed. [Ibid.][23]

Immediately afterwards a major step occurs in the history of the early federal theology. The *foedus naturale* or *foedus creationis* becomes the *foedus operum* and is placed alongside the *gratuitae promissionis foedus*:

The covenant is twofolde, the

⌐— covenante of works

└— covenant of the free promise

Genes. 4. 7. Ierem 31. 3. Rom. 10. 5. Galat. 3. 8. 9. 10. 15. 16. 17. Ephes. 2. 12.[24]

In Chapter 2 of Book IV Fenner discusses the covenant of works in greater detail:

[Of the covenant of works.]

The covenante of works, is the covenante, wher the condition annexed is perfect obedience. [ibid.]

The use of this covenante in fulfillinge praedestination is two-folde:

The first, that every mouth may be stopped, and all the world may be indangered to the condemnation of god. Rom. 3. 19.

The second use is, to the reveylinge of synne, and the miserie therof, and to worke [synne] by occasion of the flesh, and also more and more to increase it, that men may be dryven and forced to seeke restoringe in the free covenante. Rom. 3. 19. 20. et 7. 7. 8. 9. 10. 11. et 11. 32. Gal. 3. 22 et 5. 23.[25]

It is significant that Fenner relates the use of the covenant motif with predestination; in saying that the purpose of the covenant was to condemn the whole world in sin he was including Adam; both Adam and his descendants need some sort of formal cause in addition to a decree of God in order to make them odious before God; the breaking of the covenant with Adam serves this purpose. The second purpose is to increase the misery of sin so that the sinner will flee to the covenant of grace for salvation.

The rest of the chapter and of the book continue to discuss the covenant of grace:

Of the covenante of the free promise.

the couenant of the free promise, is the couenant [a] of Christ, and the blessinge that is in him, which are freely promised: [b] whence the condition is: if Christ be receyved. (a) Galat. 3. 12. 13. 14. Genes. 3. 15. et 11. 35. Deuteron. 31. 15. 16. Psalm. 74. 20. et 106. 45. 47. et 111. 5. 9. Esai. 44. 17. et 59. 21. et 61. 8. Ierem. 32. 43. 44. Ezech. 16. 6. 60. et 34. 24. 25. et 36. 26. 27. et 39. 29. et 43. 9. Hos. 2. 18. Zach. 9. 11. Malac. 3. 1. (b) Iohann. 1. 11. 12. Roman. 5. 17. Ephe. 2. 5. 6. 13.[26]

Fenner continues the emphasis of Ursinus upon Christ as mediator, who as the second Adam fulfils the obedience required of the first Adam:

Of the office of Christ

The office of Christ is that, wherby hee is made betweene god and men the alone mediatour of the free covenant. Esa. 42. 6. I Tim. 2. 5. Hebr. 9. 15. et 12. 25. Esa. 49. 8. et 61. 4. 5. 6. Ezec. 34. 24. 25. Gal. 3. 17. cap. 5.

To be a mediatour betweene god and men, is to gather togither againe into perfect fellowshipp those that disagree amonge them selves, on every part. Tim. 2. 5. Ephe. 1. 10. Col. 1. 20. Ioh. 17. 21. et 13. 6. I Ioh. 1. 3.

To be a mediatour of the free covenant is by mediation to establish the covenant of god on every part, to the salvation of the church of god. Esai 49. 8. Mal. 3. 1. Heb. 9. 15. II Sam. 7. 21. I Chr. 17. 9.[27]

Fenner did not continue the covenant of works idea in any of his other treatises, except for one, an English work published post-humously in 1589 and entitled *The Sacred Doctrine of Divinity*. This was a simple primer of theology for the average Christian reader. It starts out with the doctrine of God and immediately launches into the doctrine of predestination. Later, after discussing the law of God, Fenner deals with the doctrine of justification: man must be right with God, either through himself or through Christ:

Chap. 13: Of our owne Righteousnesse, whereof the state of Angels and Men, before and by their fall.

H[i]therto of the partes of righteousness. The severall kindes follow. Righteousness (a) is our own or from another. Our owne, which boeth Angels in heaven, and men upon earth, had perfectlie by creation . . .

a. Phil 3: 9. Rom. 9: 30, 31, 32, and 10: 3, 4, 5, 6. Gal. 3: 12. The first, requiring righteousnesse from ourselves, or by our own workes, and propounding life everlasting, if we doe it, is called The Law, or the covenant of workes, Rom. 10. 5. Gal. 3: 12. The other, sending us to Christe, and

propounding life everlasting through him, if wee beleeve in him, is called
the covenant of grace Rom. 10: 4. Gal. 3. 13, 14. Which is two-fold—Old
Testament and New Testament.[28]

An important aspect of both of Fenner's works is that for the first
time Fenner connects various Old Testament and New Testament
passages to the prelapsarian covenant. This had not been done by
Ursinus or Olevianus; in so doing he tried to give scriptural support
to what until now had been a somewhat speculative idea. The
passages which he uses are Genesis 2: 17 and 4: 7; Galatians 3: 8–10,
15–17; Romans 3: 19–20, 7: 7–11, 10: 5, and 11: 32; and Galatians 3:
22 and 5: 23. Probably the most important passage is Galatians 3.
10, which is a quotation from Deuteronomy 27: 26: 'For all who
rely on works of the law are under a curse; for it is written, "Cursed
be every one who does not abide by all things written in the book of
the law, and do them" ' (Gal. 3: 10, RSV). The curse was interpreted
as falling upon all men, not only upon Israelites who were
disobedient to God's word. All men are disobedient to God's law,
and therefore they have been disobedient to the Book of the
Covenant; therefore they have broken the prelapsarian covenant
which God made with all men. That is the manner in which the
federal theologian interpreted Galatians 3. Fenner was the first to
articulate this concept in the English vernacular.

Fenner was the assistant and disciple of Thomas Cartwright, who
had studied under Ursinus at the University of Heidelberg.
Probably Cartwright was the source for Fenner's doctrine of the
Edenic covenant. Certainly Cartwright gave advice to Fenner about
the *Sacra theologia* before it was published in 1585. If we examine
Cartwright's works, we do indeed find that he himself taught the
idea of the prelapsarian covenant; however, his works which allude
to the doctrine were not published until 1604 and 1611. Thus, they
would not influence the thinking of the theological world and
general public until that date. However, because Cartwright was so
closely connected with Fenner, we can safely assume either that he
influenced Fenner or that Fenner influenced him. Because Cartwright was the older of the two and was also the Heidelberg
student, we can be fairly certain that he was the one who taught
Fenner the prelapsarian covenant idea. Certainly what was published in 1604 was written before Cartwright's death in 1603, so
whether Cartwright's works dealing with the prelapsarian covenant
were composed before our cut-off date of 1590 is not of great

importance; we can be sure that Cartwright was dealing with the idea before 1590.

A Methodicall Short Catechisme (1604)[29] is a piece of work very similar to Fenner's *Sacra theologia* and *The Sacred Doctrine of Divinitie*. It is influenced mildly by Ramism, and starts off with the doctrine of God, then moves to the kingdom of God, which consists of the decree and the execution of the decree. It then moves on, predictably, to predestination, which is the specific decree itself:

What decree of God is that, which is specially to be considered:
That of men and angels, called predestination.
What is predestination?
It is the decree of God touching the everlasting estate of men and angels.
What are the parts of predestination?
Election and Reprobation.
What is election?
It is the eternall predestination of certaine men and angels to life, to the praise of his glorious grace.
What is reprobation?
It is the eternall predestination of certaine men and angels to destruction, to the praise of his glorious justice.
So much of the decree.[30]

Cartwright then moves on to the execution of the decree, which consists of creation and providence. For Cartwright the Fall and the repair of men and the perseverance of certain angels in righteousness is an especially important part of the doctrine of providence. It is through the word that God, in his providence, repairs men's souls, and it is through the law of that word that the covenant of works is revealed, whereby men are convicted of sin and shown that, while God requires of them the duty of Adam, they must flee to the covenant of grace for mercy and help:

What is sinne?
It is the transgression of God's law.
What is the first sinne of man?
The eating of the fruite that was forbidden; from whence also doe come other sinnes, originall and actuall.
What is due to these sinnes?
    Guilt, and ⎤
    Punishment ⎦

What is the guilt of sinne?
The desert of sinne whereby we are subiect to God's wrath.

What is the punishment of sinne?

Everlasting death begun here, and to be accomplished in the life to come.

What is that which God hath ordained for the repaire of man?

His word.

What is his word?

It is a doctrine of saving men's soules, written by divine inspiration . . .

What are the parts of the word?

The law and gracious promise (otherwise called the covenant of workes, and covenant of grace), which from the comming of Christ is called the Gospell.

What doth the law (containing the covenant of works) crave of us?

All such duties as were required of Adam in his innocencie, and all such as are required since, by reason of his fal, with reward of life everlasting to the doers of them, and curses to him that doth them not.

Is any man able to do them all?

No, not in the least point.

What then availeth the law to us?

Very much: first to shew us our sinnes and punishment thereof, thereby to drive us to Christ; and secondly, to teach us how to walke when we are come to him.[31]

Seven years later Cartwright's other work was published: *Christian Religion: svbstantially, methodicallie, plainlie and profitablie Treatised.* This work follows roughly the outline of Cartwright's *Catechisme.* The prelapsarian covenant, however, is not mentioned until after the exposition of the Decalogue and before the exposition of the offices of Christ:

What followeth to be spoken of?

The covenant of grace.

Seeing by the covenant of workes life everlasting is propounded, what need is there that the covenant of grace should be set before us?

Because, as hath beene said, the covenant of works cannot through the infirmitie of our flesh give life unto any: And therefore if God should iustifie any by it, he should be uniust, as one that should give the kingdome of heaven to wicked men.[32]

At this point the prelapsarian covenant is related to the doctrine of justification, and does not involve the doctrine of predestination at all. Further on, there will be hints via the doctrine of the sacraments that the Edenic relationship is a covenantal one:

How then commeth it to passe, that the outward elements which the minister giveth: have the names of the spirituall things they set foorth?

It is ordinary and usual in the scripture, to give the name of the thing signed and signified to the signe: as it is called the tree of life, which was but a signe of life. And in the sacraments of the Old Testament, circumcision is called the covenant, and the Lambe or kid the Passover, whereof only they were signes.[33]

The second phase of the federal theology, as articulated by Olevianus, Fenner, and Cartwright, occurred between 1584 and 1590. After 1590 it is impossible to draw historical relationships; the idea of covenant, and specifically the prelapsarian covenant, started to appear in Reformed thinking all over northern Europe. Olevianus was the first to allude to it after the work of Ursinus was published posthumously in 1584. However, it is not a central facet of his work. Dudley Fenner was the high point and the watershed of the second phase: he is the one who serves as the bridge between the early federal theology and the federal theology of the seventeenth century. His work of explicit definition, geometric design, and combination of the federal theology with High Calvinistic theology, especially with regard to the execution of the decrees of God and the manifestation of the law of God, gave the federal theology its basic form. It was Fenner who set off the prelapsarian covenant against the postlapsarian covenant, utilizing the binary nature of Ramistic methodology. Fenner also related the idea to various scriptural texts. Fenner's friend Cartwright probably taught Fenner the idea, even though Cartwright's federalistic works were not published until after his death. Cartwright's *A Methodicall Shorte Catechism* follows the general outline of Fenner's *Sacra theologia*, and is an example of how the idea was popularized in the vernacular languages.

Notes

1. Bierma, 'The Covenant Theology of Caspar Olevian'.
2. Cf. E. Bizer, *Frühorthodoxie und Rationalismus* (Zurich, 1963); J. Bohatec, *Die cartesianische Scholastik in der Philosophie und reformierten Dogmatik des 17. Jahrhunderts* (1912; repr. Hildesheim, 1966) and 'Die Methode der reformierten Dogmatik', *ThStKr* 81 (1908), 272–302; W. T. Costello, *The Scholastic Curriculum at Early Seventeenth Century Cambridge* (Cambridge, Mass., 1958); J. P. Donnelly, 'Italian Influences on the Development of Calvinist Scholasticism', *SCJ* 7 (1976), 81–101; O. Fatio, *Méthode et théologie* (Geneva, 1976); L. W. Gibbs, *William Ames: Technometry* (Philadelphia, 1979) and 'William Ames's Technometry', *JHI* 33 (1972), 615–24; N. W. Gilbert, *Renaissance Concepts of Method* (New York, 1960); Good, 'Peter Ramus and his Significance for the [Heidelberg] Catechism', in *The Heidelberg Catechism in its Newest Light*, 102–20; F. P. Graves, *Peter Ramus and the*

Educational Reformation of the Sixteenth Century (New York, 1912); W. S. Howell, *Logic and Rhetoric in England 1500–1700* (Princeton, 1956); H. Kearney, *Scholars and Gentlemen* (London, 1970), 46–70; Kickel, *Vernunft und Offenbarung*; Miller, *The New England Mind*, i. 111–53; Moltmann, 'Zur Bedeutung des Petrus Ramus für Philosophie und Theologie im Calvinismus'; J. S. O'Malley, *Pilgrimage of Faith* (Metuchen, NJ, 1973), 16–30; Ong, *Ramus*; P. Petersen, *Geschichte der aristotelischen Philosophie im protestantischen Deutschland* (Leipzig, 1921); J. G. Rechtien, 'Thought Patterns: The Commonplace Book as Literary Form in Theological Controversy during the English Renaissance' (Diss. Saint Louis University, 1975); K. L. Sprunger, 'Ames, Ramus, and the Method of Puritan Theology', *HThR* 59 (1966), 133–51, and 'Technometria: A Prologue to Puritan Theology', *JHI* 29 (1968), 115–22; H. E. Weber, *Die philosophische Scholastik des deutschen Protestantismus im Zeitalter der Orthodoxie* (Leipzig, 1907). For discussions of the application of Ramistic methodology to Reformed (specifically English Puritan) doctrine, see the following: J. T. Johnson, *A Society Ordained by God* (Nashville, 1970), 199–208; D. K. McKim, *Ramism in William Perkins' Theology* (New York, 1987); Fiering, *Moral Philosophy*.

3. Melanchthon, *Opera*, xxi. 59–230.

4. Q. Breen, 'The Terms "Loci Communes" and "Loci" in Melanchthon', *ChH* 16 (1947), 197–209; Rechtien, 'Thought Patterns'; H.-G. Gadamer, *Wahrheit und Methode* (Tübingen, 1965), 162–5; English translation: *Truth and Method* (New York, 1975), 153–6, 515–16.

5. The best exposition of what happened at a formal disputation can be found in Fiering, *Moral Philosophy*. While Ramists did not consider themselves 'Aristotelians', in actuality their theory can be regarded as a species of Aristotelianism because they retained much of the Aristotelian system of thought; what was different was their method.

6. 'Quod Sathan dixerat, Eritis sicut Elohim, id Elohim repetit, aitque: Factus est sicut vnus ex nobis. Haec ideo tantum vt appareat eorum impudentia et excaecatio, qui iam negatione illius veritatis a vero Deo, redemptionisque foedere se abduci patiuntur, cuius affirmatione, Dei ore comprobata, in peruersum tamen finem detorta, Sathan initio hominem a Deo et creationis foedere abduxit', Olevianus, *De substantia foederis*, 9.

7. 'Videmus enim vt Sathan quo primum foedus seu coniunctionem, quae inter Deum et hominem conditum ad Dei imaginem intercedebat, euerteret, proposuerit homini spem aequalitatis cum Deo ipsiusque proprietatibus quam expetere homini fas non erat: atque ita primos parentes una cum ipsorum haeredibus in aeternum exitium praecipitarit. Causa igitur dissidii omnis inter Deum et homines est peccatum, hoc est voluntaria et plane libera defectio a Deo, totiusque hominis corruptio vna cum iis quae inde emergunt actualibus peccatis', ibid. 9–10.

8. 'Et cum non tantum in integrum nos restituere Deo esset propositum, sed in ius filiorum Dei longe excellentius et firmius quam quod in prima hominis creatione acceperamus: ideo Filium incarnatum summi huius et eterni foederis voluit esse fundamentum: Requirebatur, inquam, Filius incarnatus, vt non tantum pro dissoluto creationis foedere fieret expiatio, et eiusdem instauratio: sed etiam expiationis semel factae perpetua esset duratio, et restitutio in ius amplius et excellentius ad Ro. 5. v. 17', ibid. 26.

9. 'Ac primum quidem etsi Dominus non vno modo per verbum electos suos fidem adducat, tamen vt plurimum foedus gratuitum sic administrat Deus Pater, Filius et Spiritus Sanctus, ut pro aeterna sua sapientia corda electorum ad id percipiendum praeparet, aliis autem omnem excusationem adimat osten-

dendo quod fuerit naturale foedus, seu naturalis obligatio inter Deum, quatenus est creator, et homines ad ipsius imaginem conditos: hoc nimirum, vt quemadmodum se Deus ipsis patefacerat partim interne in sua imagine, partim externe in speculo opificii huius mundi, ita vicissim ab ipsis honoraretur et glorificaretur. Huius naturalis obligationis testimonium Deus extare voluit partim in lege nature inscripta mentibus, partim in lege scripta in duabus tabulis, vtraque, iure creationis nos obligante (illa in vniversum omnes homines, altera peculiariter etiam eos quibus lata erat) vel ad obedientiam vel ad poenam, hoc est, maledictionem seu damnationem propter inobedientiam seu ανομιαν donec fiat reconciliatio et quidem prolato iam futuri iudicii praeiudicio, partim in conscientia, in qua Deus tribunal suum erexit, partim legis sancione ore Dei enunciata Deut. 27, v. 26 . . .

    'Actuale peccatum est quicquid in actionibus sive internis ut cogitationibus cor ipsum pungentibus, sive externis ut dictis et factis, pugnat cum Lege Dei Rom. 3 et 7. Deut. 27. v. 26. Illa omnia sunt venena lethalia et inimicitiae contra Deum, ac pugnant cum foedere naturali inter Deum et nos seu conformitate illa cum Deo, quae lucebat in ipsius imagine', ibid. 251 and 254.

10. 'In ipso generis humani exordio serpens ille antiquus a verbo legis, atque ita a creationis foedere falsa interpretatione hominem abduxit (neque enim ante lapsum opus habebat Evangelio) cuius legis in imagine Dei lucentis summa erat, ut diligeret Dominum Deum suum ex tota anima (sicut et Moses summam repetit, Nunc Israel quid aliud requirit a te Deus quam ut se diligas ex toto corde tuo) et in testimonium dilectionis illius ab unius arboris usu abstineret dando Deo laudem sapientiae etc', ibid. 270.

11. 'What Olevianus has done is to move the drama of God's covenant-making in history onto the stage of the individual's experience of salvation. *Sub lege* and *sub gratia* are not just two stages in redemptive history for Olevianus but two stages in the life of every believer. The legal covenant is abrogated in history at the advent of Jesus Christ but also, in a personal way, in the life of every Christian at his conversion. . . . Olevianus appeals to the covenant of grace not primarily to explain the continuity of salvation history in the two testaments or to defend the practice of paedo-baptism but to assure the believer of the security of his salvation', Bierma, 'The Covenant Theology of Caspar Olevian', 223 and 226.

12. Cf. Knappen, *Tudor Puritanism*, 372–4.

13. R. Bayne, 'Fenner, Dudley (1558?–1587)', *DNB* xviii. 317–19.

14. *The Artes of Logike and Retorike*; cf. ch. 4 n. 23 above. Cf. also Moltmann, 'Zur Bedeutung des Petrus Ramus'.

15.   Liber I: De theologia
    Theologia est scientia veritatis quem est de Deo, ad recte beateque vivendum. Tit. 1. 1; I Tim. 2. 16 et 6. 4; II Tim. 2. 18 Ioan 1. 2. 3

    eius duo:┌─ Primum de Deo

           └─ Secundum de actionibus Dei

    Psalm 78. 7 Prover. 2. 5. 10 Iud 1. 10. Colos. 2. 2 Deut 32. 2. 3. 4.

Fenner, *Sacra theologia* (1589), fo. 1. I was able to secure a microfilm of the section on the covenant from the 1585 edition. There is no difference between the two, except that the pagination is different. The section on the covenant in the 1585 edition is 87–116; the section on the covenant in the 1589 edition begins on fo. 39. The English translation is that by J. Starke, Lambeth Palace MS 465, London. I am grateful to M. McGiffert for loaning me his microfilmed copy. The English quotation in the text is from Starke, 1.

16.   Liber II: De actionibus Dei

Secunda pars theologie, est que, precipit de actionibus Dei.

Actio Dei est ipsius effectus in omnibus ad gloriam suam patefaciendam Roma. 11. 35

Actio Dei duplex est:

Decretum Eph 1. 11

Executio decreti Act. 4. 28

Decretum est actio Dei pro voluntate sua omnia omniumque circumstantias omnes, certo, immutabilique consilio ab aeterno in sese definiens. Act 2. 23 et 15. 18. Rom. 11. 32. 35

Huic subiicitur praedestinatio Rom. 8. 28. 29. 30
Praedestinatio est decretum Dei de aeterna praecipuarum creaturarum salute et condemnatione. I Thes. 5. 9. I Pet. 2. 8 Iud. 4. Rom. 9. 22. 23. Act. 4. 28 Mat. 45 (*sic*); 14. 41.
Quo referentur reliqua omnia tanquam ad finem proximum cuius etiam finis proximum (ut et aliarum omnium postremus) gloria Dei. Rom. 9. 17.   1. 21. 23. 24. Prov. 16. 4.

Ibid., fo. 5; English translation: Starke, 5.

17.   Eius duae species

┌─ Decretum electionis

└─ Decretum reprobationis

Decretum electionis, est praedestinatio ex certos . . . constituens eligere ad salutem aeternam, propriis mediis perficienda ad gloriam gratiae ipsius Ephe. 1. 4. 5. 6. 7.

Decretum reprobationis, est praedestinatio ex proposito ad odium certos constituens reiicere ad damnationem aeternam, ex ipsarum merito, propriis mediis perficiendam ad gloriam iustitiae ipsius. I. Ths. 5. 9. I. Pet. 2. 8. Iud. 4.

Ibid.; English translation: Starke, 6.

18.   Hactenus de sanctitate naturae creaturarum praecipuarum.

Sequiter [*sic*] de sanctitate actionum eorum.

Ea est obedientia.

Obedientia, est conformatio perfecta, omium (*sic*) motum et actionum purae creaturae, ad totum opus approbatum perficiendum, ad gloriam Dei. I. Cor. 6. 20. et 10. 31 Col. 3. 17. I Sam. 15. 22. I. Cor. 7. 17. 18. 19. Mat. 6. 10. Num. 15. 39. Psal. 103. 20

Ibid., fo. 9; English translation: Starke, 12.

19.   De Hom. sanct.

Eius autem leges sunt:

┌─ Communes Iud. 23. 24

└─ Speciales I. Thes. 9. 21. 23.

Universae sanctitatis lex communis haec est, (a) omnia corporis membra eorumque singulorum actiones omnes: (b) totaque denique totius hominis natura omnia aptissima adiumenta et instrumenta ad suam sanctitatem extrinsecus exprimenda sunto. (a) Prov. 4. 22. 23. 24. etc. Rom. 6. 19. Psalm. 119. 36. 37. Iob. 31. 1. (b) I. Cor. 6. 20. et 3. 16.

Ibid., fo. 14; English translation: Starke, 19.

20. Sequuntur de alimento

vel ⎡ communi hominib. et reliquis animantibus ex herbis concesso Genes. II. 29. 30. 31

⎣ Proprio homine, ex omni fructu arboris horti, excepto arboris scientiae boni et mali, cap. 2. 17.

Atque haec sunt specialia de verbo Dei specialia de verbi adiunctis sunt ⎡ Signum arboris vitae.

⎣ Verbi sanctio de non comedando [*sic*] fructu arboris scientiae boni et mali

Signum arboris vitae, est signum gratuitum donum vitae Dei aeternae a patre in Filium per spir. Sanctum homini obedientiam praestanti, obsignans, Gen. 2. 9. et 3. 22. 24. Apoc. 2. 7 I Ioh. 14. Prov. 8. 30. 31.

Ibid., fo. 31; English translation: Starke, 40–1.

21. Liber Tertius: De Corrupta rerum conditione Lapsus et peccatum, etsi in praedestinationis impletione, ut (a) media a Deo tum decernuntur, tum disponuntur; (b) et in iis particulares actiones omnes ab ipso efficaciter agantur, (c) tamen ipsa a Deo voluntario tantum permissa, ad ultimum finem diriguntur

(a) Rom. 2: 32. I Petr. 2. 8. Matth. 25. 41. cum Esa. 54. 16. (b) Rom. 11: 36 Eph. 2. 11. Exo. 10. 1. 20. et 2. 10. et 14. I Sam. 2. 25. II Sam. 12. 11. Psal. 105. 25. Ioan. 12. 40. Gen. 3. (c) Iac. i. 13. Act. 14. 16.

Ibid., fo. 32; English translation: Starke, 42.

22. Liber Quartus: De foedere Dei et Christo Atque hactenus de peccato, ita ut ex his et singularum imaginis Dei partium analogia, omnium peccatorum natura facillime definiri, et secerni possit, modo adhibeatur in scripturarum lectione et meditatione diligentia.

Hactenus etiam de lapsu, praedestinacionis implendae medio communi in conditione corrupta: sequitur de secundo, nempe foedere Dei.

Malach 2. 10. 11. Genes. 3. 7. cum Roman 2. 14. 15. Genes. 4. 7. Roman 9. 4. 5. Ephes. 2. 12. Galat. 3. 19.

Foedus Dei est foedus cum homine eiusque semine ictum de vita et morte Genes. 2. 17. et 3. 15. et 17. 1. Galat. 3. 10. 11. Marc. 16. 26.

Ibid., fo. 39; 1585 edn., 87; English translation: Starke, 50–1.

23. Foederis membra sunt

⎡ actio Dei stipulantis   ⎤   Rom. 2. 12. 26.

⎣ actio hominis stipulationem ⎦   Gen. 17. 1. Ex. 23. 8.
   recipientis

Deut. 26. 17. 18. Marc. 16. 16.

Actio Dei stipulantis, est primum membrum foederis, quo Deus stipulatur se fore hominibus in Deum, ad benedictionem vitae, conditionem annexam impletam habuerint: sin minus contra.
Ibid.

Actio hominem stipulationem recipientis: est secundum membram foederis, quo homo recipit se fore Deo in populam ad benedictionem vitae, prout conditionem annexam impletam habuerit. Ibid.

Ibid., fos. 39–40; 1585 edn., 87–8; English translation: Starke, 51.

24. Foedus duplex est ⌐Operum foedus

    └Gratuitae promissionis foedus

Genes. 4. 7. Ierem 31. 3. Rom. 10. 5. Galat. 3. 8. 9. 10. 15. 16. 17. Ephes. 2. 12.

Ibid., fo. 40; 1585 edn., 88; English translation: Starke, 51.

25. De operum foedere

Operum foedus, est foedus ubi conditio annexa est perfecta obedientia. ibid.

Huius foederis usus in praedestinatione implenda duplex est:

Primus, ut omne os obturetur et obnoxius fiat totus mundus condemnationi Dei Rom. 3. 19.

Secundus, ad peccatum eiusque miseriam patefaciendum et carnis occasione operandum, etiam magis magisque augendum, ut ad restaurationem in foedere gratuito quaerendam impellantur. Rom. 3. 19. 20. et 7. 7. 8. 9. 10. 11. et 11. 32. Gal. 3. 22 et 5. 23.

Ibid., fo. 40; 1585 edn., 88–9; English translation: Starke, 51.

26. De foedere gratuite promissionis

Foedus gratuitae promissionis, est foedus (a) de Christo et ευλογια in ipso extante, gratuito promissis, (b) ubi conditio est, si recipiatur christus. (a) Galat. 3. 12. 13. 14. Genes. 3. 15. et 11. 35. Deuteron. 31. 15. 16. Psalm. 74. 20. et 106. 45. 47. et 111. 5. 9. Esai. 44. 17. et 59. 21. et 61. 8. Ierem. 32. 43. 44. Ezech. 16. 6. 60. et 34. 24. 25. et 36. 26. 27. et 39. 29. et 43. 9. Hos. 2. 18. Zach. 9. 11. Malac. 3. 1. (b) Iohann. 1. 11. 12. Roman. 5. 17. Ephe. 2. 5. 6. 13.

Ibid.

27. De munere Christi

Munus Christi, est quo solus factus est inter Deum et homines mediator gratuiti foederis Esa. 42. 6. I Tim. 2. 5. Hebr. 9. 15. et 12. 25. Esa. 49. 8. et 61. 4. 5. 6. Ezec. 34. 24. 25. Gal. 3. 17. cap. 5.

Mediatorem esse inter Deum et homines, est ipsos inter se undique dissidentes, in perfectam recolligere Tim. 2. 5. Ephe. 1. 10. Col. 1. 20. Ioh. 17. 21. et 13. 6. I Ioh. 1. 3. Mediatorem esse gratuiti foederis est. mediatione foedus Dei omni ex parte sancire ad salutem Ecclesiae Dei Esai 49. 8. Mal. 3. 1. Heb. 9. 15. II Sam. 7. 21. I Chr. 17. 9.

Ibid., fo. 42; 1585 edn., 92–83 (*sic*, for 93); English translation: Starke, 53.

28. Fenner, *The Sacred Doctrine of Divinitie*, 30–1.

29. Cartwright, *A Methodicall Short Catechisme*; for details see biographical sketch above in ch. 4.

30. Ibid. 340.

31. Ibid.

32. Cartwright, *Christian Religion*, 123–4.

33. Ibid. 178.

6

Conclusion

For as many as are of the workes of the Law, are vnder the curse: for it is written, Cursed is euerie man that continueth not in all things, which are written in the boke of the Law, to do them. And that no man is iustified by the Law in the sight of God, it is euident: for the iust shal liue by faith. And the Law is not of faith: but the man that shal do those things, shal liue in them. Christ hathe redeemed vs from the curse of the Law, when he was made a curse for vs (for it is written, Cursed is euerie one that hangeth on [a] tre) That the blessing of Abraham might come on the Gentiles through Christ Iesus, that we might receiue the promes of the Spirit through faith.

Galatians 3: 10–14 (Geneva Bible, 1560)

All the word of God appertains to some covenant; for God speaks nothing to man without the covenant. . . .

Every reasonable creature must of necessity be liable to one of both covenants, either that of works, or this of grace . . . Man must be under some one covenant. Adam, in the state of innocency, was under the covenant of works. Man, after the fall abideth under the covenant of works; and to this day life is promised him under condition of works done by strength of nature.

Robert Rollock, *A Treatise of God's Effectual Calling* (1597)[1]

IN 1536 Heinrich Bullinger and other representatives from the Reformed Swiss cantons met at Basle and composed the First Helvetic Confession. Its fifth article dealt with the scope and purpose of Scripture:

The Purpose of Scripture. The point of this whole scriptural canon is this, that God wishes goodness to the race of men, and that God has declared that benevolence through Christ his Son. This comes to us and is received by us through faith alone, and is expressed in love to our neighbours.[2]

For Bullinger and his colleagues the purpose of Scripture was to show forth the grace of God in Jesus Christ. Over one hundred years later the Westminster Assembly of Divines approved the

Larger Catechism, which also gives a statement about the principal scope and purpose of Scripture:

5. Q. What do the scriptures principally teach?
A. The scriptures principally teach, what man is to believe concerning God, and what duty God requires of man.[3]

The rest of the Larger Catechism is divided under these two headings; Questions 6–90 deal with the subject 'What man ought to believe concerning God', while Questions 91–196 deal with 'What [the Scriptures] require as the duty of man'.

There is a definite shift noticeable between these two confessions—two documents separated by a century of theological and ecclesiastical history. The first teaches that the Scriptures principally expound grace; the second teaches that the Scriptures principally expound duty. Even responding to God's grace is a duty of all men, according to the Westminster standards. This shift in emphasis is largely the product of the federal theology, and its emphasis on the fundamental relationship between God and man as found in the Garden of Eden, articulated by the covenant of works, and characterized by Adamic duty which is binding upon Adam and all his descendants. The First Helvetic Confession is concerned only with the fallen world and the grace needed to correct this world, a grace revealed by Scripture. The Westminster documents are much more cosmic in character: they are concerned with (1) the prelapsarian world of Eden and its covenant head, Adam; (2) the postlapsarian world and its covenant head, Jesus Christ—the second Adam who applies the gracious work of redemption to his people; and (3) the post-judgement world of the new heavens and the new earth, where Christ reigns in eternity and where man is perfect, unable to fall into sin again.

Certainly the overwhelming predominance of the federal theology in Puritan thinking and Puritanism's emphasis on duty which is required through Adam and the Edenic covenant must have something to do with the 'Puritan–Presbyterian character', with its emphasis upon diligence, duty, and discipline.[4] However, the seeds of the federal theology are not to be found in ethics or morals; it only affected these areas. Its origin and rise must be seen within the context of the flow of the history of Reformed theology in the sixteenth and seventeenth centuries.[5]

Two questions plagued the Reformed Churches of Europe and

later of New England: the question of predestination and the question of the sacraments. It is out of the questions concerning predestination that the federal theology flowed, for one of the great themes of sixteenth-century intellectual thought is that of theodicy. The proposal of a covenant before the Fall in Eden must be seen as part of a series of discussions concerning the sovereignty of God.

While the roots of this discussion run deep into medieval theology, a good starting-point might be Luther and Erasmus's discussion of the freedom of the will in 1524–5.[6] Following that controversy came Calvin's arguments with Pighius and others over the doctrine of predestination, specifically as it related to the Fall. With the growing influence of Theodore Beza the doctrine of God's decrees was transferred from the doctrine of Christ to the doctrine of the Godhead, as evidenced by Beza's 1555 work *Svmma totius Christianismi* and by the final edition of Calvin's *Institutes* (1559). During the next few years High Calvinism gained greater influence and authority, and with it rose an allied interest in scholastic methodology and natural theology.

The placing of the decrees of God under the Godhead tended to lead to controversies about the *purpose* of predestination: God's sovereign purpose was no longer simply to manifest his love in Jesus Christ the Son of God. Instead this change led to discussion about the exact number of elect faithful decided upon by God before the foundation of the world, the nature and extent of the Atonement, and most importantly, the question by laymen and theologians as to whether they were of that elect number, whether the Atonement included them, and whether simply being a member of the visible Church was sufficient for salvation. In such questions we can find the seeds of seventeenth-century English Puritanism and its concern with the morphology of conversion, which continued into the Evangelical awakening of the eighteenth century.

By 1562 Ursinus had proposed a prelapsarian covenant in Eden, which was the first really clear articulation of the federal theology by a Reformed theologian. This proposal came against a background of re-examination of the meaning and translation of the words *berith*, *diatheke*, *foedus* and *testamentum*. However, the idea lay dormant until 1584; perhaps it did not become powerful because it was not published extensively until that time.

At the same time that the first seeds of the federal theology were being planted, the same forces, emanating from Heidelberg and the

Palatinate, were pursuing more 'pietistic' emphases in quiet and subdued opposition to the extreme supralapsarianism of Bezan High Calvinism. The Heidelberg Catechism, written in 1562–3 by Ursinus and Olevianus, is composed in the first person; it affirms Calvinist orthodoxy, yet at the same time emphasizes in the first question that the believer has the comfort of belonging to Christ, and that no matter what happens—whether it be the Fall or an event in the fallen world—all things work together under the control of a loving heavenly father.[7] In contrast to the Heidelberg Catechism are the charts of Beza's *Svmma totius Christianismi*, which seemed to box God and his work into neat little squares. Both parties, Heidelberg and Geneva, believed that God works in the created world via secondary causation.

The influence of scholasticism would rise in the next twenty years. Girolamo Zanchius, another professor at Heidelberg, would use Aristotelian methodology to analyse the very essence of God and his sovereign decrees. Most of his works were published between 1570 and 1580. For Zanchius, God no longer had a hidden secret side which could be used to explain Adam's Fall, the misery of man, and reprobation. A distinction was made between the decrees and the working out of the decrees, and Zanchius appeared to teach that everything about God was open and available for analysis.[8]

1584–90 was the second stage in the rise of the federal theology, and right after that period further questions were raised about soteriology, especially in England and the Netherlands. While William Perkins would preach High Calvinism in combination with 'experimental' theology, the doctrine of temporary faith, and the 'practical syllogism', the Lutheran 'Saxon Visitation Articles' of 1592 served as precursors to Arminian doctrine:

Article IV.

On Predestination and the Eternal Providence of God. The pure and true Doctrine of our Churches on this Article.

I. That Christ died for all men, and, as the Lamb of God, took away the sins of the whole world.

II. That God created no man for condemnation; but wills that all men should be saved and arrive at the knowledge of truth. He therefore commands all to hear Christ, his Son, in the gospel; and promises, by his hearing, the virtue and operation of the Holy Ghost for conversion and salvation.

III. That many men, by their own fault, perish: some, who will not hear the gospel concerning Christ; some, who again fall from grace, either by fundamental error, or by sins against conscience.

IV. That all sinners who repent will be received into favor; and none will be excluded, though his sins be red as blood; since the mercy of God is greater than the sins of the whole world, and God hath mercy on all his works.[9]

These articles are set over and against the 'false and erroneous doctrines of the Calvinists':

On Predestination and the Providence of God.

I. That Christ did not die for all men, but only for the elect.

II. That God created the greater part of mankind for eternal damnation, and wills not that the greater part should be converted and live.

III. That the elected and regenerated can not lose faith and the Holy Spirit, or be damned, though they commit great sins and crimes of every kind.

IV. That those who are not elect are necessarily damned, and cannot arrive at salvation, though they be baptized a thousand times, and receive the Eucharist every day, and lead as blameless a life as ever can be led.[10]

Furthermore, during this same time disputations about justification included discussion about the active and/or passive obedience of Christ, and the federal theology's emphasis on the first and second Adam contributed to this discussion.[11]

Inevitably, the dispute between Arminius and the High Calvinists erupted, which led to distinct differentiations between infra-lapsarian and supralapsarian Calvinists and to the publication of the Remonstrant Articles in 1610.[12] During this period Reformed theologians had already adopted the covenant of works/covenant of grace interplay and were articulating it all over northern Europe. They were also beginning to work out some of its implications in other areas.

Finally, the Westminster Assembly put the stamp of orthodox approval on the federal theology and fully included it in the Confession and the Catechisms, all three of which are fundamental documents for Reformed orthodoxy and served as the foundation for Puritan and Presbyterian thinking in the Old World as well as the New World. Without doubt the federal theology must be included in this historical flow and should be seen as an explanation of the working out of the decrees of God, especially with regard to one question: that of God's sovereignty and Adam's Fall.

The early federal theology between 1560 and 1590 developed in two stages: the first stage culminated in 1562, after a tumultuous decade of discussion about how Adam's sin worked into God's plan and could be reconciled with God's nature. The second stage is 1584–90, when the idea was developed and combined with the Ramistic system of organization by such men as Dudley Fenner. Since the Ramistic system was dominated by dichotomies, the covenant of grace started to appear as a 'foil' to the covenant of works. After 1590 the idea of the prelapsarian covenant appeared all over Reformed Protestant Europe and the whole area of covenant thinking took on especial importance in all areas of life in the seventeenth century.

The rise of the federal theology has nothing to do with sacramental theology, the theology of Church and State and their internal and external relationships, the threat of Pelagianism, or the morphology of conversion. Its rise came primarily as a result of questions about God, his nature, and his relationship to man and the universe. It seems to stem from systematic, dogmatic thinking, not from exegetical study of Scripture. None of the sixteenth-century commentaries on Genesis 1–3 mention the prelapsarian covenant until after 1590.

The federal theology, however, did have implications, and in the area of covenant thinking these are sometimes more important and more far-reaching than its origins. The theology of the sacraments, the relationship between Church and State, the morphology of conversion, the problem of Pelagianism, the doctrine of creation and the subsequent rise of science, the celebration of the Christian sabbath, the doctrine of justification, and Christian ethics are all areas in which the federal theology would leave its mark during the seventeenth and eighteenth centuries. These implications, and the history of the federal theology itself, provide important potential areas of further research, especially in the period 1590–1662. However, our conclusion is that the federal theology's distinguishing characteristic—the prelapsarian covenant with Adam—had its origins in the predestinarian discussions which took place during the sixteenth century.

Notes

1. R. Rollock, *Tractatvs de vocatione efficaci* (Edinburgh, 1597). English translation: *A Treatise of God's Effectual Calling*, trans. H. Holland (London,

1603); reprinted in *Select Works of Robert Rollock*, ed. W. Gunn, vol. i (Edinburgh, 1849), 5–288; these quotations are from pp. 33 and 51–2 of that edition.

2. 'V. Scopus Scripturae. Status hujus Scripturae canonicae totius is est, bene Deum hominum generi velle, et eam benevolentiam, per Christum Filium suum declarasse. Quae fide sola ad nos perveniat recipiaturque, caritate vero erga proximos exprimatur', *Confessio Helvetica Prior*, in Schaff, *Creeds*, iii. 212–13; cf. *BSRK* 102.

3. 'The Larger Catechism', *BSRK* 613.

4. Cf. Rolston, 'Responsible Man' and *John Calvin versus the Westminster Confession*.

5. Some of this stream of thinking is noted by Muller, 'Predestination and Christology'.

6. Cf. ch. 2 above.

7. 'Der Heidelberger Katechismus', in *BSRK* 682–719; cf. also Schaff, *Creeds*, iii. 307–55.

8. Cf. Grundler, 'Thomism and Calvinism' and *Gotteslehre*.

9. 'Art. IV
   'De praedestinatione et aeterna providentia Dei. Pura et vera doctrina nostrarum ecclesiarum de hoc articulo.
   'I. Quod Christus pro omnibus hominibus mortuus sit, et ceu agnus Dei totius mundi peccata sustulerit.
   'II. Quod Deus neminem ad condemnationem condiderit, sed velit, ut omnes homines salvi fiant et ad agnitionem veritatis perveniant; propterea omnibus mandat, ut Filium suum Christum in evangelio audiant, et per hunc auditum promittit virtutem et operationem Spiritus Sancti ad conversionem et salutem.
   'III. Quod multi homines propria culpa pereant; alii, qui evangelium de Christo nolunt audire, alii, qui iterum excidunt gratia, sive per errores contra fundamentum sive per peccata contra conscientiam.
   'IV. Quod omnes peccatores, poenitentiam agentes, in gratiam recipiantur, et nemo excludatur, etsi peccata ejus rubeant ut sanguis; quandoquidem Dei misericordia major est quam peccata totius mundi, et Deus omnium suorum operum misereretur', *Articuli Visitatorii—The Saxon Visitation Articles*, Schaff, *Creeds*, iii. 185.

10. 'Falsa et erronea doctrina Calvinistarum.
    'De praedestinatione et providentia Dei.
    'I. Christum non pro omnibus hominibus, sed pro solis electis mortuum esse.
    'II. Deum potissimam partem hominum ad damnationem aeternam creasse, et nolle, ut potissima pars convertat ut et vivat.
    'III. Electos et regenitos non posse fidem et Spiritum Sanctum amittere aut damnari, quamvis omnis generis grandia peccata et flagitia committant.
    'IV. Eos vero, qui electi non sunt, necessario damnari, nec posse pervenire ad salutem, etiamsi millies baptizarentur et quotidie ad eucharistiam accederent, praeterea vitam tam sancte atque inculpate ducerent, quantum unquam fieri potest', Ibid. 189.

11. A. Ritschl, *Die christliche Lehre von der Rechtfertigung und Versöhnung* (Bonn, 1870), nos. 31–47, 205–337; English translation: *A Critical History of the Christian Doctrine of Justification and Reconciliation*, trans. J. S. Black (Edinburgh, 1872), 196–319.

12. 'Articuli Arminiani sive Remonstrantia', Schaff, *Creeds*, iii. 545–9.

Appendix
A Bibliography of the Federal Theology and the Covenant Idea before 1750

THE following bibliography emerged out of the frustration I encountered when trying to begin my research on the idea of the covenant and the federal theology. The books on the topic have been few, and have usually dealt with only certain specialized areas of the field. Articles that dealt with the subject cited only the most popular of earlier articles. I searched in vain for a comprehensive bibliography to guide my explorations.

The following appendix is intended to aid further research in the field. I am sure that I have missed items, but this is the most comprehensive bibliography of the European and American use of the covenant idea before 1750 that I know of. I have made no effort to cover the material that deals with the ancient Near East; that is a world unto itself. Likewise, the Lutheran discussion of Law and Gospel is only sparingly covered. The year 1750 was chosen because that marks a time when the early modern world began to be transformed into the modern world, and the abandonment of early modern theology for modern theology was beginning. The community of Reformed Churches continued to use the covenant idea, but as each year passed it became more and more restricted to that community, and that community became more isolated in the face of modern culture.

A bibliography of the covenant idea after 1750 awaits another time and another place. With the discoveries in the Middle East, and a renewed interest in the entire corpus of ideas that involve covenant, a project such as that would be a tremendous help in the attempt to understand the whole nature of bonding, both between God and man and between man and man.

1690

VITRINGA, CAMPEGIUS, *Doctrina Christianae religionis per aphorismos summatim descripta editio sexta* (Franeker, 1690; repr. Leiden, 1776), ii. 230–91.

1719

WEISSMAN, CHRISTIAN EBERHARD, *Introductio in memorabilia ecclesiastica historiae sacrae Novi Testamenti* (Stuttgart, 1719; repr. Magdeburg, 1745), ii. 697–704, 1101–4.

1841

HAGENBACH, KARL R., *Lehrbuch der Dogmengeschichte*, ii (Leipzig, 1841), no. 2, sec. 221. There were various revised German and revised English editions of this work. The discussions of the federal theology did not substantially change in any of them.

1849

GOEBAL, MAX, *Geschichte des christlichen Lebens in der rheinisch-westphälischen evangelischen Kirche* (Coblenz, 1849–52), i. 352–94; ii. 145–60.

1851

EBRARD, JOHANNES HEINRICH AUGUST, *Christliche Dogmatik*, i (1st edn., Königsberg, 1851), nos. 40–3; English translation (portions): 'German Reformed Dogmatics', trans. B. C. Wolff, *MercQR* 9 (1857), 249–72; 10 (1858), 58–83; 2nd edn., Königsberg, 1863.

1852

SCHWEIZER, ALEXANDER, 'Moses Amyraldus: Versuch einer Synthese des Universalismus und des Partikularismus', *ThJ* (1852), 41–101, 155–207.

1854

EBRARD, JOHANNES HEINRICH AUGUST, 'Cocceius und seine Schule', *RE* (1st edn.), ii (1854), 762–8.

1855

SCHNECKENBURGER, MATTHIAS, *Vergleichende Darstellung des lutherischen und reformirten Lehrbegriffs*, ii (Stuttgart, 1855), no. 22.

1857

GASS, WILHELM, *Geschichte der protestantischen Dogmatik . . .*, ii (Berlin, 1857), 252–323.

HEPPE, HEINRICH, *Dogmatik des deutschen Protestantismus im sechzehnten Jahrhundert*, i (Gotha, 1857), 139–204.

SCHWEIZER, ALEXANDER, *Die theologisch-ethischen Zustande der zweiten Halfte des 17. Jahrhunderts in der zürcherischen Kirche* (Zurich, 1857).

SUDHOFF, KARL, *C. Olevianus und Z. Ursinus: Leben und ausgewählte Schriften* (LASRK 8; Elberfeld, 1857), 88–91.

1861

HEPPE, HEINRICH, *Die Dogmatik der evangelisch-reformirten Kirche . . .* (Schriften zur reformirten Theologie, 2; Elberfeld, 1861), 204–31; rev. 2nd edn. (Neukirchen, 1935), 224–54; English translation: *Reformed Dogmatics: Set out and Illustrated From the Sources*, ed. Ernst Bizer, trans. G. T. Thompson (London, 1950), 281–319.

1865

DIESTEL, LUDWIG, 'Studien zur Föderaltheologie', *JDTh* 10 (1865), 209–76.
FRANK, GUSTAV, *Geschichte der protestantischen Theologie* (Leipzig, 1865), ii. 240–74.

1867

DORNER, ISAAK AUGUST, *Geschichte der protestantischen Theologie, besonders in Deutschland* . . . (Munich, 1867), 456–69; English translation: *History of Protestant Theology, Particularly in Germany*, trans. George Robson and Sophia Taylor (Edinburgh, 1871), ii. 32–49.

1868

FISHER, GEORGE PARK, 'The Augustinian and the Federal Theories of Original Sin Compared', *NE* 27 (1868), 468–516; repr. in George Park Fisher, *Discussions in History and Theology* (New York, 1880), 355–409.
'Scoto-Calvinism and Anglo-Puritanism: An Irenicum' (n.a.), *BFER* 17 (1868), 255–75.

1869

DIESTEL, LUDWIG, *Geschichte des Alten Testamentes in der christlichen Kirche* (Jena, 1869), 286–306, 527–34.

1870

RITSCHL, ALBRECHT B., *Die christliche Lehre von der Rechtfertigung und Versöhnung*, i (Bonn, 1870), nos. 7–41, 205–337; English translation: *A Critical History of the Christian Doctrine of Justification and Reconciliation*, trans. John S. Black (Edinburgh, 1872), 186–319.

1871

WING, C. P., 'Federal Theology', *CBTEL* iii (1871), 515–20.

1874

SEPP, CHRISTIAAN, *Het godgeleerd Onderwijs in Nederland gedurende de 16e en 17e eeuw*, ii (Leiden, 1874), 219–358.

1877

SCHAFF, PHILIP, *The History of the Creeds*, vol. i of *The Creeds of Christendom* (New York, 1877; repr. Grand Rapids, 1977), 484–9, 773–4.

1878

EBRARD, JOHANNES HEINRICH AUGUST, 'Cocceius und seine Schule', *RE* (2nd edn.), iii (1878), 291–6.

1879

BERGH, WILLEM VAN DEN, *Calvijn over het genade verbond* (The Hague, 1879).

HEPPE, HEINRICH, *Geschichte des Pietismus und der Mystik in der reformirten Kirche, namentlich der Niederlande* (Leiden, 1879), 205–40.

LINDSAY, T. M., 'The Covenant Theology', *BFER* 28 (1879), 521–37.

1880

MITCHELL, ALEXANDER, 'The Theology of the Reformed Church With Special Reference to the Westminster Standards', in *Report of Proceedings of the Second General Council of the Presbyterian Alliance* (Philadelphia, 1880), 474–84.

1882

EBRARD, JOHANNES HEINRICH AUGUST, 'Cocceius, Johannes', *SchHE* (1st edn.), i (1882), 503–4.

VAN ZANDT, A. B., 'The Doctrine of the Covenants Considered as the Central Principle of Theology', *PresRev* 3 (1882), 28–39.

1884

WALKER, GEORGE LEON, 'Jonathan Edwards and the Half-Way Covenant', *NE* 182 (1884), 601–14.

1887

GOOSZEN, MAURITS ALBRECHT, 'Bijdrage tot de kennis van het gereformeerd Protestantisme', *Geloof en Vrijheid*, 21 (1887), 505–54.

1888

T'HOOFT, ANTONIUS JOHANNES VAN, *De theologie van Heinrich Bullinger in betrekking tot de Nederlandsche Reformatie* (Amsterdam, 1888).

1889

BAUR, AUGUST, *Zwinglis Theologie: ihr Werden und ihr System*, ii (1889), 229–45.

1890

GOOSZEN, MAURITS ALBRECHT, *De Heidelbergsche Catechismus: Textus receptus met toelichtende teksten; Bijdrage tot de kennis van zijne wordingsgeschiedenis en van het gereformeerd protestantisme* (Leiden, 1890).

1891

EBRARD, JOHANNES HEINRICH AUGUST, 'Cocceius, Johannes', *SchHE* (2nd edn.), i (1891), 503–4.

VOS, GEERHARDUS, *De verbondsleer in de gereformeerde theologie* (Grand Rapids, 1891; repr. Rotterdam, 1939); English translation: 'The Doctrine of the Covenant in Reformed Theology', trans. S. Voorwinde and

Willem Van Gemeren, in *Redemptive History and Biblical Interpret-ation: The Shorter Writings of Geerhardus Vos*, ed. Richard B. Gaffin (Philipsburg, NJ, 1980), 234–67.

1896

FISHER, GEORGE PARK, *History of Christian Doctrine* (International Theological Library, 4; New York, 1896), 347–51.
MÜLLER, E. F. K., 'Cocceius (gest. 1669) und seine Schule', *RE* (3rd edn.), iv (1896), 186–94.

1897

MITCHELL, ALEXANDER F., *The Westminster Assembly: Its History and Standards* (Philadelphia, 1897), 354, 387–8.

1899

DOUMERGUE, ÉMILE, *Jean Calvin: Les hommes et les choses de son temps*, 7 vols. (Lausanne, 1899–1927).

1903

NEWMAN, ALBERT HENRY, *A Manual of Church History*, i (Philadelphia, 1903), 574–7.
WARFIELD, BENJAMIN B., 'Hosea VI: 7: Adam or Man', *The Bible Student*, 8 (1903), 1–10; repr. in *Selected Shorter Writings*, ed. John E. Meeter, (Philipsburg, NJ, 1970), 116–29.

1904

BURRAGE, CHAMPLIN, *The Church Covenant Idea: Its Origin and Development* (Philadelphia, 1904).
HASTIE, WILLIAM, *The Theology of the Reformed Church in its Funda-mental Principles*, ed. William Fulton (Edinburgh, 1904).
KORSPETER, (?), 'Zu Bullingers Gedächtnis', *RKZ* 27 (1904), 237–9.
LIECHTENHAN, RUDOLF, 'Bericht über die am 22. Juni abgehaltene Jahresversammlung der schweizerischen theologisch-kirchlichen Gesell-schaft', *Kirchenblatt für die reformierte Schweiz*, 19 (1904), 108 ff.
SCHULTHESS-RECHBERG, GUSTAV VON, *Heinrich Bullinger, der Nachfolger Zwinglis* (SVRG 82; Halle and Zurich, 1904).

1907

LANG, AUGUST, *Der Heidelberger Katechismus und vier verwandte Katechismen (Leo Juds und Microns kleine Katechismen sowie die zwei Vorarbeiten Ursinus)* (QGP 3; Leipzig, 1907; repr. Darmstadt, 1967).
MCCRIE, CHARLES GRIEG, *The Confessions of the Church of Scotland* (7th series of the Chalmers Lectures; Edinburgh, 1907), 66–73.

1908

BLODGETT, JOHN T., 'The Political Theory of the Mayflower Compact', *PubColSocMass* 12 (1908–9), 204–13.

BOHATEC, JOSEF, 'Die Methode der reformierten Dogmatik', *ThStKr* 81 (1908), 272–302, 383–401.

KORFF, EMANUEL VON, *Die Anfänge der Föderaltheologie und ihre erste Ausgestaltung in Zürich und Holland* (Bonn, 1908).

1909

GOOSZEN, MAURITS ALBRECHT, 'Aanteekeningen der toelichting von den strijd over de Praedestinatie in het Gereformeerd Protestantisme: Heinrich Bullinger', *Geloof en Vrijheid*, 43 (1909), 1–42, 393–454.

MÜLLER, E. F. K., 'Johannes Cocceius and his School', *NSHE* iii (1909), 149–50.

1910

ORR, JAMES, 'Calvinism', *ERE* iii (1910), 146–55.

SCHEEL, OTTO, 'Föderaltheologie', *RGG* (1st edn.), ii (1910), 922–4.

1911

BROWN, W. ADAMS, 'Covenant Theology', *ERE* iv (1911), 216–24.

MCGIFFERT, ARTHUR C., *Protestant Thought before Kant* (New York, 1911), 153–4.

1914

ALTHAUS, PAUL, *Die Prinzipien der deutschen reformierten Dogmatik im Zeitalter der aristotelischen Scholastik* (Leipzig, 1914; repr. Darmstadt, 1967).

LUMSDEN, JOHN (comp. and ed.), *The Covenants of Scotland . . .* (Paisley, Scotland, 1914).

1916

FOSTER, HERBERT D., 'The Political Theories of Calvinists before the Puritan Exodus to America', *AHR* 21 (1916), 481–503; repr. in *Collected Papers of Herbert D. Foster* (New York, printed privately, 1929), 77–105.

1923

SCHRENK, GOTTLOB, *Gottesreich und Bund im älteren Protestantismus, vornehmlich bei Johannes Cocceius* (BFChTh.M 5; Gütersloh, 1923).

1926

RITSCHL, OTTO, *Dogmengeschichte des Protestantismus*, iii (Göttingen, 1926), 412–58.

STOLZENBURG, A. F., *Die Theologie des Jo. Franc. Buddeus und des Chr.*

Matth. Pfaff: Ein Beitrag zur Geschichte der Aufklärung in Deutschland (NSGTK 22; Berlin, 1926), 321–78.

1927

RITSCHL, OTTO, *Dogmengeschichte des Protestantismus*, iv (Göttingen, 1927), 384–8, 466–8.

SCHRENK, GOTTLOB, 'Bund: III. Föderaltheologie, dogmengeschichtlich', *RGG* (2nd edn.), i (1927), 1364–7.

1928

BRONKEMA, FRED, 'The Doctrine of Common Grace in Reformed Theology, or New Calvinism and the Doctrine of Common Grace' (Diss. Harvard, 1928), 74–7.

1929

FLEMING, SANDFORD, 'The Place of Children in the Life and Thought of the New England Churches: 1620–1847' (Diss. Yale, 1929).

1931

MILLER, PERRY, 'Thomas Hooker and the Democracy of Connecticut', *NEQ* 4 (1931), 663–712; repr. in *Errand into the Wilderness* (Cambridge, Mass., 1956), 16–47.

MÖLLER, GRETE, 'Föderalismus und Geschichtsbetrachtung im XVII. und XVIII. Jahrhundert', *ZKG* 50 (1931), 393–440.

NORDMANN, WALTER, 'Im Widerstreit von Mystik und Föderalismus', *ZKG* 50 (1931), 146–185.

SCHNEIDER, HERBERT W., *The Puritan Mind* (London, 1931).

1932

BOS, FLORIS HENDRIK, '[Piscators] Beitrag zur Weiterführung der Bundestheologie', in *Johann Piscator: Ein Beitrag zur Geschichte der reformierten Theologie* (Kampen, 1932), 223–30.

SIMON, MATTHIAS, 'Die Beziehung zwischen Altem und Neuem Testament in der Schriftauslegung Calvins', *RKZ* 82 (1932), 3. 17–21, 4. 25–8, 5. 33–5.

1933

LANGRAF, ARTUR, 'Die Gnadenökonomie des Alten Bundes nach der Lehre der Frühscholastik', *Zeitschrift für katholische Theologie*, 57 (1933), 215–53.

MILLER, PERRY, 'The Half-Way Covenant', *NEQ* 5 (1933), 676–715.

—— *Orthodoxy in Massachusetts, 1630–1650* (Cambridge, Mass., 1933).

1935

DIEMER, N., *Het scheppingsverbond met Adam (het verbond der werken), bij de theologen der 16e, 17e, en 18e eeuw in Zwitserland, Duitschland,*

Nederland en Engeland ..., with a preface by F. W. Grosheide (Kampen, 1935).

MILLER, PERRY, 'The Marrow of Puritan Divinity', *PubColSocMass* 32 (1935), 247–300; repr. in *Errand into the Wilderness* (Cambridge, Mass., 1956), 48–98; repr. in Alden T. Vaughan and Francis J. Bremer (edd.), *Puritan New England: Essays on Religion, Society and Culture* (New York, 1977), 44–65.

1936

MORISON, SAMUEL E., *The Puritan Pronaos* (New York, 1936), 155–9.

TÖRÖK, ISTVÁN, 'Die Bewertung des Alten Testamentes in der Institutio Calvins', in Varga Zsigmond (ed.), *Kálvin és a Kálvinizmus* (Debrecen, Hungary, 1936), 121–39.

1937

HENDERSON, GEORGE DAVID, *Religious Life in Seventeenth-Century Scotland* (Cambridge, 1937), 73–5, 158–89, 260, 286–95.

MILLER, PERRY, 'The Puritan Theory of the Sacraments in Seventeenth Century New England', *Catholic Historical Review*, 22 (1937), 409–25.

1938

BAUER, KARL, *Aus der grossen Zeit der theologische Fakultät zu Heidelberg* (VVKGB 14; Lahr in Baden, 1938), 25–8.

BERKHOF, LOUIS, *Reformed Dogmatics* (2nd edn.) (Grand Rapids, 1938), 211–13; the first edition did not have a section on the covenant; the third and following editions were published under the title *Systematic Theology*.

MILLER, PERRY, AND JOHNSON, THOMAS (edd.), *The Puritans* (New York, 1938), 'Introduction'; repr. in *Errand into the Wilderness* (Cambridge, Mass., 1956), 141–52; rev. edn. of *The Puritans*, 2 vols. (New York, 1963).

NIESEL, WILHELM, *Die Theologie Calvins* (EETh 6; Munich, 1938), 36–49, 86–103; English translation: *The Theology of Calvin*, trans. Harold Knight (Munich, 1938; repr. Philadelphia, 1956), 39–53, 92–109.

SCHENCK, LEWIS BEVANS, 'Infant Baptism in the Presbyterian Church in America' (Diss. Yale, 1938). Later revised and published; see Schenck, 1940.

WENGER, JOHN C., 'The Theology of Pilgrim Marpeck', *MennQR* 12 (1938), 205–56.

1939

KNAPPEN, MARSHALL M., *Tudor Puritanism: A Chapter in the History of Idealism* (Chicago, 1939), 395–6.

MILLER, PERRY, *The Seventeenth Century*, vol. i of *The New England Mind* (Cambridge, Mass., 1939).
VISSER, HUGO BASTIAAN, *De geschiedenis van de Sabbatstrijd onder de gereformeerden in de zeventiende eeuw* (Utrecht, 1939).

1940

SCHENCK, LEWIS BEVANS, *The Presbyterian Doctrine of Children in the Covenant: An Historical Study of the Significance of Infant Baptism in the Presbyterian Church in America* (YSRE 12; New Haven, 1940). Based on dissertation; see Schenck, 1938.

1942

CHRISTY, WAYNE HERRON, 'John Cotton: Covenant Theologian' (MA thesis, Pittsburgh-Xenia Theological Seminary, 1942).
DE JONG, PETER YMEN, 'The Covenant Idea in New England Theology' (Diss. Hartford Seminary Foundation, 1942). Later published; see De Jong, 1945.

1943

LINCOLN, CHARLES FRED, 'The Development of the Covenant Theology', *BS* 100 (1943), 134–63.
SLOSSER, GAIUS J., *The Westminster Assembly and Standards, 1643–1652* (Pittsburgh, 1943; printed privately), 7, 19.

1944

BEACH, WALDO, 'The Meaning and Authority of Conscience in Protestant Thought of Seventeenth Century England' (Diss. Yale, 1944).

1945

DE JONG, PETER YMEN, *The Covenant Idea in New England Theology 1620–1847* (Grand Rapids, 1945). Based on earlier dissertation; see De Jong, 1942.
JONES, R.T., 'The Church Covenant in Classical Congregationalism', *The Presbyter*, 7 (1945), 9–22.

1948

MCKEE, WILLIAM WAKEFIELD, 'The Idea of Covenant in Early English Puritanism, 1580–1643' (Diss. Yale, 1948).
MILLER, PERRY, 'Religion and Society in the Early Literature of Virginia', *WMQ*, 3rd ser., 5 (1948), 492–522; 6 (1949), 24–41; repr. in *Errand into the Wilderness* (Cambridge, Mass., 1956), 99–140.
WELLES, JUDITH B., 'John Cotton, 1584–1652, Churchman and Theologian' (Diss. Edinburgh, 1948).

1949

CHURCH, LESLIE, *More about the Early Methodist People* (London, 1949), 247–77.

1950

BOHATEC, JOSEF, *Budé und Calvin: Studien zur Gedankenwelt des französischen Frühhumanismus* (Graz, 1950), 36–7, 246–53, 450–4, 482–3.

BROWN, PAUL E., 'The Principle of the Covenant in the Theology of Thomas Goodwin' (Diss. Drew, 1950).

WENDEL, FRANÇOIS, 'Ancien et Nouveau Testament', in *Calvin: Sources et évolution de sa pensée religieuse* (Études d'Histoire et de Philosophie Religieuses Publiées par la Faculté de Théologie Protestante de l'Université de Strasbourg, 41; Paris, 1950), 156–60; English translation: 'The Old and New Testaments', in *Calvin: The Origins and Development of his Religious Thought*, trans. Philip Mairet (New York, 1963), 208–14.

1951

DILLISTONE, FREDERICK W., 'The Covenant Conception in Calvin', in *The Structure of Divine Society* (Philadelphia, 1951), 117–29.

—— 'Federalism in the Seventeenth Century', in *The Structure of Divine Society* (Philadelphia, 1951), 130–44.

JOHNSTON, O. R., 'The Puritan Use of the Old Testament', *EQ* 23 (1951), 183–209.

KÖHLER, WALTHER, *Dogmengeschichte als Geschichte des christlichen Selbstbewusstseins: Das Zeitalter der Reformation* (Zurich, 1951).

MOLTMANN, JÜRGEN, 'Gnadenbund und Gnadenwahl: Die Prädestinationslehre des Moyse Amyraut, dargestellt im Zusammenhang der heilsgeschichtlich-foederaltheologischen Tradition der Akademie von Saumur' (Diss. Göttingen, 1951).

TRINTERUD, LEONARD J., 'The Origins of Puritanism', *ChH* 20 (1951), 37–57.

1952

GEIGER, MAX, *Die Basler Kirche und Theologie im Zeitalter der Hochorthodoxie* (Zurich, 1952), 313–40, 399–405.

LINCOLN, CHARLES FRED, 'The Covenants' (Diss. Dallas Theological Seminary, 1952).

STERN, MARVIN, 'The Puritans in Massachusetts, 1630–1685' (Honors thesis, Harvard College, 1952).

1953

BURRELL, SIDNEY, 'Kirk, Crown and Covenant: A Study in the Scottish Backgrounds of the English Civil War' (Diss. Columbia, 1953).

CALAMENDREI, MAURO, 'Theology and Political Thought of Roger Williams' (Diss. University of Chicago, 1953).

GENDEREN, JAN VAN, *Herman Witsius: Bijdrage tot de kennis der gereformeerde theologie* (The Hague, 1953).

JOHNSTON, O. R., 'The Means of Grace in Puritan Theology', *EQ* 25 (1953), 202–23.

MCLELLAND, JOSEPH C., 'The Doctrine of the Sacraments in the Theology of Peter Martyr Vermigli (A.D. 1500–1562)' (Diss. Edinburgh, 1953). Later revised and published; see McLelland, 1957.

MILLER, PERRY, *From Colony to Province*, vol. ii of *The New England Mind* (Cambridge, Mass., 1953).

MOLTMANN, JÜRGEN, 'Prädestination und Heilsgeschichte bei Moyse Amyraut', *ZKG* 65 (1953/1954), 270–303.

SMITH, (ALECK) LEWIS, 'Changing Conceptions of God in Colonial New England' (Diss. State University of Iowa, 1953).

WEST, W. M. S., 'A Study of John Hooper: With Special Reference to his Contact with Henry Bullinger' (Diss. Zurich, 1953).

—— 'John Hooper and the Origins of Puritanism', *The Baptist Quarterly*, NS 15 (1953–4), 346–68; 16 (1955–6), 22–46, 67–88.

1954

BRAUER, JERALD C., 'Reflections on the Nature of English Puritanism', *ChH* 23 (1954), 99–108.

HIGHFILL, W. LAWRENCE, 'Faith and Works in the Ethical Theory of Richard Baxter' (Diss. Duke, 1954), 10–11, 60–107, 263–301.

MURRAY, JOHN, *The Covenant of Grace: A Biblico-Theological Study* (London, 1954).

NIEBUHR, H. RICHARD, 'The Idea of Covenant and American Democracy', *ChH* 23 (1954), 126–35; repr. in Michael McGiffert (ed.), *Puritanism and the American Experience* (Reading, Mass., 1969), 219–25.

OBERHOLZER, EMIL, JUN., 'Saints in Sin: A Study of the Disciplinary Action of the Congregational Churches of Massachusetts in the Colonial and Early National Periods' (Diss. Columbia, 1954). Revised and published; see Oberholzer, 1956.

SNIJDERS, GERRIT, *Friedrich Adolph Lampe* (Harderwijk, 1954), 74–80.

1955

AMON, MARIE C., 'Influence of Political Philosophy on Education in Seventeenth-Century New England' (Diss. Saint Louis University, 1955).

BAKER, FRANK, 'The Beginnings of the Methodist Covenant Service', *LQHR* 180 (1955), 215–20.

BARTH, KARL, *Die kirchliche Dogmatik*, iv, part 1 (Zurich, 1955), sec. 57, no. 2, 57–70; English translation: *Church Dogmatics*, ed. Geoffrey W.

Bromiley and Thomas F. Torrance, iv, part 1 (Edinburgh, 1956), sec. 57, no. 2, 54–66.

EMERSON, EVERETT H., 'Thomas Hooker and the Reformed Theology: The Relationship of Hooker's Conversion Preaching to its Background' (Diss. Louisiana State, 1955).

FARRELL, FRANK E., 'Richard Sibbes: A Study in Early Seventeenth Century English Puritanism' (Diss. Edinburgh, 1955).

HALLER, WILLIAM, *Liberty and Reformation in the Puritan Revolution* (New York, 1955), 18–20, 298–300.

HENDERSON, GEORGE D., 'The Idea of the Covenant in Scotland', *EQ* 27 (1955), 2–14; repr. in *The Burning Bush: Studies in Scottish Church History* (Edinburgh, 1957), 61–74.

HUTTER, KARL, *Der Gottesbund in der Heilslehre des zürcher Theologen Johann Heinrich Heidegger* (Gossau, 1955).

KOKŠA, GEORG, *Die Lehre des Scholastiker des XVI. und XVII. Jahrhunderts von der Gnade und dem Verdienst der älttestamentlichen Gerechten* (Rome, 1955).

KRAELING, EMIL G., *The Old Testament since the Reformation* (New York, 1955), 44.

MILLER, PERRY, 'The Social Context of the Covenant', *Bulletin of the Congregational Library*, 6 (1955), no. 2, 17–23.

REITER, PAUL C., 'The Ecclesiology of Covenant Theology' (MA thesis, Dallas Theological Seminary, 1955).

SHIPLEY, DAVID, 'Wesley and some Calvinistic Controversies', *Drew Gateway*, 25 (1955), 205–9.

SIMPSON, ALAN, 'The Covenanted Community', in *Puritanism in Old and New England* (Chicago, 1955), 19–38; repr. in John M. Mulder and John F. Wilson (edd.), *Religion in American History: Interpretive Essays* (Englewood Cliffs, NJ, 1978), 17–28.

SMITH, H. SHELTON, 'The Federal Doctrine of Original Sin', in *Changing Conceptions of Original Sin: A Study in American Theology since 1750* (New York, 1955), 1–9.

STAEDTKE, JOACHIM, 'Die Juden im historischen und theologischen Urteil des Schweizer Reformators Heinrich Bullingers', *Judaica*, 11 (1955), 236–56.

VAN TIL, CORNELIUS, 'Covenant Theology', *TCERK* i (1955), 306.

WENGER, JOHN C., 'Covenant Theology', *MennEnc* i (1955), 726–7.

ZUCK, LOWELL HUBERT, 'Anabaptist Revolution through the Covenant in Sixteenth Century Continental Protestantism' (Diss. Yale, 1955).

1956

BRUGGINK, DONALD J., 'The Theology of Thomas Boston' (Diss. Edinburgh, 1956).

DRUMMOND, ANDREW L., *The Kirk and the Continent* (Edinburgh, 1956).

EMERSON, EVERETT H., 'Calvin and Covenant Theology', *ChH* 25 (1956), 136–44.

KRAUS, HANS-JOACHIM, *Geschichte der historisch-kritischen Erforschung des Alten Testaments von der Reformation bis zur Gegenwart* (Neukirchen, 1956), 49–51.

MILLER, PERRY, *Errand into the Wilderness* (Cambridge, Mass., 1956).

MOLTMANN, JÜRGEN, 'Bund: III. Dogmengeschichtlich (Foederaltheologie)', *EKL* i (1956), 621–3.

OBERHOLZER, EMIL, JUN., *Delinquent Saints: Disciplinary Action in the Early Congregational Churches of Massachusetts* (Columbia Studies in the Social Sciences, 590; New York, 1956). Based on dissertation; see Oberholzer, 1954.

PRINS, P., 'Verbond en verkiezing bij Bullinger en Calvijn', *GThT* 56 (1956), 97–111.

1957

EENIGINBERG, ELTON M., 'The Place of the Covenant in Calvin's Thinking', *RefR(H)* 10 (1957), no. 4, 1–22.

GAUSTAD, EDWIN S., *The Great Awakening in New England* (New York, 1957), 7–8.

JACOBS, P., 'Bund: IV. Foederaltheologie, dogmengeschichtlich', *RGG* (3rd edn.), i (1957), 1518–19.

McCOY, CHARLES SHERWOOD, 'The Covenant Theology of Johannes Cocceius' (Diss. Yale, 1957).

McLELLAND, JOSEPH C., 'Covenant Theology: A Reevaluation', *CJT* 3 (1957), 182–8.

—— *The Visible Words of God: An Exposition of the Sacramental Theology of Peter Martyr Vermigli, A.D. 1500–1562* (Grand Rapids, 1957). Based on earlier dissertation; see McLelland, 1953.

MOSSE, GEORGE L., *The Holy Pretence: A Study in Christianity and Reason of State from William Perkins to John Winthrop* (Oxford, 1957), 88–102.

NUTTALL, GEOFFREY F., *Visible Saints: The Congregational Way 1640–1660* (Oxford, 1957), 73–82.

WALSER, PETER, *Die Prädestination bei Heinrich Bullinger im Zusammenhang mit seiner Gotteslehre* (SDGSTh 11; Zurich, 1957).

1958

BASS, WILLIAM W., 'Platonic Influences on Seventeenth-Century English Puritan Theology as Expressed in the Thinking of John Owen, Richard Baxter, and John Howe' (Diss. University of Southern California, 1958), 56–61, 103–15, 189–98, 265–6, 284–5.

BATTIS, EMERY J., 'Troublers in Israel: The Antinomian Controversy in the Massachusetts Bay Colony, 1636–1638', 2 vols. (Diss. Columbia, 1958). Later revised and published; see Battis, 1962.

BOORSTIN, DANIEL J., 'The Puritan Tradition: Community above Ideology', *Com.* 26 (1958), 288–99.

BURRELL, SIDNEY A., 'The Covenant Idea as a Revolutionary Symbol', *ChH* 27 (1958), 338–50.

[Church of Scotland], 'Report of the Special Commission on Baptism', *Reports to the General Assembly with the Legislative Acts* (1958), 645–763. This is the second part of a report in three parts. Parts 1 and 3 can be found in the *Reports to the General Assembly with the Legislative Acts* (1957), 647–705; (1959), 630–661.

OESTRICH, GERHARD, 'Die Idee des religiösen Bundes und die Lehre vom Staatsvertrag', in Wilhelm Burges and Carl Hinrichs (edd.), *Zur Geschichte und Problematik der Demokratie: Festgabe für Hans Herzfeld* (Berlin, 1958), 11–32; repr. in Hans Hubert Hofmann (ed.), *Die Entstehung des modernen souveränen Staates* (Berlin, 1967), 137–51, and in Gerhard Oestrich, *Geist und Gestalt des frühmodernen Staates: Ausgewählte Aussätze* (Berlin, 1969), 157–78.

WOLF, HANS HEINRICH, *Die Einheit des Bundes: Das Verhältnis von Altem und neuem Testament bei Calvin* (BGLRK 10; Neukirchen, 1958).

ZIFF, LARZER, 'The Social Bond of Church Covenant', *AQ* 10 (1958), 454–62.

1959

BRUGGINK, DONALD J., 'Calvin and Federal Theology', *RefR(H)* 13 (1959), no. 1, 15–22.

FAST, HEINOLD, *Heinrich Bullinger und die Täufer: Ein Beitrag zur Historiographie und Theologie im 16. Jahrhundert* (Schriftenreihe des Mennonitischen Geschichtsvereins, 7; Weierhof, 1959).

MILLER, CHARLES, 'The Spread of Calvinism in Switzerland, Germany and France', in John H. Bratt (ed.), *The Rise and Development of Calvinism* (Heritage Hall Publications, 2; Grand Rapids, 1959), 27–62.

TORRANCE, THOMAS F., *The School of Faith: The Catechisms of the Reformed Church* (London, 1959), xliii–cxxvi.

VISSER, P. C., *Zondagsrust en zondagsheiliging* (Kampen, 1959), 12.

WILCOX, WILLIAM GEORGE, 'New England Covenant Theology: Its English Precursors and Early American Exponents' (Diss. Duke, 1959).

1960

COLLINS, GEORGE N. M., 'Covenant Theology' *Baker's Dictionary of Theology* (Grand Rapids, 1960), 144.

—— 'Federal Theology', *Baker's Dictionary of Theology* (Grand Rapids, 1960), 217–18.

DESCHNER, JOHN, *Wesley's Christology* (Dallas, 1960), 112–13.

EUSDEN, JOHN D., 'Natural Law and Covenant Theology', *NatLF* 5 (1960), 1–30.

EVANS, E. LEWIS, 'Bundestheologie', *WKL* (Stuttgart, 1960), 196–8.

GERSTNER, JOHN H., 'The Covenantal Frame of Reference', in *Steps to Salvation: The Evangelistic Message of Jonathan Edwards* (Philadelphia, 1960), 173–88.

McNEILL, JOHN T., 'Note 1 to "The Similarity of the Old and New Testaments", Book II, Chapter x of the *Institutes of the Christian Religion*', in John Calvin, *Institutes of the Christian Religion*, i (LCC 20; Philadelphia, 1960), 428.

OKI, HIDEO, 'Ethics in Seventeenth Century English Puritanism' (Diss. Union Theological Seminary, NYC, 1960).

1961

BARNES, GEOFFREY L., 'A Comparison of the Content and Meaning of the Divine Service in the Understanding of John Owen (Representing 17th Century English Puritanism) and John Cotton, Thomas Hooker and John Norton (as Representing the First Generation of New England Divines)' (Master of Sacred Theology thesis, Hartford Seminary Foundation, 1961).

BEACHY, ALVIN J., 'The Concept of Grace in the Radical Reformation' (Diss. Harvard, 1961). Later published; see Beachy, 1977.

CHALKER, W. H., 'Calvin and some Seventeenth Century English Calvinists' (Diss. Duke, 1961).

DENHOLM, ANDREW T., 'Thomas Hooker: Puritan Preacher, 1586–1647' (Diss. Hartford Seminary Foundation, 1961).

GEORGE, CHARLES H. AND GEORGE, KATHERINE, *The Protestant Mind of the English Reformation, 1570–1640* (Princeton, 1961), 183–8.

GULLEY, FRANK, 'The Influence of Heinrich Bullinger and the Tigurine Tradition upon the English Church in the Sixteenth Century' (Diss. Vanderbilt, 1961).

MØLLER, JENS G., 'Melanchthons naturretslære og føderalteologiens gerningspagt', *DTT* 24 (1961), 79–92.

POLMAN, A. D. R., 'Verbond', in *Christlijke Encyclopedie*, vi (1961), 460–3.

—— 'Verbondstheologie', ibid. 464.

STAEDTKE, JOACHIM, 'Bullinger's Bedeutung für die protestantische Welt', *Zwing.* 11 (1961), 372–88.

WILLIAMS, COLIN, *John Wesley's Theology Today* (Nashville, 1960), 84–7.

1962

BATTIS, EMERY, *Saints and Sectaries: Anne Hutchinson and the Antinomian Controversy in the Massachusetts Bay Colony* (Chapel Hill, 1962), 23–6. Based on dissertation; see Battis, 1958.

BOTOND-BLAZEK, JOSEPH B., 'An Inquiry into the Legal Enforcement of Sexual Morality in 17th-Century Massachusetts' (Diss. UCLA, 1962).

GUSTAFSON, JAMES M., 'A Study in the Problem of Authority in Congregational Church Order' (1962; typescript located in Yale Divinity School Library; call number: UC63. G978).

HOEKEMA, ANTHONY A., 'Calvin's Doctrine of the Covenant of Grace', *RefR(H)* 15 (1962), 1–12.

STAEDTKE, JOACHIM, *Die Theologie des jungen Bullinger* (SDGSTh 16; Zurich, 1962).

—— 'Die Theologie Heinrich Bullingers', *Kirchenbote: Blatt der evangelisch-reformierten Kirche in Nordwestdeutschland*, 7, no. 4 (April, 1962), 2–4.

TOFT, DANIEL JOHN, 'Zacharias Ursinus: A Study in the Development of Calvinism' (MA thesis, University of Wisconsin, 1962), 61–85.

WILLIAMS, GEORGE H., *The Radical Reformation* (Philadelphia, 1962).

1963

BREWARD, IAN, 'The Life and Theology of William Perkins, 1558–1602' (Diss. Manchester, 1963).

CAMERON, JAMES KERR (ed.), *Letters of John Johnston (c.1565–1611) and Robert Howie (c.1565–c.1645)* (Saint Andrews University Publications, 54; Edinburgh, 1963).

COENEN, LOTHAR, 'Gottes Bund und Erwählung', in Lothar Coenen (ed.), *Handbuch zum Heidelberger Katechismus* (Neukirchen, 1963), 126–35.

DOW, NORMAN, 'A Select Bibliography on the Concept of Covenant', *AusSemBul* 78 (1963), 52–62.

FULCHER, JAMES RODNEY, 'Puritan Piety in Early New England: A Study in Spiritual Regeneration from the Antinomian Controversy to the Cambridge Synod of 1648 in the Massachusetts Bay Colony' (Diss. Princeton University, 1963).

LITTLE, DAVID, 'The Logic of Order: an Examination of the Sources of Puritan-Anglican Controversy and of their Relation to Prevailing Legal Conceptions of Corporation in the Late 16th and Early 17th Century in England' (Diss. Harvard Divinity School, 1963). Later revised and published; see Little, 1969.

McCOY, CHARLES SHERWOOD, 'Johannes Cocceius: Federal Theologian', *SJTh* 16 (1963), 352–70.

McDONAUGH, THOMAS M. *The Law and the Gospel in Luther: A Study of Martin Luther's Confessional Writings* (Oxford Theological Monograph; Oxford, 1963).

MØLLER, JENS G., 'The Beginnings of Puritan Covenant Theology', *JEH* 14 (1963), 46–67.

MONK, ROBERT C., 'John Wesley: his Puritan Heritage; A Study of the Christian Life' (Diss. Princeton Theological Seminary, 1963), 154–68, 299–302. Later published; see Monk, 1966.

MORGAN, EDMUND S., 'The Half-Way Covenant', *Visible Saints: The History of a Puritan Idea* (New York, 1963), 113–38; repr. in John M. Mulder and John F. Wilson (edd.), *Religion in American History: Interpretive Essays* (Englewood Cliffs, NJ, 1978), 29–44.

PETTIT, NORMAN, 'The Image of the Heart in Early Puritanism: the

Emergence in England and America of the Concept of Preparation for Grace' (Diss. Yale, 1963). Later published; see Pettit, 1966.

ROBINSON, LEWIS MILTON, 'A History of the Half-Way Covenant' (Diss. University of Illinois, 1963).

SOMMERVILLE, C. J., 'Conversion, Sacrament and Assurance in the Puritan Covenant of Grace, to 1650' (MA thesis, University of Kansas, 1963).

SPRUNGER, KEITH L., 'The Learned Doctor Ames' (Diss. University of Illinois, Urbana–Champaign, 1963). Later revised and published; see Sprunger, 1972.

STAEDTKE, JOACHIM, 'Das Glaubensbuch der reformierten Kirche. Vierhundert Jahre Heidelberger Katechismus', *Neue Zürcher Zeitung*, no. 326 (27 January, 1963).

VAN DYKEN, SEYMOUR, 'Samuel Willard, 1640–1707: Preacher of Orthodoxy in an Era of Change' (Diss. Princeton Theological Seminary, 1963). Later published; see Van Dyken, 1972.

WALSER, PETER, 'Glaube und Leben bei Heinrich Bullinger', *Zwing.* 11 (1963), 607–16.

WALZER, MICHAEL, 'Puritanism as a Revolutionary Ideology', *History and Theory*, 3 (1963), 59–90.

WILLIAMS, J. RODMAN, 'The Covenant in Reformed Theology', *AusSemBul* 78 (1963), 24–38.

1964

BARITZ, LOREN, *City on a Hill: A History of Ideas and Myths in America* (New York, 1964).

BURRELL, SIDNEY, 'The Apocalyptic Vision of the Early Covenanters', *ScHR* 43 (1964), 1–24.

CLEBSCH, WILLIAM A., *England's Earliest Protestants 1520–1535* (New Haven, 1964).

FISCH, HAROLD, *Jerusalem and Albion: The Hebraic Factor in Seventeenth-Century Literature* (New York, 1964), 93–114, 225–53.

HASLER, RICHARD A., 'Thomas Shepard: Pastor-Evangelist (1605–1649): A Study in the New England Puritan Ministry' (Diss. Hartford Seminary Foundation, 1964).

NEW, JOHN F. H., *Anglican and Puritan: The Basis of their Opposition 1558–1640* (Stanford, 1964), 91–4, 127–8.

TWEED, ROBERT B., 'Donald Cargill, Covenanter (162?–1681): A Background Study with Special Reference to his Family Connections and other Formative Influences' (Diss. Edinburgh, 1964).

WATKINS, HAROLD K., 'The Ecclesiastical Contributions of Increase Mather to Late Seventeenth and Early Eighteenth Century Puritan Thought' (Diss. Pacific School of Religion, 1964).

YULE, GEORGE, 'Developments in English Puritanism in the Context of the Reformation', in *Studies in the Puritan Tradition: A Joint Supplement of the Congregational and Presbyterian Historical Societies* (Chelmsford, 1964), 8–27.

1965

BEARDSLEE, JOHN W., III (ed. and trans.), *Reformed Dogmatics: J. Wollebius; G. Voetius; F. Turretin* (LPT; New York, 1965).

BURSTYN, HAROLD S., and HAND, ROBERT S., 'Puritanism and Science Reinterpreted', in *Actes du XIe Congrès International d'Histoire des Sciences* (1965), no. 2, 139–43.

CHERRY, C. CONRAD, 'The Puritan Notion of the Covenant in Jonathan Edwards' Doctrine of Faith', *ChH* 34 (1965), 328–41.

MORGAN, EDMUND S., *Puritan Political Ideas 1558–1794* (Indianapolis, 1965), xx–xxv, xl–xlii.

MORGAN, IRVONWY, *The Godly Preachers of the Elizabethan Church* (London, 1965), 120–3.

ROSENMEIER, JESPER, 'The Image of Christ: The Typology of John Cotton' (Diss. Harvard, 1965).

RYRIE, CHARLES C., *Dispensationalism Today* (Chicago, 1965), 178–83.

STEARNS, RAYMOND P., 'The Half-Way Covenant and New England History', *Bulletin of the Congregational Library*, 17 (1965–6), no. 3, 8–14.

VON ROHR, JOHN, 'Covenant and Assurance in Early English Puritanism', *ChH* 24 (1965), 195–203.

WALZER, MICHAEL, *The Revolution of the Saints: A Study in the Origins of Radical Politics* (Cambridge, Mass., 1965), 55–7, 82–5, 167–71, 212–15, 221, 261.

WILLIAMS, RAY S., 'The American National Covenant, 1730–1800' (Diss. Florida State University, 1965).

1966

BEEBE, DAVID LEWIS, 'The Seals of the Covenant: The Doctrine and Place of the Sacraments and Censures in the New England Puritan Theology Underlying the Cambridge Platform of 1648' (Diss. Pacific School of Religion, 1966), 122–46.

BLANKE, FRITZ, 'Entstehung und Bedeutung des Zweiten Helvetischen Bekenntnisses', in *400 Jahres Zweites Helvetisches Bekenntnis, Geschichte und ökumenische Bedeutung* (Zurich and Stuttgart, 1966), 13–25.

CHERRY, C. CONRAD, 'Covenant Relation', in *The Theology of Jonathan Edwards: A Reappraisal* (Garden City, NY, 1966), 107–23.

DANIEL, E. RANDOLPH, 'Reconciliation, Covenant and Election: A Study in the Theology of John Donne', *AThR* 48 (1966), 14–30.

LEITH, JOHN H., 'Creation and Redemption: Law and Gospel in the Theology of John Calvin', in Paul C. Empie and James I. McCord (edd.),

Marburg Revisited: A Reexamination of Lutheran and Reformed Traditions (Minneapolis, 1966), 141–52.

MACKENZIE, J. ROSS, 'The Covenant Theology: A Review Article', *JPH* 44 (1966), 198–204.

MAIR, NATHANIEL HARRINGTON, 'Christian Sanctification and Individual Pastoral Care in Richard Baxter' (Diss. Union Theological Seminary, NYC, 1966).

MALEFYT, CALVIN S. D., 'The Changing Concept of Pneumatology in New England Trinitarianism' (Diss. Harvard 1966).

MONK, ROBERT C., *John Wesley: His Puritan Heritage* (New York, 1966), 96–106, 216–18. Based on earlier dissertation; see Monk, 1963.

OBERMAN, HEIKO A., *Forerunners of the Reformation* (New York, 1966), 123–41.

PETTIT, NORMAN, *The Heart Prepared: Grace and Conversion in Puritan Spiritual Life* (New Haven, 1966). Based on dissertation; see Pettit, 1963.

PLOTKIN, FREDERICK S., 'Sighs from Sion: A Study of Radical Puritan Eschatology in England, 1640–1660' (Diss. Columbia, 1966).

PREUS, JAMES SAMUEL NESBITT, 'Promissio: Its Hermeneutical Function in the Middle Ages and the Young Luther' (Diss. Harvard Divinity School, 1966). Later revised and published; see Preus, 1969.

RUPP, E. GORDON, 'Patterns of Salvation in the First Age of the Reformation', *ARG* 57 (1966), part 1/2, 52–66.

SHEALY, WILLIAM ROSS, JUN., 'The Power of the Present: The Pastoral Perspective of Richard Baxter, Puritan Divine, 1615–1691' (Diss. Drew, 1966), 112–49.

SOMMERVILLE, C. J., 'Conversion versus the Early Puritan Covenant of Grace', *JPH* 44 (1966), 178–97.

STAEDTKE, JOACHIM (ed.), *Glauben und Bekennen; Vierhundert Jahre Confessio Helvetica Posterior: Beiträge zu ihrer Geschichte und Theologie* (Zurich, 1966).

1967

ARMSTRONG, BRIAN G., 'The Calvinism of Moise Amyraut: The Warfare of Protestant Scholasticism and French Humanism' (Diss. Princeton Theological Seminary, 1967). Later revised and published; see Armstrong, 1969.

BURG, BARRY R., 'Richard Mather (1596–1669): The Life and Work of a Puritan Cleric in New England' (Diss. University of Colorado, 1967). Later revised and published; see Burg, 1982.

BUSCH, EBERHARD, 'Der Beitrag und Ertrag der Föderaltheologie für ein geschichtliches Verständnis der Offenbarung', in Felix Christ (ed.), *Oikonomia; Heilsgeschichte als Thema der Theologie: Festschrift für Oscar Cullmann* (Hamburg-Bergstadt, 1967), 171–90.

FOSTER, MARY CATHERINE, 'Hampshire County, Massachusetts, 1729–1754: A Covenant Society in Transition' (Diss. Michigan, 1967).

GREAVES, RICHARD L., 'John Bunyan and Covenant Thought in the Seventeenth Century', *ChH* 36 (1967), 151–69.

HOEKEMA, ANTHONY A., 'The Covenant of Grace in Calvin's Teaching', *CTJ* 2 (1967), 133–61.

MORGAN, EDMUND S., *Roger Williams: The Church and the State* (New York, 1967).

NUCKOLS, THOMAS W., 'A Holy Commonwealth: The Political Thought of Richard Baxter' (Diss. Duke, 1967).

OBERMAN, HEIKO A., 'Wir sein pettler. Hoc est verum: Bund und Gnade in der Theologie des Mittelalters und der Reformation', *ZKG* 78 (1967), 232–52.

POPE, ROBERT G., 'The Half-Way Covenant: Church Membership in the Holy Commonwealths, 1648–1690' (Diss. Yale, 1967). Later revised and published; see Pope, 1969.

PREUS, JAMES S., 'Old Testament *Promissio* and Luther's New Hermeneutic', *HThR* 60 (1967), 145–61.

PRIEBE, VICTOR LEWIS, 'The Covenant Theology of William Perkins' (Diss. Drew, 1967).

REINITZ, RICHARD M., 'Symbolism and Freedom: The Use of Biblical Typology as an Argument for Religious Toleration in Seventeenth Century England and America' (Diss. Rochester, 1967).

TANIS, JAMES, *Dutch Calvinistic Pietism in the Middle Colonies: A Study in the Life and Theology of Theodorus Jacobus Freylinghuysen* (The Hague, 1967), 116–22.

TOON, PETER, *The Emergence of Hyper-Calvinism in English Nonconformity 1689–1765* (London, 1967), 20–8.

1968

DAVIDSON, EDWARD H., 'The Covenant and God's Incentives', in *Jonathan Edwards: The Narrative of a Puritan Mind* (Cambridge, Mass., 1968), 37–56.

EUSDEN, JOHN, 'Introduction', in *The Marrow of Theology: William Ames 1576–1633* (Boston, 1968), 51–5.

GREAVES, RICHARD L., 'The Origins and Early Development of English Covenant Thought', *The Historian*, 31 (1968), 21–35.

HAENDLER, KLAUSE, 'Gesetz und Evangelium: Eine ausgewählte Bibliographie', in Ernst Kinder and Klaus Haendler (edd.), *Gesetz und Evangelium: Beiträge zur gegenwärtigen theologischen Diskussion* (WdF 142; Darmstadt, 1968), 357–423.

JOHNSON, JAMES T., JUN., 'A Society Ordained by God: A Study of English Puritan Marriage Doctrine in the First Half of the Seventeenth Century' (Diss. Princeton University, 1968). Later published; see Johnson, 1970.

KLASSEN, WILLIAM, *Covenant and Community: The Life, Writings and Hermeneutics of Pilgrim Marpeck* (Grand Rapids, 1968).

KOCH, ERNST, *Die Theologie der Confessio Helvetica Posterior* (BGLRK 27; Neukirchen, 1968).

NAGY, BARNABAS, 'Bullingers Bedeutung für das östliche Europa: Ein Forschungsbericht', in *Reformation 1517–1567; Wittenberger Vorträge: Im Auftrage des Vorbereitenden Ausschusses für die zentralen kirchlichen Veranstaltungen*, ed. Ernst Kähler (Berlin, 1968), 84–119.

PRIMUS, J. H., 'The Role of the Covenant Doctrine in the Puritanism of John Hooper', in G. C. Berkouwer *et al.* (edd.), *Opstellen aangeboden aan Prof D. Nauta* (Leiden, 1968), 182–96.

1969

ARMSTRONG, BRIAN G., *Calvinism and the Amyraut Heresy: Protestant Scholasticism and Humanism in Seventeenth-Century France* (Madison, 1969). Based on dissertation; see Armstrong, 1967.

ASHMALL, DONALD, 'John Smyth, John Robinson and the Church' (Master of Sacred Theology thesis, Andover Newton Theological School, 1969).

BREEN, TIMOTHY H., 'The Character of the Good Ruler: A Study of Puritan Political Ideas in New England, 1630–1730' (Diss. Yale, 1969). Later published; see Breen, 1970.

EHALT, DAVID R., 'The Development of Early Congregational Theory of the Church with Special Reference to the Five "Dissenting Brethren" at the Westminster Assembly' (Diss. Claremont, 1969).

FÖRSTER, WINFRIED, *Thomas Hobbes und der Puritanismus: Grundlagen und Grundfragen seiner Staatslehre* (BPW 8; Berlin, 1969), 74–126.

GREAVES, RICHARD L., *John Bunyan* (Courtenay Studies in Reformation Theology, 2; Grand Rapids, 1969), 97–121.

KRAUS, HANS-JOACHIM, *Geschichte der historisch-kritischen Erforschung des Alten Testaments* (2nd edn., Neukirchen, 1969), 53–5.

LITTLE, DAVID, *Religion, Order and Law: A Study in Pre-Revolutionary England* (New York, 1969), 71, 257–8. Based on dissertation; see Little, 1963.

OZMENT, STEVEN E., *Homo Spiritualis: A Comparative Study of the Anthropology of Johannes Tauler, Jean Gerson and Martin Luther (1509–16) in the Context of their Theological Thought* (SMRT 6; Leiden, 1969).

POPE, ROBERT G., *The Half-Way Covenant: Church Membership in Puritan New England* (Princeton, 1969). Based on dissertation; see Pope, 1967.

PREUS, JAMES S., *From Shadow to Promise: Old Testament Interpretation from Augustine to the Young Luther* (Cambridge, Mass., 1969). Based on dissertation; see Preus, 1966.

TRIPP, DAVID, *The Renewal of the Covenant in the Methodist Tradition* (London, 1969).

WILSON, JOHN F., *Pulpit in Parliament: Puritanism During the English Civil Wars, 1640–1648* (Princeton, 1969), 166–96.

1970

BAKER, JOSEPH WAYNE, 'Covenant and Society: The *Respublica Christiana* in the Thought of Heinrich Bullinger' (Diss. University of Iowa, 1970). Later revised and published; see Baker, 1980 (two works).

BREEN, TIMOTHY H., *The Character of the Good Ruler: A Study of Puritan Political Ideas in New England, 1630–1730* (New Haven, 1970). Based on dissertation; see Breen, 1969.

BREWARD, IAN (ed.), *The Work of William Perkins* (The Courtenay Library of Reformation Classics, 3; Appleford, Abingdon, England, 1970).

COOLIDGE, JOHN S., *The Pauline Renaissance in England: Puritanism and the Bible* (Oxford, 1970), 99–140.

'Covenant Theology', in T. C. O'Brien (ed.), *Corpus Dictionary of Western Churches* (Washington, 1970), 240.

DAVIES, HORTON M., *Worship and Theology in England: From Cranmer to Hooker, 1534–1603* (Princeton, 1970), 283, 335, 344, 430–2, 444.

'Federal Theology', in T. C. O'Brien (ed.), *Corpus Dictionary of Western Churches* (Washington, 1970), 322.

GRESCHAT, MARTIN, 'Der Bundesgedanke in der Theologie des späten Mittelalters', *ZKG* 81 (1970), 44–63.

GUEGUEN, JOHN A., 'Political Order and Religious Liberty: A Puritan Controversy' (Diss. University of Chicago, 1970).

HALL, DAVID D., 'Understanding the Puritans', in Herbert J. Bass (ed.) *The State of American History* (Chicago, 1970), 330–49.

HOLIFIELD, E. BROOKS, 'The Covenant Sealed: The Development of Puritan Sacramental Theology in Old and New England 1570–1720' (Diss. Yale, 1970). Later published; see Holifield, 1974.

JOHNSON, JAMES T., *A Society Ordained by God: English Puritan Marriage Doctrine in the First Half of the Seventeenth Century* (Nashville, 1970). Based on dissertation; see Johnson, 1968.

JONES, JAMES W., III, 'The Beginnings of American Theology: John Cotton, Thomas Hooker, Thomas Shepard and Peter Bulkeley' (Diss. Brown, 1970).

MCGIFFERT, MICHAEL, 'American Puritan Studies in the 1960s', *WMQ*, 3rd ser., 27 (1970), 36–67.

MARSDEN, GEORGE M., 'Perry Miller's Rehabilitation of the Puritans: A Critique', *ChH* 39 (1970), 91–105.

MEIGS, JAMES T., 'The Half-Way Covenant: A Study in Religious Transition', *Found.*, 13 (1970), 142–58.

METZ, WULF, *Necessitas satisfactionis? Eine systematische Studie zu den Fragen 12–18 des Heidelberger Katechismus und zur Theologie des Zacharias Ursinus* (SDGSTh 26; Zurich, 1970).

ROLSTON, HOLMES, III, 'Responsible Man in Reformed Theology: Calvin versus the Westminster Confession', *SJTh* 23 (1970), 129–56.

STOEVER, WILLIAM KENNETH BRISTOW, 'The Covenant of Works in

Puritan Theology: The Antinomian Crisis in New England' (Diss. Yale, 1970). Later revised and published; see Stoever, 1978.

TORRANCE, JAMES BRUCE, 'Covenant or Contract? A Study of the Theological Background of Worship in Seventeenth-Century Scotland', *SJTh* 23 (1970), 51–76.

1971

COTTRELL, JACK WARREN, 'Covenant and Baptism in the Theology of Huldreich Zwingli' (Diss. Princeton Theological Seminary, 1971).

COURTENAY, WILLIAM J., 'Covenant and Causality in Pierre D'Ailly', *Spec.* 46 (1971), 94–119.

'Covenant Theology' (n.a.), *WDCH* (1971), 243.

FISCH, HAROLD, *Hamlet and the Word: The Covenant Pattern in Shakespeare* (New York, 1971).

GIBBS, LEE W., 'The Puritan Natural Law Theory of William Ames', *HThR* 64 (1971), 37–57.

GILDRIE, RICHARD P., 'Salem, 1626–1668: History of a Covenant Community' (Diss. University of Virginia, 1971). Later published; see Gildrie, 1975.

GOULDING, JAMES A., 'The Controversy Between Solomon Stoddard and the Mathers: Western versus Eastern Massachusetts Congregationalism' (Diss. Claremont, 1971).

JOHNSON, JAMES T., 'The Covenant Idea and the Puritan View of Marriage' *JHI* 32 (1971), 107–18.

KINCAID, JOHN, 'The American Vocation and its Current Discontents', *Publius*, 1 (1971), 115–40.

LEWIS, STEPHEN C., 'Edward Taylor as a Covenant Theologian' (Diss. New York University, 1971).

LOWRIE, ERNEST B., 'A Complete Body of Puritan Divinity: An Exposition of Samuel Willard's Systematic Theology' (Diss. Yale, 1971). Later published; see Lowrie, 1974.

MCLOUGHLIN, WILLIAM G., *New England Dissent, 1630–1833: The Baptists and the Separation of Church and State*, 2 vols. (Cambridge, Mass., 1971).

MILLER, GLENN T., 'The Rise of Evangelical Calvinism: A Study in Jonathan Edwards and the Puritan Tradition' (Diss. Union Theological Seminary, NYC, 1971).

MUNSON, CHARLES ROBERT, 'William Perkins: Theologian of Transition' (Diss. Case Western Reserve, 1971).

STEINMETZ, DAVID C. 'Heinrich Bullinger (1504–1575): Covenant and the Continuity of Salvation History', in David C. Steinmetz (ed.), *Reformers in the Wings* (Philadelphia, 1971), 133–42.

TOON, PETER, *God's Statesman: The Life and Work of John Owen* (Exeter, England, 1971), 169–71.

TRINTERUD, LEONARD J. (ed.), *Elizabethan Puritanism* (LPT; New York, 1971), 302–14.

1972

BREEN, T. H., 'English Origins and New World Development: The Case of Covenanted Militia in Seventeenth-Century Massachusetts', *PastPres* 57 (1972), 74–96.

HAGEN, KENNETH, 'From Testament to Covenant in the Early Sixteenth Century', *SCJ* 3 (1972), 1–24.

MCGIFFERT, MICHAEL, 'Introduction', in *God's Plot: The Paradoxes of Puritan Piety; Being the Autobiography and Journal of Thomas Shepard* (Amherst, Mass., 1972), 3–32.

MOHR, JAMES D., 'Heinrich Bullinger's Opinions concerning Martin Luther' (Diss. Kent State, 1972).

MURRAY, JOHN, 'Covenant Theology', *EC* iii (1972), 199–216; repr. in *Collected Writings of John Murray*, iv: *Studies in Theology; Reviews* (Edinburgh, 1982), 216–40.

ROLSTON, HOLMES, III, *John Calvin versus the Westminster Confession* (Richmond, 1972).

SPRUNGER, KEITH L., *The Learned Doctor William Ames: Dutch Backgrounds of English and American Puritanism* (Urbana, 1972), 148–52. Based on dissertation; see Sprunger, 1963.

STURM, ERDMAN, *Der junge Zacharias Ursin: Sein Weg vom Philippismus zum Calvinismus (1534–1562)* (BGLRK 33; Neukirchen, 1972), 253–9.

THOMAS, GEOFFREY, 'Covenant Theology—a Historical Survey', in *Becoming a Christian: Papers Read at the 1972 Westminster Conference* (London, 1972), 5–21.

THUNDYIL, ZACHARIAS, *Covenant in Anglo-Saxon Thought* (Madras, India, 1972), 97–120.

VAN DYKEN, SEYMOUR, *Samuel Willard: Preacher of Orthodoxy in an Era of Change* (Grand Rapids, 1972), 100–19. Based on dissertation; see Van Dyken, 1963.

WARD, HARRY M., *Statism in Plymouth Colony* (Port Washington, NY, 1972), 3–14, 52–63.

1973

BÜSSER, FRITZ, 'Die Prophezei: Die Anfänge der theologischen Fakultät Zürich', *Neue Zürcher Zeitung*, no. 512 (4 November 1973).

FAULENBACH, HEINER, *Weg und Ziel der Erkenntnis Christi: Eine Untersuchung zur Theologie des Johannes Coccejus* (BGLRK 36; Neukirchen, 1973).

GREAVES, RICHARD L., 'John Knox and the Covenant Tradition', *JEH* 24 (1973), 23–32.

JONES, JAMES W., *The Shattered Synthesis: New England Puritanism before the Great Awakening* (New Haven, 1973), 21–4, 47–9, 60–4.

LEITH, JOHN H., *Assembly at Westminster: Reformed Theology in the Making* (Richmond, 1973), 91–5.

O'MALLEY, J. STEVEN, *Pilgrimage of Faith: The Legacy of the Otterbeins* (American Theological Library Association Monograph Series, 197, no. 4; Metuchen, NJ, 1973).

SELEMENT, GEORGE, 'The Covenant Theology of English Separatism', *JAAR* 41 (1973), 66–74.

TOIVIAINEN, KALEVI, *Kirkko ja valtio: Confessio Helvetica posteriorin mukaan* (Suomalaisen Teologisen Kirjallisuusseuran Julkaisuja, 89; Helsinki, 1973).

TORRANCE, JAMES BRUCE, 'The Contribution of McLeod Campbell to Scottish Theology', *SJTh* 26 (1973), 295–311.

WOOLEY, BRUCE C., 'Reverend Thomas Shepard's Cambridge Church Members, 1636–1649: A Socio-Economic Analysis' (Diss. Rochester, 1973).

1974

AHLUWALLE, HARSHARAN S., 'Salvation New England Style: A Study of Covenant Theology in Michael Wigglesworth's *The Day of Doom*', *Indian Journal of American Studies*, 4, no. 1–2 (1974), 1–12.

BAKER, J. WAYNE, 'Heinrich Bullinger and the Idea of Usury', *SCJ* 5 (1974), 49–70.

CLOUSE, ROBERT G., 'Covenant Theology', *NIDCC* (1974), 267.

FISCH, HAROLD, 'Shakespeare and the Puritan Dynamic', *SS* 27 (1974), 81–92.

FOSTER, MARY C., 'Theological Debate in a Revival Setting: Hampshire County in the Great Awakening', *Fides et Historia*, 6, no. 2 (1974), 31–47.

HAGEN, KENNETH, *A Theology of Testament in the Young Luther: The Lectures on Hebrews* (SMRT 12; Leiden, 1974).

HOLIFIELD, E. BROOKS, *The Covenant Sealed: The Development of Puritan Sacramental Theology in Old and New England 1570–1720* (New Haven, 1974). Based on dissertation; see Holifield, 1970.

LOWRIE, ERNEST BENSON, *The Shape of the Puritan Mind: The Thought of Samuel Willard* (New Haven, 1974), 96–185. Based on dissertation; see Lowrie, 1971.

MACLEOD, DONALD, 'Federal Theology: An Oppressive Legalism?', *Banner of Truth*, 125 (1974), 21–8.

REED, MICHAEL D., 'Edward Taylor: The Poetry of Defiance' (Diss. University of Oregon, 1974).

STROUT, CUSHING, *The New Heavens and the New Earth: Political Religion in America* (New York, 1974), ch. 4.

VENINGA, JAMES FRANK, 'Covenant Theology and Ethics in the Thought of John Calvin and John Preston', 2 vols. (Diss. Rice, 1974).

WEDDLE, DAVID L., 'Jonathan Edwards on Men and Trees, and the Problem of Solidarity', *HThR* 67 (1974), 155–75.

1975

AVIS, P. D. L., 'Moses and the Magistrate: A Study in the Rise of Protestant Legalism', *JEH* 26 (1975), 149–72.

BOGUE, CARL W., *Jonathan Edwards and the Covenant of Grace* (Diss. Free University of Amsterdam, 1975; published Cherry Hill, NJ, 1975).

COTTRELL, JACK WARREN, 'Is Bullinger the Source for Zwingli's Doctrine of the Covenant?', in Ulrich Gäbler and Erland Herkenrath (edd.), *Heinrich Bullinger 1504–1575, Gesammelte Aufsätze zum 400. Todestag*, i: *Leben und Werk* (ZBRG 7; Zurich, 1975), 75–83.

DAVIES, HORTON M., *Worship and Theology in England: From Andrewes to Baxter and Fox, 1603–1690* (Princeton, 1975), 6, 168, 173–4, 247, 311–14, 320, 360 n., 365, 417–18, 419, 433, 440.

GILDRIE, RICHARD P., *Salem, Massachusetts 1626–1683: A Covenant Community* (Charlottesville, 1975). Based on dissertation; see Gildrie, 1971.

GREVE, LIONEL, 'Freedom and Discipline in the Theology of John Calvin, William Perkins and John Wesley: An Examination of the Origin and Nature of Pietism' (Diss. Hartford Seminary Foundation, 1975).

LAUGHLIN, PAUL ALAN, 'The Brightness of Moses's Face: Law and Gospel, Covenant and Hermeneutics in the Theology of William Tyndale' (Diss. Emory, 1975).

POLIZZOTTO, CAROLYN M., 'Types and Typology: A Study in Puritan Hermeneutics' (Diss. London, 1975).

STAEDTKE, JOACHIM, 'Die Geschichtsauffassung des jungen Bullinger', in Ulrich Gäbler and Erland Herkenrath (edd.), *Heinrich Bullinger 1504–1575. Gesammelte Aufsätze zum 400. Todestag*, i: *Leben und Werk* (ZBRG 7; Zurich, 1975), 65–74.

STOEVER, WILLIAM KENNETH BRISTOW, 'Nature, Grace and John Cotton: The Theological Dimension in the New England Antinomianism Controversy', *ChH* 44 (1975), 22–34.

WARD, JAMES F., 'Consciousness and Community: American Idealist Social Thought from Puritanism to Social Science' (Diss. Harvard, 1975).

1976

BOGUE, CARL, 'Jonathan Edwards on the Covenant of Grace', R. C. Sproul (ed.), *Soli Deo Gloria: Essays in Reformed Theology* (Nutley, NJ, 1976), 134–45.

FORRER, RICHARD, 'The Puritan Religious Dilemma: The Ethical Dimensions of God's Sovereignty', *JAAR* 44 (1976), 613–28.

ISBELL, R. SHERMAN, 'The Origin of the Concept of the Covenant of Works' (Master of Theology thesis, Westminster Theological Seminary, 1976).

KATSH, ABRAHAM I., 'The Impact of the Bible on American Legislation', in J. Armenti (ed)., *The Papin Festschrift*, ii (Villanova, Pa., 1976), 386–98.

KENDALL, R. T., 'The Nature of Saving Faith from William Perkins (d. 1602) to the Westminster Assembly (1643–49)' (Diss. Oxford, 1976). Later published; see Kendall, 1979.

LUCAS, PAUL R., *Valley of Discord: Church and Society along the Connecticut River 1636–1745* (Hanover, NH, 1976).

LUISI, MIRIAM P., 'The Community of Consent in the Thought of Jonathan Edwards' (Diss. Fordham, 1976).

MCGIFFERT, MICHAEL, 'The Problem of the Covenant in Puritan Thought: Peter Bulkeley's *Gospel Covenant*', *NEHGR* 130 (1976), 107–29.

MULLER, RICHARD A., 'Predestination and Christology in Sixteenth Century Reformed Theology' (Diss. Duke, 1976). Later revised and published; see Muller, 1986.

RILEY, PATRICK, 'Three 17th Century German Theorists of Federalism: Althusius, Hugo and Leibniz', *Publius*, 6 (1976), 7–41.

SPEAR, WAYNE RENWICK, 'Covenanted Uniformity in Religion: The Influence of the Scottish Commissioners upon the Ecclesiology of the Westminster Assembly' (Diss. Pittsburgh, 1976).

1977

BEACHY, ALVIN J., *The Concept of Grace in the Radical Reformation* (BHRef 17; Nieuwkoop, 1977). Based on dissertation; see Beachy, 1961.

EMERSON, EVERETT H., *Puritanism in America, 1620–1750* (Boston, 1977).

GREVEN, PHILIP, *The Protestant Temperament: Patterns of Child-Rearing, Religious Experience and the Self in Early America* (New York, 1977).

HAMM, BERNDT, *Promissio, pactum, ordinatio: Freiheit und Selbstbindung Gottes in der scholastischen Gnadenlehre* (BHTh 54; Tübingen, 1977).

PROZESKY, MARTIN H., 'The Emergence of Dutch Pietism', *JEH* 28 (1977), 29–37.

SOLBERG, WINTON U., *Redeem the Time: The Puritan Sabbath in Early America* (Cambridge, Mass., 1977), 35–40, 145–51.

STAEDTKE, JOACHIM, 'Bullinger's Theologie: Eine Forsetzung der Zwinglischen?', in *Bullinger-Tagung 1975*, ed. U. Gäbler and Endre Zsindely (Zurich, 1977), 87–98.

TOLMIE, MURRAY, *The Triumph of the Saints: The Separate Churches of London, 1616–1649* (Cambridge, 1977), 13–15, 24, 26, 59, 66, 90, 112, 196.

TORRANCE, JAMES BRUCE, 'The Covenant Concept in Scottish Theology and Politics and its Legacy' (Inaugural Lecture, 20 October 1977, King's College, University of Aberdeen, Aberdeen, Scotland; mimeograph made available to me by the Revd Paul Copeland, Wishaw, Scotland). Later published; see Torrance, 1981.

WILSON-KASTNER, PATRICIA, 'Jonathan Edwards: History and the Covenant', *Andrews University Seminary Studies*, 15 (1977), 205–16.

ZARET, DAVID, 'An Analysis of the Development and Content of the Contractual Theory of Pre-Revolutionary Puritanism' (Diss. Oxford, 1977). Later revised and published; see Zaret, 1985.

1978

BROMILEY, GEOFFREY W., *Historical Theology: An Introduction* (Grand Rapids: 1978).

KNOX, R. BUICK, 'The History of Doctrine in the Seventeenth Century', in Hubert Cunliffe-Jones (ed.), *A History of Christian Doctrine* (Edinburgh, 1978), 437–8.

MULLER, RICHARD A., 'Perkins' *A Golden Chaine*: Predestinarian System or Schematized *Ordo Salutis*?', *SCJ* 9 (1978), 68–81.

MURPHY, SUSAN, 'In Remembrance of Me: Sacramental Theology and Practice in Colonial New England' (Diss. University of Washington, 1978).

SMITH, MORTON H., 'The Church and Covenant Theology', *JETS* 21 (1978), 47–65.

STOEVER, WILLIAM KENNETH BRISTOW, *'A Faire and Easie Way to Heaven': Covenant Theology and Antinomianism in Early Massachusetts* (Middletown, Conn., 1978). Based on dissertation; see Stoever, 1970.

WATTS, MICHAEL, *The Dissenters* (Oxford, 1978), 3, 25, 29–31, 42, 52, 55, 62, 75, 261.

1979

ANDERSON, PHILIP J., 'Presbyterianism and the Gathered Churches in Old and New England, 1640–1662: The Struggle for Church Government in Theory and Practice' (Diss. Oxford, 1979).

BUTLER, CHARLES J., 'Religious Liberty and Covenant Theology' (Diss. Temple, 1979).

COPELAND, ROBERT, and HEMPHILL, BRUCE, 'Historical Study: Covenanting and the Ordination Queries', Reformed Presbyterian Church of North America, *Minutes of the Synod and Yearbook, 1979* (Pittsburgh, 1979), 113–21.

CURRIE, MARY M., 'The Puritan Half-Way Covenants: A Contemporary Issue', *AusSemBul*, 95 (1979), 29–39.

FERGUSON, SINCLAIR B., 'The Doctrine of the Christian Life in the Teaching of Dr. John Owen (1616–1683)' (Diss. Aberdeen, 1979). Later revised and published; see Ferguson, 1987.

HALL, BASIL, 'The Early Rise and Gradual Decline of Lutheranism in England (1520–1600)', in Derek Baker (ed.), *Reform and Reformation: England and the Continent c. 1500–c. 1750* (SCH(L) subs., 2; Oxford, 1979), 103–32.

HIGGINS, LESLEY HALL, 'Radical Puritans and Jews in England, 1648–1672' (Diss. Yale, 1979).

HILL, CHRISTOPHER, 'Covenant Theology and the Concept of "A Public Person" ', in Alkis Kontos (ed.), *Powers, Possessions and Freedoms: Essays in Honor of C. B. MacPherson* (Toronto, 1979), 3–22.

HÖPFL, HARRO, and THOMPSON, MARTYN P., 'The History of Contract as a Motif in Political Thought', *AHR* 84 (1979), 919–45.

HÜGLIN, THOMAS, 'Johannes Althusius: Medieval Constitutionalist or Modern Federalist?', *Publius*, 9 (1979), 9–42.

KANTROW, ALAN M., 'Jacob's Ladder: Anglican Traditionalism in the New England Mind' (Diss. Harvard, 1979).

KENDALL, R. T., *Calvin and English Calvinism to 1649* (Oxford Theological Monograph; Oxford, 1979). Based on dissertation; see Kendall, 1976.

LEAHY, FREDERICK S., *The Theological Basis for Covenanting* (Pittsburgh, The Reformed Presbyterian Theological Seminary, 1979).

LETHAM, ROBERT W. A., 'Saving Faith and Assurance in Reformed Theology: Zwingli to the Synod of Dort' (Diss. Aberdeen, 1979).

LYALL, FRANCIS, 'Of Metaphors and Analogies: Legal Language and Covenant Theology', *SJTh* 32 (1979), 1–18.

MORGAN, JOHN, 'Puritanism and Science: A Reinterpretation', *HistJ* 22 (1979), 535–60.

NERI, D., 'Antiassolutismo e federalismo nel pensiero di Althusius', *Pensiero Polit.* 12 (1979), 393–409.

NORTH, GARY, 'From Covenant to Contract: Pietism and Secularism in Puritan New England, 1691–1720', *JCR* 6 (1979–80), no. 2, 155–94.

O'BRIEN, T. C., 'Federal Theology', *EDR* ii (1979), 1332.

OKI, HIDEO, 'From William Ames (1576–1633) towards Milton concerning the Developmental of the Puritan Covenant Theology', *MCJN* 3 (1979), 2–3.

STOUT, DOUGLAS ANDREW, 'The Origins and Early Development of the Reformed Idea of Covenant' (Diss. Cambridge, 1979).

WILBURN, RALPH G., 'Background for Disciple Theology in North America: From Colonial Covenant Theology to the Great Revivals', *Lexington Theological Quarterly*, 14 (1979), 19–32.

1980

BAKER, J. WAYNE, *Covenant and Community in the Thought of Heinrich Bullinger* (Philadelphia, Center for the Study of Federalism, Temple University, 1980).

—— *Heinrich Bullinger and the Covenant: The Other Reformed Tradition* (Athens, Ohio, 1980). Based on dissertation; see Baker, 1970.

BIERMA, LYLE DEAN, 'The Covenant Theology of Caspar Olevian' (Diss. Duke, 1980).

BUTLER, CHARLES J., *Covenant Theology and the Development of Religious Liberty* (Philadelphia, Center for the Study of Federalism, Temple University, 1980).

ELAZAR, DANIEL J., *From Biblical Covenant to Modern Federalism: The Federal Theology Bridge* (Philadelphia, Center for the Study of Federalism, Temple University, 1980).

—— 'The Political Theory of Covenant: Biblical Origins and Modern Developments', *Publius*, 10 (1980), 3–30.

ELAZAR, DANIEL J., and KINCAID, JOHN (edd.), 'Covenant, Polity and Constitutionalism', *Publius*, 10 (1980), no. 4.

FISCH, HAROLD, *Covenant Motifs in Seventeenth Century English Literature* (Philadelphia, Center for the Study of Federalism, Temple University, 1980).

HÜGLIN, THOMAS O., 'Althusius, Federalism, and the Notion of the State', *Pensiero Polit.* 13 (1980), 225–32.

—— *Covenant and Federalism in the Politics of Althusius* (Philadelphia, Center for the Study of Federalism, Temple University, 1980).

JONGE, CHRISTIAAN DE, 'De Irenische Ecclesiologie van Franciscus Junius (1545–1602)' (Diss. Leiden, 1980; published Nieuwkoop, 1980; BHRef 30).

KARLBERG, MARK WALTER, 'The Mosaic Covenant and the Concept of Works in Reformed Hermeneutics: A Historical-Critical Analysis with Particular Attention to Early Covenant Eschatology' (Diss. Westminster Theological Seminary, 1980).

—— 'Reformed Interpretation of the Mosaic Covenant', *WThJ* 43 (1980), 1–57.

KINCAID, JOHN (comp.), *Working Bibliography on Covenant and Politics* (revised edn.: Philadelphia, Center for the Study of Federalism, Temple University, 1980).

LACHMAN, DAVID, 'The Marrow Controversy: 1718–1723; An Historical and Theological Analysis' (Diss. St Andrews, 1980).

LUTZ, DONALD, 'From Covenant to Constitution in American Political Thought', *Publius*, 10 (1980), 101–33.

MCCOY, CHARLES SHERWOOD, *History, Humanity and Federalism in the Theology and Ethics of Johannes Cocceius* (Philadelphia, Center for the Study of Federalism, Temple University, 1980).

MCGIFFERT, MICHAEL, 'Covenant, Crown and Commons in Elizabethan Puritanism', *JBS* 20 (1980), 32–52 (repr. Philadelphia, Center for the Study of Federalism, Temple University, 1980).

MULLER, RICHARD A., 'Covenant and Conscience in English Reformed Theology: Three Variations on a 17th Century Theme', *WThJ* 42 (1980), 308–34.

OSTERHAVEN, M. EUGENE, 'Calvin on the Covenant', *RefR(H)* 33 (1980), 136–49; repr. in Donald K. McKim (ed.), *Readings in Calvin's Theology* (Grand Rapids, 1984), 89–106.

OSTROM, VINCENT, 'Hobbes, Covenant and Constitution', *Publius*, 10 (1980), 83–100.

REED, MICHAEL D., 'Early American Puritanism: The Language of its Religion', *American Imago*, 37 (1980), 278–333.

1981

CONFORTI, JOSEPH A., *Samuel Hopkins and the New Divinity Movement: Calvinism, the Congregational Ministry, and Reform in New England between the Great Awakenings* (Grand Rapids, 1981).

FAULENBACH, HEINER, 'Coccejus, Johannes (1603–1669)', *TRE* viii (1981), 132–40.

FIERING, NORMAN, *Jonathan Edwards's Moral Thought and its British Context* (Chapel Hill, 1981), 73, 343.

FOSTER, MARSHALL and SWANSON, MARY-ELAINE, *The American Covenant: The Untold Story* (Thousand Oaks, California, 1981).

JAMIESON, JOHN F., 'Jonathan Edwards's Change of Position on Stoddardeanism', *HThR* 74 (1981), 79–99.

KELLER, KARL, 'The Loose, Large Principles of Solomon Stoddard', *Early American Literature*, 16 (1981), 27–41.

LILLBACK, PETER ALAN, 'Ursinus' Development of the Covenant of Creation: A Debt to Melanchthon or Calvin?', *WThJ* 43 (1981), 247–88.

LOCHER, GOTTFRIED W., *Zwingli's Thought: New Perspectives* (SHCT 25; Leiden, 1981).

McGIFFERT, MICHAEL, 'William Tyndale's Conception of Covenant', *JEH* 32 (1981), 167–84.

MULLER, RICHARD A., 'The Spirit and the Covenant: John Gill's Critique of the *Pactum Salutis*', *Found.* 24 (1981), 4–14.

PAUL, ROBERT S., 'The Covenant in Church History', *AusSemBul* 96 (1981), 38–50.

PARMER, PHILL W., ' "Like Little Paul in Person, Voice and Grace": A Comparative Study of Edward Taylor and St. Paul' (Diss. Louisiana State, 1981).

PAUL, ROBERT S., 'Social Justice and the Puritan "Dual Ethic" ', in *Intergerini Parietis Septum (Ephesians 2: 14): Essays Presented to Markus Barth on his Sixty-Fifth Birthday*, ed. Dikran Y. Hadidian (Pittsburgh Theological Monograph Series, 33; Pittsburgh, 1981), 251–84.

SHAW, MARK RANDOLPH, 'The Marrow of Practical Divinity: A Study in the Theology of William Perkins' (Diss. Westminster Theological Seminary, 1981), 111–53.

TORRANCE, JAMES BRUCE, 'The Covenant Concept in Scottish Theology and Politics and its Legacy', *SJTh* 34 (1981), 225–43 (repr. Philadelphia, Center for the Study of Federalism, Temple University, 1980). Based on inaugural lecture; see Torrance, 1977.

YULE, GEORGE, *Puritans in Politics: The Religious Legislation of the Long Parliament 1640–1647* (The Courtenay Library of Reformation Classics, 13; Appleford, Abingdon, England, 1981), 25–6, 42–4, 65–6.

ZENS, JON, 'An Examination of the Presuppositions of Covenant and Dispensational Theology', in *Studies in Theology and Ethics* (Malin, Oregon, 1981), 1–50.

1982

BELL, M. CHARLES, 'Saving Faith and Assurance of Salvation in the Teaching of John Calvin and Scottish Theology' (Diss. Aberdeen, 1982). Later published; see Bell, 1985.

BREYMEYER, RICHARD, 'Ein unbekannter Katalog der Bibliothek des Johannes Coccejus—der Schlüssel zum Buchbesitz des bedeutendsten reformierten Theologen des 17. Jahrhunderts', *Linguistica Biblica*, 52 (1982), 7–40.

BURG, BARRY, *Richard Mather* (Boston, 1982). Based on dissertation; see Burg, 1967.

COHEN, CHARLES LLOYD, 'The Heart and the Book: Faith, the Bible, and the Psychology of Puritan Religious Experience' (Diss. University of California, Berkeley, 1982). Later published; see Cohen, 1986.

DOUGLAS, WALTER B., 'The Sabbath in Puritanism', in *The Sabbath in Scripture and History*, ed. Kenneth A. Strand (Washington, DC, 1982), 229–43.

FERGUSON, SINCLAIR B., 'The Teaching of the Confession', in A. I. C. Heron (ed.), *The Westminster Confession in the Church Today* (Edinburgh, 1982), 28–39.

GWYN, DOUGLAS, 'The Apocalyptic Word of God: The Life and Message of George Fox (1624–1691)' (Diss. Drew, 1982).

KENDALL, R. T., 'The Puritan Modification of Calvin's Theology', in W. Stanford Reid (ed.), *John Calvin: His Influence in the Western World* (Grand Rapids, 1982), 199–214.

LILLBACK, PETER A., 'Calvin's Covenantal Response to the Anabaptist View of Baptism', *Christianity and Civilization*, 1 (1982), 185–232.

McGIFFERT, MICHAEL, 'Grace and Works: The Rise and Division of Covenant Divinity in Elizabethan Puritanism', *HThR* 75 (1982), 463–502.

MULLER, RICHARD A., 'The Federal Motif in Seventeenth Century Arminian Theology', *Nederlands Archief voor Kerkgeschiedenis*, 62 (1982), 102–22.

SELL, ALAN P. F., *The Great Debate: Calvinism, Arminianism and Salvation* (West Sussex, England, 1982).

SPRUNGER, KEITH L., *Dutch Puritanism: A History of English and Scottish Churches of the Netherlands in the Sixteenth and Seventeenth Centuries* (SHCT 31; Leiden, 1982).

STOUT, HARRY S., 'Word and Order in Colonial New England', in Nathan O. Hatch and Mark A. Noll (edd.), *The Bible in America* (New York, 1982), 19–38.

TORRANCE, JAMES B., 'Calvinism and Puritanism in England and Scotland: Some Basic Concepts in the Development of "Federal Theology" ', South African Congress for Calvin Research, *Calvinus Reformator: His Contribution to Theology, Church and Society* (Potchefstroom, 1982), 264–86.

—— 'Strengths and Weaknesses of the Westminster Theology', in A. I. C. Heron (ed.), *The Westminster Confession in the Church Today* (Edinburgh, 1982), 40–54.

WALLACE, DEWEY D., *Puritans and Predestination: Grace in English Protestant Theology 1525–1695* (Studies in Religion; Chapel Hill, 1982), 197–8.

1983

BIERMA, LYLE D., 'Federal Theology in the Sixteenth Century: Two Traditions?', *WThJ* 45 (1983), 304–21.

GLEASON, RONALD N., 'Calvin and Bavinck on the Lord's Supper', *WThJ* 45 (1983), 273–303.

GOETERS, J. F. GERHARD, 'Föderaltheologie', *TRE* xi (1983), 246–52.

HELM, PAUL, 'Calvin and the Covenant: Unity and Continuity', *EQ* 55 (1983), 65–81.

LANE, TONY, 'The Quest for the Historical Calvin', *EQ* 55 (1983), 95–113.

LETHAM, ROBERT W. A., 'The *Foedus Operum*: Some Factors Accounting for its Development', *SCJ* 14 (1983), 457–67.

McGIFFERT, MICHAEL, 'God's Controversy with New England', *AHR* 88 (1983), 1151–74.

McKIM, DONALD K., 'William Perkins and the Theology of the Covenant', in Horton M. Davies (ed.), *Studies of the Church in History* (Allison Park, Pa., 1983), 85–101.

MASON, ROGER, 'Covenant and Commonweal: The Language of Politics in Reformation Scotland', in Norman MacDougall (ed.), *Church, Politics and Society, Scotland 1408–1929* (Edinburgh, 1983), 97–126.

SHAW, MARK R., 'Drama in the Meeting House: The Concept of Conversion in the Theology of William Perkins', *WThJ* 45 (1983), 41–72.

TORRANCE, JAMES B., 'The Incarnation and "Limited Atonement" ', *EQ* 55 (1983), 83–94.

1984

BREITENBACH, WILLIAM, 'The Consistent Calvinism of the New Divinity Movement', *WMQ*, 3rd ser., 41 (1984), 241–64.

COGGINS, JAMES R., and WHITE, B. R., 'The Theological Positions of John Smyth', *BQ* 30 (1984), 247–64.

GURA, PHILIP F., *A Glimpse of Sion's Glory: Puritan Radicalism in New England, 1620–1660* (Middletown, Conn., 1984).

HIGGINS, JOHN R., 'Aspects of the Doctrine of the Holy Spirit during the Antinomian Controversy of New England with Special Reference to John Cotton and Anne Hutchinson' (Diss. Westminster Theological Seminary, 1984).

HOSKINS, RICHARD J., 'The Original Separation of Church and State in America', *Journal of Law and Religion*, 2 (1984), 221–39.

KLUNDER, JACK D., 'The Application of Holy Things: A Study of the Covenant Preaching in the Eighteenth Century Dutch Colonial Church' (Diss. Westminster Theological Seminary, 1984).

LOVIN, ROBIN W., 'Equality and Covenant Theology', *Journal of Law and Religion*, 2 (1984), 241–62.

MONTGOMERY, MICHAEL S. (comp.), *American Puritan Studies: An Annotated Bibliography of Dissertations, 1882–1981* (Bibliographies and Indexes in American History, 1; Westport, Conn., 1984).

OAKLEY, FRANCIS J., *Omnipotence, Covenant and Order: An Excursion in the History of Ideas from Abelard to Leibniz* (Ithaca, NY, 1984).

PELIKAN, JAROSLAV, 'The History of the Covenant', in *Reformation of Church and Dogma (1300–1700)*, vol. iv of *The Christian Tradition: A History of the Development of Doctrine* (Chicago, 1984).

PREUS, KLEMET, 'Jonathan Edwards: A Case of Medium-Message Conflict', *Concordia Theological Quarterly*, 48 (1984), 279–97.

SCOBEY, DAVID M., 'Revising the Errand: New England's Ways and the Puritan Sense of the Past', *WMQ*, 3rd ser., 41 (1984), 3–31.

SHAWCROSS, JOHN T., 'Milton and the Covenant: The Christian View of Old Testament Theology', in James H. Sims and Leland Ryken (edd.), *Milton and Scriptural Tradition: The Bible into Poetry* (Columbia, Mo., 1984), 160–91.

SPINKS, BRYAN D., *From the Lord and 'the best Reformed Churches': A Study of the Eucharistic Liturgy in the English Puritan and Separatist Traditions, 1550–1633* (Rome, 1984).

VAN BIBBER, JAMES J., 'The Concepts of Church Membership and Ministry in the Covenantal Theology of Jonathan Edwards' (Diss. Southwestern Baptist Theological Seminary, 1984).

WEIR, DAVID A., '*Foedus Naturale*: The Origins of Federal Theology in Sixteenth Century Reformation Thought' (Diss. St Andrews, 1984). Revised and published; see Weir, 1989.

1985

BELL, M. CHARLES, *Calvin and Scottish Theology: The Doctrine of Assurance* (Edinburgh, 1985). Based on dissertation; see Bell, 1982.

HICKS, JOHN M., 'The Theology of Grace in the Thought of Jacobus Arminius and Philip van Limborch: A Study in the Development of Seventeenth-Century Dutch Arminianism' (Diss. Westminster Theological Seminary, 1985).

KLAAREN, EUGENE M., *Religious Origins of Modern Science: Belief in Creation in Seventeenth-Century Thought* (Lanham, Md., 1985).

LILLBACK, PETER A., 'The Binding of God: Calvin's Role in the Development of Covenant Theology' (Diss. Westminster Theological Seminary, 1985).

MULLER, RICHARD A., *A Dictionary of Latin and Greek Theological Terms Drawn Principally from Protestant Scholastic Theology* (Grand Rapids, 1985).

POTTER, MARY LANE, 'The "Whole Office of the Law" in the Theology of John Calvin', *Journal of Law and Religion*, 3 (1985), 117–39.

PRESTWICH, MENNA (ed.), *International Calvinism, 1541–1715* (Oxford, 1985).

ZARET, DAVID, *The Heavenly Contract: Ideology and Organization in Pre-Revolutionary Puritanism* (Chicago, 1985). Based on dissertation; see Zaret, 1977.

1986

BOUGHTON, LYNNE C., 'Supralapsarianism and the Role of Metaphysics in Sixteenth-Century Reformed Theology', *WThJ* 48 (1986), 63–96.

BURCHILL, CHRISTOPHER J., 'On the Consolation of a Christian Scholar: Zacharias Ursinus (1534–83) and the Reformation in Heidelberg', *JEH* 37 (1986), 565–83.

COHEN, CHARLES LLOYD, *God's Caress: The Psychology of Puritan Religious Experience* (New York, 1986). Based on dissertation; see Cohen, 1982.

GERSTNER, JONATHAN N., 'The Thousand Generation Covenant: Dutch Reformed Covenant Theology and the Colonists of South Africa' (Diss. University of Chicago, 1986).

LAPLANCHE, FRANÇOIS, *L'Écriture, Le Sacré, et L'Histoire: Érudits et Politiques Protestants Devant la Bible en France au XVIIᵉ Siècle* (Studies of the Institute of Intellectual Relations Between the West-European Countries in the Seventeenth Century, 12; Amsterdam, 1986).

McCOY, MICHAEL R., 'In Defense of the Covenant: The Sacramental Debates of Eighteenth Century New England' (Diss. Emory, 1986).

McSWAIN, JAMES B., 'The Controversy over Infant Baptism in England, 1640–1700' (Diss. Memphis State, 1986).

MULLER, RICHARD A., *Christ and the Decree: Christology and Predestination in Reformed Theology from Calvin to Perkins* (Studies in Historical Theology, 2; Durham, NC, 1986). Based on dissertation; see Muller, 1976.

STEPHENS, W. P., *The Theology of Huldrych Zwingli* (Oxford, 1986).

STOUT, HARRY S., *The New England Soul: Preaching and Religious Culture in Colonial New England* (New York, 1986).

VON ROHR, JOHN, *The Covenant of Grace in Puritan Thought* (American Academy of Religion, Studies in Religion, 45; Atlanta, 1986).

1987

FERGUSON, SINCLAIR B., *John Owen on the Christian Life* (Edinburgh, 1987). Based on dissertation; see Ferguson, 1979.

LUTZ, DONALD S., and WARREN, JACK D., *A Covenanted People: The Religious Tradition and the Origins of American Constitutionalism* (Providence, RI, The John Carter Brown Library, 1987).

PARRY, G. J. R., *A Protestant Vision: William Harrison and the Reformation of Elizabethan England* (Cambridge Studies in the History and Theory of Politics; Cambridge, 1987).

VISSER, DERK, 'The Covenant in Zacharias Ursinus', *SCJ* 18 (1987), 531–44.

WHITTEMORE, ROBERT C., *The Transformation of the New England Theology* (American University Studies, Ser. vii, Theology and Religion, 23; New York, 1987).

1988

HESSELINK, I. JOHN, 'Law and Gospel or Gospel and Law? Calvin's Understanding of the Relationship', in Robert V. Schnucker (ed.), *Calviniana: Ideas and Influence of Jean Calvin (Sixteenth Century Essays and Studies)*, 10 (1988), 13–32.

HUGHES, RICHARD T. AND ALLEN, C. LEONARD, *Illusions of Innocence: Protestant Primitivism in America, 1630–1875* (Chicago, 1988).

MCGIFFERT, MICHAEL, 'From Moses to Adam: The Making of the Covenant of Works', *SCJ* 19 (1988), 131–55.

REID, W. STANFORD, 'John Knox's Theology of Political Government', *SCJ* 19 (1988), 529–40.

TORRANCE, JAMES B., 'Interpreting the Word by the Light of Christ or the Light of Nature? Calvin, Calvinism and Barth', in Robert V. Schnucker (ed.), *Calviniana: Ideas and Influence of Jean Calvin (Sixteenth Century Essays and Studies)*, 10 (1988), 255–67.

1989

DELBANCO, ANDREW, *The Puritan Ordeal* (Cambridge, Mass., 1989).

WEIR, DAVID A., *The Origins of the Federal Theology in Sixteenth-Century Reformation Thought* (Oxford, 1990). Based on earlier dissertations; see Weir, 1984.

Researchers in this area should be aware of the following two journals which deal especially with the covenant idea:

Covenant Letter
Publius: The Journal of Federalism

Both are published by the Center for the Study of Federalism, Room 512, Gladfelter Hall, Temple University, Philadelphia, Pa., 19122, USA.

Keith Thomas discusses the opposite kind of covenant—the covenant with Satan—in his 1971 volume *Religion and the Decline of Magic* (New York, 1971), 438.

Bibliography of Works Cited and Consulted

PRIMARY SOURCES

ALTHUSIUS, JOHANNES, *Politica methodice digesta, et exemplis sacris et profanis illustrata* (Herborn, 1603); critical edn. ed. Joachim Friedrich (Cambridge, Mass., 1932); English translation (abridged): *The Politics of Johannes Althusius* (London, 1964).

AUGUSTINE OF HIPPO, *De civitate Dei . . .*, vol. vii of *Sancti Aurelii Augustini Hipponensis episcopi opera omnia* (Paris, 1838); English translation: *Concerning the City of God against the Pagans*, trans. Henry Bettenson, ed. David Knowles (Baltimore, 1967).

Die Bekenntnisschriften der reformierten Kirche, ed. E. F. K. Müller (Leipzig, 1903).

BEZA, THEODORE, *A briefe Declaraccion of the chiefe poyntes of Christian religion, set forth in a Table of Predestination* (Geneva, 1556).

—— *Ad sycophantarum quorvndam calvmnias . . .* (Geneva, 1558); repr. in *Volumen . . . tractationum theologicarum . . .* (Geneva, 1582), i. 337–424.

—— *Theodori Bezae responsio ad defensiones et reprehensiones Sebastiani Castellionis, quibus suam Noui Testamenti interpretationem defendere aduersus Bezam . . .* (Geneva, 1563).

—— *Theodori Bezae Vezelii, volumen . . . tractationum theologicarum . . .*, 3 vols. (Geneva, 1582).

Biblia cum concordantiis Veteris et Novi Testamenti, et sacrorum canonum . . . (Leiden, 1523).

Biblia sacra iuxta Vulgatam versionem, 2 vols. (Stuttgart, 1969).

The Book of Concord, or the Symbolical Books of the Evangelical Lutheran Church, ed. Henry E. Jacobs (Philadelphia, 1882–3).

BUDAEUS, G., et al., *Dictionarium Graecolatinum supra omnes editiones postremo . . .* (Basle, 1572).

BULLINGER, HEINRICH, *De testamento seu foedere Dei unico et aeterno brevis expositio . . .* (Zurich, 1534); repr. in *In Epistolas Apostolorvm Canonicas Septem Commentarii Heinrychi Bvllingeri. Additi sunt ad finem libelli duo, alter De Testamento Dei Unico et Aeterno . . .* (Zurich, 1558).

BUXTORF, JOHANNES, *Lexicon Hebraicum et Chaldaicum: complectens omnes voces, tam primas quam derivatas, quae in Sacris Bibliis, Hebraea, et ex parte Chaldaea lingua scriptis extant . . . editio quinta . . .* (Basle, 1645).

CALVIN, JOHN, *Opera quae supersunt omnia . . .*, ed. G. Baum, E. Cunitz, and E. Reuss, 59 vols. (*CR*, vols. xxix–lxxxvii; Brunswick, 1863–1900).

—— *Calvin's Calvinism*, trans. Henry Cole, 2 vols. (London, 1856–7; repr. 2 vols. in 1, Grand Rapids, 1950).

—— *Commentaries on the Twelve Minor Prophets*, trans. John Owen, i (Edinburgh, 1846).

—— *Theological Treatises*, ed. and trans. J. K. S. Reid (LCC 22; Philadelphia, 1954).

—— *The Institutes of the Christian Religion*, ed. John T. McNeill, trans. Ford Lewis Battles, 2 vols. (LCC 20–1; Philadelphia, 1960).

—— *Concerning the Eternal Predestination of God*, ed. J. K. S. Reid (London, 1961).

CARTWRIGHT, THOMAS, *Cartwrightiana*, ed. Albert Peel and Leland H. Carlson (Elizabethan Nonconformist Texts, 1; London, 1951).

—— 'Epistle in Latin to Dudley Fenner, 3 Sept. 1583', in Dudley Fenner, *Sacra theologia sive veritas quae est secundum pietatem ad unicae et verae methodi leges descripta, et in decem libros per Dudleium Fennerum digesta* (London and Geneva, 1585).

—— *A Methodicall Short Catechisme . . .* (1604); printed in numerous editions of John Dod and Robert Cleaver, *A Plaine and Familiar Exposition of the Ten Commandments, with a Methodicall Short Catechisme*; the text used in this book was the 18th edn. (London, 1630).

—— *Christian Religion: svbstantially, methodicallie, plainlie and profitablie Treatised*, ed. William Bradshaw (London, 1611).

CASIMIR, JOHANN, *Briefe des Pfalzgrafen Johann Casimir mit verwandten Schriftstücken*, ed. Friedrich von Bezold, 3 vols. (Munich, 1882–1903).

CASTELLIO, SEBASTIAN (ed. and trans.), *Biblia; interprete Sebastiano Castalione. Una cum eiusdem annotationibus . . .* (Basle, 1554).

CASTELLIO, SEBASTIAN, *Sebastiani Castellionis defensio suarum translationum Bibliorum, et maxime Noui Foederis* (Basle, 1562).

—— *Sebastiani Castellionis Dialogi IIII.* (Aresdorff [Arensdorf, Germany], 1578; Gouda, 1613).

COCCEIUS, JOHANNES, *Lexicon et commentarius sermonis Hebraici et Chaldaici Veteris Testamenti. Accedunt interpretatio vocum germanica, belgica ac graeca ex LXX interpretibus . . .* (Leiden, 1669).

The [Westminster] Confession of Faith; The Larger and Shorter Catechisms . . . With The Sum of Saving Knowledge . . . Covenants, National and Solemn League; Acknowledgement of Sins, and Engagement to Duties; Directories for Publick and Family Worship; Form of Church Government, etc.; Of Publick Authority in the Church of Scotland; With Acts of Assembly and Parliament, Relative To, and Approbative of, the Same (Belfast, 1933).

'The Confutation of the Errors of the Careless by Necessity' (n.a.), Baptist Historical Society, *Transactions*, 4 (1914–15), 88–123.

The Creeds of Christendom, ed. Philip Schaff, 3 vols. (New York, 1877; repr. Grand Rapids, 1977).

ERASMUS, DESIDERIUS, *De libero arbitrio* ΔIATPIBH . . ., ed. Johannes von Walter (Basle, Antwerp, and Cologne, 1524; repr. in QGP 8, Leipzig, 1910; English translation in Desiderio Erasmus and Martin Luther, *Luther and Erasmus: Free Will and Salvation*, trans. and ed. E. Gordon Rupp, A. N. Marlow, Philip S. Watson, and B. Drewery (LCC 17; Philadelphia, 1969), 33–97.

ERASMUS, DESIDERIO, and LUTHER, MARTIN, *Luther and Erasmus: Free Will and Salvation*, trans. and ed. E. Gordon Rupp, A. N. Marlow, Philip S. Watson, and B. Drewery (LCC 17; Philadelphia, 1969).

ESTIENNE, HENRY, *Thesaurus Graecae linguae Henr. Stephano constructus*, iii (Geneva, 1572).

ESTIENNE, ROBERT (trans.), *Biblia* . . . (Paris, 1545).

ESTIENNE, ROBERT, *Phrases Hebraicae, seu loqvendi genera Hebraica quae in Veteri Testamento passim leguntur, ex commentariis Hebraeorum, aliisque doctissimorum virorum scriptis explicata. Thesauri linguae Hebraicae altera pars* (Geneva, 1558).

FENNER, DUDLEY, *A brief Treatise vpon the first Table of the Lawe, orderly disposing the principles of Religion, whereby we may examine ourselves* (Middelburg, 1576).

—— *The Artes of Logike and Retorike, plainly set foorth in the English toonge . . . togeather with examples for the practise of the same for Methode in the government of the familie, prescribed in the worde of God: And for the whole in the resolution or opening of certain parts of Scripture, according to the same* (Middelburg, 1584); repr. in *Four Tudor Books on Education*, ed. Robert D. Pepper (Gainesville, Florida, 1966), 143–80.

—— *Sacra theologia sive veritas quae est secundum pietatem ad unicae et verae methodi leges descripta, et in decem libros per Dudleium Fennerum digesta* (London and Geneva, 1585; 2nd edn. London and Geneva, 1589); English translation by J. Starke, Lambeth Palace MS 465, London.

—— *The Sacred Doctrine of Divinitie, Gathered ovt of the worde of God. Togither with an explication of the Lordes Prayer* (London, 1599 [*sic*, for 1589]).

The Harmony of Protestant Confessions . . ., ed. and trans. Peter Hall (London, 1844).

HYPERIUS, ANDREAS, *Andreae Hyperii methodi theologiae siue praecipuorum Christianae religionis locorvm commvnivm* . . . (Basle, 1568).

JUD, LEO, *et al.* (trans.), *Biblia sacrosancta Testamenti Veteris et Noui* . . . (2nd edn. Zurich, 1544).

JUNIUS, FRANCISCUS, *Opera theologica Francisci Ivnii bitvrigis sacrarvm literarvm professoris eximii. Quorum nonnulla nunc primum publicantur. Praefixa est vita auctoris*, 2 vols. (Geneva, 1608).

—— *D. Francisci Junii opuscula theologica selecta*, ed. Abraham Kuyper (Bibliotheca Reformata, 1; New York, 1882).

LUTHER, MARTIN, *De servo arbitrio*, in *D. Martin Luthers Werke*, xviii (Weimar, 1908), 551–787; English translation in Desiderio Erasmus and Martin Luther, *Luther and Erasmus: Free Will and Salvation*, trans. and ed. E. Gordon Rupp, A. N. Marlow, Philip S. Watson, and B. Drewery (LCC 17; Philadelphia, 1969), 99–334.

MELANCHTHON, PHILIP, *Loci Communes 1555*, ed. Clyde L. Manschrek; Introduction by Hans Engelland (LPT; New York, 1965).

—— *Opera quae supersunt omnia*, ed. Henricus Ernestus Bindseil, *CR*, vols. xxi–xxii (Brunswick, 1854–5).

MÜNSTER, SEBASTIAN, *Dictionarium Hebraicvm, iam vltimo ab autore Sebastiano Munstero recognitum, et ex rabinis, praesertim ex radicibus Dauid Kimhi, auctum et locupletatum* (Basle, 1523, 1539).

MUSCULUS, WOLFGANG, *Loci communes sacrae theologiae, iam recens recogniti et emendati* . . . (Basle, 1560); English translation: *Common-places of Christian Religion gathered by Wolfgang Musculus*, trans. J. Man (London, 1563).

OLEVIANUS, CASPAR, *Expositio symbolica apostolici* . . . (Frankfurt, 1576).

—— *In epistolam D. Pauli Apost. ad Galatas notae* . . . (Geneva, 1578).

—— *Notae Gasparis Oleuiani in evangelia* . . . (Herborn, 1579).

—— *In epistolas ad D. Pauli Apostoli ad Philippenses et Colossenses, notae* . . . (Geneva, 1580).

—— *In epistolam D. Pauli Apostoli ad Romanos notae, ex Gasparis Oleuiani concionibus excerptae et a Theodoro Beza editae: cum praefatione eiusdem Bezae* (Geneva, 1579; 2nd edn. 1584).

—— *De substantia foederis gratuiti inter Deum et electos, itemque de mediis, quibus ea ipsa substantia nobis communicatur, libri duo praelectionibus Gasparis Oleuiani excerpti* (Geneva, 1585; 2nd edn. 1589, 'priore emendatior').

PAGNINUS, SANCTUS, *Thesaurus linguae sanctae* . . . (Lyons, [1529]).

PIGHIUS, ALBERT, *De libero hominis arbitrio et diuina gratia, libri decem, nunc primum in lucem editi* (Cologne, 1542).

Reformed Confessions of the Sixteenth Century, ed. Arthur C. Cochrane (Philadelphia, 1966).

REUCHLIN, JOHANNES, *De rudimentis linguae Hebraicae una cum lexico* (n.p., 1506).

ROLLOCK, ROBERT, *Tractatvs de vocatione efficaci* . . . (Edinburgh, 1597); English translation: *A treatise of Gods effectual calling* . . ., trans. Henry Holland (London, 1603); repr. in *Select Works of Robert Rollock*, ed. William Gunn, i (The Wodrow Society, 15; Edinburgh, 1849), 5–288.

TREMELLIUS, IMMANUEL, and JUNIUS, FRANCISCUS (trans.), *Testamenti Veteris Biblia Sacra, sive libri canonici* . . . (London, 1580).

URSINUS, ZACHARIAS, *Volumen tractationum theologicarum* (Neustadt, 1584).

—— *Organi Aristotelei, libri quinque priores a Doct. Zacharia Ursino Uratislauiensi, per quaestiones perspicue et erudite expositi, ita ut provectioribus quoque, docti commentarii usum praestare possint. Eiusdem Ursini, de Petri Rami dialectica et rhetorica iudicium, ad illustrissimum Principem Fridericum III, Electorem Palatinatum etc., perscriptum anno 1570. Omnia nunc primum in lucem edita*, ed. Johannes Jungnitz (Neustadt, 1586).

—— *Zachariae Ursini, Uratislaviensis, scholasticarum in materiis theologicis exercitationum liber* (Neustadt, 1589).

—— *D. Zachariae Ursini theologi celeberrimi, sacrarum literarum olim in academia Heidelbergensi et Neustadiana doctoris et professoris fidelissimi, opera theologica* . . . *tribvta in tomos tres*, ed. Quirinus Reuterus (Heidelberg, 1612).

—— 'Zacharias Ursins Briefe an Crato von Crafftheim nach den in Breslau befindlichen Urschriften', ed. W. Becker, *TARWPV* 8 (1889), 79–121.

—— 'Ein Brief an Henricus Stephanus', ed. C. Krafft, *TARWPV*, 8 (1889), 121–3.

—— 'Zacharias Ursinus Briefe an Crato von Crafftheim nach den Breslau befindlichen Urschriften', ed. W. Becker, *TARWPV* 12 (1892), 41–107 (continuation of Becker, 1889, above).

—— 'Briefe des Heidelberger Theologen Zacharias Ursinus aus Heidelberg und Neustadt a. H.', ed. H. Rott, *NHdJb* 14 (1906), 39–172.

—— 'Briefe des Heidelberger Theologen Zacharias Ursinus (1534–1583)', ed. G. A. Benrath, *HdJb* 8 (1964), 93–141.

—— 'Das Stammbuch des Zacharias Ursinus (1553–1562 und 1581)', ed. Wilhelm H. Neuser, *BPfKG* 31 (1964), 101–55.

—— 'Briefe des Heidelberger Theologen Zacharias Ursinus aus Wittenberg und Zürich (1560/1561)', *HdJb* 14 (1970), 85–119.

—— See ch. 3 n. 9 for a listing of various commentaries on the Heidelberg Catechism. These commentaries were compiled by students of Ursinus's, based on their lecture notes from his classes.

ZAMORENSIS, ALPHONSUS, *Uocabularium Hebraicum et Chaldaicum totius Veteris Testamentum; cum alijs tractatibus prout infra prefatione continetur in academia complutensi nouiter impressum*, vol. vi of *Uetus Testamentum multiplici lingua nunc primo impressum* (Alcalá, 1515).

SECONDARY SOURCES

Reference Works

Allgemeine deutsche Biographie, 56 vols. (Leipzig, 1875–1912).

Allgemeines Gelehrten-Lexicon, ed. Christian G. Jöcher, 11 vols. (Leipzig, 1750; repr. Hildesheim, 1960).

Alumni Cantabrigienses, part 1, 4 vols. (Cambridge, 1922–7).

Athenae Cantabrigienses, 3 vols. (Cambridge, 1858–1913).

Biographisch woordenboek van protestantsche godgeleerden in Nederland, 5 vols. (The Hague, 1903–43).

The Cambridge History of the Bible, iii (Cambridge, 1963).

Cyclopaedia of Biblical, Theological, and Ecclesiastical Literature, 12 vols. (New York, 1867–87).

Dictionary of Latin and Greek Theological Terms, Drawn Principally from Protestant Scholastic Theology, ed. Richard A. Muller (Grand Rapids, 1985).

Dictionary of National Biography . . . from the Earliest Times to 1900, 22 vols. (London, 1885–1901).

Dictionnaire de biographie française, i– (Paris, 1933–).

Dignorum laude virorum . . ., 5 vols. (Heidelberg and Frankfurt, 1615–20; repr. Frankfurt, 1705 and 1706).

The Encyclopedia of Christianity, vols. i– (Wilmington, Delaware, 1964–).

Encyclopaedia of Religion and Ethics, 13 vols. (New York, 1908–27).

Encyclopedic Dictionary of Religion, 3 vols. (Washington, 1979).

Evangelisches Kirchenlexicon, 3 vols. (Göttingen, 1956–9).

La France protestante ou Vies des protestants français, 9 vols. (Paris, 1846–59).

Neue deutsche Biographie, i– (Berlin, 1953–).

The New International Dictionary of New Testament Theology, 3 vols. (Exeter, England, 1975–8).

The New International Dictionary of the Christian Church (Grand Rapids, 1974).

The New Schaff-Herzog Encyclopedia of Religious Knowledge, 13 vols. (New York, 1908–14).

Nieuw nederlandsch biografisch woordenboek, 10 vols. (Leiden, 1911–37).

Realencyklopädie für protestantische Theologie und Kirche (1st edn., 22 vols., Hamburg, 1854–68; 2nd edn., 18 vols., Leipzig, 1877–88; 3rd edn., 24 vols., Leipzig, 1896–1913).

Die Religion in Geschichte und Gegenwart (Tübingen: 1st edn., 5 vols., 1909–13; 2nd edn., 5 vols., 1927–31; 3rd edn., 7 vols., 1957–65).

A Religious Encyclopaedia or Dictionary of Biblical, Historical, Doctrinal and Practical Theology (New York, 2nd edn., 3 vols., 1882–3; 3rd edn., 4 vols., 1891).

Theological Dictionary of the New Testament, 10 vols. (Grand Rapids, 1964–76).

Theological Dictionary of the Old Testament, vols. i– (Grand Rapids, 1974–).

Theologische Realencyklopädie, i– (Berlin, 1977–).

Theologisches Begriffslexicon zum Neuen Testament, 3 vols. (Wuppertal, 1967–71).

Theologisches Wörterbuch zum Alten Testament, i– (Stuttgart, 1973–).
Theologisches Wörterbuch zum Neuen Testament, 11 vols. (Stuttgart, 1933–79).
Twentieth Century Encyclopedia of Religious Knowledge, 2 vols. (Grand Rapids, 1955).
Weltkirchen Lexicon (Stuttgart, 1960).
The Westminster Dictionary of Church History (Philadelphia, 1971).

Books, Articles, Dissertations, and Manuscripts

ADAM, GOTTFRIED, *Der Streit um Prädestination im ausgehenden 16. Jahrhundert: Eine Untersuchung zu den Entwürfen von Samuel Huber und Aegidius Hunnius* (BGLRK 30; Neukirchen, 1970).

AGNEW, DAVID, *The Theology of Consolation* (Edinburgh, published privately, 1880).

ALTHAUS, PAUL, *Die Prinzipien der deutschen reformierten Dogmatik im Zeitalter der aristotelischen Scholastik* (Leipzig, 1914; repr. Darmstadt, 1967).

ALTINGIUS, HENRICUS, 'Historiae Ecclesiae Palatine', in *Monumenta pietatis . . .*, ed. Ludwig Christian Mieg, i (Frankfurt, 1702), 129–250.

Archiv für die Geschichte der Stadt Heidelberg (Heidelberg, 1868–70).

ARMSTRONG, BRIAN G., *Calvinism and the Amyraut Heresy: Protestant Scholasticism and Humanism in Seventeenth-Century France* (Madison, 1969).

BAINTON, ROLAND, and LOCKWOOD, DEAN P., 'Classical and Biblical Scholarship in the Age of the Renaissance and Reformation', *ChH* 10 (1941), 125–43.

BAKER, DEREK (ed.), *Reform and Reformation: England and the Continent c. 1500–c. 1750* (SCH(L) subs. 2; Oxford, 1979).

BAKER, J. WAYNE, 'Covenant and Society: The *Respublica Christiana* in the Thought of Heinrich Bullinger' (Diss. University of Iowa, 1970).

—— *Covenant and Community in the Thought of Heinrich Bullinger* (Philadelphia, Center for the Study of Federalism, Temple University, 1980).

—— *Heinrich Bullinger and the Covenant: The Other Reformed Tradition* (Athens, Ohio, 1980).

BANGS, CARL, 'Arminius and the Reformation', *ChH* 30 (1961), 155–70.

—— *Arminius: A Study in the Dutch Reformation* (Nashville, 1971).

BARON, HANS, 'Religion and Politics in the German Imperial Cities during the Reformation', *EHR* 52 (1937), 405–27, 614–33.

—— 'Calvinist Republicanism and its Historical Roots', *ChH* 8 (1939), 30–42.

BARTH, KARL, *Die kirchliche Dogmatik*, ii, part 1 and iv, part 2 (Zurich, 1955); English translation: *Church Dogmatics*, ed. Geoffrey W. Bromiley and Thomas F. Torrance (Edinburgh, 1956–7).

BAUER, KARL, *Aus der grossen Zeit der theologische Fakultät zu Heidelberg* (VVKGB 14; Lahr in Baden, 1938).

BEEBE, DAVID LEWIS, 'The Seals of the Covenant: The Doctrine and Place of the Sacraments and Censures in the New England Puritan Theology Underlying the Cambridge Platform of 1648' (Diss. Pacific School of Religion, 1966).

BENRATH, GUSTAV ADOLPH, 'Die Eigenart der pfälzischen Reformation und die Vorgeschichte des Heidelberger Katechismus', *HdJb* 7 (1963), 13–32.

—— 'Die Universität der Reformationszeit', *ARG* 57 (1966), 32–51.

BENRATH, K., 'Celio, Secundus Curio (1503–1569)', *NSHE* iii (1909), 325–6.

BENZ, RICHARD, *Heidelberg: Schicksal und Geist* (Constance, 1961).

BERGH, WILLEM VAN DEN, *Calvijn over het genade verbond* (The Hague, 1879).

BIERMA, LYLE DEAN, 'The Covenant Theology of Caspar Olevian' (Diss. Duke, 1980).

BIZER, ERNST, *Historische Einleitung zur Heinrich Heppes Dogmatik* (Neukirchen, 1958).

—— *Frühorthodoxie und Rationalismus* (ThSt(B) 71; Zurich, 1963).

BLANKE, FRITZ, 'Calvins Urteil über Zwingli', in *Aus der Welt der Reformation*, ed. Fritz Blanke, 5th edn. (Zurich, 1960), 18–47.

BOHATEC, JOSEF, 'Die Methode der reformierten Dogmatik', *ThStKr* 81 (1908), 272–302.

—— 'Calvin's Vorsehungslehre', in *Calvinstudien: Festschrift zum 400. Geburtstage Johann Calvins*, ed. Josef Bohatec (Leipzig, 1909), 339–441.

—— *Die cartesianische Scholastik in der Philosophie und reformierten Dogmatik des 17. Jahrhunderts* (Leipzig, 1912; repr. Hildesheim, 1966).

BORGEAUD, CHARLES, 'Cartwright and Melville at the University of Geneva, 1569–1574', *AHR* 5 (1899), 282–90.

BOUGHTON, LYNNE C., 'Supralapsarianism and the Role of Metaphysics in Sixteenth-Century Reformed Theology', *WThJ* 48 (1986), 63–96.

BRACKENRIDGE, R. DOUGLAS, 'The Development of Sabbatarianism in Scotland, 1560–1650', *JPH* 42 (1964), 149–65.

BRATT, JOHN H. (ed.), *The Rise and Development of Calvinism* (Heritage Hall Publications, 2; Grand Rapids, 1959).

BRAUER, JERALD C., 'Reflections on the Nature of English Puritanism', *ChH* 23 (1954), 99–108.

BRAY, JOHN S., 'The Value of Works in the Theology of Calvin and Beza', *SCJ* 4 (1973), 77–86.

—— *Theodore Beza's Doctrine of Predestination* (Nieuwkoop, 1975).

BREEN, QUIRINUS, 'The Terms "Loci Communes" and "Loci" in Melanchthon', *ChH* 16 (1947), 197–209.

BREEN, TIMOTHY H., *The Character of the Good Ruler: A Study of Puritan Political Ideas in New England, 1630–1730* (New Haven, 1970).

BREWARD, IAN (ed.), *The Work of William Perkins* (The Courtenay Library of Reformation Classics, 3; Appleford, Abingdon, England, 1970).

BRISTLEY, ERIC D., 'Bibliographica Catechismus Heidelbergensis: An Historical Bibliography of Editions, Translations, Commentaries, Sermons and Historical Studies of the Heidelberg Catechism, 1563' (1983; manuscript on file, Westminster Theological Seminary Library, Philadelphia, Pa.).

BROOK, BENJAMIN, *Memoir of the Life and Writings of Thomas Cartwright* (London, 1845).

BROWN, W. ADAMS, 'Covenant Theology', *ERE* iv (1911), 216–24.

BRYCE, JAMES, *The Holy Roman Empire* (London, 1894).

BUCHANAN, GEORGE W., *The Consequences of the Covenant* (Supplements to *Novum Testamentum*, 20; Leiden, 1970).

BUISSON, FERDINAND, *Sébastien Castellion: Sa vie et son œuvre (1515–1563); Étude sur les origines du protestantisme libéral français*, 2 vols. (Paris, 1892).

BURCHILL, CHRISTOPHER J., 'On the Consolation of a Christian Scholar: Zacharias Ursinus (1534–83) and the Reformation in Heidelberg', *JEH* 37 (1986), 565–83.

—— 'Girolamo Zanchi: Portrait of a Reformed Theologian and His Work', *SCJ*, 15 (1984), 185–207.

BURRAGE, CHAMPLIN, *The Church Covenant Idea: Its Origin and Development* (Philadelphia, 1904).

BURSTYN, HAROLD S., and HAND, ROBERT S., 'Puritanism and Science Reinterpreted', *Actes du XIᵉ Congrès International d'Histoire des Sciences* (1965), no. 2, 139–43.

BUTLER, CHARLES J., 'Religious Liberty and Covenant Theology' (Diss. Temple, 1979).

CALDWELL, PATRICIA, *The Puritan Conversion Narrative: The Beginnings of American Expression* (Cambridge, 1983).

CAMERON, JAMES KERR (ed.), *Letters of John Johnston (c.1565–1611) and Robert Howie (c.1565–c.1645)* (Saint Andrews University Publications, 54; Edinburgh, 1963).

CARNEY, FREDERICK S., 'The Associational Theory of Johannes Althusius: A Study in Calvinist Constitutionalism' (Diss. University of Chicago, 1960).

Cartwright and His Contemporaries (n.a.) (English Puritan Divines in the Reign of Queen Elizabeth; London, 1848).

CHADWICK, OWEN, 'The Making of the Reforming Prince: Frederick III, Elector Palatine', in R. Buick Knox (ed.), *Reformation, Conformity and Dissent* (London, 1977).

CHERRY, C. CONRAD, 'The Puritan Notion of the Covenant in Jonathan Edwards' Doctrine of Faith', *ChH* 34 (1965), 328–41.

CLASEN, CLAUS-PETER, *The Palatinate in European History 1559–1660* (Oxford, 1963).

CLEBSCH, WILLIAM A., *England's Earliest Protestants 1520–1535* (New Haven, 1964).

COENEN, LOTHAR (ed.), *Handbuch zum Heidelberger Katechismus* (Neukirchen, 1963).

COHEN, CHARLES LLOYD, *God's Caress: The Psychology of Puritan Religious Experience* (New York, 1986).

COLLINSON, PATRICK, 'The Authorship of *A Brieff Discours off the Troubles begonne at Franckford*', *JEH* 9 (1958), 188–208.

—— 'The Beginnings of English Sabbatarianism', in C. W. Dugmore and C. Duggan (edd.) (SCH(L) 1; London, 1964), 207–21.

—— *The Elizabethan Puritan Movement* (London, 1967).

COLVILE, FREDERICK LEIGHT, *The Worthies of Warwickshire who Lived between 1500 and 1800* (London, 1870).

COOLIDGE, JOHN S., *The Pauline Renaissance in England: Puritanism and the Bible* (Oxford, 1970).

COPINGER, W.A., *A Treatise on Predestination, Election and Grace: Historical, Doctrinal and Practical; to which is Added a Bibliography of the Subject* (London, 1889).

COSTELLO, WILLIAM THOMAS, *The Scholastic Curriculum at Early Seventeenth Century Cambridge* (Cambridge, Mass., 1958).

COTTRELL, JACK WARREN, 'Covenant and Baptism in the Theology of Huldreich Zwingli' (Diss. Princeton Theological Seminary, 1971).

—— 'Is Bullinger the Source for Zwingli's Doctrine of the Covenant?', in Ulrich Gäbler and Erland Herkenrath (edd.), *Heinrich Bullinger, 1504–1575, Gesammelte Aufsätze zum 400. Todestag*, i: *Leben und Werk* (ZBRG 7; Zurich, 1975), 75–83.

Covenant Letter (Philadelphia, Center for the Study of Federalism, Temple University).

CREMEANS, CHARLES D., *The Reception of Calvinistic Thought in England* (Illinois Studies in the Social Sciences, 31; Urbana, 1949).

CROSS, CLAIRE, 'Continental Students and the Protestant Reformation in England in the Sixteenth Century', in Derek Baker (ed.), *Reform and Reformation: England and the Continent c.1500–c. 1750* (SCH(L) subs. 2; Oxford, 1979), 35–58.

CUNO, FRIEDRICH WILHELM, *Johann der Aeltere von Nassau-Dillenburg, ein fürstlicher Reformator, nach den Hauptmomenten seines Lebens geschildert* (Halle, 1869).

—— *Blätter der Erinnerung an Dr. Kaspar Olevianus* (Barmen, 1887).

—— *Franciscus Junius der Ältere, Professor der Theologie und Pastor (1545–1602)* (Amsterdam, 1891; repr. Geneva, 1971).

—— *Daniel Tossanus der Ältere*, 2 vols. (Amsterdam, 1898).

CURTIS, MARK H., *Oxford and Cambridge in Transition* (Oxford, 1959).
Bèze', *RThPh*, 3rd ser., 16 (1966), 365–77.

DANTINE, JOHANNES, 'Die Prädestinationslehre bei Calvin und Beza' (Diss. University of Göttingen, 1965).

—— 'Les Tabelles sur la doctrine de la prédestination par Théodore de Bèze', *RThPh*, 3rd ser., 16 (1966), 365–77.

DE JONG, PETER YMEN, *The Covenant Idea in New England Theology 1620–1847* (Grand Rapids, 1945).

DELORMEAU, CHARLES ÉMILE, *Sébastien Castellion: Apôtre de la tolérance et de la liberté de conscience, 1515–1563* (Neuchâtel, 1963).

DENNISON, JAMES T., JUN., 'The Puritan Doctrine of the Sabbath in England 1532–1700' (Master of Theology thesis, Pittsburgh Theological Seminary, 1973).

—— 'The Perpetuity and Change of the Sabbath', in R. C. Sproul (ed.), *Soli Deo Gloria: Essays in Reformed Theology; Festschrift for John H. Gerstner* (Nutley, NJ, 1976), 146–55.

DIBON, PAUL, *L'Enseignement philosophique dans les universités à l'époque précartésienne (1575–1650)*, vol. i of *La Philosophie néerlandaise au Siècle d'Or* (Publications de l'Institut Française d'Amsterdam Maison Descartes, 2; Paris, 1954).

DIEMER, N., *Het scheppingsverbond met Adam (het verbond der werken), bij de theologen der 16e, 17e, en 18e eeuw in Zwitserland, Duitschland, Nederland en Engeland*, with a Preface by F. W. Grosheide (Kampen, 1935).

DIETEL, WILLIAM M., 'Puritanism vs. Anglicanism: A Study of Theological Controversy in Elizabethan England' (Diss. Yale, 1956).

DIJK, KLAAS, *De strijd over Infra- en Supralapsarisme in de Gereformeerde Kerken van Nederland* (Kampen, 1912).

DILLISTONE, FREDERICK W., 'The Covenant Conception in Calvin', in *The Structure of Divine Society* (Philadelphia, 1951), 117–29.

—— 'Federalism in the Seventeenth Century', in *The Structure of Divine Society* (Philadelphia, 1951), 130–44.

DOCHNAHL, FRIEDRICH JAKOB, and TAVERNIER, KARL, *Chronik von Neustadt an der Haardt nebst den umliegenden Orten und Burgen mit besonderer Berücksichtigung der Weinjahre* (Pirmasens, 1900).

DODWELL, CHARLES REGINALD (ed.), *The English Church and the Continent* (London, 1959).

DOERR, WILHELM (ed.), *Semper Apertus: Sechshundert Jahre Ruprecht-Karls Universität Heidelberg, 1386–1986, 6 vols. (New York, 1985)*.

DONNELLY, JOHN PATRICK, SJ, *Calvinism and Scholasticism in Vermigli's Doctrine of Man and Grace* (SMRT 13; Leiden, 1976).

—— 'Italian Influences on the Development of Calvinist Scholasticism', *SCJ* 7 (1976), 81–101.

DORNER, ISAAK AUGUST, *Geschichte der protestantischen Theologie, besonders in Deutschland . . .* (Munich, 1867); English translation: *History of Protestant Theology, Particularly in Germany*, ii, trans. George Robson and Sophia Taylor (Edinburgh, 1871).

DOUMERGUE, ÉMILE, *Jean Calvin: Les hommes et les choses de son temps*, 7 vols. (Lausanne and Neuilly-sur-Seine, 1899–1927).

DRUMMOND, ANDREW L., *The Kirk and the Continent* (Edinburgh, 1956).

DUMBRELL, WILLIAM J., *Covenant and Creation: A Theology of the Old Testament Covenants* (Nashville, 1984).

ELAZAR, DANIEL J., *From Biblical Covenant to Modern Federalism: The Federal Theology Bridge* (Philadelphia, Center for the Study of Federalism, Temple University, 1980).

—— 'The Political Theory of Covenant: Biblical Origins and Modern Developments', *Publius*, 10 (1980), 3–30.

ELLIOT, JOHN HUXTABLE, *Europe Divided 1559–1598* (New York, 1968).

EULAU, H., 'Theories of Federalism under the Holy Roman Empire', *APSR* 35 (1941), 643–64.

EUSDEN, JOHN D., 'Natural Law and Covenant Theology', *NatLF* 5 (1960), 1–30.

EVANS, R. J. W., *Rudolf II and his World: A Study in Intellectual History 1576–1612* (Oxford, 1973).

—— *The Wechel Presses: Humanism and Calvinism in Central Europe 1572–1627* (Past and Present Supplement 2; Oxford, 1975).

FATIO, OLIVIER, *Méthode et théologie: Lambert Daneau et les débuts de la scolastique réformée* (THR 147; Geneva, 1976).

'Festschrift zur 350Jährigen Wiederkehr Gründung der Hohen Schule zu Herborn', *NA* 55 (1935), 1–184.

FIERING, NORMAN, *Moral Philosophy at Seventeenth-Century Harvard: A Discipline in Transition* (Chapel Hill, 1981).

FISCHER, BONIFATIUS, OSB, *Novae Concordantiae Bibliorum Sacrorum iuxta Vulgatam versionem critice editam*, ii and v (Stuttgart, 1977).

FISHER, GEORGE PARK, *History of Christian Doctrine* (International Theological Library, 4; New York, 1896).

FOSTER, HERBERT D., *Collected Papers of Herbert D. Foster* (New York, printed privately, 1929).

FULCHER, JAMES RODNEY, 'Puritan Piety in New England: A Study in Spiritual Regeneration from the Antinomian Controversy to the Cambridge Synod of 1648 in the Massachusetts Bay Colony' (Diss. Princeton University, 1963).

GADAMER, HANS-GEORG, *Wahrheit und Methode* (Tübingen, 1960); English translation of 2nd German edn.: *Truth and Method* (New York, 1975).

GALDON, JOSEPH A., SJ, *Typology and Seventeenth-Century Literature* (The Hague, 1975).

GARDY, FRÉDÉRIC, *Bibliographie des œuvres théologiques, littéraires, historiques et juridiques de Théodore de Bèze* (THR 41; Geneva, 1960).

GEESINK, W., 'Franciscus Junius (1545–1602)', in *Calvinisten in Holland* (Rotterdam, 1887; repr. Geneva, 1970), 1–50.

GEORGE, CHARLES H. and GEORGE, KATHERINE, *The Protestant Mind of the English Reformation: 1570–1640* (Princeton, 1961).

GERSTNER, JOHN H., and GERSTNER, JONATHAN NEIL, 'Edwardsean Preparation for Salvation', *WThJ* 42 (1979–80), 5–71.

GIBBS, LEE W., 'The Puritan Natural Law Theory of William Ames', *HThR* 64 (1971), 37–57.

—— 'William Ames's Technometry', *JHI* 33 (1972), 615–24.

—— *William Ames: Technometry* (Philadelphia, 1979).

GIERKE, OTTO VON, *Johannes Althusius und die Entwicklung der naturrechtlichen Staatstheorien* (Untersuchungen zur Deutschen Staats- und Rechtsgeschichte, 7; Breslau, 1913); English translation: *The Development of Political Theory*, trans. Bernard Freyd (New York, 1939).

—— *Die Staats- und Korporationslehre der Neuzeit*, vol. iv of *Das deutsche Genossenschaftsrecht* (Berlin, 1913); English translation: *Natural Law and the Theory of Society 1500–1800*, trans. E. Barker (Cambridge, 1934; repr. 2 vols. into 1, 1950).

GILBERT, NEAL W., *Renaissance Concepts of Method* (New York, 1960).

GILLET, J. F. A., *Crato von Crafftheim und seine Freunde: Ein Beitrag zur Kirchengeschichte*, 2 vols. (Frankfurt, 1860–61).

—— 'Friedrich III, Kurfürst von der Pfalz, und der Reichstag zu Augsburg im J. 1566', *HZ* 19 (1868), 38–102.

GIRAN, ÉTIENNE, *Sébastien Castellion et la réforme calviniste: Les deux réformées* (Haarlem, 1913).

GLAWISCHNIG, ROLF, *Niederlande, Kalvinismus und Reichsgrafenstand 1559–1584: Nassau-Dillenburg unter Graf Johann VI* (Schriftendes Hessischen Landesamtes für geschichtliche Landeskunde, 36; Marburg, 1973).

GODFREY, W. ROBERT, 'Tensions within International Calvinism: The Debate on the Atonement at the Synod of Dort, 1618–1619' (Diss. Stanford, 1974).

GOEBAL, MAX, *Geschichte des christlichen Lebens in der rheinisch-westphälischen evangelischen Kirche*, i–ii (Coblenz, 1849–52).

—— 'Dr. Caspar Olevianus, 1535–1587', trans. Henry Harbough, *MercQR* 7 (1855), 294–306.

—— 'Dr. Zacharias Ursinus', trans. Henry Harbough, *MercQR* 7 (1855), 629–36.

GOETERS, J. F. G., 'Entstehung und Frühgeschichte des Katechismus', in Lothar Coenen (ed.), *Handbuch zum Heidelberger Katechismus* (Neukirchen, 1963), 3–23.

GOETERS, WILHELM, *Die Vorbereitung des Pietismus in der reformierten Kirche der Niederlande bis zur labadistischen Krisis 1670* (Leipzig, 1911; repr. Amsterdam, 1974).

GÖTZ, JOHANN B., *Die erste Einführung des Kalvinismus in der Oberpfalz 1559–1576*, RGST 60 (1933).

—— *Die religiösen Wirren in der Oberpfalz von 1576 bis 1620*, RGST 66 (1937).

GOOD, JAMES I., *The Origin of the Reformed Church in Germany* (Reading, Pa., 1887).

—— *The Heidelberg Catechism in its Newest Light* (Philadelphia, 1914).

GOOSZEN, MAURITS ALBRECHT, *Heinrich Bullinger en de strijd over de Praedestinatie* (Rotterdam, 1909).

GRAVES, FRANK P., *Peter Ramus and the Educational Reformation of the Sixteenth Century* (New York, 1912).

GREAVES, RICHARD L., 'John Bunyan and Covenant Thought in the Seventeenth Century', *ChH* 36 (1967), 151–69.

—— 'The Origins and Early Development of English Covenant Thought', *The Historian*, 31 (1968), 21–35.

—— 'John Knox and the Covenant Tradition', *JEH* 24 (1973), 23–32.

—— 'The Origins of English Sabbatarian Thought', *SCJ* 12 (1981), 19–34.

GRÜN, HUGO, 'Geist und Gestalt der Hohen Schule Herborn', *NA* 65 (1954), 130–47.

—— 'Die theologische Fakultät der Hohen Schule Herborn 1584–1817', *JHKGV* 19 (1968), 57–145.

GRUNDLER, OTTO, 'Thomism and Calvinism in the Theology of Girolamo Zanchi (1516–1590)' (Diss. Princeton Theological Seminary, 1961).

—— *Die Gotteslehre Girolamo Zanchis und ihre Bedeutung für seine Lehre von der Prädestination* (BGLRK 20; Neukirchen, 1965).

GUHRT, J., and BECKER, O., 'Bund', *TBLNT* i. 157–65; English translation: 'Covenant, Guarantee, Mediator', *NIDNTT* i. 365–76.

GÜMBEL, JAKOB THEODOR, *Die Geschichte der protestantischen Kirche der Pfalz* (Kaiserslautern, 1885).

HAGEN, KENNETH, 'From Testament to Covenant in the Early Sixteenth Century', *SCJ* 3 (1972), 1–24.

—— *A Theology of Testament in the Young Luther: The Lectures on Hebrews* (SMRT 12; Leiden, 1974).

HAGENBACH, KARL R., *Lehrbuch der Dogmengeschichte*, ii (Leipzig, 1841).

HALL, BASIL, 'Calvin Against the Calvinists', in G. E. Duffield (ed.), *John Calvin* (Courtenay Studies in Reformation Theology, 1; Appleford, Abingdon, England, 1966), 12–37.

HANBURY, BENJAMIN, *The Ecclesiastical Polity . . . of R. Hooker: . . . Accompanied by . . . a Life of T. Cartwright* (London, 1830).

HARGROVE, O. T., 'The Doctrine of Predestination in the English Reformation' (Diss. Vanderbilt, 1966).

—— 'The Predestinarian Offensive of the Marian Exiles at Geneva', *HMPEC* 42 (1973), 111–23.

—— 'The Predestinarian Controversy Among the Marian Protestant Figures', *HMPEC* 47 (1978), 131–51.

HARRISON, ARCHIBALD W., *The Beginnings of Arminianism to the Synod of Dort* (London, 1926).

—— *Arminianism* (London, 1937).

HÄUSSER, LUDWIG, *Geschichte der rheinischen Pflaz . . .*, ii (Heidelberg, 1845; repr. of 1856 edn., Pirmasens, 1970).

HAUTZ, JOHANN FRIEDRICH, *Geschichte der Universität Heidelberg*, ii: *1556–1803* (Mannheim, 1864).

HEILER, CARL, 'Der Herborner Student, 1584–1817', *NA* 55 (1935), 1–100.

HELM, PAUL, 'Calvin and the Covenant: Unity and Continuity', *EQ* 55 (1983), 65–81.

HENDERSON, GEORGE DAVID, 'The Idea of the Covenant in Scotland', *EQ* 27 (1955), 2–14; repr. in *The Burning Bush: Studies in Scottish Church History* (Edinburgh, 1957), 61–74.

HENSS, WALTER, 'Der zeitgeschichtliche Hintergrund des Heidelberger Katechismus im Spiegel der Heidelberger Sammlungen', *Ruperto-Carola*, 15 (1963), 32–44.

HEPPE, HEINRICH, *Geschichte des deutschen Protestantismus in den Jahren 1555–1581*, 4 vols. (Marburg, 1852–9).

—— *Dogmatik des deutschen Protestantismus im sechzehnten Jahrhundert*, i (Gotha, 1857).

—— *Der kirchliche Verkehr Englands mit dem evangelischen Deutschland im sechzehnten Jahrhundert: Ein Beitrag zur Geschichte des evangelischen Bundes* (Marburg, 1859); English translation: *The Reformers of England and Germany in the Sixteenth Century: Their Intercourse and Correspondence; A Historical Sketch and Original Documents*, trans. H. Schmettau and B. H. Cowper (London, 1859).

—— *Die Dogmatik der evangelisch-reformirten Kirche . . .* (Schriften zur reformirten Theologie, 2; Elberfeld, 1861; rev. 2nd edn. Neukirchen, 1935); English translation of rev. 2nd edn.: *Reformed Dogmatics: Set out and Illustrated from the Sources*, ed. Ernst Bizer, trans. G. T. Thompson (London, 1950).

HICKS, JOHN M., 'The Theology of Grace in the Thought of Jacobus Arminius and Philip van Limborch: A Study in the Development of Seventeenth-Century Dutch Arminianism' (Diss. Westminster Theological Seminary, 1985).

HILL, CHRISTOPHER, 'Seventeenth-Century English Society and Sabbatarianism', in J. S. Bromley and E. H. Kossman (edd.), *Britain and the Netherlands*, ii (Historische studies uitgegeven vanwege het Instituut voor Geschiedenis der Rijksuniversiteit te Utrecht, 20; Groningen, 1964), 84–108.

—— *Society and Puritanism in Pre-Revolutionary England* (London, 1964).

HILLERS, DELBERT R., *Covenant: The History of a Biblical Idea* (Baltimore, 1969).

HINKE, W. J., 'The Origin of the Heidelberg Catechism', *Reformed Church Review*, 4th ser., 17 (1913), 156–66.

HINZ, GERHARD (ed.), *Aus des Geschichte der Universität Heidelberg und ihrer Fakultäten* (Ruperto-Carola Sonderband Jahrgang 13; Heidelberg, 1961).

—— (ed.) *Die Ruprecht-Karl-Universität Heidelberg* (West Berlin, 1965).

HOEKEMA, ANTHONY A., 'Calvin's Doctrine of the Covenant of Grace', *RefR(H)* 15 (1962), 1–12.

—— 'The Covenant of Grace in Calvin's Teaching', *CTJ* 2 (1967), 133–61.

HOENDERDAAL, GERRIT J., 'Arminius . . . Arminianismus', *TRE* iv (1979), 63–9.

HOLIFIELD, E. BROOKS, *The Covenant Sealed: The Development of Puritan Sacramental Theology in Old and New England 1570–1720* (New Haven, 1974).

HOLLWEG, WALTER, *Heinrich Bullingers Hausbuch: Eine Untersuchung über die Anfänge der reformierten Predigtliteratur* (BGLRK 8; Neukirchen, 1956).

—— *Neue Untersuchungen zur Geschichte und Lehre des Heidelberger Katechismus*, 2 vols. (BGLRK 13 and 28; Neukirchen, 1961 and 1968).

T'HOOFT, ANTONIUS JOHANNES VAN, *De theologie van Heinrich Bullinger in betrekking tot de Nederlandsche Reformatie* (Amsterdam, 1888).

HÖPFL, HARRO, and THOMPSON, MARTYN P., 'The History of Contract as a Motif in Political Thought', *AHR* 84 (1979), 919–45.

HOWELL, W. S., *Logic and Rhetoric in England 1500–1700* (Princeton, 1956).

HÜGLIN, THOMAS O., 'Johannes Althusius: Medieval Constitutionalist or Modern Federalist?', *Publius*, 9 (1979), 9–42.

—— 'Althusius, Federalism, and the Notion of the State', *Pensiero Polit.* 13 (1980), 225–32.

—— *Covenant and Federalism in the Politics of Althusius* (Philadelphia, Center for the Study of Federalism, Temple University, 1980).

ISBELL, R. SHERMAN, 'The Origin of the Concept of the Covenant of Works' (Master of Theology thesis, Westminster Theological Seminary, 1976).

ITTERZON, GERRIT PIETER VAN, *Franciscus Gomarus* (The Hague, 1930).

JANSSEN, JOHANNES, *Geschichte des deutschen Volkes seit dem Ausgang des Mittelalters*, iv–vi (Freiburg im Breisgau, 1891–3); English translation: *History of the German People at the Close of the Middle Ages*, trans. A. M. Christie, vii–ix, xiii–xiv (London, 1905–9).

JEDIN, HUBERT, *Studien über die Schriftstellertätigkeit Albert Pigges*, RGST 55 (1931).

JOHNSON, A. F., 'Books Printed at Heidelberg for Thomas Cartwright', *The Library*, 5th ser., 2 (1947–8), 284–6.

JOHNSON, JAMES T., *A Society Ordained by God: English Puritan Marriage Doctrine in the First Half of the Seventeenth Century* (Nashville, 1970).

JONES, HYWEL, *Thomas Cartwright 1535–1603* (London, 1970).

JONGE, CHRISTIAAN DE, 'Franciscus Junius (1545–1602) and the English Separatists at Amsterdam', in Derek Baker (ed.), *Reform and Reformation: England and the Continent c.1500–c.1750* (SCH(L) subs. 2; Oxford, 1979), 165–74.

—— 'De Irenische Ecclesiologie van Franciscus Junius (1545–1602)' (Diss. Leiden, 1980; published Nieuwkoop, 1980; BHRef 30).

KAMPSCHULTE, FRANZ W., *Johann Calvin: Seine Kirche und sein Staat in Genf*, 2 vols. (Leipzig, 1869–99).

KARLBERG, MARK WALTER, 'The Mosaic Covenant and the Concept of Works in Reformed Hermeneutics: A Historical-Critical Analysis with Particular Attention to Early Covenant Eschatology' (Diss. Westminster Theological Seminary, 1980).

KARST, THEODOR, *Das kürpfalzische Oberamt Neustadt an der Haardt* (Veröffentlichungen zur Geschichte von Stadt und Kreis Neustadt an der Weinstrasse; Schriftenreihe der Bezirksgruppe Neustadt im historischen Verein der Pfalz, l; Speyer, 1960).

—— 'Pfalzgraf Johann Casimir und die Neustadter: Ein Verfassungskonflikt im Spiegel einer geschichtlichen Sage', *MHVPf* 76 (1978), 129–46.

KATZ, DAVID S., *Sabbath and Sectarianism in Seventeenth-Century England* (Brill's Studies in Intellectual History, 10; Leiden, 1988).

KEARNEY, HUGH, *Scholars and Gentlemen: Universities and Society in Pre-Industrial Britain, 1500–1700* (London, 1970).

KEEP, DAVID F., 'Henry Bullinger, 1504–1575', *LQHR* (1966), 133–46.

KENDALL, R. T., *Calvin and English Calvinism to 1649* (Oxford Theological Monograph; Oxford, 1979).

KEVAN, ERNEST F., *The Grace of Law: A Study in Puritan Theology* (London, 1964; repr. Grand Rapids, 1976).

KICKEL, WALTER, *Vernunft und Offenbarung bei Theodor Beza: Zum Problem des Verhältnisses von Theologie, Philosophie und Staat* (BGLRK 25; Neukirchen, 1967).

KLINE, MEREDITH, *Treaty of the Great King: The Covenant Structure of Deuteronomy* (Grand Rapids, 1963).

KLUCKHOHN, AUGUST, *Friedrich der Fromme, Kurfürst von der Pfalz, der Schützer der reformirten Kirche 1559–1576* (Nördlingen, 1879).

KNAPPEN, MARSHALL M., *Tudor Puritanism: A Chapter in the History of Idealism* (Chicago, 1939).

KOCH, ERNST, *Die Theologie der Confessio Helvetica Posterior* (BGLRK 27; Neukirchen, 1968).

KORFF, EMANUEL VON, *Die Anfänge der Föderaltheologie und ihre erste Ausgestaltung in Zürich und Holland* (Bonn, 1908).

KRUMM, JOHN M., 'Continental Protestantism and Elizabethan Anglicanism (1570–1595)', in Franklin H. Littell (ed.), *Reformation Studies: Essays in Honor of Roland Bainton* (Richmond, 1962), 129–44.

KUHN, MANFRED, *Pfalzgraf Johann Casimir von Pfalz-Lautern 1576–1583* (Schriften zur Geschichte von Stadt und Landkreis Kaiserslautern, 3; Otterbach-Kaiserslautern, 1960).

KUYPER, ABRAHAM, 'Praefatio', *D. Francisci Junii opuscula theologica selecta*, ed. Abraham Kuyper (Bibliotheca Reformata, l; New York, 1882), pp. v–xx.

KYLE, RICHARD, 'The Concept of Predestination in the Thought of John Knox', *WThJ* 46 (1984), 53–77.

LANG, AUGUST, *Der Heidelberger Katechismus und vier verwandte Katechismen (Leo Juds und Microns kleine Katechismen sowie die zwei Vorarbeiten Ursinus)* (QGP 3; Leipzig, 1907; repr. Darmstadt, 1967).

—— *Die Reformation und das Naturrecht*, BFChTh 13 (1909), 284–333; English translation: 'The Reformation and Natural Law', trans. J. G. Machen, in William P. Armstrong (ed.), *Calvin and the Reformation* (New York, 1909), 56–98.

—— *Der Heidelberger Katechismus zum 350jährigen Gedächtnis seiner Entstehung* (SVRG 113; Leipzig, 1913).

LAUGHLIN, PAUL ALAN, 'The Brightness of Moses's Face: Law and Gospel, Covenant and Hermeneutics in the Theology of William Tyndale' (Diss. Emory, 1975).

LEAPER, WYNEFREDE A., 'The Growth of Sabbatarianism in England from 1558 to 1658' (MA thesis, National University of Ireland, 1919).

LETHAM, ROBERT W. A., 'Saving Faith and Assurance in Reformed Theology: Zwingli to the Synod of Dort', 2 vols. (Diss. Aberdeen, 1979).

—— 'The *Foedus Operum*: Some Factors Accounting for its Development', *SCJ* 14 (1983), 457–67.

—— 'Theodore Beza: A Reassessment', *SJTh* 40 (1987), 25–40.

LEVY, MAX, *Der Sabbath in England; Wesen und Entwicklung des englischen Sonntags* (Kölner Anglistische Arbeiten, 18; Leipzig, 1933).

LILLBACK, PETER ALAN, 'Ursinus' Development of the Covenant of Creation: A Debt to Melanchthon or Calvin?', *WThJ* 43 (1981), 247–88.

—— 'The Binding of God: Calvin's Role in the Development of Covenant Theology' (Diss. Westminster Theological Seminary, 1985).

LINSENMANN, A. P., 'Albertus Pighius und sein theologischer Standpunkt', *ThQ* 48 (1866), 571–644.

LITTELL, FRANKLIN H., 'What Calvin Learned at Strassburg', in John H. Bratt (ed.), *The Heritage of John Calvin* (Heritage Hall Lectures, 1960–70, no. 2; Grand Rapids, 1973), 74–86.

LITTLE, DAVID, *Religion, Order and Law: A Study in Pre-Revolutionary England* (New York, 1969).

LOVEJOY, ARTHUR O., 'Milton and the Paradox of the Fortunate Fall', *ELH* 4 (1937), 161–79.

LOVIN, ROBIN W., 'Covenantal Relationships and Political Legitimacy', *JR* 60 (1980), 1–6.

McCARTHY, DENNIS J., SJ, 'Covenant in the Old Testament: The Present State of Inquiry', *Catholic Biblical Quarterly*, 27 (1965), 217–40.

—— *Der Gottesbund im Alten Testament* . . . (Stuttgart, 1967); English translation: *Old Testament Covenant: A Survey of Current Opinions* (Richmond, 1972).

—— *Treaty and Covenant: A Study in Form in the Ancient Oriental Documents and in the Old Testament* (Analecta Biblica Investigationes Scientificae in Res Biblicas, 21a; new edn., Rome, 1978).

McCOMISKEY, THOMAS E., *The Covenants of Promise: A Theology of the Old Testament Covenants* (Grand Rapids, 1985).

McCOY, CHARLES SHERWOOD, 'The Covenant Theology of Johannes Cocceius' (Diss. Yale, 1957).

—— 'Johannes Cocceius: Federal Theologian', *SJTh* 16 (1963), 352–70.

—— *History, Humanity and Federalism in the Theology and Ethics of Johannes Cocceius* (Philadelphia, Center for the Study of Federalism, Temple University, 1980).

McGIFFERT, MICHAEL, 'Covenant, Crown and Commons in Elizabethan Puritanism', *JBS* 20 (1980), 32–52.

—— 'William Tyndale's Conception of Covenant', *JEH* 32 (1981), 167–84.

—— 'From Moses to Adam: The Making of the Covenant of Works', *SCJ* 19 (1988), 131–55.

McKEE, WILLIAM WAKEFIELD, 'The Idea of Covenant in Early English Puritanism 1580–1643' (Diss. Yale, 1948).

McKIM, DONALD K., *Ramism in William Perkins' Theology* (American University Studies, Ser. vii, Theology and Religion, 15; New York, 1987).

McLELLAND, JOSEPH C., 'The Reformed Doctrine of Predestination According to Peter Martyr', *SJTh* 8 (1955), 255–74.

McNEILL, JOHN T., 'Natural Law in the Thought of Luther', *ChH* 10 (1941), 211–27.

—— 'Natural Law in the Teaching of the Reformers', *JR* 26 (1946), 168–82.

—— *History and Character of Calvinism* (New York, 1954).

MAEHLY, JAKOB, *Sebastian Castellio: Ein biographischer Versuch nach den Quellen* (Basle, 1862; repr. Geneva, 1971).

MARSDEN, GEORGE M., 'Perry Miller's Rehabilitation of the Puritans: A Critique', *ChH* 39 (1970), 91–105.

MASSELINK, EDWARD J., *The Heidelberg Story* (Grand Rapids, 1964).

MELLES, G., *Albertus Pighius en zijn strijd met Calvijn over het liberum arbitrium* (Kampen, 1973).

MENK, GERHARD, 'Der doppelte Johannes Althusius—eine ramistische Dichotomie? Ein biographischer Beitrag', *NA* 87 (1976), 135–42.

—— 'Kalvinismus und Pädagogik: Matthias Martinius (1572–1630) und der Einfluss der Herborner Hohen Schule auf Johann Amos Comenius', *NA* 91 (1980), 77–104.

—— *Die Hohe Schule Herborn in ihrer Frühzeit (1584–1660): Ein Beitrag zum Hochschulwesen des deutschen Kalvinismus im Zeitalter der Gegenreformation* (Wiesbaden, 1981).

MERULA, PAUL, 'Vita . . . Francisci Junii', in F. Junius, *Opera theologica* . . . (Geneva, 1608), i/B, pp. 1–28.

METZ, WULF, *Necessitas satisfactionis? Eine systematische Studie zu den Fragen 12–18 des Heidelberger Katechismus und zur Theologie des Zacharias Ursinus* (SDGSTh 26; Zurich, 1970).

MILLER, CHARLES, 'The Spread of Calvinism in Switzerland, Germany and France', in John H. Bratt (ed.), *The Rise and Development of Calvinism* (Heritage Hall Publications, 2; Grand Rapids, 1959), 27–62.

MILLER, PERRY, *Orthodoxy in Massachusetts, 1630–1650* (Cambridge, Mass., 1933).

—— 'The Marrow of Puritan Divinity', *PubColSocMass* 32 (1935), 247–300.

—— *The New England Mind*; i: *The Seventeenth Century*; ii: *From Colony to Province* (Cambridge, Mass., 1939 and 1953).

—— ' "Preparation for Salvation" in Seventeenth Century New England', *JHI* 4 (1943), 253–86.

Mitteilungen des historischen Vereins der Pfalz (Speyer, 1876–).

MOELLER, BERND, *Reichsstadt und Reformation* (SVRG 180; Gütersloh, 1962).

—— *Villes d'Empire et Réformation* (Albert Chenou Travaux d'Histoire éthico-politique 10; Geneva, 1966); English translation: *Imperial Cities and the Reformation*, trans. H. C. E. Midelfort and M. U. Edwards, Jun. (Philadelphia, 1972).

MOELLER, WILHELM ERNST, *Reformation und GegenReformation*, vol. iii of *Lehrbuch der Kirchengeschichte* (Leipzig, 1894); English translation: *Reformation and Counter Reformation*, vol. iii of *The History of the Christian Church*, trans. J. H. Freese (New York, 1900).

MOGI, SOBEI, *The Problem of Federalism: A Study in the History of Political Theory*, 2 vols. (New York, 1931).

MØLLER, JENS G., 'The Beginnings of Puritan Covenant Theology', *JEH* 14 (1963), 46–67.

MOLTMANN, JÜRGEN, 'Zur Bedeutung des Petrus Ramus für Philosophie und Theologie im Calvinismus', *ZKG* 68 (1957), 295–318.

—— *Prädestination und Perseveranz: Geschichte und Bedeutung der reformierten Lehr 'de perseverantia sanctorum'* (BGLRK 12; Neukirchen, 1961).

MORAW, PETER and KARST, THEODOR, *Die Universität Heidelberg und Neustadt an der Haardt* (Veröffentlichungen zur Geschichte von Stadt und Kreis Neustadt an der Weinstrasse; Speyer, 1963).

MORGAN, JOHN, 'Puritanism and Science: A Reinterpretation', *HistJ* 22 (1979), 535–60.

MOSSE, GEORGE L., *The Holy Pretence: A Study in Christianity and Reason of State from William Perkins to John Winthrop* (Oxford, 1957).

MÜLLER, ALBERT *Daniel Tossanus' Leben un Wirken* (Flensburg, 1882).

MÜLLER, E. F. K., 'Cocceius (gest. 1669) und seine Schule', *RE* (3rd edn.), iv (1896), 186–94.

MULLER, RICHARD A., 'Predestination and Christology in Sixteenth Century Reformed Theology' (Diss. Duke, 1976).

—— 'Perkins' *A Golden Chaine*: Predestinarian System or Schematized *Ordo Salutis*?', *SCJ* 9 (1978), 68–81.

—— 'Covenant and Conscience in English Reformed Theology: Three Variations on a 17th Century Theme', *WThJ* 42 (1980), 308–34.

—— 'The Spirit and the Covenant: John Gill's Critique of the *Pactum Salutis*', *Found.* 24 (1981), 4–14.

—— 'The Federal Motif in Seventeenth Century Arminian Theology', *Nederlands Archief voor Kerkgeschiedenis*, 62 (1982), 102–22.

—— *Christ and the Decree: Christology and Predestination in Reformed Theology from Calvin to Perkins* (Studies in Historical Theology, 2; Durham, NC, 1986).

MURRAY, R. H., *The Political Consequences of the Reformation: Studies in Sixteenth Century Political Thought* (London, 1926).

MUSS-ARNOLT, WILLIAM, 'Puritan Efforts and Struggles, 1550–1663: A Bio-Bibliographical Study; II', *AJT* 23 (1919), 471–99.

Nassauische Annalen: Jahrbuch des Vereins für Nassauische Altertums-kunde und Geschichtsforschung (Wiesbaden, 1827–).

NERI, D., 'Antiassolutismo e federalismo nel pensiero di Althusius', *Pensiero Polit.* 12 (1979), 393–409.

Neues Archiv für die Geschichte der Stadt Heidelberg und der rheinischen Pfalz (Heidelberg, 1890–).

NEUSER, WILHELM H., 'Die Erwählungslehre im Heidelberger Katechismus', *ZKG* 75 (1964), 309–26.

—— 'Die Väter des Heidelberger Katechismus', *ThZ* 35 (1979), 177–94.

NEVIN, JOHN W., 'Zacharias Ursinus', *MercQR* 3 (1851), 490–512.

NEW, JOHN F. H., *Anglican and Puritan: The Basis of their Opposition 1558–1640* (Stanford, 1964).

NICHOLSON, E. W., *God and His People: Covenant and Theology in the Old Testament* (New York, 1986).

NIESEL, WILHELM, *Die Theologie Calvins* (EETh 6; Munich, 1938); English translation of 2nd German edn.: *The Theology of Calvin*, trans. Harold Knight (Philadelphia, 1956).

NIJENHUIS, W., 'Varianten binnen Nederlandse Calvinisme in de zestiende eeuw', *TvG* 89 (1976), 358–73; English translation: 'Variants within Dutch Calvinism in the Sixteenth Century', *The Low Countries History Yearbook: Acta Historiae Neerlandica*, 12 (1979), 48–64.

NUTTALL, GEOFFREY F., *Visible Saints: The Congregational Way 1640–1660* (Oxford, 1957), 73–82.

OBERMAN, HEIKO AUGUSTINUS, 'Wir sein pettler. Hoc est verum: Bund und Gnade in der Theologie des Mittlealters und der Reformation', *ZKG* 78 (1967), 232–52.

OESTRICH, GERHARD, 'Die Idee des religiösen Bundes und die Lehre vom Staatsvertrag', in Wilhelm Burges and Carl Hinrichs (edd.), *Zur Geschichte und Problematik der Demokratie: Festgabe für Hans Herzfeld* (Berlin, 1958), 11–32; repr. in Hans Hubert Hofmann (ed.), *Die Entstehung des modernen souveränen Staates* (Berlin, 1967), 137–51, and in Gerhard Oestrich, *Geist und Gestalt des frühmodernen Staates: Ausgewählte Aussätze* (Berlin, 1969), 157–78.

O'MALLEY, J. STEVEN, *Pilgrimage of Faith: The Legacy of the Otterbeins* (American Theological Library Association Monograph Series, 197, no. 4; Metuchen, NJ, 1973).

ONG, WALTER J., SJ, *Ramus: Method, and the Decay of Dialogue; From the Art of Discourse to the Art of Reasoning* (Cambridge, Mass., 1958).

ORR, JAMES, 'Calvinism', *ERE* iii (1910), 146–55.

OSTERHAVEN, M. EUGENE, 'Calvin on the Covenant', *RefR(H)* 33 (1980), 136–49.

OSTROM, VINCENT, 'Hobbes, Covenant and Constitution', *Publius*, 10 (1980), 83–100.

OZMENT, STEVEN, *Mysticism and Dissent: Religious Ideology and Social Protest in the Sixteenth Century* (New Haven, 1973).

—— *The Reformation in the Cities: The Appeal of Protestantism to Sixteenth-Century Germany and Switzerland* (New Haven, 1975).

PAMP, FREDERICK E., JUN., 'Studies in the Origins of English Arminianism' (Diss. Harvard, 1951).

PARKER, KENNETH L., 'The English Sabbath: 1558–1640' (Diss. Cambridge, 1984).

PARKER, T. H. L., 'The Approach to Calvin', *EQ* 16 (1944), 165–72.

PASSERIN D'ENTREVES, A., *Natural Law: An Introduction to Legal Philosophy* (London, 1951).

PEARSON, ANDREW FORRET SCOTT, *Thomas Cartwright and Elizabethan Puritanism 1535–1603* (Cambridge, 1925).

—— *Church and State: Aspects of Sixteenth Century Puritanism* (Cambridge, 1928).

PETERSEN, PETER, *Geschichte der aristotelischen Philosophie im protestantischen Deutschland* (Leipzig, 1921).

PETTIT, NORMAN, *The Heart Prepared: Grace and Conversion in Puritan Spiritual Life* (New Haven, 1966).

PIDOUX DE MADUÈRE, PIERRE A., *Albertus Pighius, adversaire de Calvin* (Lausanne, 1932).

PLATH, UWE, *Calvin und Basel in den Jahren 1552–1556* (BSHST 22; Zurich, 1974).

PLATT, JOHN, *Reformed Thought and Scholasticism: The Arguments for the Existence of God in Dutch Theology, 1575–1650* (SHCT 29; Leiden, 1982).

POPE, ROBERT G., *The Half-Way Covenant: Church Membership in Puritan New England* (Princeton, 1969).

PORTER, H. C., *Reformation and Reaction in Tudor Cambridge* (Cambridge, 1958).

PRESS, VOLKER, *Calvinismus und Territorialstaat: Regierung und Zentralbehörden der Kurpfalz 1559–1619* (KHS 7; Stuttgart, 1970).

PRESTWICH, MENNA (ed.), *International Calvinism, 1541–1715* (Oxford, 1985).

PRIEBE, VICTOR LEWIS, 'The Covenant Theology of William Perkins' (Diss. Drew, 1967).

PRIMUS, JOHN H., 'Calvin and the Puritan Sabbath: A Comparative Study', in David E. Holwerda (ed.), *Exploring the Heritage of John Calvin* (Grand Rapids, 1976), 40–75.

PRINS, P., 'Verbond en verkiezing bij Bullinger en Calvijn', *GThT* 56 (1956), 97–111.

PRINS, R., 'The Image of God in Adam and the Restoration of Man in Jesus Christ: A Study in Calvin', *SJTh* 25 (1972), 32–44.

QUELL, GOTTFRIED and BEHM, JOHANNES, 'διαθήκη', *ThWNT* ii. 106–37; English translation: 'διαθήκη', *TDNT* ii. 106–34.

RAITT, JILL (ed.), *Shapers of Religious Traditions in Germany, Switzerland and Poland 1560–1600* (New Haven, 1981).

RECHTIEN, JOHN G., 'Thought Patterns: The Commonplace Book as Literary Form in Theological Controversy during the English Renaissance' (Diss. Saint Louis University, 1975).

REITSMA, JOHANNES, *Franciscus Junius, een levensbeeld uit de eersten tijd der kerkhervorming* (Groningen, 1864).

RETH, ANNO VON, *Herborn, Dillenburg, Haiger: Geographische Untersuchungen an benachbarten Kleinstädten* (Marburger Geographische Schriften, 42; Marburg/Lahn, 1970).

RICHARDS, GEORGE W., *The Heidelberg Catechism: Historical and Doctrinal Studies* (Sworder Memorial Lectures, 1911; Philadelphia, 1913).

RILEY, PATRICK, 'Three 17th Century German Theorists of Federalism: Althusius, Hugo and Leibniz', *Publius*, 6 (1976), 7–41.

RITSCHL, ALBRECHT B., *Die christliche Lehre von der Rechtfertigung und Versöhnung* (Bonn, 1870); English translation: *A Critical History of the Christian Doctrine of Justification and Reconciliation*, trans. John S. Black (Edinburgh, 1872).

RITSCHL, OTTO, *System und systematische Methode in der Geschichte des wissenschaftlichen Sprachgebrauchs und der philosophischen Methodologie* (Bonn, 1906).

ROLSTON, HOLMES, III, 'Responsible Man in Reformed Theology: Calvin versus the Westminster Confession', *SJTh* 23 (1970), 129–56.

—— *John Calvin versus the Westminster Confession* (Richmond, 1972).

ROSENMEIER, JESPER, 'New England's Perfection: The Image of Adam and the Image of Christ in the Antinomian Crisis, 1634–1638', *WMQ*, 3rd ser., 27 (1970), 435–59.

ROTH, F. W. E., 'Zur Geschichte der Heidelberger Buchdruckereien und Verlagsgeschäfte 1558–1618', *NAGH* 4 (1901), 226–55.

SARPI, PAOLO, *Istoria del Concilio Tridentino*, ed. Corrado Vivanti, i (Turin, 1974); English translation of the 3rd edn.: *The Historie of the Councel of Trent*, trans. Nathanael Brent (London, 1640).

SCHAFF, PHILIP, 'Die ältesten Ausgaben des Heidelberger Katechismus', *ZHTh* 37 (1867), 113–24.

—— *The History of the Creeds* (New York, 1877; vol. i of *The Creeds of Christendom*; repr. Grand Rapids, 1977).

SCHLOSSER, HEINRICH, 'Die Bedeutung der Hohen Schule Herborn für die Geschichte des deutschen Geistes', *NA* 55 (1935), 101–12.

—— 'Caspar Olevianus', *Nassauische Lebensbilder*, 1 (1940), 67–73.

SCHMIDT, D., 'Girolamo Zanchi', *ThStKr* 32 (1859), 625–708.

SCHMIDT, MARTIN, 'Biblizismus und natürliche Theologie in der Gewissenslehre des englischen Puritanismus', *ARG* 42 (1951), 198–219, and 43 (1952), 70–187.

SCHOTTENLOHER, KARL, *Pfalzgraf Ottheinrich und das Buch: Ein Beitrag zur Geschichte der evangelischen Publizistik; mit Anhang: Das Reformationsschrifttum in der Palatina*, RGST 50/51 (1927).

SCHRENK, GOTTLOB, *Gottesreich und Bund im älteren Protestantismus, vornehmlich bei Johannes Cocceius* (BFChTh.M 5; Gütersloh, 1923).

SCHWEIZER, ALEXANDER, 'Sebastian Castellio als Bestreiter der calvinischen Prädestinationslehre der bedeutendste Vorgänger des Arminius', *ThJb(T)* 10 (1850), 1. 1–27.

—— *Die protestantischen Centraldogmen in ihrer Entwicklung innerhalb der reformirten Kirche*, 2 vols. (Zurich, 1854–6).

SEISEN, J. D., *Geschichte der Reformation zu Heidelberg von ihren ersten Anfangen bis zur Abfassung des Heidelberger Katechismus: Eine Denkschrift zur dreihundertjährigen Jubelfeier daselbst am 3. Januar 1846* (Heidelberg, 1846).

SIGMUND, PAUL, *Natural Law in Political Thought* (Cambridge, Mass., 1971).

SIMON, MATTHIAS, 'Die Beziehung zwischen Altem und Neuem Testament in der Schriftauslegung Calvins', *RKZ* 82 (1932), 3. 17–21, 4. 25–8, 5. 33–5.

SIMPSON, ALAN, 'The Covenanted Community', in *Puritanism in Old and New England* (Chicago, 1955), 19–38; repr. in John M. Mulder and John F. Wilson (edd.), *Religion in American History: Interpretive Essays* (Englewood Cliffs, NJ, 1978), 17–28.

SMITHEN, FREDERICK, *Continental Protestantism and the English Reformation* (London, 1927).

SMOUT, T. C. (ed.) *Scotland and Europe, 1200–1800* (Edinburgh, 1986).

SOLBERG, WINTON U., *Redeem the Time: The Puritan Sabbath in Early America* (Cambridge, Mass., 1977).

SOMMERVILLE, C. J., 'Conversion, Sacrament and Assurance in the Puritan Covenant of Grace, to 1650' (MA thesis, University of Kansas, 1963).

—— 'Conversion versus the Early Puritan Covenant of Grace', *JPH* 44 (1966), 178–97.

SPIJKER, W. VAN'T, 'Natuur en Genade in de Reformatorische Theologie', *Theologia Reformata*, 22 (1979), 176–90.

SPRUNGER, KEITH L., 'Ames, Ramus, and the Method of Puritan Theology', *HThR* 59 (1966), 133–51.

—— 'Technometria: A Prologue to Puritan Theology', *JHI* 29 (1968), 115–22.

—— *Dutch Puritanism: A History of English and Scottish Churches of the Netherlands in the Sixteenth and Seventeenth Centuries* (SHCT 31; Leiden, 1982).

—— 'English and Dutch Sabbatarianism and the Development of Puritan Social Theology, 1600–1660', *ChH* 51 (1982), 24–38.

STAEDTKE, JOACHIM, 'Der zürcher Prädestinationsstreit von 1560', *Zwing.* 9 (1953), 536–45.

STAMER, LUDWIG, *Das Zeitalter der Reform (1556–1685)*, vol. iii, part 1 of *Kirchengeschichte der Pfalz* (Speyer, 1955).

STAUFFER, RICHARD, *Dieu, la création, et la Providence dans la prédication de Calvin* (BSHST 33; Berne, 1978).

STEINMETZ, DAVID C. (ed.), *Reformers in the Wings* (Philadelphia, 1971).

STEITZ, H., *Geschichte der evangelischen Kirche in Hessen und Nassau* (Marburg, 1977).

STEUBING, JOHANN H., *Kirchen- und Reformations-Geschichte der Oranien-Nassauischen Lande* (Hadamer, 1804).

—— 'Lebensnachrichten von den Herborner Theologen: I. Caspar Olevian und Johannes Piscator', *ZHTh* 11 (1841), 4. 74–138.

STOEVER, WILLIAM KENNETH BRISTOW, 'The Covenant of Works in Puritan Theology: The Antinomian Crisis in New England' (Diss. Yale, 1970).

—— 'Nature, Grace and John Cotton: The Theological Dimension in the New England Antinomianism Controversy', *ChH* 44 (1975), 22–34.

—— *'A Faire and Easie Way to Heaven': Covenant Theology and Antinomianism in Early Massachusetts* (Middletown, Conn., 1978).

STOUT, HARRY S., *The New England Soul: Preaching and Religious Culture in Colonial New England* (New York, 1986).

STRUVE, BURKHARD GOTTHELF, *Ausführlicher bericht von der pfaltzischen kirchen-historie . . .* (Frankfurt, 1721).

STRYPE, JOHN, *Annals and Life of Whitgift*, 3 vols. (Oxford, 1822).

STÜCKELBERGER, HANS MARTIN, 'Calvin und Castellio', *Zwing.* 7 (1939), 91–128.

STURM, ERDMAN, *Der junge Zacharias Ursin: Sein Weg vom Philippismus zum Calvinismus (1534–1562)* (BGLRK 33; Neukirchen, 1972).

SUDHOFF, KARL, 'Sudhoff's Olevianus', trans. H. Rust, *MercQR* 8 (1856), 163–98.

—— *C. Olevianus und Z. Ursinus: Leben und ausgewahlte Schriften* (LASRK 8; Elberfeld, 1857).

TAYLOR, W. C., 'Scottish Students in Heidelberg, 1386–1662', *ScHR* 5 (1907–8), 67–75, 250–1.

THOLUCK, F. A. G., *Das akademische Leben des siebzehnten Jahrhunderts* (Halle, 1853–4).

THOMPSON, BARD, 'The Palatinate Church Order', *ChH* 23 (1954), 340–57.

—— (ed.), *Essays on the Heidelberg Catechism* (Philadelphia, 1963).

THUNDYIL, ZACHARIAS, *Covenant in Anglo-Saxon Thought* (Madras, 1972).

TIPSON, LYNN BAIRD, JUN., 'The Development of a Puritan Understanding of Conversion' (Diss. Yale, 1972).

TOEPKE, GUSTAV (ed.), *Die Matrikel der Universität Heidelberg von 1386 bis 1662*, ii *(1554–1662)* (Heidelberg, 1886; repr. Nendeln, Liechtenstein, 1976).

TOFT, DANIEL JOHN, 'Zacharias Ursinus: A Study in the Development of Calvinism' (MA thesis, University of Wisconsin, 1962).

—— 'Shadows of Kings: The Political Thought of David Pareus, 1548–1622' (Diss. University of Wisconsin, 1970).

TOON, PETER, *The Emergence of Hyper-Calvinism in English Non-conformity 1689–1765* (London, 1967).

—— *God's Statesman: The Life and Work of John Owen* (Exeter, 1971).

TÖRÖK, ISTVÁN, 'Die Bewertung des Alten Testamentes in der Institutio Calvins', in Varga Zsigmond (ed.), *Kálvin és a Kálvinizmus* (Debrecen, Hungary, 1936), 121–39.

TORRANCE, JAMES BRUCE, 'Covenant or Contract? A Study of the Theological Background of Worship in Seventeenth-Century Scotland', *SJTh* 23 (1970), 51–76.

—— 'Calvinism and Puritanism in England and Scotland: Some Basic Concepts in the Development of "Federal Theology" ', South African Congress for Calvin Research, *Calvinus Reformator: His Contribution to Theology, Church and Society* (Potchefstroom, 1982), 264–86.

—— 'Strengths and Weaknesses of the Westminster Theology', in A. I. C. Heron (ed.), *The Westminster Confession in the Church Today* (Edinburgh, 1982), 40–54.

—— 'The Incarnation and "Limited Atonement" ', *EQ* 55 (1983), 83–94.

TRINKAUS, CHARLES, 'The Problem of Free Will in the Renaissance and Reformation', *JHI* 10 (1949), 51–62.

TRINTERUD, LEONARD J., 'The Origins of Puritanism', *ChH* 20 (1951), 37–57.

TYACKE, NICHOLAS, *Anti-Calvinists: The Rise of English Arminianism, c.1590–1640* (Oxford, 1987).

VANDERMOLEN, RONALD J., 'Providence as Mystery, Providence as Revelation: Puritan and Anglican Modifications of John Calvin's Doctrine of Providence', *ChH* 47 (1978), 27–47.

VENINGA, JAMES FRANK, 'Covenant Theology and Ethics in the Thought of John Calvin and John Preston', 2 vols. (Diss. Rice, 1974).

VISSER, DERK, *Zacharias Ursinus: The Reluctant Reformer; His Life and Times* (New York, 1983).

—— (ed.), *Controversy and Conciliation: The Reformation and the Palatinate. 1559–1583* (Pittsburgh Theological Monographs, NS 18; Allison Park, Pa., 1986).

—— 'The Covenant in Zacharias Ursinus', *SCJ* 18 (1987), 531–44.

VON ROHR, JOHN, 'Covenant and Assurance in Early English Puritanism', *ChH* 24 (1965), 195–203.

—— *The Covenant of Grace in Puritan Thought* (American Academy of Religion, Studies in Religion, 45; Atlanta, 1986).

VOS, GEERHARDUS, *De verbondsleer in de gereformeerde theologie* (Grand Rapids, 1891; repr. Rotterdam, 1939); English translation: 'The Doctrine of the Covenant in Reformed Theology', trans. S. Voorwinde and Willem Van Gemeren, in *Redemptive History and Biblical Interpretation: The Shorter Writings of Geerhardus Vos*, ed. Richard B. Gaffin (Phillipsburg, NJ, 1980), 234–67.

WALLACE, DEWEY D., *Puritans and Predestination* (Chapel Hill, 1982).

WALSER, PETER, *Die Prädestination bei Heinrich Bullinger im Zusammenhang mit seiner Gotteslehre* (SDGSTh 11; Zurich, 1957).

WARFIELD, BENJAMIN BRECKENRIDGE, *Calvin and Calvinism* (New York, 1931).

WEBER, HANS EMIL, *Die philosophische Scholastik des deutschen Protestantismus im Zeitalter der Orthodoxie* (APG(F) 1; Leipzig, 1907).

—— *Reformation, Orthodoxie und Rationalismus*, 3 vols. (BFChTh.M 35, 45, and 51; Gütersloh, 1937–51; repr. Darmstadt, 1966).

WEINFIELD, M., 'berith', *ThWAT* i. 781–808; English translation: 'Berith', *TDOT*, ii. 253–79.

WEISERT, HERMANN, *Die Rektoren der Ruperto Carola zu Heidelberg und die Dekane ihrer Fakultäten, 1386–1968* (Heidelberg, 1968).

WENDEL, FRANÇOIS, *Calvin: Sources et évolution de sa pensée religieuse* (Études d'Histoire et de Philosophie Religieuses Publiées par la Faculté de Théologie Protestante de l'Université de Strasbourg, 41; Paris, 1950); English translation: *Calvin: The Origins and Development of his Religious Thought*, trans. Philip Mairet (New York, 1963).

WEST, W. M. S., 'John Hooper and the Origins of Puritanism', *BQ* 15 (1954), 8. 346–68; 16 (1955), 1. 22–46, 2. 67–88.

WHITAKER, WILFRED B., *Sunday in Tudor and Stuart Times* (London, 1933).

WILCOX, WILLIAM GEORGE, 'New England Covenant Theology: Its English Precursors and Early American Exponents' (Diss. Duke, 1959).

WILEY, DAVID NEELD, 'Calvin's Doctrine of Predestination: His Principal Soteriological and Polemical Doctrine' (Diss. Duke, 1971).

WILLIAMS, ARNOLD, *The Common Expositor: An Account of the Commentaries on Genesis 1527–1633* (Chapel Hill, 1948).

WILLIAMS, LLOYD G., *'Digitus Dei*: God and Nation in the Thought of John Owen; A Study in English Puritanism' (Diss. Drew, 1981).

WILLIAMS, NORMAN POWELL, *The Ideas of the Fall and of Original Sin* (London, 1929).

WILSON, J. DOVER, 'Richard Schilders and the English Puritans', *TBSL* 11 (1909–11), 65–134.

WINKELMANN, EDUARD (ed.), *Urkundenbuch der Universitaet Heidelberg*, 2 vols. (Heidelberg, 1886).

WOLF, HANS HEINRICH, *Die Einheit des Bundes: Das Verhältnis von Altem und Neuem Testament bei Calvin* (BGLRK 10; Neukirchen, 1958).

WOLF, K., 'Aus dem Briefwechsel Christoph Pezels mit Graf Johann dem Älteren von Nassau-Dillenburg', *ARG* 34 (1937), 177–234.

WOLTERS, ALBRECHT JULIUS CONSTANTIN, *Der Heidelberger Katechismus in seiner ursprünglichen Gestalt* (Bonn, 1864).

YULE, GEORGE, 'Developments in English Puritanism in the Context of the Reformation', in *Studies in the Puritan Tradition: A Joint Supplement of the Congregational and Presbyterian Historical Societies* (Chelmsford, 1964), 8–27.

ZEDLER, GOTTFRIED and SOMMER, HANS (edd.), *Die Matrikel der Hohen Schule und des Paedagogiums zu Herborn* (Wiesbaden, 1908).

Index

debate, debates 63, 104, 123, 184
    see also argumentation; disputation;
    logic; syllogism
Decalogue 4, 6, 20, 33, 41, 99, 100, 104,
    105, 119, 138, 140, 146
decree, decrees, decrees of God, decretal
    15, 16, 18, 19, 28, 57, 63, 64, 66, 67,
    69, 72–4, 76, 78, 79, 80, 85, 86, 87,
    92, 104, 108, 120, 121, 130, 138, 139,
    140, 141, 142, 145, 147, 155–7 194
    see also double decree; hidden decree;
    order of God's decrees;
    predestination
Defensio sanae (Calvin, John) 64
Defensio (Castellio, Sebastian) 59, 61,
    64, 77, 88
Delbanco, Andrew 195
Delormeau, Charles Émile 90
Denholm, Andrew T. 174
Dennison, James T., Jun. 41
Deschner, John 173
determinism, deterministic 20, 23, 47,
    108
    see also hyper-Calvinism
Deuteronomy, Book of 39, 53, 55, 57,
    60, 75, 92, 115, 136, 138, 142, 143,
    144, 149, 151, 152
dialectic 29, 42, 134
Dialogi IIII (Castellio, Sebastian) 83,
    90, 97
diatheke 35, 51, 56–9, 61, 109, 129, 155
Dibon, Paul 131
Dictionarium Hebraicum (Münster,
    Sebastian) 53, 60
Dictionary of National Biography
    (*DNB*) 128, 129, 149
Dictionnaire de biographie française
    (*DBF*) 129
Diemer, N. 13, 24, 25, 29, 45, 48, 49, 87,
    166
Diestel, Ludwig 162
Dietel, William M. 95
Dignorum laude virorum (*DLV*) 109,
    128–30
Dijk, Klaas 46
Dillistone, Frederick W. 43, 169
dipleural covenant 100
    see also covenant and related
    subheadings; bilateral covenant;
    conditional covenant; contract;
    mutual covenant
disobedience 5, 14, 28, 49, 136
disputation, disputations, 63, 115, 123,
    132, 134, 148, 157

see also argumentation; debate; logic;
    syllogism
Dochnahl, Friedrich Jakob 132
Dodwell, Charles Reginald 38
Doerr, Wilhelm 132
dogmatics 1, 2, 22, 24, 38, 46–8, 63, 91,
    101, 105, 120, 122, 158, 161, 167,
    170, 177
    see also Reformed dogmatics
Donne, John 177
Donnelly, John Patrick, SJ 46, 147
donum superadditum 24
doppelbund 24
    see also covenant and related
    subheadings
Dorner, Isaak August 131, 132, 162
double decree 80
    see also decree; double predestination;
    predestination
double predestination 18, 23, 32, 50, 80
    see also predestination; single
    predestination
double covenant 27, 32
    see also doppelbund
Douglas, Walter B. 188, 191
Doumergue, Émile 88, 89, 164
Dow, Norman 175
Drummond, Andrew L. 38, 171
du Jon
    see Junius, Franciscus
Dumbrell, William J. 60
duty 28, 49, 81, 140, 145, 154

earth 7, 12, 13, 21, 55, 82, 84, 133, 143,
    154, 184
Easter Eve 64
Ebrard, J. H. A. 161–3
ecclesiology 62, 171, 186
Eden, Garden of 4, 6, 7, 9, 27, 29, 49, 84,
    99, 105, 109, 140, 154, 155, 177
    see also Edenic state; innocence, state
    of; paradisal state; paradise;
    prelapsarian state; tree of the
    knowledge of good and evil; tree of
    life
Edenic state 15, 24, 27, 28, 34, 55, 62,
    105, 140
    see also Eden, Garden of; innocence,
    state of; paradisal state; paradise;
    prelapsarian state
Edinburgh 122, 126
Edwards, Jonathan 163, 174, 177, 179,
    182, 185–7, 190, 193
Eeniginberg, Elton M. 172